John Woolman's Path
to the Peaceable Kingdom

EARLY AMERICAN STUDIES

SERIES EDITORS
Daniel K. Richter, Kathleen M. Brown,
Max Cavitch, and David Waldstreicher

Exploring neglected aspects of our colonial, revolutionary, and early national history and culture, Early American Studies reinterprets familiar themes and events in fresh ways. Interdisciplinary in character, and with a special emphasis on the period from about 1600 to 1850, the series is published in partnership with the McNeil Center for Early American Studies.

A complete list of books in the series is available from the publisher.

John Woolman's Path to the Peaceable Kingdom

A Quaker in the British Empire

Geoffrey Plank

PENN

UNIVERSITY OF PENNSYLVANIA PRESS

PHILADELPHIA

Published by
University of Pennsylvania Press
Philadelphia, Pennsylvania 19104-4112
www.upenn.edu/pennpress

Printed in the United States of America on acid-free paper
10 9 8 7 6 5 4 3 2 1

Library of Congress Cataloging-in-Publication Data
Plank, Geoffrey Gilbert, 1960–
    John Woolman's path to the peaceable kingdom : a Quaker in the
British Empire / Geoffrey Plank. — 1st ed.
        p.   cm. — (Early American studies)
    Includes bibliographical references and index.
    ISBN 978-0-8122-4405-2 (hardcover : alk. paper)
    1. Woolman, John, 1720–1772. 2. Quakers—United States—
Biography. 3. Abolitionists—United States—Biography. 4. Society
of Friends—United States—History—18th century. 5. Antislavery
movements—United States—History—18th century. I. Title. II. Series:
Early American studies.
BX7795.W7P53   2012
289.6092—dc23   2011032479
[B]

For Ina

Contents

Introduction

In 1847 THE poet John Greenleaf Whittier published a series of essays entitled "Quaker Slaveholding, and How it Was Abolished." Whittier identified 1742 as a critical year, when "an event, simple and inconsiderable in itself, was made the instrumentality of exerting a mighty influence upon slavery in the Society of Friends." Some time during that year a shopkeeper in Mount Holly, New Jersey, sold a woman as a slave and asked his clerk to write up the bill of sale.

> On taking up his pen, the young clerk felt a sudden and strong scruple in his mind. The thought of writing an instrument of slavery for one of his fellow creatures oppressed him. God's voice against the desecration of His image spoke in his soul. He yielded to the will of his employer, but, while writing the instrument, he was constrained to declare, both to the buyer and the seller, that he believed slavekeeping inconsistent with the Christian religion. This young man was JOHN WOOLMAN. The circumstance above named was the starting point of a life-long testimony against slavery.[1]

Whittier's essays detailed John Woolman's antislavery work and suggested that he was the most influential opponent of slavery in his era, and indeed that his individual efforts had culminated with the Quakers resolving to denounce slaveholding and the slave trade.

In the decades following 1742, Woolman became one of the most insistent opponents of slavery in the British Empire. He began writing his first antislavery essay, *Some Considerations on the Keeping of Negroes*, in 1746, but he withheld the piece from publication for several years, apparently waiting until the time was propitious for obtaining approval from the Quakers' oversight bodies. It appeared as a pamphlet in 1754.[2] Later that year Philadelphia Yearly Meeting published *An Epistle of Caution and Advice concerning the Buying and Keeping of Slaves*, its pivotal corporate declaration against slaveholding.[3] From that time forward Woolman was part of an ever-expanding community of Quakers campaigning against slavery. He traveled from North Carolina to Massachusetts visiting Quaker meetings, holding private conferences with slaveholding Friends, writing further essays and petitioning Quaker meetings. Working within the administrative structures of the Society of Friends, he coordinated his actions with other reformers. Together they used the meetings' disciplinary procedures to convince recalcitrant Quakers to free their slaves.

Whittier was neither the first nor the last writer to praise Woolman, but among the early commentators he was one of the most articulate, influential and well-informed.[4] He knew very well that Woolman did not initiate the antislavery movement on his own. As historians Jean R. Soderlund and Gary Nash have explained in detail, some Quakers began protesting against slavery as early as the seventeenth century, and during Woolman's lifetime there were hundreds of other American Quakers who actively opposed slaveholding.[5] Whittier knew about Woolman's predecessors and contemporaries, but he chose to emphasize Woolman's contributions for strategic reasons. In 1833, when Whittier became an abolitionist, the Quakers in North America were divided into antagonistic groups. They disagreed with each other on questions of doctrine and religious practice as well as their response to the escalating political controversy surrounding slavery in the United States. Despite their differences, however, virtually all America's Quakers revered Woolman. The Quakers knew Woolman through his journal and in some Quaker circles he was admired more for his piety than for his stance against slaveholding. Whittier sought to take advantage of Woolman's famous spirituality. He made a promise to the great abolitionist William Lloyd Garrison that he would invoke Woolman's "holy" memory to convince America's recalcitrant Quakers to support immediate emancipation.[6] Whittier praised Woolman repeatedly over the next thirty-nine years, using increasingly extravagant language. By the end of the American Civil War, he was asserting that Woolman had been a world-historical figure with few equals. Whittier credited Woolman with initiating "a far-reaching moral, social, and political revolution, undoing the evil work of centuries" and claimed that his influence could be seen "wherever a step in the direction of emancipation has been taken in this country [the United

States] or in Europe."[7] One later writer, following Whittier's lead, compared Woolman's historical significance to that of Napoleon.[8]

Whittier's rhetorical calculations paralleled in some ways the deliberations that Woolman himself engaged in. Woolman understood the power of saintliness, and he was constantly alert to the ways in which his words might be received. In order to enhance the impact of his presence and message, he adapted his statements and actions for particular audiences. He spoke and behaved differently in the south, for example, than he did in New Jersey and Pennsylvania. But even when he worked tactically and chose not to press a point because the argument would be futile, he did not believe that he was merely setting priorities and choosing which battles were worth fighting. He never thought that any partial victory would be enough. Indeed the broad range of controversies he joined—concerning drunkenness, quartering of soldiers, theatrical performances, fine furniture, labor relations, smallpox inoculation, Indian affairs, abuse of horses, wartime taxation, and many other questions in addition to slavery—stemmed from his insistence that humanity should reform itself comprehensively. He thought that all people should strive to establish that kingdom foreseen by the prophet Isaiah, where every creature, even the members of the "animal race," as Woolman described them, lived together in harmony, without predation, competition, or any other kind of conflict. This religious vision inspired Woolman's detailed and sweeping critique of the material culture and economy of the British Empire.

Woolman saw the imperial economy as a machine, and he believed (much like the seventeenth-century political economists who promoted imperialism) that the various parts of the British Empire served specialized functions that supported one another. He argued that purchasing the products of slave labor promoted slave-raiding and warfare in Africa and that concentrating wealth in the hands of the landed elite on the American East Coast had the effect of pushing landless whites onto Indian lands in the west. He therefore saw from his home in Mount Holly nearly all the evils of the far-flung empire around him. To divorce himself, symbolically at least, from the destructive operations of the imperial economy, he behaved in a way that struck many of his contemporaries as strange. He sometimes traveled on foot to avoid the ostentation and cruelty of riding horses and to dramatize his sense of kinship with slaves. Similarly in the 1760s he would not eat sugar, and he refused to wear dyed cloth, which for him represented luxury, exploitation, and waste. Gradually and deliberately he developed a way of structuring the routines of his daily life in order to provide lessons for those around him. At various moments,

Woolman considered the clothes he wore, his manner of speaking, the gifts he accepted and refused, the way he walked, where he slept, the food he ate, and his choice of spoons as freighted with moral and political significance. In his physical life, he sought to propound a critique of the imperial economy. He also sought to point the way toward a better future, the one foretold in biblical prophesy. Woolman's behavior confused many of his contemporaries, but after his death, with the posthumous publication of his journal, his reputation soared. He came to be revered as "the Quaker saint," and he was singled out as the most important early leader of the Quaker antislavery movement.

The effusive praise that Woolman has received, both as a saint and as a pioneering opponent of slavery, has unfortunately impeded our ability to comprehend his engagement with other Quakers, and it was those relationships which gave meaning and structure to his work as a reformer.[9] Historian Thomas P. Slaughter's biography *The Beautiful Soul of John Woolman, Apostle of Abolitionism* draws on and contributes to a long tradition of presenting Woolman as a unique prophetic figure who stood alone against the evils of his day. This literature has exaggerated the distance separating Woolman and his neighbors in Mount Holly from the secular currents of eighteenth-century life, and it has also consistently exalted him above the community of like-minded reformers who acted in concert to convince the Society of Friends to denounce slaveholding.[10]

In order to devote sustained attention to Woolman's community life, the influences that worked on him, and the problems that animated him, this book is organized into thematic chapters. Instead of presenting a simple chronological narrative, it starts with his conception of the course of history and proceeds through his understanding of the process of inspiration, his fidelity to Quaker discipline, and his thoughts on work, slavery, and warfare. The final three chapters examine demonstrative behavior, ocean-going travel, and death. From Woolman's perspective, all these issues were interrelated. The chapters have been placed in an order that elucidates how his engagement with one question informed his thoughts on another. They track the evolution of his ideas and concerns. Woolman's priorities changed during his career, but he was consistent in his effort to remain faithful to the fundamental tenets and practices of Quakerism.

When addressing Friends meetings, Woolman invoked long-standing Quaker traditions. He manifested a readiness to defer to the meetings' oversight bodies if his views were deemed unsound or excessively divisive, because he did not believe that he could do any good in the long run working outside the regular channels of the Society of Friends. He took many initiatives, but he never acted alone. The records of the Quaker meetings, Woolman's correspondence, and the letters of his contemporaries, business and probate records, travelers' journals, and the wide-ranging literature produced by the meetings situate Woolman within his religious society and demonstrate his engagement with the full spectrum of controversies engulfing eighteenth-century American Quakerism.[11] These records also reveal his familiarity with developments across the British Empire. Woolman wanted the meetings to improve themselves so that they could serve as model communities and influence others, and he believed that eventually the Quakers would help remake the world. He stubbornly maintained that this was possible even though the meetings sometimes infuriated him.

Woolman became a minister in 1741, when he was twenty-one, and from that time until his death in 1772 his work for the Society of Friends dominated his life. He helped manage the Mount Holly Quaker Meeting and attended worship there twice a week. He assumed important posts in regional Quaker meetings in the New Jersey capital, and Philadelphia. He traveled extensively as a minister, and at the end of his life he crossed the Atlantic to England. Nonetheless, although he worked hard in his ministerial capacity, he was never paid for his labor performed, because the Quakers condemned the "hireling ministry." Therefore, he had to find other work to support himself and his family.

Woolman's economic enterprises drew him much farther into the world of commerce than anyone would know just from reading his celebrated journal. His journal concentrates on his spiritual life, and its hold on our imaginations has made it difficult to recognize the complexity of his business operations. He was unhappy as an entrepreneur because he worried that the pursuit of profit compromised him. In the late 1750s, he tried to reform himself, but before that time as a shopkeeper and pork producer he obtained supplies from several continents and raised meat for the West Indies. He kept detailed, extensive records of his transactions in his ledger books, which open up a window into the social history of colonial New Jersey and reveal that colony's ties to the wider world.

When Woolman's grandparents arrived in New Jersey in the 1670s and 1680s, there were fewer than 10,000 settlers in the colony. The population had more than tripled by the time of Woolman's birth, and it grew beyond 100,000 during his lifetime.[12] As the settlers became more numerous, they also, as a group, grew steadily richer.[13] Diets improved, the housing stock became grander and more permanent, and consumer goods proliferated. As the colonists acquired wealth, they inevitably confronted a new moral order, a commercial culture that accepted, validated, and indeed promoted pursuit of self-interest in the marketplace. The idea that "private vices" could produce "public benefits" was a new concept in the eighteenth century, and although it was gaining force and empowering those who embraced it, it disturbed the consciences of many like Woolman who adhered to older models of civic responsibility, customary restraints in trading practices, and religious codes that condemned hubris, jealousy and greed.[14]

When Woolman attended Friends Meetings he met some who agreed with his prescriptions for reform at a fine level of detail, but he also encountered wealthy slaveholders, heavy drinkers, militiamen, and at least one privateer. While the Quakers valued unity, they faced mounting challenges to their sense of tradition and community, partly as a consequence of the expansion of the Atlantic economy. The increasing concentration of wealth, the presence of second- and third-generation slaves and freed people living with Quaker families, and the Delaware Valley's intimate economic ties to the sugar producing islands of the Caribbean made many local Friends skeptical about the moral foundations of their social order. Some Quakers had started to ask painful questions as early as the seventeenth century, but the reformers became better organized, more numerous, and more persistent during Woolman's lifetime, especially after Pennsylvania and New Jersey mobilized to participate in the Seven Years' War.[15]

The Seven Years' War was an unprecedented crisis for the Quakers of New Jersey and Pennsylvania. As professed pacifists, they believed that God required them to stay peaceful, but the outbreak of fighting along their frontiers seemed to prove that they had failed. Many believed that God was punishing them for neglecting or mistreating Indians and for a number of other transgressions including living ostentatiously and maintaining slaves. These views were not universally shared, however. There were others among the Quakers who responded to the war by concluding that pacifism was no longer a tenable option. Their legal obligations, their fidelity to the king, and their need to protect their home communities required them to participate in military action. Some of those who thought this way took up arms, hired substitute soldiers, or offered supplies to the troops. Pacifist Quakers brought disciplinary action against Friends who supported the war effort. The controversies that ensued divided the meetings and contributed to a purging that was already underway. Seeking to regain God's favor, Woolman and his fellow reformers demanded that the meetings maintain strictures against a wide range of bad behavior including military service, slaveholding, drunkenness, horse-racing, reading pernicious books, and marrying outside the Society of Friends.

After Britain's victory in the Seven Years' War, Woolman and other Quaker reformers positioned themselves as defenders of the Indians and campaigned for restraint in the settlement of the empire's recently conquered western lands. The Quakers' stance brought the wrath of their neighbors upon them, and the violence that ensued provides one indication among many that the questions dividing Quaker meetings were disturbing non-Quakers as well. As historian Christopher Brown has demonstrated, the expansion of the British Empire following the Seven Years' War triggered a wide-ranging transatlantic debate about the status of conquered peoples and the future relationships among the empire's diverse populations and lands. Polemicists and schemers took a fresh look at the empire as a whole. Proposals affecting North America implicated the Caribbean as well, and the discussion of the French and the Indians expanded to include black slaves. By the late 1760s, a significant number of non-Quakers were questioning the future of slavery in the British Empire.[16]

The debates that preoccupied Woolman affected everyone living in the British colonies in North America. Some passages in his journal, supplemented with other evidence, give an indication of how wide-ranging and pervasive the arguments became. During his travels through Virginia in 1757, Woolman entered into extended conversations with strangers he met on obscure country roads. A few of them had already formed strong opinions about the impact of the slave trade on the lives of the people of Africa. Woolman also met the father of a young man whose protest against the conduct of the Seven Years' War gained the attention of both George Washington and the governor of Virginia. Whether they supported the current direction of imperial policy or opposed it, these Virginians were aware of the controversies that surrounded the expansion of British power in North America and globally.

During the 1750s and 1760s, increasing numbers of English-speaking settlers in North America discovered that their economic activities were tied to those of peoples on distant shores of the Atlantic. The expansion of long-distance commerce caused considerable anxiety in the American colonies, leading some to ask new questions and seek new ways to express themselves by deploying their power as consumers. When Woolman and his fellow reformers publicly renounced the produce of the Caribbean, they invoked the Quakers' long-standing advisories against taking plunder from war zones and drinking excess quantities of rum. Associating those issues with the problem of slavery, some Delaware Valley Quakers had been expressing misgivings about participating in the Caribbean economy for decades. Many more started to avoid sugar and rum in the 1760s, and, in general, when they explained their decision, they focused on the connection between those products and slavery. Woolman, in particular, asked the Friends to calculate in detail the influence they might be having on the sugar islands (consciously or not) through their consumer behavior.

Woolman thus helped pioneer a form of protest that has gained power and influence steadily to the present day. He resolved to spend his money only in a manner that was consistent with the public good. His behavior in some ways prefigured and anticipated the later actions of the American Patriots who, during the imperial crisis of the late 1760s, subscribed to non-importation agreements and vowed not to purchase British goods. Like Woolman, the Patriots recognized the global impact of consumer expenditure. They asked the American colonists to temper their instinct for self-indulgence, become conscientious, and spend in ways that would send a political message and advance a righteous cause.[17] The Quakers were ahead of the Patriots in thinking about the leverage that they believed they had acquired as a consequence of the integration of the imperial economy. They also exerted a comparable historical influence. Although they never challenged the authority of the British parliament or monarchy, Woolman and his associates were as radical as the most ambitious Patriots. Within a generation after Woolman's death their movement had affected a change in the structure of society as revolutionary as anything associated with the formation of the United States.[18]

Nonetheless, it is important to remember that Woolman was never the paramount leader of the abolitionists. He was certainly no Napoleon, but by examining him closely in his social context we can learn a great deal about colonial America, the Quakers on both sides of the ocean, and the combination of religious conviction and communal tension that gave energy to the early days of organized opposition to slavery and its place in the imperial economy. Woolman's experiences illuminate the world in which he lived, and his life remained important, and indeed gained significance, after the eighteenth century. Those who measure a figure's historical significance on the basis of his or her influence should consider the lasting power of Woolman's carefully crafted life story. Woolman wrote his journal as a service to his society, and he strove to make sure that the episodes he recounted in the text advanced useful messages and promoted the divinely inspired project of the Society of Friends. Even while he was composing new entries he gave drafts of his finished chapters to other ministers, and he authorized them to delete or alter passages they considered unwise. After Woolman's death, his full journal was edited meticulously by Quaker committees prior to its publication. The account of Woolman's life contained in the journal is an unusually powerful story. But as historians we cannot understand it, or any other aspect of Woolman's career, without examining the community he was born into, and the religious society that shaped him and ultimately invested his life with a meaning that transcended his peculiar historical circumstances, turning him into an antislavery hero and the Quakers' saint.

Chapter 1

Past Ages: History

The apprehension of there being less steadiness and firmness
amongst people in this age than in past ages often troubled me
while I was a child.
 —John Woolman, *Journal*, chapter 1

IN 1755, WHEN at age thirty-five John Woolman began to write an account
of his life, he started with a Saturday afternoon when he was a schoolchild,
perhaps as young as six. The children were dismissed from their lessons, and
Woolman joined a group walking in the direction of his family's farm. None
of the boys and girls were in a hurry to get to their homes. After going a short
distance along the road, most of them ran into the fields to play, but Woolman did not follow them. He kept on walking by himself until he was "out of
sight," and then he sat down on the ground and opened his Bible. He wanted
to see how the Scriptures ended and turned to the last chapter of Revelation.
In his journal Woolman recounts reading, "He showed me a river of water,
clear as crystal, proceeding out of the throne of God and the Lamb, etc." Being
as young as he was, he may not have worked his way through the next twenty
verses to reach the end of the Bible, but undoubtedly he made it to the end
of the next verse, which reads, "on either side of the river, was there the tree
of life, which bare twelve manner of fruits, and yielded her fruit every month,
and the leaves of the tree were for the healing of the nations." He repeated
what he read, looked up, and decided that he wanted to see that place by the
river "which I then believed God had prepared for his servants." Recalling that
moment nearly thirty years later, he declared, "The place where I sat and the
sweetness that attended my mind remains fresh in my memory."[1]

That was Woolman's first epiphany, the beginning of a lifelong series of visionary events—he called them "gracious visitations"—that would punctuate, direct and inform his "experience of the goodness of God." As long as he lived he remembered vividly where this first experience took place. The small circle of ground by a path near a ridge overlooking Rancocas Creek in Burlington County, New Jersey, became lodged in his mind alongside the promise of the millennium. As he grew older, learned more about his family, studied Quaker history, and read further in the Bible, he became more convinced that the landscape around him was charged with historic and cosmic significance.

Not far from where he sat, his family lived in a brick house at the crest of a slope overlooking the creek. There was a barn by the house with poultry in the barnyard, hogs rooting, and sheep, cows, and horses grazing nearby. There were hayfields and plots of corn on the property, as well as woodlots and a productive apple orchard. Like his grandfather and father before him, Woolman referred to the place as a "plantation."[2]

His grandfather, also named John Woolman, had been one of the first English settlers in the region. In 1678, joining hundreds of other Quaker migrants, he had come to West Jersey from Gloucestershire at twenty-three. Shortly after he arrived, the proprietors of the new colony granted him a share that allowed him to claim a parcel of unoccupied land. The property he chose was well located. The plot abutted the southern boundary of Burlington, the colonial capital, and the banks of Rancocas Creek, which emptied into the Delaware River only four miles downstream. Woolman's grandfather took possession of the land in 1681, and soon thereafter built a house near the marshes by the side of the creek. He married and raised a family, cleared and planted fields, bought livestock, and in 1703 built the brick house that stood at the top of the ridge with a commanding view of the farm. He died in 1718, and John Woolman his grandson, born two years later, was named for him.[3]

Viewed across the fields from where the boy sat, the property might have looked large and prosperous, but Woolman never associated his home with comfort or ease. The house was crowded. At age seven John had three older sisters, one younger sister, and two younger brothers. Four more boys and two girls would be added to the family before he left home. Woolman's parents, Samuel and Elizabeth, faced enormous challenges maintaining the farm, feeding and supporting their proliferating offspring, and setting aside money and land to secure their sons' and daughters' futures. John held a special place as the first-born son. Though the Quakers strove to treat their children equally, for pragmatic reasons Samuel and Elizabeth prepared John to take over the farm in the event of their deaths. As he grew toward manhood John stayed with his parents and assumed increasing responsibility in helping to manage the family's estate, while his younger brother Abner, still a "lad," went away in the summers to work in the Pine Barrens on a construction crew building saw mills.[4]

In comparison with other settlers in British-colonial America, the Quakers who came to the Delaware Valley were unusually intent on acquiring land to distribute to as many of their sons as possible. This impulse stemmed from their devotion to the country life and their professed conviction that all their sons were equal in the eyes of God. If land could not be secured for every boy in a family, some other kind of provision would be made.[5] With seven sons, Samuel Woolman confronted a challenge larger than that faced by most of his neighbors. Though he already owned a large farm, he acquired extensive additional properties, including a large tract in Evesham to the south and nearly 400 acres in Morris County to the north. The outlying lands remained uncultivated. Samuel held them in reserve in order to provide for his younger sons' futures.[6] He was never able to acquire enough land for all the boys, but he wanted to allow as many of them as possible to become farmers, and he hoped to keep the family's original plantation intact and bequeath it to John.

John was an oldest son like his father and grandfather before him, and during his childhood he expected to inherit the land and continue their way of living. Looking back on his early years he judged that he was educated "pretty well for a planter."[7] Nearly as soon as he was able, his parents put him to work, directing him to help them care for animals. "In my youth I was used to hard labor," he remembered.[8] Samuel taught him the practical details of livestock husbandry, but the lessons he recalled most vividly related to the moral implications of farm work. John's father told him to "fear the Lord" and maintain a "spirit of tenderness" toward all the "creatures of which we had the command."[9]

As a family the Woolmans read the Bible carefully. On Sunday afternoons after returning home from Quaker meeting, Samuel and Elizabeth gathered their children and asked them to read biblical passages one at a time. John remembered that he "found comfort in reading the Holy Scriptures." Those afternoons strengthened his love for his mother, father, brothers, and sisters, and deepened his sense of obligation toward them all. He particularly revered his father. Once when John was ten or eleven years old, his father went away from home, and when his mother tried to discipline him he made what he remembered as "an undutiful reply." On the following Sunday the family went to

Quaker meeting together. John walked home alongside his father, and when the two of them were alone, his father reprimanded him for his disobedience. John walked home silently, went alone into the house, and prayed. From that moment forward, he declared in his journal, he never "spoke unhandsomely" to either of his parents again.[10]

Samuel and Ellizabeth watched their children closely. On one occasion after Quaker meeting, John's oldest sister Elizabeth and two of the other girls in the family resolved among themselves that they wanted to visit "some other young women at some distance off." John suspected that the company of those other girls would have done his sisters "no good." The young Elizabeth and her sisters asked for permission to go, but they were refused. Elizabeth accepted her parents' judgment, and later that day when the two younger girls were complaining, she cut them short and said that their mother and father had acted "for their good."[11] John agreed. By the time he was eleven he was already convinced that children were dangerously vulnerable to corruption, and this was a conviction he retained for the rest of his life.[12] Parents could never fully control their young sons and daughters, but he always considered it "very grievous" when pious fathers saw their educational efforts wasted or perverted by sons and daughters who took advantage of their upbringing and instead of serving God chose iniquity.[13]

Even as a boy John wanted to be good and do good, and with these goals in mind he worked on the farm. He studied the scriptures and other "religious books," and attended Quaker meetings. Alone, for example during his "winter evenings," he explored his father's library which contained not only "books of divinity" but also treatises on law and navigation.[14] Gradually he developed a conception of his family's place in the wider world.

The landscape around the Woolmans' farm was scattered with clues to its historical significance. Nearly all the prominent buildings were made of brick in a distinctive style. Since the seventeenth century, Quaker landowners in southern New Jersey had built their houses out of brick. They had designed and constructed their Meeting Houses in a similar manner so that together their homes and places of worship gave their towns, villages and farmland an appearance that was recognizably Quaker.[15] The Quakers who settled along Rancocas Creek erected their meeting house the same year that the elder John Woolman built his brick home. The meeting house stood to the west of the plantation only a few hundred yards away.[16]

Most of the farms in the area were patchworks like the Woolman lands, with hayfields, meadows, crops, orchards, gardens, and woods. The soil was

Figure 1. House in Mount Holly, New Jersey, built for John Woolman's brother Asher in 1756. It is typical of Quaker architectural style. Courtesy New Jersey State Archives, Department of State.

not particularly good for raising grain. Local families raised pork, mutton, and beef, and they made butter and cheese. They had several ways to get their produce to market. Rancocas Creek was navigable, and at the mouth of the creek the Delaware River was wide, providing easy access to the port of Burlington to the north and Philadelphia to the southwest. Small boats passed by the Woolmans' farm going to and from the Delaware. Burlington County's rural families also used roads and footpaths through the region, carrying produce in carts or driving livestock overland to Burlington or to the ferry port across the river from Philadelphia. Pork was the region's biggest money-earner and its most important contribution to the economy of the British Empire. In *The History of Nova Caesarea*, published in 1765, Burlington historian Samuel Smith declared that pork was the local staple and that the county's farmers raised it primarily "for the West-India market." Smith boasted that Burlington County pork had a good reputation "through all the islands" of the Caribbean.[17]

Standing on the riverbank a few miles from his house, John could watch ships anchoring off the docks at Burlington, loading barrels of salted pork, and sailing south toward the ocean. He first saw the sea when he was still a young man. His younger brother Uriah moved to Philadelphia in his twenties and entered into business selling produce overseas, an occupation that brought him into frequent contact with ship captains.[18] His brother Abner, by contrast, stayed closer to his ancestral home. New Jersey was small and no one was ever far from the ocean, but Abner did not see the open water until 1760, when he was thirty-six.[19]

A census taken in 1726 counted 4,129 people in Burlington County: 3,872 whites and 257 of African descent. Nearly half the inhabitants were under sixteen, and the population was growing steadily through the time of Woolman's childhood. Census-takers returned in 1745 and counted 6,369 whites and 434 blacks. Burlington City, the county seat and provincial capital, was older than Philadelphia and although it was considerably smaller, in some ways it rivaled its downstream neighbor. Burlington was a center of government, it had a capacious and busy port, and it was a hub of American Quakerism. The most important annual gathering of Quakers in the Delaware Valley, Philadelphia Yearly Meeting, met every other year in Burlington. The region was steadily growing more diverse, and by 1745, according to the census, "Quakers and reputed Quakers" constituted less than half of Burlington County's population.[20] Nonetheless, of all Burlington's religious communities, the Friends had made the most visible mark on the landscape. In the 1760s Smith counted 19 church buildings in the county: two Episcopalian chapels, one Baptist, one Presbyterian, and 15 Quaker meeting houses.[21] Woolman grew up surrounded by physical reminders of his heritage, but he sensed that his ancestors' way of life and the customs that had sustained them, both as a religious society and as a farming community, were losing their hold on his world.

In 1730 a consortium of investors opened an iron works in the town of Mount Holly, four miles upstream from the Woolman farm on Rancocas Creek. Within a few years they had built a furnace, two forges, and several houses for their workers on 400 acres of meadows and woodland. Agents for the operation recruited laborers not only in Mount Holly but across the river from Burlington in Bristol, Pennsylvania, and in Philadelphia. They purchased the contracts of servants bound for terms of years, including some men born in the colonies and others newly arrived from Ireland and Britain. They also employed African-born and American slaves.[22] At the time of Woolman's birth there had been slaves and other bound servants living in houses scattered across Burlington County. Nearly one of every five households in the county contained slaves.[23] But household servants generally lived in the homes of their masters. The men and women who lived and worked in Mount Holly were different, and posed a more visible challenge to the rural social order. Mount Holly became a destination for runaways and the center of a visible, cosmopolitan community that welcomed young men and women who lived outside families, including bound servants and slaves.[24]

The iron works in Mount Holly were a local manifestation of a pattern of development overtaking the economy of the entire Delaware Valley. While the region continued to derive most of its income from agricultural exports, engaging in overseas commerce was speculative and dangerous, and as a consequence wealthy colonists in Pennsylvania and New Jersey had no secure way to reinvest their earnings. Increasingly through the eighteenth century, they formed partnerships and launched enterprises that might have seemed prohibitively risky in a more stable economic environment. Some of the new businesses, particularly in the iron industry, made substantial profits.[25] New fortunes were made, and the gap between rich and poor became more obvious. The diversification of the economy helped finance a rise in expenditure for fine clothing, jewelry, books, and furniture.[26] At the same time, economic development brought tens of thousands of indigent non-Quakers into the region, some bound by contract to labor for a term of years, and others enslaved.

There is no way to know in detail how Woolman thought about these developments when he was a boy, but looking back on his childhood from the perspective of the 1750s he remembered feeling apprehensive. Though he expressed deep satisfaction with the Quaker community that had brought him up, he declared that he had been frequently disturbed by a sense that he lived in an era of weakness and moral decline. He wrote, "The apprehension of there being less steadiness and firmness amongst people in this age than in past ages often troubled me while I was a child."[27] His uneasiness lingered. Woolman remained wistful for the rest of his life.

*   *   *

When he meditated on the course of his life, Woolman was always mindful of the legacies bequeathed to him by his father and grandfather. Whether he was making plans, assessing the good he had done, or recognizing his failings, he kept his family and his religious heritage in mind. As an adult when he reviewed records left by Quakers who had died, he declared that he looked forward to the day when he might join them among the worthy departed. He wanted to emulate the best of his predecessors, including men and women from the recent and the distant past. In 1767 Woolman was a member of the Burlington Quarterly Meeting of Ministers and Elders, and he wrote this comment at the bottom of a list of that meeting's current membership: "As looking over the minutes made by persons who have put off this body hath sometimes revived in me a thought how ages pass away, so this list may probably revive a like thought in some when I and the rest of the persons above named are centered in another state of being."[28]

Even as a boy Woolman deduced from what he "heard and read" that there had been times in the past when people "walked in uprightness before God in a degree exceeding any that I knew or heard of."[29] He continued to believe that the faithful of previous generations had outshone those who lived in his own age. The idea did not depress him, but rather inspired him to effort. As a reformer he sought to restore the righteousness that had been lost. At various moments over the course of his lifetime, he said his contemporaries should follow examples set by the first Quaker settlers of the Delaware Valley, the original English founders of the Quaker movement, the early Protestant reformers who broke with the Catholic Church, the early Christians, Jesus, the prophets, and Moses. He thought Quakers should emulate Adam and Eve.

Woolman never thought that in the circumstances of the mid-eighteenth century it would be possible or even wise to try to live precisely as the ancients had lived. Like other Quakers, he believed that every age faced its own challenges, and that God would always help humanity cope by providing his people with new revelations.[30] He hoped to become one of his own era's prophets. That aspiration, paradoxically, only strengthened his sense of kinship with people from history. Though he felt disturbed by the events of the eighteenth century, he felt indebted to the good people who had come before him, and contemplating the direction of his own life, he looked for guidance by meditating on lives from the past.

When he surveyed the past looking for exemplary righteous communities, the most recent he could recognize were the early Quaker settlers of New Jersey and Pennsylvania. They had proven themselves by establishing friendly relations with the Indians and more generally by adhering to the fundamental principles of Quakerism. After visiting frontier communities himself, Woolman came to the conclusion that the struggle to survive, clear farmland, and build new towns in the forest promoted austerity and plain living. Righteous colonists in newly settled regions were likely to live like "disciples of Christ."[31] God had recognized the devotion of the first Quakers in the Delaware Valley. He had favored them and their good fortune proved it.

Woolman believed that "our gracious father, who at the same time beholds the situation of all his creatures," had "opened a way" for some Europeans to move away from their "thick-settled land." As he described this process in the early 1770s, God had "given us room" in the Americas.[32] Woolman argued that the early colonists and their progeny had been able to make a good life for themselves in America and also that their arrival, in the long run, would work for the benefit of the Indians. He described humanity as "one great family, consisting of various parts, divided by great waters." Everyone on earth was descended from Adam and Eve, but one branch of that great family—the Indians—had become isolated in the Americas after the flood. "Within a few ages past," the Europeans had discovered how to cross the Atlantic, and this knowledge had presented them with an unprecedented opportunity. Christ had long ago commanded his followers to "preach the gospel to distant countries," and therefore as soon as "crossing the seas" became possible it became a "necessity." But not all "professed Christians" had been equal to the charge. Contrasting New Jersey and Pennsylvania with places like Peru and Virginia, Woolman argued that the original colonization of the Delaware Valley had been a uniquely blessed historical event because the settlers had been faithful servants of God.[33]

When he reviewed the history of his home region Woolman never acknowledged that Swedish and Dutch colonists had preceded the Quakers by decades, nor did he mention the English conquest of New Netherland, which had made it possible for Charles II to grant charters to the first proprietors of West Jersey and Pennsylvania. According to Woolman's account of events, the Quakers had sailed up the Delaware alone without military support or any other colonists preparing the ground for them. They had met only Indians in the valley, and the outcome of that encounter had been nothing less than miraculous.

In Woolman's lifetime, Burlington County retained many reminders of the transformative events of the seventeenth century. When he was young there were still several compact Indian communities in western New Jersey, though they no longer dominated the landscape. Indians also lived and worked, alone or in small groups, among the colonists.[34] While the Quakers felled trees, constructed barns, and erected brick and stone buildings, uncut tracts of forest remained. In 1765 Woolman lived adjacent to lands that were described in newspaper advertisements as "well timbered" and suitable for clearing and making "meadow."[35] In the 1760s Smith reported that the colony's woods contained panthers, bears, wildcats, wolves, rattlesnakes, gray foxes, red foxes, raccoons, otters, beavers, squirrels, rabbits, minks, groundhogs, and deer. In general the wild animals were in retreat, however, and Smith noted that the "most voracious" of them had been driven away from the "old settled places."[36] Woolman believed that God had directed this transformation. In an essay published in 1754, he invoked the early years of the Quaker colonies in order to profess gratitude for God's overriding influence. "Respecting our progress in this land, the time is short since our beginning was small and number few, compared with the native inhabitants." The colonists had survived with divine protection, and against the apparent odds they had done well. "The wilderness and solitary deserts in which our fathers passed the days of their pilgrimage are now turned into pleasant fields. The natives are gone from before us, and we establish peaceably in the possession of the land, enjoying our civil and religious liberties."[37]

Woolman was convinced that the Quakers had received divine assistance in America, but he also sensed that God's favors had come with conditions attached. Even as a young man, he believed that the Quakers held no exclusive claim on Providence. At nineteen or twenty, when he was still living in his parents' house, he received what he described as a revelation informing him that "sincere, upright-hearted people in every society who truly loved God were accepted of him."[38] Years later in an epistle he drafted for Philadelphia Yearly Meeting, he provided an extended discussion of God's role in history. He insisted that all the "empires and kingdoms of the earth" were subject to God's "almighty power," and that the events recorded in the Bible demonstrated that the Lord judged societies "in a national capacity." While God did not "at all times suddenly execute his judgments on a sinful people in this life," justice would always ultimately prevail. Therefore the world's evil "provinces and kingdoms" were doomed to "drink the cup of adversity as a reward of their doings." History proved that the only safe course for any people to take was to follow God's directions and rely on him. The faithful would be rewarded. It was only "righteousness which exalteth a nation."[39] Woolman believed this not only on the basis of his reading, but also from looking at the land around him and from speaking with a few old Friends who had been present at the founding of New Jersey and Pennsylvania. Though he does not mention them in his journal, his maternal grandparents Henry and Elizabeth Burr had come separately to New Jersey in the 1680s, and it is clear from other evidence that Woolman knew his grandfather well.[40]

Throughout his life he respected the elderly, and he recorded in his journal one instructive encounter with an ancient Friend, a dramatic moment which made an impression not only on Woolman but on many other Quakers in the Delaware Valley. At Philadelphia Yearly Meeting in 1764, an eighty-three-year-old man named John Smith rose to speak. Born in New England, Smith became a Quaker while still a child. In his youth he suffered for his convictions. In 1704 he was imprisoned in Massachusetts for seven months because he refused to enlist for Major Benjamin Church's military raid against Acadia. Two years later, he sailed to England where he ran afoul of a naval press-gang. Smith was forced on board a warship where he remained, nominally a member of the crew, for six weeks. During that time he underwent "sufferings" and "trials," but he refused to cooperate, and eventually he was released, whereupon he made his way quickly to Pennsylvania. In 1764 Smith was visibly old and ill. He told the meeting that he expected to die soon and he wanted to give them a final piece of advice, much as an ailing parent might want to instruct a child. He reminded those around him that early in the century the Quakers had been "a plain, low-minded people," but in the Delaware Valley by the 1720s they had "increased in wealth" and begun "conforming to the fashions of the world." They had lost some of their humility and "their meetings in general" were "not so lively and edifying." By the 1740s many Friends were "very rich." They wore "costly garments" and silver watches, even at worship. Partly as a result, "the powerful overshadowings of the Holy Ghost were less manifest in the Society." As for the 1760s, Smith declared, "the barrenness manifest amongst us is a matter of much sorrow." He was right, at least as far as his health was concerned. Smith never returned to Yearly Meeting, and he died in 1766.[41]

Woolman believed that the early Quakers, like John Smith, had been tested and strengthened through suffering. Their perseverance and fidelity to their principles had proved that they were better Christians than the comfortable Friends of the middle years of the eighteenth century. Smith was unusual from Woolman's perspective in that he had been born in the colonies and had undergone his early trials in Massachusetts. Generalizing about Quaker history, Woolman asserted that the Quakers in England and Wales suffered more than their colonial counterparts. By standing fast in the face of persecution they had proven themselves and demonstrated that they were better able to resist the bad influence of their non-Quaker neighbors. He believed that among all his Quaker predecessors, the most diligent, patient, and faithful were those who had joined the Society of Friends while still in England and Wales. Pennsylvania and New Jersey had been founded well because they were settled by British Friends.[42]

Woolman studied the early English Quakers. In his journal he records that as a child he spent some "leisure time" reading "the history of the first rise of our society."[43] As an adult he possessed his own copy of William Sewel's 721-page *History of the Rise, Increase, and Progress of the Christian People called Quakers*.[44] He owned that book along with other works by prominent seventeenth-century English Quakers including William Penn, Robert Barclay and William Dewsbury. And he lent these works to his neighbors.[45] As a minister Woolman asked the Delaware Valley Quakers to "look unto the Rock from whence we were hewn" and follow their English ancestors' example.[46] He thought that a great "work of reformation" had begun in England and he wanted to see it "spread amongst the nations."[47]

Woolman knew that in some respects England had been a hostile place for the first Quakers. The early Friends had faced persecution, but eventually God had intervened in English politics and "providentially delivered" them.[48] From that time forward the Friends had enjoyed a kind of freedom "unknown in many parts of the world." Under the influence of Providence, the English government granted the Quakers "liberty of conscience" and in effect presented them with an opportunity to disseminate "the pure gospel ministry without interruption from outward power."[49] The "free exercise of religion" was a "pure gift," and Woolman declared that it required "our deepest gratitude and most careful attention."[50] He thought that English liberty placed an obligation on the Quakers not only to be thankful but also worthy. "A trust is committed to us, a great and weighty trust." If the Friends abused their freedom and misbehaved, they would lose the favor that they had received from Providence and take a "step back toward the wilderness, one step toward undoing what God in infinite love hath done through his faithful servants in a work of several ages."[51]

During Woolman's lifetime, the Delaware Valley Quakers uniformly insisted that liberty of conscience could only be preserved through the continuation of Britain's system of government. They therefore repeatedly declared their devotion to the king. The first Philadelphia Yearly Meeting session Woolman attended as a representative of Burlington, in 1746, ended with an effusive declaration of support for George II. The Quakers had only a few weeks earlier learned of the military defeat of the rebel Catholic Charles Edward Stuart and his supporters. The meeting formally sent a letter to London expressing their "thankfulness and humility" and acknowledging "the gracious interposition of the divine Providence" in delivering "our King and our fellow subjects in Great Britain from the difficulties and dangers to which they have been exposed, by the base, wicked and perfidious attempts of unreasonable and ungrateful men, who had combined against our happiness and were desperately engaged in attempting the subversion of our liberties in order to subject us to the tyranny of a Popish Pretender, and to the superstition and idolatry of the Church of Rome." The Yearly Meeting called on Quakers everywhere to demonstrate "by the whole course of their conduct" their "fidelity and loyalty to our King, who on this occasion hath manifested a pastoral care for the safety and protection of all his faithful subjects, and whose favorable notice, in continuing to us the free enjoyment of our religion and civil liberties, we have abundant cause humbly and dutifully to acknowledge."[52]

It may seem incongruous for pacifist Quakers to praise the British monarch in the aftermath of the notoriously bloody Battle of Culloden, but the Friends' peace testimony was seldom interpreted in the eighteenth century as prohibiting the use of force to uphold the rule of law.[53] Rebellion was a crime, and Friends generally accepted the government's authority to suppress insurrection. To be sure, as Woolman would later discover, the Quakers disagreed among themselves over the meaning of their commitment to peace, but even when discussing the Anglo-French wars, Quaker meetings in America went out of their way to express fidelity to the crown, publicly praying that God would use his own means to protect the British people and preserve their system of government. They issued these declarations in part to disabuse those who suspected that the Quakers were disloyal, but the meetings did not make these statements merely to placate their critics. Compared to other colonists in North America, they maintained unusually close ties with England.

Friends meetings in Britain and America exchanged correspondence and ministerial visits on a regular basis, and as a group the American Quakers felt that they knew England well. Woolman expressed his love for the English countryside long before he ever saw it.[54] His affection for England stemmed in part from its association with the origins of Quakerism, but when he surveyed human history and contemplated the legacies bequeathed to him by earlier generations, he felt indebted to the English in general and not merely to the seventeenth-century Quakers. He was particularly mindful of the struggles and accomplishments of the English Protestants of the sixteenth century. He felt moved by the story of Bishop Hugh Latimer, for example, who during the reign of Queen Mary I faced prosecution for his Protestant beliefs. When the criminal court announced its sentence and informed him that he would be burned alive at the stake, Latimer praised God for allowing him to die a martyr. He told the courtroom, "I thank God most heartily that he hath prolonged my life to this end, that I may in this case glorify him by this kind death." After reading Latimer's words in John Foxe's *Book of Martyrs*, Woolman copied them out and added the following commentary: "It is worthy of remembrance that people in different ages, deeply baptized into the nature of that work for which Christ suffered, have joyfully offered up their liberty and lives for the promoting of it in the earth."[55]

Bishop Latimer died for a cause that transcended the boundaries of England. Woolman knew that the English did not initiate the Protestant Reformation. He acknowledged that the "reformation from popery" had been "a gradual progress from age to age." Successive generations of reformers had been able to "proceed further," each cohort "laboring in those works of righteousness appointed for them in their day." Therefore when he searched for heroes in the era before the sixteenth century, he looked beyond Britain to continental Europe. He celebrated the life and work of the fifteenth-century Bohemian reformer Jan Hus, for example, who was widely regarded as a precursor to Luther.[56]

Woolman assumed a tolerant disposition as a young man, and as an adult he admired the Catholic mystic Thomas à Kempis, whose work he lent out to customers in his shop.[57] Nonetheless, like other Protestants in his day, he categorically rejected the institutional pretensions of the Roman Catholic Church. The "Bishop of Rome," he complained, "assumes a power that does not belong to any officer in the church of Christ."[58] Woolman considered the pontiff sinfully arrogant, and he associated the Catholic Church with repression and violence. "How deeply affecting is the condition of many upright hearted people who are taken into the papal inquisition? What lamentable cruelties, in deep vaults, in a private way, are exercised on many of them? And how lingering is that death by a small slow fire, which they have frequently endured, who have been faithful to the end?"[59] Woolman vowed never to make any statement or take any action that might bolster the ecclesiastical power of the Pope. "If I should knowingly do anything tending to strengthen him in that capacity, it would be great iniquity."[60] He thought the basic task of the Reformation had been to repair the damage done by the Catholics in the Middle Ages and restore the ways of the ancient church.

Woolman studied the lives of the early Christians alongside those of George Fox and the other early Quakers for specific guidance on conduct. He believed that both groups were inspired by the same spirit. He took it for granted, for example, that the Christians in the Roman Empire dressed in a way that conformed to Quaker standards of simplicity, and that they refused to participate in "heathenish" ceremonies much in the same way that the early

Figure 2. Title page of William Cave's *Primitive Christianity*, a work Woolman frequently cited in his writings on the early church. Courtesy Library Company of Philadelphia.

Quakers refused to doff their hats.[61] He thought that early Christianity was, in effect, an older version of Quakerism and quite possibly a better one, closer to the teachings of Jesus. Eager to study early Christian customs, he read and reread William Cave's *Primitive Christianity: or, The Religion of the Ancient Christians in the First Ages of the Gospel.*[62] Using Cave as his principal source, he found instruction in the lives of several early Christian figures including Polycarp of Smyrna, Tertullian, Origen, and Clement of Alexandria.[63]

Behind those early Christians stood Jesus, who from Woolman's perspective presented the strictest, and potentially the most intimidating, exemplar of moral behavior. Woolman insisted that Jesus had set "an example of humility and plainness" for all those who believed in him. He thought he knew what the savior had looked like, and he asserted that Jesus was "not only meek and low of heart, but his outward appearance was plain and lowly." Following Christ's example required the rejection of "selfish customs in food, in raiment, in houses, and all things else." Woolman warned his fellow Quakers, "Think not his pattern too plain or too coarse for you."[64] Like Thomas à Kempis, he thought everyone should strive to imitate Christ.

Woolman accepted the narrative of human events contained in the Bible beginning with the lives of Adam and Eve and continuing through the great flood, the destruction of the tower of Babel, the scattering of the world's peoples, and the tumultuous history of Israel.[65] The Bible gave Woolman a record of specific ancient incidents, and also provided an indication of how history worked, describing the forces that influenced human affairs and the ways that ordinary people experienced them. Woolman assumed that the same dynamics that had operated in biblical times continued to prevail in the eighteenth century. He incorporated scriptural passages into nearly everything he wrote, including his private correspondence, his lessons for children, his essays, his journal, and even his account books. He constantly tested his ideas and observations against the truths revealed in the scriptures.

Woolman trusted the insights of the seers and wise men of the Bible, and he hoped to replicate their experience. He never thought that they had had better access to God than he did. On the contrary, he prepared himself in an effort to make sure that if he received a divine call he would be ready to assume prophetic authority. From his earliest days as a minister, when he confronted potentially hostile audiences, he comforted himself by recounting the experiences of other prophets. He kept in mind that the "messages of the prophet Jeremiah were so disagreeable to the people" that "he became the object of their reproach." He also compared himself to Moses.[66]

The naming practices of Woolman's Quaker neighbors reflected the Bible's hold on their imaginations. Sometime after 1753, Woolman recorded the names of the male members of the Mount Holly Meeting. He copied out 47 names, 40 of which were biblical. The meeting's membership included eight Johns, six Josephs, four Samuels, three Jacobs, three Josiahs, three Thomases, two Solomons, an Aaron, an Abram, a Benajah, a Benjamin, a Daniel, a David, a Hezekiah, a Jeremiah, a Job, and a Zachariah.[67] When they named their own children, Woolman's parents followed a similar pattern. John had brothers named Abraham, Abner, Asher, Eber, Jonah, and Uriah, and sisters named Elizabeth, Esther, Hannah, Rachel, and Sarah. Of the thirteen children only one, Patience, did not carry a biblical name.[68] It was not unusual for Quakers to identify with figures from the Old Testament. In his influential seventeenth-century treatise on Quaker theology, Robert Barclay had written, "God hath seen meet that herein [that is, in the Scriptures] we should, as in a looking-glass, see the conditions and experiences of the saints of old; that finding our experience answering to theirs, we might thereby be the more confirmed and comforted."[69]

Over the centuries in many countries, religious communities have drawn strength from Old Testament stories chronicling the integrity, courage, and resilience of a few of the chosen people. According to the Bible many of the descendants of Abraham faltered, but even in the face of military conquest, captivity, and forced exile, at least a small number refused to abandon their nation's distinctive ways. Like most readers of the Bible, Woolman loved those tales of heroism, but when he turned to the first pages of the scriptures his thoughts focused on less self-consciously divisive themes. As Woolman understood them, the early chapters of Genesis outlined a history and a set of cultural antecedents that every nation shared.

Like other Quakers before him, he was fascinated by the design, partial construction, and demolition of the Tower of Babel.[70] Prior to that moment in history, all humanity had shared a common language. Things had changed radically after the architects of Babel, seeking "self-exaltation," declared "Let us build a tower and a city." Woolman conflated Babel with Babylon, and he associated both places with "the confusion of languages" and a decadent, avaricious, urban way of life. In his most ambitious exegesis on human history, he described Babel as a "city of business," and proceeded immediately to quote the words of an angel in Revelation: "Come out of Babylon my people."[71] From his early childhood onward, at least since that afternoon when he sat under a tree and read the last chapter of the Bible, he had been convinced that

God had prepared a "pure habitation" for his servants.[72] On the basis of other scriptural passages he came to believe that, in that future paradise, all people would speak the same language, or at a minimum everyone would be able to understand one another, and no one would live in a commercial city. Only under these circumstances could the "true harmony of mankind" be restored.

History began, of course, with Adam and Eve. Woolman closely identified himself with humanity's first parents. They had seen life in Paradise, and after their fall and expulsion from the garden, they had set to work trying to regain what they had lost. In their early days in the wilderness, Adam and Eve had "no house, no tools for business, no garments but what their Creator gave them, no vessels for use, nor any fire to cook roots or herbs." Nonetheless God had guided them and given them "means for their happy living in this world." Woolman noticed some similarity between the landscape that Adam and Eve occupied and the wilds of America, and he considered the two of them models of Quaker-style simplicity, diligence, and faith.[73]

Woolman understood the standard Christian teaching that good had come from Adam and Eve's fall. The difficulties of life outside Paradise had given the faithful an opportunity to prove through many trials their love of God. Humanity's sins also made it possible for God to show his love through the sacrifice of Jesus.[74] There was nothing in these doctrines, however, that could weaken Eden's hold on Woolman's imagination. He wanted to peer into the past as far as he could see, and observing the world around him, especially as a boy, he noticed remnants of Paradise nearly everywhere he looked.

Woolman's experience of farm life confirmed his reading of Genesis. He believed that the structure, appearance, and appeal of plants and animals provided evidence of God's original plan for creation. He was convinced that there was a "superiority in men over the brute creatures." He thought that some animals were "so manifestly dependent on men for a living, that for them to serve us in moderation so far as relates to the right use of things looks consonant to the design of our Creator."[75] He observed that sheep in particular "are pleasant company on a plantation, their looks are modest, their voice is soft and agreeable; their defenseless state exposeth them a prey to wild beasts, and they appear to be intended by the great Creator, to live under our protection, and supply us with matter for warm and useful clothing."[76] The sheep's amiability, helplessness and good service proved that the animal deserved and needed humanity's attention.

Domestic animals played an essential role in Woolman's conception of moral order. They demanded love and care while implicitly calling on their keepers to behave responsibly. They also modestly accepted their place in God's creation. As an adult, when he was feeling anxious, impatient, or upset, Woolman found comfort walking through fields. "The sight of innocent birds in the branches and sheep in the pastures, who act according to the will of their Creator, hath at times tended to mitigate my trouble." Pasturelands reminded him not only of Eden but also of God's promise of a better future, because Woolman's understanding of history was circular. He believed that it was the task of Christianity to reverse the effects of Adam and Eve's fall, "to repair the breach made by disobedience, to finish sin and transgression."[77] Eventually God would lead his servants to "that holy mountain on which they neither *hurt nor destroy*!"[78] On the slopes of that mountain, according to Isaiah, even wild animals would live as if they had been raised on a farm. "The wolf also shall dwell with the lamb, and the leopard shall lie down with the kid; and the calf and the young lion and the fatling together . . . and the cow and the bear shall feed; their young ones shall lie down together; and the lion shall eat straw like an ox."[79] Long before he left his father's farm, Woolman had come to believe that loving animals was an integral part of the Christian life. He insisted that "the flame of life was kindled in all animal and sensitive creatures" and that "the love and reverence of God the Creator" required the faithful "to exercise true justice and goodness, not only toward all men but also toward all the brute creatures." "To say we love God as unseen and at the same time exercise cruelty toward the least creature moving by his life, or by life derived from him, was a contradiction in itself."[80]

Woolman began to attach religious significance to livestock-keeping as a child, and as an adult he sought to make other children cognizant of the moral significance of animals. In the 1760s, he became a schoolteacher and composed an inexpensive primer entitled *A First Book for Children* which he intended for rural households where the boys and girls had not yet entered school.[81] The earliest lessons in the primer provided an idealized vision of a working farm. These were the first sentences Woolman expected the young students to copy out:

> The Sun is up my Boy,
> Get out of thy Bed,
> Go thy way for the Cow,
> Let her eat the Hay.
> Now the Sun is set,
> And the Cow is put up,

The Boy may go to his Bed.
Go not in the Way of a bad Man;
Do not tell a Lie my Son.

The primary purpose of this lesson was to teach the child how to write correctly, but the words also conveyed a message about the care of domestic animals.

The second writing lesson began with comments on birds and sheep:

The Dove doth no harm,
The Lamb doth no harm,
A good boy doth no harm.
The Eye of the Lord is on them that fear him. He will love them,
    and do them good.
He will keep their Feet in the Way they go, and save them
    from the Paths of Death.

While the first lesson centered on human responsibility toward animals, this second presented animals as models of good behavior. That message was reinforced in Woolman's third lesson, which focused on creatures in the wild:

The Lark will fly in the Field,
The Cat doth run after the Mouse,
The Chub swims in the Brook,
And the good Boy will love to do good in his place.

Children should find their place within God's moral order: this lesson was repeated in the next lesson, which brought the students back to the barnyard.

The Cow gives us Milk,
The Sheep spares us Wool,
The Hen lays Eggs,
The good Boy and the good Girl learn their Books.
Good Boys do well.
Bad Boys go to Ruin.

After that last, sobering warning, animals disappeared from the primer. Woolman did not use their lives to illustrate evil. In a lesson plan he wrote for his own classroom, he composed this model sentence for his students to copy: "A viper is poison but not like bad company."[82] He wanted the children to know that animals were better than evil people, even if the animal in question was a poisonous snake.

As a reformer Woolman called for the better treatment of domestic animals. He protested, for example, against the abuse of draft animals in North America's fields and on the continent's roads. "Oxen and horses are often seen at work when, through heat and too much labor, their eyes and the emotion of their bodies manifest that they are oppressed. Their loads in wagons are frequently so heavy that when weary with hauling it far, their drivers find occasion in going up hills or through mire to raise their spirits by whipping to get forward."[83] He also expressed concern that destitute families underfed their cattle. "I have seen poor creatures in distress, for want of good shelter and plentiful feeding, when it did not appear to be in the power of the owners to do much better for them, being straightened in answering the demands of the wealthy."[84] On some farms during long winters "the grain intended for the cow is found necessary to be eaten in the family." To illustrate the suffering that resulted, he described the lament of a dairy cow. "I knew her voice, and the sound thereof was the cry of hunger."[85]

Woolman was not the only Quaker reformer in the eighteenth century to profess a concern for the proper care of animals. Along with Woolman, the antislavery campaigners Benjamin Lay, Joshua Evans, and Anthony Benezet objected to the mistreatment of draft animals and livestock. Indeed Lay, Evans, and Benezet took a step Woolman never publicly took, and became vegetarian.[86] Compared to some others Woolman was relatively moderate, but his way of discussing animals accorded with a cultural trend that affected many others in the Delaware Valley. Still, in his journal he insisted that he learned about the religious significance of animals not from a widespread public discussion, but from an intimate set of conversations he had as a boy with his father. It is an explanation that receives corroboration from the writings of Woolman's brother Abner. Before he died in 1771, Abner gave John a manuscript journal containing what he thought were the most important religious messages of his life.

Abner was four years younger than John, and as the sixth child and third boy in the family he did not get as much attention from his father as John did. Nonetheless he received the rudiments of the same education. Although Abner spent the summers of his childhood hired out to work on sawmills, he regretted leaving home, and would have preferred to stay with his father to help maintain the farm. Recounting his younger days, he remembered that he used to think that he could see the world almost as it had appeared when it was first created by God. "I looked upon the visible part of creation in a degree of the light and power in which it was made." He thought that when seen in this way, even trees could "afford us an innocent pleasure in this life, if the mind be fully subdued, and above all things delighted in adoring the great creator." Like his brother John, when he was troubled Abner found consolation meditating upon the "vast globe, the lights in the firmament, the depths of the sea, the many sorts of grain, plants, and herbs." All these things "set forth the power of an Almighty being." Abner watched "multitudes of birds with a pleasant harmonious voice" and heard them singing God's praise. He saw "four footed beasts" living in "fatness and delight" and he was convinced that they were fed by God.[87]

Abner argued that "if we look on the face of the earth" it was easy to discern the intentions of "the great creator of the whole universe." The "great variety of pleasant healthful fruits" and "plants and herbs" were the food that God had provided Adam and Eve in their "state of innocency." "Alas," he wrote, "by giving way to selfish desires" man had become "degenerated and alienated from his maker. . . . In this dark fallen state, what vast havoc doth he make with the creation? What numberless numbers of animals are oppressed and destroyed by man, and how oft doth men oppress and afflict each other?"[88] He asserted that Christians should admire and emulate the "meek spirit of a dove," and the innocence of a lamb.[89]

Abner believed that those who cared for children and animals should follow the example Adam and Eve had set when they lived in Paradise. "When thou undertakes the management of the young, or other creatures, O then remember the innocency of man, when the Almighty gave him dominion over the inferior part of the creation! And labor for that innocent state, therein to govern with tenderness and mercy." He linked an admonition from Deuteronomy, "Thou shalt not muzzle the ox when it treadeth out the corn," with the general charge that he believed God had given Adam and Eve, to take dominion over "the inferior part of the creation" but at the same time to be "merciful." He argued that God had delegated responsibility over the animals to humanity, but that people remained answerable to God if they viciously exploited the charge. He was not, however, vegetarian. In his journal he gave specific instructions on the slaughtering of animals, admonishing his readers to perform the operation without inflicting unnecessary pain. "When thou taketh away the life of a creature, let awfulness [awe] cover thy mind, let the execution be quick and with as little pain as possible, always remembering that the Lord hath a regard for every part of his creation, and that thou as a steward must account to him for all thy conduct toward them."[90]

As a campaigner for the better treatment of animals, John Woolman was very much like Abner. Although some in the twentieth century have claimed that he was a vegetarian, he never explicitly opposed the consumption of meat, and indeed his account books make it clear that he sold beef almost continuously, as a shopkeeper and then as a small farmer, from the early 1750s until the last year of his life.[91] His interest in the treatment of animals and the limits of his advocacy for them illustrate a fundamental characteristic of his ministry. His ideas may have carried radical implications, but at heart, from his childhood forward, he was conservative. Woolman's vision of the ideal social order was modeled not only on Eden but also on the way of life he knew as a boy on his father's farm.

Chapter 2

Deserts and Lonely Places:
Social Diversion and Solitary Meditation

I sought deserts and lonely places and there with tears did confess
my sins to God and humbly craved help of him.
—Woolman, *Journal*, chapter 1

ON A SPRING day when he was approximately nine, Woolman was walking down the road toward a neighbor's house when he saw a mother robin sitting by her nest. She flew off the instant she saw him, but did not go far for fear of abandoning her chicks. Instead she "flew about," and "with many cries expressed concern" for her young ones. Woolman responded just as she feared. He began throwing stones at her and eventually hit and killed her. At first he was pleased, but then he was struck with remorse. To free the motherless chicks from a slow death, he climbed the tree and killed them. In his account of this episode, written years after the event, Woolman honored the mother bird, "an innocent creature" who cared for, nourished, and sought to protect her young. He also expressed sympathy for the suffering of the chicks. He believed that his action had confirmed a lesson from Proverbs, that the "tender mercies of the wicked are cruel." He concluded that God had placed a "principle in the human mind" directing people to "exercise goodness toward every living creature." Those who rejected this principle, he suggested, would be shunted off into a "contrary disposition."[1]

Woolman was in his thirties when he recounted this story in his journal. As a boy he may not have been able to articulate the meaning of the episode so clearly, but as an adult he found many occasions to reiterate the rule stated in that proverb. A "wrong beginning," he declared, "leads into many difficulties, for to support one evil, another becomes customary. Two produces more, and the further men proceed in this way the greater the dangers, their doubts and fears, and the more painful and perplexing are their circumstances."[2] Woolman wrote his journal with didactic purposes in mind, and in this instance he was making a statement in favor of moral consistency. It was a lesson that he was careful to validate by referring to the scriptures, but there was more to the story than could be encapsulated in the language of the proverb.

Woolman hoped that his readers would pay attention not only to his precepts, but also to the way that he came to them. In this instance he believed that an instructive incident had led to the discovery of a divinely sanctioned truth. Although he read widely and peppered all his writings with citations of the scriptures and other texts, he maintained that words could never adequately convey the knowledge he had gained through experience, and he thought that his discoveries could only be understood fully by those who had "trodden in the same path" as he did.[3] He had faith in the value of living observantly, and this was typical of Quakers in his era. The Friends in general were adamant that no one could achieve religious understanding simply by reading books. In a similar vein they insisted that listening to the advice of one's parents, elders, teachers, and ministers would never be enough to instill spiritual insight.[4]

Like other Quaker children, Woolman was taught at an early age that God could speak to him directly, and throughout his life he listened for God's voice in his "inward ear," in the "language of the Holy One spoken in my mind."[5] He strove to be attentive because he believed that God sent him messages in innumerable ways. Sometimes he was startled by spectacular visions and on one occasion he heard an angel chanting, but more commonly he received "the fresh instructions of Christ" through his experience of living "from day to day."[6]

Those who knew Woolman remarked on the care he took in watching the world around him. His son-in-law John Comfort recalled an afternoon he spent in Woolman's apple orchard inspecting the trees. Comfort looked at one tree and said, "This is a tree full of caterpillars." Woolman paused before he responded, and then he said, "Not quite full." Comfort was exasperated at being corrected. When he recounted this incident years later, he declared that his father-in-law never accepted any "inaccuracy of expression" and never said anything that was less than "strictly and literally true."[7] Yet while the story testifies to Woolman's precise use of language, it also reflects the kind of attention he paid to living creatures and other physical things. Caterpillars mattered to him not simply because they damaged trees, but also because they might serve as God's agents on earth. In an essay Woolman composed near the time of this encounter with Comfort, he asserted that God had occasionally sent pests and "devouring creatures" to Pennsylvania and New Jersey to punish Quaker colonists after they had sinned.[8]

Woolman's world was scattered with messages sent by angels who, as William Cave described them, had "the government of fruits and seasons, and the productions of animals committed to them."[9] Woolman imagined the angels working in harmony, almost always invisible, selflessly performing the will of God.[10] He received lessons from them in droughts, hailstorms, and soaking rains. "I have at times," he wrote, "beheld the vehement operation of lightening as a messenger from HIM who created all things."[11] Woolman's childhood encounter with the robins was more traumatic than most of his other outdoor moments of insight, but in other respects it fit a pattern that began that afternoon when he tarried on the hillside on his way home from school, one that would continue for the rest of his life. By the time he reached adulthood, he had learned to go outside in order to receive messages from above.

In his journal he describes an evening when he was approximately 18. After reading the writings of "a pious author," he left his parents' house and "walking out alone I humbly prayed." He felt that God "helped" him on that occasion, and in times of trouble from that time forward, he "sought deserts and lonely places" in order to pray for consolation and instruction. Woolman recounted the experiences of others, both Quakers and non-Quakers, who received wisdom on the road "far from home on a lonesome journey" or sleeping in a field at night. He recalled how he would walk outside repeatedly, literally begging God for guidance. On one particularly difficult day, he walked "in a solitary wood" inwardly crying for divine direction. He did not receive the resolution he was seeking on that first occasion, but a few weeks later a message from God, supported by a Bible verse, came into his mind as he "walked on the road."[12] Woolman was hardly unique in seeking spiritual enlightenment outdoors. His brother Abner, as a young man, frequently went out "alone in the fields and other places in prayer to God."[13] Woolman's neighbor Joshua Evans recorded in his journal that he "often sought retirement by night and by day in lonely places, frequently in the woods."[14]

Walking was a powerful metaphor for Quakers, "a phrase frequently used in scripture, to represent our journey through life." According to Woolman's understanding of "walking," the word could be applied broadly "to comprehend the various affairs and transactions properly relating to our being in the world." Like other Quaker ministers, he frequently paraphrased 1 John 1:7, "if we walk in the light, as he is in the light, we have fellowship one with another."[15] He also associated the walking metaphor with Isaiah, indicating that the prophet used the word "walking" as a way to refer to "the journey through life, as a righteous journey."[16] But walking was more than a metaphor. Woolman considered it essential for health. One of the lessons he gave as a schoolteacher stressed the value of walking and breathing clean air.

> Clear air is food for the lungs
> Air once taken should be refined
> Hard frost refines the air
> North wind refines the air
> Tempests in summer refine the air[17]

Woolman advocated walking because he believed that the things he encountered outdoors, including both the animals and the weather, might teach him something. He thought that standing under the open sky brought him, in a material sense, closer to God.

Sleeping could be, in many ways, like walking alone through the country. Just as the woods and fields were places to go for divine instruction, so dreams could serve as avenues for inspiration. Woolman experienced his first "night vision" at nine, when he dreamed that he was standing at the door of his father's house looking out over a "pleasant green" while strange bodies moved across the sky. Later in life he had a dream in which he sat by a window and saw a supernatural spectacle outside. In other dreams, celestial beings visited him when he was outdoors, and in one of his most dramatic visions, angels carried him into the sky.[18]

On a page in his ledger book, Woolman copied out the opening stanza of a poem attributed to the English dissenting minister Isaac Watts, entitled "A Wonderful Dream." The first lines read,

> When the bright monarch of the day
> Withdraws from human sight
> And night had spread her sable veil
> And put the day to flight . . .

The poet went on to recount a dream Woolman might have described as a "night vision." The dreamer saw himself dead. He was watching his funeral procession

Figure 3. Various illustrations appeared at the end of printed editions of *A Wonderful Dream*. This image of death and an angel appeared in the 1765 imprint. Courtesy American Antiquarian Society.

when an angel descended, took him by the hand, and led him above the moon and stars to "tread the upper sky." He met the devil on that heavenly plain, and although the devil tried to scare him, he maintained his faith. Soon afterward, he was admitted into the presence of Jesus, who told him that it was too soon for him to die. Christ directed the dreamer "to live on earth . . . and fight the glorious fight/ Against the devil, world and sin/ and put them all to flight." Reinspired, the dreamer started out on his return to earth, but then the devil reappeared and once again tried to shake his resolve. He responded, "I fear you not," and the angel who had guided him up to heaven took him back home. The two talked for a while outside the door of the house before the dreamer woke up. The next morning the man in the poem "perus'd the holy scriptures" and located descriptions of "each shining form" he had seen in his dream.[19]

Watts was not a Quaker, but Woolman was often attracted to the writings of non-Quakers whose views seemed to correspond with the teachings of the Society of Friends. The Quakers had faith in the instructive power of dreams. They took notes on them and shared their recollections and interpretations with family members and neighbors.[20] Quaker ministers described their dreams at meetings for worship and consulted with one another about the messages that their "night views" might contain and convey.[21] Sometimes the images and messages were difficult to interpret, and like the sleeper in the poem, the Quakers were anxious to reassure themselves that they understood their dreams in ways that conformed to the teachings of scripture.[22]

In the dream Woolman remembered from age nine, he saw the moon rise in the west and speed backward across the sky. It dropped a small cloud which landed near his father's house and became a "beautiful green tree." Then the sun rose and under its heat the tree withered. Shortly thereafter "a being, small in size, full of strength and resolution," appeared, "moving swift from the north, southward." Woolman identified the creature as a "sun worm." After Woolman died, Philadelphia Yearly Meeting appointed a committee to edit his journal ahead of publication, and the committee deleted this dream from the text.[23] The editors retained some of Woolman's accounts of other dreams, including a few of his own and some he learned about from other dreamers, but the reports of "night visions" that were approved for publication had much clearer moral lessons in them. Woolman may have thought that there was a message embedded in his vision of the "sun worm," but whatever that lesson was, it was too cryptic and idiosyncratic for the Overseers of the Press. In eighteenth-century Quaker circles, a dream's principal value was its ability to instruct.

What was true for dreams also applied to the insights one received walking alone in the open air. Woolman and others like him may have gone out by themselves into the countryside to receive inspiration, but they did not think that the truths they discovered in "lonely places" were only for their private edification. On the contrary, spiritual lessons had a social purpose, and God meant for them to be shared. Although Woolman was alone when he killed the robins, for example, the lesson that he drew from that experience had universal moral implications. Equally significantly, Woolman's way of telling the story contained an implicit warning about the behavior of nine-year-olds. Yes, they were capable of divine insight, and a boy might receive holy inspiration standing still and alone by a tree, but beware of children in groups. They are apt to be stupid, cruel, and destructive when they run in gangs.

From the moment the mother robin first saw Woolman approaching from a distance, she thought she knew what a child like him would do, and when he came nearer he behaved exactly as she expected. His pleasure at having killed her reflected his pride, and it is easy to imagine that at that instant he anticipated boasting about his accomplishment to his peers. As he later revealed more clearly in his journal, Woolman belonged to a circle of mischievous, shallow-minded, strutting young boys. Precisely because children are prone to be gregarious, Woolman viewed late childhood as a period of acute risk. Like other Quaker reformers in his era, he warned parents that their sons and daughters were susceptible to evil influence and could take bad cues from the behavior of those around them.[24] He similarly advised schoolteachers to instruct only "a small number of children" at a time. The teachers should "gently lead" their pupils "without giving countenance to pride or evil emulation among them."[25] But every school day must end, and at some time in the afternoon, perhaps only during their return home from classes, the children would be left in their own company, and fall under each others' sway. For a dutiful boy with righteous parents and good teachers, this was a moment of spiritual danger. If walking alone was a potential form of worship, running, especially in groups as boys commonly do, was a sacrilege. Throughout his life Woolman condemned "hurry," and when he wrote of his adolescent years, he described himself "running" on a road with many companions, speeding away from "heavenly things."[26]

Memories from his childhood troubled Woolman for his entire life. As an adult, he confessed, "While I meditate on the gulf toward which I traveled, and reflect on my youthful disobedience, for these things I weep; mine eye runneth down with water." He declared that during the worst years of his youth his "chief study" had been to "promote mirth." "Serious reflections were uneasy to me, and youthful vanities and diversions my greatest pleasure." He became "foolish." On that singular, memorable morning, his youthful bravado led him to kill some birds, but otherwise even according to his own estimation his sins were relatively innocuous. He never used "profane language," nor did he ever engage in "scandalous conduct." Nonetheless he believed that he was wicked, because he enjoyed the company of "wanton young people": "I perceived a plant in me which produced much wild grapes . . . vanity was added to vanity, and repentance to repentance." Looking back on those years he perceived that he had become "alienated from the Truth," and he was racing toward "destruction."[27]

Years later in his work as a Quaker minister, Woolman joined with many others to campaign against a variety of activities that they described as "diversion."[28] The reformers used that word precisely, and they believed that it referred to something terrible. "Diversion" shunted people off from the right path and led them away from God. Young people were particularly prone to diversion. In a missive Woolman wrote on behalf of Philadelphia Yearly Meeting, he advised Quaker children to "devote the flower of youth to the services of our creator." If they maintained their devotion, "standing in the meekness of wisdom," they would "remain unshaken" and "choose rather to suffer affliction with the faithful, than to decline from the [Friends'] precious testimony" by consorting with "libertine people."[29] As a schoolteacher Woolman warned children about the dangers of aimless fun. In one lesson, he directed a group of students to copy out in their books, "Happy hours are quickly followed by amazing vexations."[30]

Woolman remembered a great struggle that raged within him during his childhood, one that pitted Satan against the divine. He usually tried to be good, but when he failed to "pray rightly" he left himself vulnerable and "the tempter when he came found entrance."[31] On such occasions Woolman encountered the devil as an intruder, a powerful, supernatural, external influence on his soul. He saw the devil as "the stranger" or "the enemy."[32] But he also recognized that evil could spread simply through human agency, because people made bad choices, behaved badly and influenced each other through the force of example. Human societies could generate demonic forces "like dark matter gathering into clouds over us."[33] The consequences could be horrific. Woolman believed that "one person in society continuing to live contrary to true wisdom" was likely to encourage others to embrace evil. He compared the result to "a wild vine which, springing from a single seed and growing strong, the branches extend, and their little twining holders twist round all herbs and boughs of trees where they reach, and are so braced and locked in, that without much labor or great strength they cannot be disentangled."[34]

When Woolman discussed the evil work that children could do, he concentrated on the ways they influenced one another. He was particularly concerned about trickery and gossip, and his classroom lessons stressed the perils of idle chatter:

A whisper separateth friends
Unwise talk cometh from the unwise
Turn away thine ear from vanity . . .[35]

In these admonitions, Woolman warned his students against repeating his own sins. He had been a joker as a child. According to his own account, he had tried to exceed his friends "in the art of foolish jesting."[36] As an adult he wept when he remembered those years, not merely because he had failed to be consistently righteous, but more painfully because he believed that he had advanced the project of the devil by encouraging others in folly.

At seventeen, Woolman collapsed. "Darkness, horror and amazement" seized him and his "pain and distress of body" was so great that he doubted whether he would recover. Recounting this event in his journal, he declared that it had "pleased God to visit me with sickness."[37] He was forever grateful for that illness. Even on of his deathbed, he cried aloud, "O Lord! It was thy power that enabled me to forsake sin in my youth, and I have felt thy bruises since for disobedience, but as I bowed under them, thou healedst me."[38] Woolman's adolescent bout with illness initiated a lifelong practice of examining ailments for messages from God.[39] He monitored his own physical well-being carefully and studied his symptoms in the same way he counted caterpillars. Like many other Christians in the eighteenth century, Quakers commonly believed that God targeted individuals for illness in order to teach them lessons.[40] William Penn, in his influential and widely distributed treatise *No Cross, No Crown*, told the story of a religious scholar who after "a long life of study" fell mortally ill and a week and a half later declared, "God has learned me more of himself in ten days sickness than I could get by all my labor and studies."[41] During his illness Woolman came to believe that God had a lesson for him, but he was "filled with confusion" because he viewed himself as a sinner. "I lay and bewailed myself. I had not confidence to lift up my cries to God." Eventually he gained the ability to pray, and he described this turning point as a catharsis: "In a deep sense of my great folly I was humbled before him [God], and at length that Word which is as a fire and a hammer broke and dissolved my rebellious heart."[42]

On his sickbed at seventeen, Woolman made a promise to himself and to God that if he recovered he would forever thereafter "walk humbly" as a Christian. According to his own assessment, he was able to keep to that resolution for a "considerable time," but eventually he was drawn back into the company of "wanton young people." Those next few months were an agony for him and sharpened his understanding of the source of his trouble. He decided that if he was to "live in the life which the faithful servants of God lived in," he would have to give up going "into company as heretofore." He determined that if he was ever to live a righteous life, "all the cravings of sense must be governed by divine principle." After coming to this conclusion he felt the "power of Christ prevail over selfish desires," and he resolved to give up his old acquaintances.

"A single life," he declared, "was best for me." He did not explain this decision to his old companions, but instead allowed them to judge him "as they would, for I found it safest for me to live in private." For the next two years he continued to live on his father's farm, but by his own account he "lived retired." He led "a very private life."[43]

*   *   *

The vividness of Woolman's account of his youth reflects the importance he attached to the lessons he learned in those early years. He made it his lifelong project to honor the resolutions he made after he recovered from his illness, but he did abandon one of them. He would not lead a private life. At age twenty-two Woolman experienced a wave of "fresh and heavenly openings." He became newly alert to God's watchful care "over his creatures in general, and over man as the most noble amongst those which are visible." Woolman became "clearly convinced" that he should place his "whole trust in God" and "in all things . . . act on an inward principle of virtue."[44] The first assertive action he took after coming to this resolution was to visit a tavern.

During the week of Christmas, 1742, Woolman observed groups of men and women from Mount Holly and the surrounding area gathering in public houses where they spent their afternoons and evenings "in drinking" and playing "vain sports." The sight troubled him because he believed that revelers who engaged in such activities tended to "corrupt one another." There was one house that drew his attention more than the others. It was the source of unusually visible "disorder"; Woolman therefore resolved to enter that place and speak to its proprietor. Even though he knew he was still young and did not want to appear presumptuous, he found confidence after reading what "the Almighty said to Ezekiel respecting his duty as a watchman." God had told Ezekiel, "Son of man, I have made thee a watchman unto the House of Israel: therefore hear the word at my mouth, and give them warning from me." These words convinced Woolman to protest. He waited for a "suitable opportunity" before going into the establishment. When he entered, he saw the owner standing with a group of patrons. He explained that he wanted to speak to the man alone and asked him to step aside. As he described the event, "in the fear and dread of the Almighty I expressed to him what rested on my mind." The proprietor listened "kindly" and said very little in response. Then Woolman left. The house may or may not have fallen silent for a moment, but once the young man was gone the drinkers surely resumed

Figure 4. Three Tun Tavern, Mount Holly, New Jersey, built in the 1720s or 1730s. It was one of several successful drinking establishments in the town. Library of Congress.

their chatter, and some of them certainly continued into the night. Nonetheless, Woolman believed that he had done what had to be done and so felt relieved.[45]

In taking this action, Woolman was following closely in the footsteps of the Quaker founder George Fox. In the opening pages of his journal, Fox reported that he went to a fair when he was nineteen. He met two men there who invited him "to drink part of a Jug of Beer with them." Fox accepted a glass and drank it. Then the others suggested that they keep drinking, and to add to the fun they suggested that the first man to give up should pay for all the rounds. Upon hearing this Fox was "grieved." He remembered, "I rose up to be gone; and putting my hand into my pocket, I took out a groat, and laid it down upon the Table before them, and said, *If it be so, I'll leave you.*" Fox believed that God had taught him when he was eleven years old that he should drink only for the purpose of maintaining his health and never to make himself "wanton." But he had never taken a public stance on the issue before. Indeed, this was the first public protest he ever made. Fox had trouble sleeping that night, but according to his journal God spoke to him and gave him this advice: "Thou seest, how Young People go together into Vanity, and Old People into the Earth; and Thou must forsake all, both Young and Old, and keep out of all, and be as a Stranger unto all."[46]

As these early passages from Fox's journal indicate, the Quakers had long spoken out against excessive drinking, but they had never been particularly effective in stopping the practice. William Penn, for example, had initially hoped to ban taverns and alehouses from Pennsylvania, but he quickly bowed to reality. The early Quaker colonists established such businesses immediately upon their arrival.[47] Those early establishments had sold beer and brandy, but the regional drinking culture changed significantly in the early decades of the eighteenth century as the Delaware Valley expanded its commercial ties to the West Indies. Quaker reformers identified the 1720s as the critical turning point when New Jersey and Pennsylvania began to consume large quantities of rum.[48]

In 1726 Philadelphia Yearly Meeting issued its first warning against the improper use of rum, in a resolution specifically directed against the "pernicious custom" of distributing drams at auctions. According to the statement, Quakers who offered items for sale at auction frequently gave "rum and other strong liquors" to potential customers in order to encourage bidding and "advance the price." The meeting denounced this practice as unfair and indicated that it had led to episodes of "great intemperance and disorder."[49] Twenty-three years later, the distribution of liquor at auctions was still such a problem that the meeting felt the need to repeat its prior warning and to add a broader admonition against "drinking strong liquors to excess." Over the next few years the Yearly Meeting would complain repeatedly about rum drinking, asserting that the Quakers often made themselves drunk when they gathered to celebrate marriages and births, when they worked in groups at harvest time, and when they mourned together after burials.[50]

While some Quakers in the Delaware Valley indulged in what the Yearly Meeting described as "immoderate" and "disorderly" behavior, more commonly they drank rum for what they believed to be medicinal purposes, and in any given household the liquor might have been taken by most members of the family. Several members of the Mount Holly Friends Meeting purchased, consumed and distributed significant quantities of rum.[51] Woolman's cousin Joseph Burr, for example, bought rum on seven occasions in 1753 alone, and acquired at least a gallon each time. He could purchase as much as five gallons or half a barrel at one time.[52] There is no reason to think that Burr drank all that liquor by himself, nor is it likely that he hosted an endless succession of parties. The Delaware Valley Quakers drank rum in the winter because they believed that it could protect a person from the cold, and they drank it in the summer as a way to relieve the heat.[53] Especially in the summer and early autumn, employers gave rum to their workers, and by mid-century this custom had grown so entrenched that it was difficult to get anyone to work at harvest time without a provision of liquor. Many believed that working in the sun without the benefit of rum could be lethal.[54] Woolman acknowledged that he drank "spirits" for relief when the sun left him feeling exhausted.[55] "People much spent with labor," he wrote, "often take strong drink to revive them."[56]

The idea that liquor was necessary for the maintenance of health in the colonies vexed Woolman and other Quaker advocates of temperance, in part because they had not yet fully articulated the countervailing argument that drinking too much rum could be physically debilitating.[57] Following the lead of the Quaker reformer John Churchman, Woolman contended that the health of the people of New Jersey and Pennsylvania was becoming all too dependent on the intake of liquor. He thought that peculiar constitutional dispositions arose among the inhabitants of different lands. It was intrinsic in "the nature of people," he suggested, that as they age they grow accustomed to the "food and air" that nourished them from their youth. Therefore travelers, "by a separation from their native air and usual diet" often "grow weak and unhealthy." He thought that the colonists in America were becoming over accustomed to drinking strong liquor, and this continuing "from age to age" was likely to alter their "natures," impeding their ability to receive "the pure Truth."[58]

The fundamental problem with drinking rum was that it was difficult to live worshipfully and receive messages from God when drunk. Woolman complained that after too much liquor "the mind is not so calm nor so fitly disposed for divine meditation" as it is "when all such extremes are avoided." He disapproved of drinking for inebriation even on rare celebratory occasions, because when ordinarily sober people lapse they set a bad example which "strengthens the hands of the more excessive drinkers." Taking in too much liquor could "disorder" the "understandings" of those who drank and lead them to "neglect their duty as members in a family or civil society."[59] Abner Woolman commented, "How often we see people deprived of their reason by drinking too freely . . . many have so far given away to it that it hath been the cause of their own and their families' poverty, and that which is more dreadful, it unfits the soul for that glorious kingdom prepared for the righteous from the foundation of the world."[60] The Quaker reformer Anthony Benezet described the effect of drink in vivid terms. Those who drank too much liquor became "profane and abandoned, and to the last degree regardless of their duty to God and man; the feelings of the mind are gradually benumb'd, and an insensibility to the healing influence of religion ensues."[61] Liquor was a problem for the Quakers, but in order to understand the implications of Woolman's first protest at the public house, it is important to notice that few if any of the customers at that establishment would have been members of the Society of Friends.

Woolman entered the public house during the busy season of the year that he uneasily referred to as "the time called Christmas." The Quakers of his day did not celebrate the holiday. Quite to the contrary, they rejected the event as a display of empty, formal ritual, the antithesis of the spontaneous, inspired worship that they sought to encourage in their meetings. In the seventeenth century the Quakers made public statements against Christmas celebrations and as a consequence some Friends in England had faced violent, angry crowds every year on December 25.[62] By the eighteenth century the date passed uneventfully in most Quaker households, especially in colonial New Jersey and Pennsylvania. Nonetheless, Quaker reformers like Woolman remained upset by the festivities they saw around them. Sophia Hume, an outspoken Quaker reformer of the era, wrote an "Address to the Magistrates" in 1766 in which she derided the celebration of Christmas. Hume quoted the prophet Amos: "I hate, I despise your feast days. I will not smell your solemn assemblies, your new moons, and your appointed feasts, my soul hateth: your solemn meetings are iniquity."[63] Christmas was a holiday for other people, not Quakers.

Historians studying American Quaker reformers in the middle years of the eighteenth century have identified two potentially contradictory trends. Woolman, Churchman, Benezet and other advocates of reform demanded that their meetings pay attention to the suffering of their non-Quaker neighbors, including slaves and freedmen, Acadian refugees and American Indians. More generally they manifested a heightened engagement with the affairs of non-Quakers, and their efforts had the effect of increasing their meetings' international influence.[64] At the same time, they advocated stricter disciplinary supervision over the members of their own religious society. After the reformers gained influence in the meetings, their insistence on maintaining distinctive standards of conduct made the Quakers more peculiar and set them apart from their neighbors. This, the reformers thought, was all for the good. Like Fox before them, they sought to "keep out of all, and be as a Stranger unto all."[65]

Both of these impulses, to stand apart and to remain engaged, would have been apparent in the way Woolman comported himself on that afternoon when he spoke to the publican. He would have addressed the man as "thou," because he consistently spoke in what the Quakers described as "plain language."[66] The Quakers had adopted this form of speech in their earliest days, in the 1650s. They had done so in part because Fox and his associates believed that using the word "you" would be ungrammatical when addressing a single person. They associated "you" with flattery and deceit, and avoiding it became a matter of principle for members of the Society of Friends. Using "thou" became a practice that distinguished the Quakers from most other speakers of the English language.[67] Woolman hints that during his childhood some of the boys he played with occasionally failed to abide by the Quaker rules of speech. When he heard them speak in the "profane" way it troubled him, and even in the most sinful period of his youth he never varied in his manner of speaking.[68] As an adult he served on a committee within Philadelphia Yearly Meeting that in insistent terms directed parents to teach their children to use "plainness of speech" consistently.[69] He believed that speaking in that distinctively Quaker way would help children avoid "the snares and dangers which attend a too familiar conversation" with non-Quakers.[70] Plain language would also draw attention to them, identify them, and consequently bestow upon them a sense of responsibility. When Woolman addressed others as "thou" he implicitly declared "I am a Quaker," and he knew that others, hearing what he had to say, were likely to think of him first as a member of his religious society.

Mindful of his conspicuousness as a Quaker and the obligations it placed upon him, Woolman consistently sought to speak in a way that would promote the work of God on earth. He wanted to appear sober, but also loving, and mindful of the implications of the Quakers' peace testimony, he self-consciously sought to advance the cause of peace. Occasionally he had difficulty suppressing his angry impulses, but in general he took care to avoid appearing aggressive.[71] In general he kept his words short, said what was necessary, and left. He believed that his listeners might need time to consider the meaning of his statements and feel the instructive force of his example.

Woolman recounted in his journal another, similar visit he made to a public house late in the summer of 1763. He had seen broadsides in Mount Holly advertising a magic show to be performed at the establishment. The show had gone forward, and the magician had made such an impression on the audience that a second performance was scheduled for the next night. The show was to begin "about sunset." Woolman went to the public house and asked the owner if he could sit there. He positioned himself on a long bench by the door and engaged those who entered in conversation. As Woolman described it, he "laboured to convince them that thus assembling to see those tricks and sleights-of-hand, and bestowing their money to support men who in that capacity were of no use in the world, was contrary to the nature of the Christian religion." One of the patrons tried to present counterarguments, "endeavoring . . . to show the reasonableness of their proceedings." Woolman responded with "some texts of Scripture." After approximately an hour "calmly debating the matter," the customer "gave up the point" and Woolman left.[72]

As he grew older Woolman became more comfortable expressing his views authoritatively, but when he was a young man he often found it difficult to state his views in a way that would avoid giving others offense. He lived in a society that venerated age, and when he felt moved to object to the behavior of an older man, he recalled, "I expressed what lay upon me in a way which became my youth." Nonetheless, he was wary of compromising his beliefs for the sake of politeness. He insisted that when speaking to others who were behaving badly, "it's needful for us to take heed that their kindness, their freedom, and affability do not hinder us from the Lord's work." Furthermore, if his seriousness upset those around him, he refused to be swayed by their hostility or ridicule. "I find that to be [taken as] a fool . . . and commit my cause to God, not fearing to offend men who take offense at the simplicity of Truth, is the only way to remain unmoved at the sentiments of others. The fear of man brings a snare." "To conform a little to a wrong way strengthens the hands of such who carry wrong customs to their utmost extent." Therefore, he concluded, it was often necessary to oppose "the customs of the times" and "bear patiently the reproaches attending singularity."[73]

Woolman campaigned against idle entertainment all his life. As an adult he worked on committees that advised against the reading of "pernicious books," "the unnecessary frequenting of taverns and places of diversion," participation in lotteries, and attendance at horse races.[74] All these efforts were aimed at Quakers first, but they were intended in the long run to encourage moral reform in the entire colonial population. Philadelphia Quarterly Meeting articulated this more ambitious aim in a statement against horse racing and idle attendance at fairs. The meeting declared that by "steadily and carefully avoiding every appearance of evil and all temptations, lightness, extravagance and wantonly spending our time, we may have humble hope that others will follow us."[75] Woolman similarly expressed the hope that "in the exercise of our several gifts, and by the spirit of our conduct, we may labor to draw the minds of others toward that inward heavenly life, in which alone is true safety and felicity."[76] But he warned his fellow Quakers, if "our conduct in the affairs of life do not agree with the principles we profess, and the doctrines we publish to the world, it necessarily tends to destroy that real beauty and comeliness which adorns religion in its purity, and gives opportunity to the enemies of truth . . . to propagate their destructive tenets and alienate the minds of youth from the true inward knowledge of God."[77]

Since the seventeenth century, the Society of Friends had opposed "unprofitable plays, frivolous recreations, sportings and gamings which are invented to pass away the precious time."[78] During Woolman's era, meetings often took inspiration from the words of the Apostle Paul, and denounced all forms of self-indulgence. In 1772, at the end of the only gathering of London Yearly Meeting that Woolman attended, Britain's Quakers issued an admonitory statement citing Paul's Epistle to the Romans: "If ye live after the flesh, ye shall die: but if ye through the spirit do mortify the deeds of the body, ye shall live."[79] Though Woolman had often heard such statements, he was never convinced that the Quakers consistently lived in accordance with their precepts. Along with other reform-minded ministers, he resolved "to promote the cleansing of our camp from disorders, and the filth and rust contracted through fleshly ease and the love of the world."[80] When Philadelphia Yearly Meeting gathered in the Pennsylvania capital, Woolman complained about the "many expenses attending our entertainment in town."[81] In Philadelphia in 1762, he attended a meeting of elders and ministers where, according to another minister in attendance, "Truth's testimony against libertinism was exalted."[82]

By withdrawing from unrighteous social gatherings, denouncing rowdiness, and avoiding trivial activities, the reformers hoped to transform the society around them. Paradoxically they believed that they could maximize their influence by refusing to participate fully in the communal life of their non-Quaker neighbors. Woolman had come to a similar conclusion that December afternoon in 1742. Thus, from that time onward, in his ministerial life and in his writings, he repeatedly emphasized the power of setting a severe example. In one late essay, he cited his youthful experience, and thanked God for teaching him that "a state of inward purity may be known in this life." He believed that he had been led to "love mankind in the same love with which our Redeemer loveth us," with "resignation to endure hardships for the real good of others."[83] In another late essay published under the title *Considerations on the True Harmony of Mankind* he addressed himself to all good

Christians, and warned them not to "indulge a desire to imitate our neighbors in those things which harmonize not with the true Christian walking." "Strong are the desires I often feel, that this holy profession may remain unpolluted, and the believers in Christ may so abide in the pure inward feeling of his spirit, that the wisdom from above may shine forth in their living, as a light by which others may be instrumentally helped on their way." He admonished his readers to be "true patterns of the Christian life, who in living and walking may hold forth an invitation to others." In order to send a message through their way of living, the Christians should "come out of the entanglements of the spirit of this world." By visibly avoiding the corrupting influence of "the world," the Christians might transform it. Indeed Woolman suggested that if the faithful set a good example, their influence could ultimately span the globe, reaching "all nations and tongues" to "the utmost parts of the earth."[84]

Woolman wrote *Considerations on the True Harmony of Mankind* in 1770 and submitted it to the Quaker Overseers of the Press in Philadelphia, which approved the piece for publication and arranged for the printer Joseph Crukshank to produce several hundred copies. Woolman wrote an advertisement for the work and with the help of the Philadelphia Quakers he sent his ad to every Quaker Meeting in Pennsylvania and New Jersey. He explained that he had written the essay "under an apprehension of duty," and he encouraged the meetings to buy multiple copies, advising them that Crukshank would sell them his pamphlets in bundles of twelve.[85] In support of these efforts, Philadelphia Yearly Meeting took an active role in distributing the pamphlet, sending it to "distant places" where it was thought Woolman's message might have a "salutary effect." In 1772, a committee of the Yearly Meeting wrote to Quaker meetings in New York, Rhode Island, and Massachusetts, encouraging them to buy copies of Woolman's essay and give them along with other religious writings to their children, their servants, and any "new settlers" who came to visit them. The Pennsylvania Quakers took note of the general increase of "settlement" in the various colonies and "the poverty of many who may be religiously concerned for the right instructing of their children in the principles of truth, as professed by us." They asserted that Woolman's essay could be read for "profit," unlike those "vain books that amuse the thoughtless youth, and lead such who love to read them [away] from the simplicity of the truth."[86] The uncompromising advice contained within *Considerations on the True Harmony of Mankind*, and the pamphlet's widespread distribution highlight Woolman's belief in the universality of his precepts. He thought that everyone should avoid time-wasting, pointless conviviality and indulgent behavior. "Be not curious in useless matters," he told his students. "Employ thy time in that which is of use."[87]

By the time he wrote *Considerations on the True Harmony of Mankind* Woolman had grown accustomed to thinking of himself as a visionary who could receive socially valuable insights when he secluded himself away from human company. In his journal, he reports that when he felt uneasy with the people around him, a verse from a Psalm came to him from the "center" of his mind. The biblical passage read, "Oh Lord, I am a stranger in the earth; hide not thy face from me." Those words inspired him to work.[88] He believed that the Holy Spirit and the angels spoke to him in solitude, and sometimes after his moments alone with God's agents, he would return like a prophet with an urgent message for society as a whole.

He did not always speak immediately, however. When he was using the Bible as his text he was ready to debate almost anyone at a moment's notice, including anonymous tavern-goers and strangers he met along the road.[89] But he was more cautious about claiming authority on the basis of the inspiration he received when he was asleep or walking alone in the fields. Like other Quaker ministers, he thought that the insights he derived from dreams, waking visions, and peculiar experiences should be evaluated by other Friends before they were shared with anyone else. Sometimes he revealed his spiritual discoveries during worship at Quaker meetings. On other occasions he was more circumspect. As an adult, Woolman refined his note-taking habits and kept records of his unusual experiences, including his observations of natural phenomena and dreams.[90] He incorporated some of these memoranda into drafts of his yet-unpublished journal. Others became short manuscript essays or records he referred to in private conversation. If Woolman suspected that his insights might be useful to others, his first step was to talk to a few respected Quakers, so that together they could evaluate the meaning and value of what he had seen. When he met with such advisors, sometimes they would simply converse, but on other occasions they would huddle over papers that Woolman had written. He gave his close associates short prophetic declarations, outlines of proposed essays, and passages he was thinking of incorporating into his journal.[91] Everyone involved in these consultations understood that nothing he wrote would appear in print unless it was approved for publication by the Quaker Overseers of the Press.

Woolman sought to publish only a portion of his writings. Those pieces that he wanted to see published were vetted and edited by Quaker oversight bodies before appearing in print. Special committees were appointed to review each work, and the overseers did more than simply acquiesce in publication. When they endorsed the essays and facilitated their printing and distribution, they acted on behalf of Philadelphia Yearly Meeting, and in that capacity they declared that Woolman's advice was useful to the faithful and advanced God's purposes. After Woolman died, his journal underwent a similar editorial process. A committee of overseers in Philadelphia deleted some of the passages he had written. For example they declined to allow the publication of a few of his contentious political observations.[92] Overall, however, they approved of Woolman's perspective and officially endorsed not only the truths he believed he had uncovered, but also the process through which he had acquired his spiritual knowledge. The Overseers of the Press left standing Woolman's account of two visions in which angels spoke to him.[93] They also approved for publication Woolman's description of several divine "openings" he received as a small boy when he kept away from his schoolmates and wandered alone on the roadside near Rancocas Creek.

Beginning in his childhood, Woolman habitually sought out "deserts and lonely places," engaged in deep introspection, and cut himself off from casual sociability. At some point during his maturation, perhaps not as early as that moment after he killed the robins, but certainly by the time he wrote his first account of that episode, he came to believe that the insights he received in those moments of seclusion might prove useful to others. Eventually he became convinced that he could play a leading role in nurturing the growth of a community uncorrupted by the evils of the world. To reassure himself, he sought confirmation from trusted Friends that his discoveries were consistent with Quaker principles and the teachings of Christianity. Eventually he took his ideas to formal oversight bodies. Although as an adult he often emulated the prophets, he always deferred to the authority of his meeting. As we shall see in the next chapter, he never wanted to say or do anything in contravention of the precepts of the Society of Friends.

Chapter 3

More Than Was Required:
Quaker Meetings

> I stood up and said some words in a meeting, but not keeping
> close to the divine opening, I said more than was required of me;
> and being soon sensible of my error, I was afflicted in mind some
> weeks without any light or comfort.
> —Woolman, *Journal*, chapter 1

IN 1740 ELIZABETH Woolman, John's oldest sister, attained the age of twenty-five. Eber, the youngest of the Woolman children, had been born a year earlier, and there were now thirteen brothers and sisters living with their parents in the house by Rancocas Creek. Elizabeth decided that it was time for her to leave. This changed the dynamics of the household, because Elizabeth had taken a hand in helping to raise her younger siblings. John remembered her giving them moral advice in rhyme. Elizabeth left home just as John was considering a similar move. He was turning twenty and finding it increasingly difficult to focus his mind on "husbandry." He wanted to find "some other way of living." His journal does not indicate when this restlessness began to afflict him, but he writes that he was troubled for "a considerable time." Thus, when a shopkeeper from Mount Holly told him he was looking for a servant to help him tend the counter and keep the books, John immediately expressed interest. He took the proposal to his father, and as he described the event in his journal, "after some deliberation it was agreed for me to go."[1]

Woolman does not identify his master in his journal, and the man's name has been lost to posterity. He had originally been a tailor, but after purchasing the shop in Mount Holly he had expanded his business. While he continued to sew, alter, and repair clothing, he also sold bread and other goods, and in perhaps his most speculative venture, on one occasion he purchased the labor contracts of Scottish indentured servants and offered them for sale in Mount Holly. He and his wife lived six miles from the shop. In addition to Woolman he employed an apprentice tailor. The shopkeeper, his wife, Woolman, and the other servant were all actively engaged in the business, but Woolman was the only one living in Mount Holly and so had primary responsibility for working with customers.[2]

Even at the moment when Woolman accepted this employment, he feared the consequences of "being much in the way of company," and he prayed for divine guidance to preserve him from "taint and corruption." Work drew him into a lively community, but he still wanted to retain his humility and dedicate his life to God. As soon as he arrived in Mount Holly, his old acquaintances knew where they could find him, and they started to visit him at the shop. Woolman conjectured that they were unaware that he had permanently given up "vanities": "At these times I cried to the Lord in secret for wisdom and strength, for I felt myself encompassed with difficulties and had fresh occasion to bewail the follies of time past in contracting a familiarity with a libertine people." He felt more comfortable during his time alone, at night.[3]

Woolman's outlook improved after his old friends gave up on him, and he met others more righteous, "whose conversation was helpful."[4] He began attending the Mount Holly Quaker Meeting at its Sunday and weekday gatherings. The meeting was well established, and on good days it brought together more than 100 Friends for worship.[5] Woolman was hardly a stranger to Mount Holly, having spent his childhood only a few miles away, and almost certainly he knew some of the local Quakers. Nonetheless, the meeting was new to him, and its impact on him was profound. In those first few weeks, he went to worship in what he described as an "awful frame of mind," as he strove to become "inwardly acquainted with the language of the True Shepherd." Within a few months he felt moved by what he took to be inspiration. Specific words came to him that he thought he should share, and he rose from his bench. As he remembered that moment afterward, his initial words had reflected a "divine opening," but then he had started to ramble, digress, and explain himself, and by the time he sat down, he knew he had spoken too long. The idea pained him. "I said more than was required of me," he confessed, "and being soon sensible of my error, I was afflicted in mind some weeks." Thinking back on what he had done, he could not find "light or comfort."[6]

Woolman was a newcomer to the Mount Holly Meeting and barely twenty-one when he started to preach, but the Quakers as a group were receptive to inspired messages from young and inexperienced ministers. An Irish girl named Susannah Hatton began speaking in worship at age sixteen, and in 1737, when she was still seventeen, she crossed the Atlantic to tour America and spoke at several meetings in the Delaware Valley.[7] Some local ministers stammered and exhibited "little knowledge in the learning of schools," but so long as they were perceived to be inspired, they were respected as spiritual leaders within the Society of Friends.[8]

Nonetheless, an array of pressures inhibited Friends from casually speaking in their meetings. Since the days of Fox, the Quakers had condemned uninspired, self-important preaching. Indeed, they justified their separate existence as a religious society by arguing that preachers who lacked divine inspiration were doing the work of the devil by interposing themselves between the faithful and God. Therefore, as Woolman knew all too well, speaking inappropriately at a Quaker meeting could be a grievous sin. In Woolman's time, some Quakers in the Delaware Valley hesitated for years before rising to speak. David Ferris felt a divine call to the ministry in 1734 when he was twenty-seven, but could not muster the strength to preach for the next twenty-one years.[9] Joshua Evans recoiled in fright when he first felt moved to speak. "It appeared to me almost like death to give up in obedience to that intimation which I believed required me to speak." "I could scarcely reconcile myself to become a minister, as it seemed to be like taking me out of my element, and causing me to be plunged into the deeps." He did not want to be a hypocrite, and he dreaded "preaching to those with whom I had once rioted in folly." At the same time he feared "the consequence of giving out, or flinching. . . . This, I thought, would be terrible in the day of account."[10]

In addition to spiritually grounded inhibitions, more prosaic, social considerations kept many Quakers quiet. Members of the meetings informally assessed one another's performances after worship ended, and sometimes their judgments could be harsh. When she attended meetings in Philadelphia, English traveling minister Elizabeth Wilkinson found it difficult to speak in the presence of "so many great so many wise and eloquent." After reprimanding herself for her timidity, she managed to speak a "few words," even though she felt that she was in the presence of some who "were ready to say in themselves, stand by I am holier than thou."[11] When an elderly Quaker from a nearby town visited George Churchman's meeting and gave ministry, Churchman judged that the man's words were "not attended with the sweetness of the

true Gospel." As a result, he reported, the gathering became "low and dis-
tressing." "Oh," Churchman complained, "how quiet worship is sometimes
interrupted!"[12] In an effort to forestall such difficulties London Yearly Meeting
issued guidelines for would-be ministers. The English Quakers cautioned all
worshipers to refrain from "undue and restless behavior," and warned speakers
to avoid "all unbecoming tones, sounds, gestures, and all affectation which
are not agreeable to Christian gravity." Preachers were advised to avoid "using
unnecessary preambles" and reminded that nothing that they said should "be
offered with a view to popularity, but in humility, and the fear of the Lord."
Those who felt moved to speak were admonished not to "disturb, or interrupt
any people in their worship" and particularly advised not to break the silence
unnecessarily at the end of the gatherings "when the meeting was left well
before."[13]

Speaking badly could be excruciating, and therefore it is hardly surprising that Woolman kept his silence for several weeks after his first attempt.
In his second offering, he spoke only "a few words" and "found peace." He
drew a lesson from that experience, "to wait in silence sometimes many weeks
together" until the spirit moved him to rise. Then he might be able "to stand
like a trumpet through which the Lord speaks to his flock."[14] His ministry improved, and he soon gained the approval of the Quakers in Mount Holly and
throughout the county. Burlington Monthly Meeting appointed Woolman to
attend its regional Quarterly Meeting in September 1742, and in August 1743
the Monthly Meeting formally recognized him, along with Peter Andrews
and Josiah White, as new ministers within the Society of Friends.[15] In his
journal Woolman described how he and Andrews worked together and gradually learned how to speak as ministers. The two men "were taught by renewed
experience to labor for an inward stillness, at no time to seek for words, but to
live in the spirit of Truth and utter that to the people which Truth opened in
us."[16] In the mid-1740s one member of Burlington Monthly Meeting counted
the number of times various ministers spoke in worship, and that record confirms Woolman's assertion that he did not speak frequently.[17]

*   *   *

The Quakers seldom transcribed their ministers' words, and although Woolman would speak in meetings for worship hundreds of times over the next
twenty-nine years, the surviving records contain only a few brief quotations from him. A review of Quaker meeting records along with the diaries,

correspondence, and memoirs of those who heard him speak provides instead a few general descriptions of the topics he covered, his tone, brief quotations from his words, and a number of assessments of his ministry's impact. One Quaker who attended the Mount Holly Meeting as a boy remembered that Woolman "was a man of few words, and his public communication was generally short." Nonetheless, this boy found Woolman's messages comforting and noticed that "there was a peculiar melody in his voice."[18] The English Quakers who saw him at the very end of his career as a minster reported that he was "careful in his public appearances to feel the putting forth of the divine hand, so that the spring of the gospel ministry often flowed through him with great purity and sweetness, as a refreshing stream to the weary travelers, toward the city of God."[19]

Woolman used similar language when he described his ministry. By his own account, there were times when words flowed out of him like water through the raised gate of a dam, but at other times he spoke even though the "spring of the ministry was low." Speaking at such times was difficult, but he found over time that he obtained "inward sweetness" by working his way through the trouble.[20] Woolman often addressed his words to only a segment of his audience, and on many occasions he focused his attention on the youths in attendance at a meeting.[21] He could be stern as well as reassuring, and he frequently invoked God's judgment. In London, he gave "lively testimony," telling those around him that "divine love was yet able to cleanse us from all filthiness of flesh and spirit, which must in a degree be witnessed before we could experience a union with the divine nature." He warned the English Quakers that "God did not unite with any contrary to his nature, Christ with Belial, nor the temple of God with idols." Therefore he pleaded with them that "all might endeavor after that purity of heart so necessarily connected with our happiness."[22] On another occasion he took Matthew as his text, and succinctly reminded his fellow worshippers, "Every plant that's not of my Heavenly Father's planting shall be plucked up by the roots."[23]

Woolman's preaching was memorable, but it constituted only a fraction of his work as a minister. He attended worship at least once week, but sometimes weeks or even months would pass between his spoken messages. Nonetheless, even though he could not be relied upon to offer words on any given Sunday, he made his presence felt at meetings even when he did not say a word. Woolman was conscientious not only about joining the Friends in worship every week, but also about entering the meetinghouse at the appointed time. One Mount Holly Friend remembered, "He was not easy to go to meeting before or after the time, but believed that the hour should be observed. So he would go to the meeting house and wait till the time arrived before entering."[24] Joshua Evans was similarly self-conscious about the impact of his arrival at worship. Before he became a minister, when he attended weekday meetings he frequently took a circuitous route to the meeting house so that his neighbors would not notice him. He did not want to appear ostentatious. After Evans became a minister, by contrast, he deliberately went "on the open road" in order to set a good example.[25] Inside the meetinghouse the ministers sat apart from the other worshippers in a way that confirmed their responsibility to lead. Woolman reports that after he became a minister, he sat in the "uppermost seat" of the Mount Holly Meeting.[26] With other respected Friends around him, he sat in front of the gathered worshippers and led them into silence.[27]

Abner Woolman's journal contains some concrete descriptions of his experience of silent worship. Sometimes, sitting quietly, Abner found it difficult to concentrate on spiritual matters. He recounts one cold day when he sat by the fire at his meetinghouse. He could not warm up, and he spent the first part of the meeting worrying about how he could get home without making himself ill. Eventually, however, even these ruminations turned to worship. He decided that his fear of illness was unfounded, because "the Lord is a powerful God." "My heart was warmed," he remembered, "and immediately I felt inward comfort." Quaker worshippers tried to leave their trivial worries behind. At one good meeting, Abner reports, "my mind was released from earthly objects and my inward man strengthened in my silent sitting." Eventually "heavenly treasure appeared exceeding beautiful and desirable, and there was a language in my heart, 'O my beloved seek for it.'" That meeting reduced Abner to tears.[28]

As Abner's journal suggests, silence at a Quaker meeting could have a powerful effect. Adopting the language of Revelation, Woolman praised the "benefit of true silence" and said that it reminded him of "how incense ascended on the opening of the seventh seal, and there was silence in heaven for the space of half an hour."[29] This quiet ecstasy was sometimes a corporate experience, and for some Quakers who felt it, worship became the center of their emotional lives. Evans reports that when he started to attend worship regularly "the time between meetings seemed to be long."[30]

In 1754 Burlington Monthly Meeting, which had supervisory authority over the Mount Holly Meeting, appointed Woolman to deliver a message. The statement asserted that Friends in the area had been negligent "in attending the appointed times of meeting for religious worship." Therefore Woolman was directed to remind the Mount Holly Quakers of their duty, and to suggest to them, "if it is honorable among men to punctually attend their appointments in outward affairs, it must be much more so in relation to superior duties. . . . Religious worship being the highest concern in life, the attending on a duty of that importance with a careless indifference, not only reflects dishonor on the particular [person], but is a disgrace and disreputation to the whole."[31]

The Quakers repeatedly reminded each other that attendance at meetings for worship was an important duty, but they were also aware that their sense of societal obligation could destroy the sincerity and spontaneity that they valued in their gatherings. Quaker ministers sought to uphold their responsibilities and instill a sense of obligation in others without conveying a feeling that attendance was routine. Peter Andrews was considered an exemplary worshipper not only because he was "careful to attend meetings for worship," but also because when he arrived at the meetinghouse he "manifested a real concern to wait upon God for strength and wisdom."[32] Woolman's mentor Abraham Farrington was praised in similar terms, for being "diligent in attending meetings" while at the same time making it clear that he was "waiting for wisdom to see his duty, and strength to perform it."[33] Woolman contended that Friends should gather only "in sincerity" and with "a clear sense of duty." Analyzing his own motives for going to worship, he declared that if he felt drawn to attend "partly in conformity to custom, or partly from a sensible delight which my animal spirits feel in the company of other people," then on occasion it might be better for him to stay home.[34]

He seldom made that choice, however. Like other fervent young men and women who entered the ministry, he quickly discovered that Quaker meetings could consume most of his spare time. In addition to meetings for worship there were "disciplinary" meetings in which Friends performed administrative tasks. The Quakers did not maintain a paid clergy, but instead they asked their ministers and other respected Friends to donate their time, pool their resources, and share out the logistical and pastoral work generated by the meetings. In Woolman's section of New Jersey, the principal agency for such work was the Monthly Meeting held in Burlington, where leading Friends met to oversee the operation of the meetings in Mount Holly, Rancocas, and several other communities in and around the capital.

Woolman began attending Burlington Monthly Meeting even before he became a minister, and during his thirty years of service he performed a wide variety of tasks for that meeting. He served on committees supervising meet-inghouse construction and maintenance, and he helped deliver books and pamphlets to local meetings. He met with men and women who had been nominated for positions of responsibility, and he served on committees that were formed to speak with non-Quakers who wished to join the Society of Friends. The meeting in Burlington—like other Quaker monthly, quarterly, and yearly meetings—convened a separate women's gathering where female ministers and Friends discussed issues of particular concern to women. Wool-man advised the Burlington women's meeting on procedural issues.[35]

Most of the Monthly Meeting's tasks were performed in two steps. First a committee would investigate the matter in question and come up with a rec-ommendation, draft a minute, or give an oral report to the meeting as a whole. These committees were generally quite small, and a majority of them had only two members. The Friends appointed to serve on the committees met and performed their tasks whenever they could find an appropriate time, in antici-pation of the second stage of the decision-making process. Their word was not final. In the second stage of the process, the committee's recommendations would be submitted for approval by the Friends who attended the formal Monthly Meeting. That meeting never took a vote. The Quakers feared inter-nal antagonism and division, and they would not govern themselves by simple majority rule. On the other hand, they also knew the risks inherent in always seeking a full consensus. As Woolman told his students, "unity without good-ness is not good."[36] The Friends gathered and waited for divine guidance, and in many respects their disciplinary meetings resembled their meetings for wor-ship. As Woolman described the process, "it is the will of our heavenly father, that we with a single eye to the leadings of his holy spirit should quietly wait on him, without hurrying in the business before us."[37] As a practical matter, this meant that if a respected Friend voiced apparently sincere objections to a proposed course of action, the meeting would pause before making a decision. On at least two recorded occasions Woolman stood alone and blocked resolu-tions at Burlington Monthly Meeting, but in both cases he achieved only a delay. After a few weeks' further deliberation, both decisions went into effect.[38]

Many of the most difficult and potentially contentious issues to come be-fore the Monthly Meeting involved disciplining Friends who misbehaved. The first time Woolman became involved in such a case was in 1744, after his father was appointed to visit a Northampton, New Jersey, Quaker named Benjamin Bryant who was reported to be "frequently overtaken with strong drink." A representative from Northampton told the Friends gathered in Burlington that

Bryant had been "dealt with but doth not refrain." In response, the Monthly Meeting appointed Samuel Woolman and one other Friend to visit Bryant. They met with him, and at the next session of the Monthly Meeting reported that Bryant seemed "sorrowful, and gave some ground to hope that he would for the future be more careful." Bryant, however, wanted to prove his sobriety and asked to be visited again. Another month passed, but Samuel Woolman and the other Friend failed to report back to the Monthly Meeting on Bryant's progress, and so the meeting asked John, with the help of Josiah White, to chase down his father and the other committee member and get a report.[39] In 1750 Woolman and Josiah White were appointed to consider a similar case from Northampton involving a Friend named Samuel Gaskill. On that occasion the Northampton Friends indicated that they had already met with Gaskill about "his excessive drinking and other evil practices," but that they could not convince him to mend his ways. In contrast to the Bryant case, this time the Monthly Meeting simply accepted the Northampton meeting's judgment and directed Woolman and White to draw up a "testification" against Gaskill. Their statement against him was read aloud at a meeting for worship in Northampton and perhaps posted in a public place in that town. Gaskill was no longer recognized as a member of the Society of Friends.[40]

It was unusual for the Monthly Meeting to be so directive and confrontational in such a case. In 1752, when Woolman was assigned to the case of John Gibbs and Isaac Gibbs Jr., two Mansfield Quakers who were reputed to have neglected their duty to attend meeting for worship and to have engaged "in the frequent practice of drinking to excess," Woolman and his partners on the small committee were told to visit with the men and "inform them that unless they reform their manner of conversation and acknowledge their faults, the meeting will be under the necessity of testifying against them."[41] Instructions such as these often initiated a difficult series of visits and negotiations. John Scarborough, a minister who frequently joined Woolman on disciplinary visits, received praise for the tone he set in correcting Friends who behaved badly. "He was steadily concerned to promote good order and discipline . . . he used great plainness in admonishing transgressors, [and] seldom gave offense."[42] In his own discussions of the disciplinary process Woolman emphasized the importance of retaining humility, and in a statement he wrote jointly with Scarborough he declared, "we have in some measure learned, that the meek in spirit find an inward support on which alone we desire to rely."[43]

Quaker ministers and elders needed to be tactful when they confronted wayward Friends. They faced equally daunting challenges when they were assigned to settle disputes involving multiple parties. Woolman served on several committees formed to intervene in private contests between debtors and creditors, and in one case to mediate a squabble between the young beneficiaries of a will.[44] The Quakers prided themselves on their ability to settle disagreements amicably, and they tried to avoid lawsuits as much as possible. Sometimes, however, their efforts at arbitration failed and in those instances one or both of the parties involved might ask the Monthly Meeting for permission to take their cases to court. In 1753 Woolman and Peter Andrews served on a disciplinary committee that examined a financial dispute; they concluded that the matter was "dark and complicated" and unlikely to be "accommodated by Friendly advice." Therefore the committee recommended authorizing a lawsuit.[45] The Monthly Meeting followed this advice even though this represented a small failure for them. One reason meetings discouraged litigation was that they believed their members should be true to their word. Friends prized honesty and disowned members who were guilty of financial misconduct or fraud. In a case in 1754, the Monthly Meeting assigned Woolman alone the task of drawing up a "testification" against two Quakers who had fled their creditors and reneged on their debts.[46]

In 1755 Woolman helped Philadelphia Yearly Meeting revise a list of queries, a list that reveals the extent to which the Quakers monitored each other's conduct. In response to the queries, local meetings were directed to report whether their members were "careful to live within the bounds of their circumstances and to avoid launching into trade and business beyond their ability to manage." The meetings were to make sure that their members were "careful to avoid the excessive use of spirituous liquors" and "the unnecessary frequenting of taverns and places of diversion." The queries mandated a regularly scheduled inquiry into the Quakers' use of grammar and their clothing, to confirm that "plainness of speech, behavior and apparel" was maintained. Local meetings were particularly directed to pay attention to the circumstances of their members' children, to determine whether they were properly educated, treated well if they had stepparents, and provided for in their parents' wills.[47]

In the 1750s, as part of their campaign to encourage spiritual growth and maintain moral discipline among the Quakers, Woolman and other respected Friends began traveling to visit families in their homes. In doing so they were reviving an old tradition and responding to pressure that had been building for several years for meetings to pay closer attention to the domestic affairs of their members.[48] In 1753 Woolman joined Abraham Farrington on a series of tours in New Jersey.[49] Working together, he and Farrington concentrated on the area around Burlington, and on his own initiative Woolman traveled as far as the New Jersey shore.[50] In 1758 Philadelphia Yearly Meeting issued a general call to its monthly meetings to form committees to visit families, and earlier in the same year Burlington Monthly Meeting established a standing visiting committee with seven members. Woolman served on that committee well into the 1760s.[51]

The project of visiting Quaker families was an early manifestation of a widening movement that Jack D. Marietta has described as the "Reformation of American Quakerism."[52] The reformers' ultimate purpose was to strengthen the Quakers as a religious community, remind them of their core principles, and promote the work of salvation. When Woolman visited a family, he often gathered the household together for worship within the home. He and his associates described their visits in thoroughly religious terms. Woolman believed that a special providence sometimes directed him to a Quaker family. On one occasion when he was on the road, he and his traveling companion learned of a woman living nearby who was tormented by dreams of death and divine punishment. Woolman and his friend went to meet the woman. She had recovered her spirits by that time, but they stayed to have "some religious conversation with her and her husband." Both she and her husband valued the conversation, and it came at a propitious moment. Woolman reports that a "short time" after their visit, the woman's husband drowned.[53] In his own part of New Jersey, Abner occasionally visited families, and in his journal he describes the process he underwent before entering a home. He took his time, "inwardly waiting on the Lord for help," and proceeded only if he felt that God had directed him to do so. Then he would self-consciously maintain his focus. Once inside the house, he made sure that he spoke only "in a religious way" and refused to engage in "conversation on temporal things." He explained that "where we go on business of this nature, much other conversation is hurtful."[54]

While the committee members were going to see Quakers in their homes, they were also visiting local meetings. These gatherings presented the travelers with special challenges. Since many more people were involved, the visitors had greater difficulty influencing the tone of the encounters. No matter how patiently they waited for divine guidance before speaking, they could not supervise the others in the room. Woolman and his fellow reformers placed a premium on maintaining peace within the meetings and told the Friends that when they met to make decisions they should avoid "contention and personal reflection . . . heats and passions and doubtful disputations." They suggested

Figure 5. The building at the center is the Greater Meetinghouse, corner of Market and Second Streets, Philadelphia. Completed in 1755, for the rest of the eighteenth century it was the most common gathering place of Philadelphia Yearly Meeting. Courtesy Library Company of Philadelphia.

that in order to assure that the meetings conducted business "in the peaceable spirit and wisdom of Jesus with decency forbearance and love to each other," it might be necessary to exclude some individuals from the decision-making process. Woolman and his associates declared that the Quakers should "suffer no turbulent contentious persons among us in ordering or managing the affairs of truth."[55]

As part of an effort to secure compliance with these directives, Woolman was appointed in 1755 to a committee of thirty ministers and elders charged with visiting every Monthly and Quarterly Meeting in the Delaware Valley, and to "inspect into their care and conduct in the discipline." Woolman was a leader in this effort, and he signed on behalf of the other committee members when the group issued its final report to Philadelphia Yearly Meeting in 1758. That report declared that the committee had performed a valuable service and recommended that its work be continued. At its own behest, the committee received a new mandate, and Woolman was reappointed to serve on it in 1758 and 1759.[56] He believed that this work was important, but he also sometimes found it tedious, and long. In 1758, he helped facilitate the reorganization of the Quaker meetings immediately south of Philadelphia. For administrative reasons Chester Quarterly Meeting had to be split in two.[57] In November, Woolman attended the first-ever session of Western Quarterly Meeting at London Grove, Pennsylvania, which had been calved off from Chester. The event brought together hundreds of Quakers and consumed most of a Saturday and the following Monday, with sessions lasting as long as eight hours at a time. In his journal, after describing the gathering, Woolman erupted into a diatribe against time-wasting talk: "In three hundred minutes are five hours, and he that improperly detains three hundred people one minute, besides other evils that attend it, does an injury like that of imprisoning one man five hours without cause."[58] Nonetheless Woolman persevered, and he would return to attend Western Quarterly Meeting on several future occasions.[59]

Much of Woolman's most memorable work took place outside Mount Holly, and indeed beyond the confines of New Jersey. During his 29–year ministerial career he took at least thirty extended journeys.[60] He was hardly unusual in this respect. The Quakers had a long tradition of traveling. Between 1696 and 1741, the renowned Philadelphia minister Thomas Chalkley, for example, traversed Britain's North American colonies, made his way to the Caribbean, and traveled in Europe as far as "England, Wales, Scotland, Ireland, Holland, Friesland, and several parts of Germany." In 1737 Chalkley stopped in Mount Holly, where he convened two large "open meetings" with Quakers and "divers people, not of our profession" in attendance. One of these events was held at the meetinghouse and the other at the home of the Quaker justice of the peace and future New Jersey assemblyman Thomas Shinn.[61] When Chalkley's journal was published in 1749, Woolman was appointed to help publicize the volume.[62] Like other Quaker journals, Chalkley's emphasized the value of long-distance travel. This reflected the importance the Friends placed on maintaining unity within their far-flung religious society, staying in contact with each other, coordinating their actions, and increasing their visibility globally.

Woolman took his first such journey in 1743. Only a few weeks after Burlington Monthly Meeting named him a minister, Abraham Farrington approached him and asked him to come along on "a visit to Friends on the eastern side" of New Jersey.[63] Farrington was fifty-two and had been a minister for more than 15 years. He owned land near Mount Holly and maintained an orchard there, but he was not a wealthy man.[64] On the contrary, those who knew him commented that his "outward circumstances" were "at times difficult." Farrington's parents had been Quakers, but his father had died when he was still an infant and his mother had married a non-Quaker. At age ten he had been bound out to service in a non-Quaker family where he stayed until he reached twenty-one. In effect, therefore, Farrington was a convert to Quakerism, and this circumstance helps explain his peculiar missionary zeal.[65]

After Farrington approached him, Woolman went to speak with some other "elderly Friends" before agreeing to go. Ordinarily Friends who undertook such "religious visits" did so as representatives of their meetings. Before leaving they were expected to obtain a certificate which would serve as a letter of introduction at each Quaker Meeting they planned to attend. The process of obtaining a certificate generally took at least a month, and it was no foregone conclusion that a minister's local meeting would authorize travel. The New Jersey ministers Thomas Evans and Joshua Evans, for example, on separate occasions had difficulty obtaining certificates.[66] In this case, however, Woolman did not need a certificate as a minister because he would be going only as Farrington's companion. Woolman's account of the trip reflects his subordinate status. He felt that his mind was still "tender" in 1743, and he was "frequently silent through the meetings" the two men attended. "When I spake, it was with much care that I might speak only what Truth opened."[67]

The arrival of traveling Quaker ministers often drew crowds. This could place some social pressure on the travelers, but many itinerant Quaker ministers, remaining faithful to the precept that they should speak only when inspired, sat before those who came to see them and maintained a perfect silence.[68] During his travels Peter Andrews had many "religious meetings appointed on his account," and these gatherings were, it was said, "mostly very large." Nonetheless, "in several public meetings he had nothing to say amongst them." This was "a great disappointment to many," but in retrospect his insistence on waiting to be moved by God was judged to have performed "a signal service." Friends praised Andrews because his silence was instructive. Indeed they said that he had been divinely "led to famish that too eager desire after words."[69]

Farrington told Woolman at the outset of their journey that the two men were going to visit "Friends." Woolman was therefore mildly surprised that they went to New Brunswick, New Jersey, which was, as Woolman described it, "a town in which none of our Society dwells." There were no Quaker homes in New Brunswick to meet in, and certainly no available meeting-houses. Therefore the two men arranged to hold worship in a tavern. The event seemed to go well. At least, Woolman reported, "The room was full and the people quiet." In total the ministers spent two weeks on the road and

Woolman was continuously impressed by the number of non-Quakers they were able to gather around them. As they went through Woodbridge, Rahway and Plainfield they convened six or seven meetings among people Woolman identified as Presbyterian. At these gatherings Farrington did more talking than Woolman. Farrington was "frequently strengthened to hold forth the Word of Life amongst them."[70]

Woolman obtained his first certificates for ministerial travel in 1746. He announced to his meeting that he wanted to take to the road as a minister, specifically to visit "the back settlements of Pennsylvania and Virginia." "Several conferences" ensued, and a "considerable time passed," but eventually it was arranged for Woolman to take two ministerial trips, one across New Jersey with Peter Andrews, and another, much more extensive journey with Peter's brother Isaac. The Andrews brothers were second-generation Quakers, their father having been introduced to the religious society by Chalkley.[71] On both trips the ministers divided their time between well-established meetings and impromptu gatherings with people unaffiliated with the Society of Friends. During their short trip through New Jersey, Woolman and Peter Andrews visited Quaker meetings in Salem, Cape May, and Egg Harbor as well as the Yearly Meeting at Shrewsbury. They also held worship in places with no established Quaker meetings, in Barnegat and Manasquan.[72]

Isaac Andrews accompanied Woolman on the much longer journey across Pennsylvania as far west as the Susquehanna River and from there south through Maryland and Virginia to North Carolina. Woolman saw much that he did not like on that expedition, but he was positively impressed by the people he met on the margins of colonial settlements. On the banks of the Susquehanna, he and Isaac Andrews visited a town that had been in existence for less than ten years. The two ministers worshipped with the people there, and although the settlers were not Quakers, Woolman thought that the austere conditions of frontier life had inspired them to live simply, industriously, and soberly, much like ideal members of the Society of Friends. He was similarly pleased with what he saw in North Carolina, where Quaker meetings were just getting organized in newly established towns. Woolman was struck by the "openness" of the young people in North Carolina and believed that they were receptive to divine inspiration.[73]

On their return journey, Woolman and Isaac Andrews visited another "new settlement" in Virginia, and "had several meetings amongst the people, some of whom had lately joined in membership with our Society." Woolman judged that at least some of them were "honest-hearted Friends, who appeared to be concerned for the cause of Truth."[74] From 1746 forward he took an interest in the affairs of newly-established Quaker meetings. The Burlington Friends helped subsidize the creation of a new meeting near the northern tip of New Jersey in a place called the "Great Meadows," and in 1751 they sent Woolman to assess the progress of the settlers there. Woolman's journal hints that that visit was difficult. He had "searching laborious exercise amongst Friends in those parts," but eventually "found inward peace therein."[75] The settlement lay near contested land, and a few years later when a coalition of Indians in league with the French took up arms against the British, New Jersey's "Great Meadows" became a scene of terror, flight, and desolation.[76]

Woolman's early travels as a minister gave him valuable experience and information that he would draw upon later when he entered into controversies over slavery, imperial expansion, and the conduct of the Seven Years' War. His most important early journey, in retrospect, was the one with Isaac Andrews in 1746, which gave him his first encounter with southern slavery. He was disturbed by the plantation slave labor system, but he kept those misgivings to himself. He had other concerns to address at that time. His priority was to introduce himself to other Quakers, familiarize himself with the needs of his religious society, and discern what he could do to advance the cause of Quakerism.

During a 1747 journey north with Peter Andrews, Woolman joined a complex network of traveling ministers from Pennsylvania, Long Island, New England, and Britain, and he worshipped in dozens of established meetings in New Jersey, New York, Connecticut, Rhode Island, and Massachusetts. By his own estimation, he and Andrews traveled more than 1,500 miles. In addition to meeting Quakers, they worshipped at gatherings "made up of other Societies." In New Milford and two other towns that Woolman described as "back settlements" in Connecticut, the two ministers met several young people who had been brought up as Presbyterians but had eventually moved to Quakerism. They told Woolman that they used to attend regular church services and then meet on their own for worship afterward. The local Presbyterian minister had joined them at some of those informal meetings, but eventually found fault with their "judgment in matters of religion." The informal group had consequently broken apart, with some of the young people returning to the fold of the local church and others leaving to join the Society of Friends.[77] Woolman was fascinated by this circle of new Quakers, and he would meet others like them in his subsequent travels. When he encountered groups that had come to Quakerism apparently on their own initiative, he guessed that some among them had received direct guidance from God.

Throughout his life, Woolman was intensely interested in the geographical spread of Quakerism, through the formal process of establishing new meetings and less predictably through the spontaneous, providential arrival of groups exhibiting signs of divine inspiration. But he was also concerned, perhaps even more fervently, with the internal affairs of well-established meetings. He timed his journeys to coincide with large periodic or annual gatherings of Friends in every region he visited. In anticipation of his 1760 trip to New England, for example, he prepared a list of ten important Quaker events, though because of the difficulties of travel and scheduling conflicts, he was unable to get to all of them.[78]

When Woolman attended Virginia Yearly Meeting in 1757, he participated in a discussion of the queries each local meeting would be required to answer periodically in reports they sent to the quarterly and annual gatherings of Friends.[79] After extensive deliberations the Virginia Quakers adopted a list of fourteen questions, beginning:

1st Are all meetings for religious worship and discipline duly attended, the hour observed, and are friends preserved from sleeping or any other indecent behavior therein, particularly from chewing tobacco or taking snuff.

2d Is love and unity maintained amongst you as brethren, are tale bearing, back biting and evil reports discouraged, and when any differences arise, are endeavors used speedily to end them.

3d Are Friends careful to bring up the children under their direction in plainness of speech behavior and apparel, in frequently reading the holy scriptures, and to restrain them from reading pernicious books, and to keep them from the corrupt conversation of the world.[80]

While making a few noticeable alterations, the Virginia Quakers adopted the list of questions Woolman had helped draft for Philadelphia Yearly Meeting two years earlier.[81]

Similarly, when Woolman attended the Yearly Meeting in Newport, Rhode Island, in 1760, he was assigned to a committee that was drafting a new "Book of Discipline" for the New England Quakers. Books of Discipline were collections of Yearly Meeting resolutions that were copied out periodically and distributed to local meetings in manuscript form. The Rhode Island committee reviewed English and Pennsylvanian examples.[82] Statements that were included in Books of Discipline gained increased attention and therefore in practical terms carried greater authority. Like other reformers of his generation, Woolman thought that the Discipline, quite literally, had to be maintained. While he and his colleagues valued procedural regularity, they were equally concerned to see that all Quaker meetings, especially the supervisory monthly, quarterly, and yearly meetings, exercised their duties in a spirit of reverence and care. After visiting one Quarterly Meeting in New Jersey, for example, George Churchman complained that Friends' manner of transacting business was "light and superficial": "The want of the form was not so much the fault, as the want of a humbling sense in active members of the necessity of applying for divine wisdom to assist in judging of the present state of subordinate meetings."[83]

Traveling ministers sought to set a good example, and therefore they were often highly self-conscious about the impressions they made at disciplinary meetings. Although he disagreed with some of the local ministers at Virginia Yearly Meeting in 1757, Woolman humbly acquiesced in the meeting's decisions, and after the sessions ended he felt sure that he had been right to do so. It was best to "leave all to him who alone is able to turn the hearts of the mighty and make way for the spreading of truth."[84] He was not so restrained in Rhode Island, however, where during a discussion of gambling he spoke angrily and (in his own estimation) without charity toward "an ancient Friend." Although Woolman won that particular argument he was worried that his manner of speaking might have weakened his cause in the long run. Therefore, he stood before the meeting and expressed his regret, exhibiting, as described it, "some degree of creaturely abasement."[85]

As part of its ongoing effort to maintain good relations between distant groups of Quakers, Philadelphia Yearly Meeting repeatedly appointed Woolman to committees charged with writing formal epistles to yearly meetings outside the Delaware Valley in North America. Nearly every year from 1750 to 1763, Woolman worked with another representative of the Yearly Meeting to draft a letter to Friends in other regions, such as Rhode Island, North Carolina, Long Island, or Virginia. There was a clear pattern to the assignments he was given. The Philadelphia Quakers asked him to assist in writing epistles to meetings he had recently visited.[86]

Woolman's epistle-writing responsibilities shifted in 1764, when Philadelphia Yearly Meeting asked him to help draft its annual epistle to London. He would keep that assignment for the next eight years, and in that capacity he

Figure 6. In 1760 Woolman attended New England Yearly Meeting in this building, the Old Friends Meetinghouse in Newport, Rhode Island. Library of Congress.

would work not only with influential Philadelphia Quakers, but also with several Friends who had either lived in Britain or had traveled there extensively, including John Churchman, William Horne, John Hunt, George Mason, and Joseph White.[87] Partly as a consequence of this work, by the time Woolman himself traveled to England in 1772 he felt confident that he knew enough about English Quakerism to participate immediately in their disciplinary proceedings. Many of those who saw him at London Yearly Meeting in 1772 were impressed by his readiness to contribute to its discussions. One English Quaker privately praised "the simplicity, solidity and clearness of many of his remarks."[88] Another observed that his advice was "solid and weighty."[89] In talking to the English Quakers about their manner of doing business, Woolman did not confine himself to generalities. He threw his support behind a specific proposal then circulating in various parts of England, to establish new regional, consultative meetings to assess whether the Friends were "living up to our principles."[90]

The attention Woolman paid to institutional structures and Quaker disciplinary process stemmed directly from the concern that had animated him since the first day he spoke at the Mount Holly Meeting. He did not believe that ministers should do "more than was required." In 1772 he wrote two extended essays providing advice to Quaker ministers, one on discipline and the other on vocal ministry at meetings for worship.[91] In both pieces Woolman drew on his own experience, pleading for ministers to wait for divine guidance before speaking or correcting anyone. He warned them not to be proud, selfish, spiteful, or greedy, to be wary of self-indulgent impulses, and never to take any self-satisfied pleasure in their work. He argued that ideally, Quaker ministers should perform their duties only during those hours when they felt overwhelmed by inspiration. In his essay on discipline, he argued that ministers would perform their duties perfectly if they waited in silence and spoke only when they could honestly say, "It is no longer I that live, but Christ that liveth in me." Then, he suggested, "right judgment" would be known.[92]

Living up to the demands that the Quaker reformers set for themselves required an enormous amount of sacrifice. Family life suffered as Quaker ministers attended midweek, weekly, monthly, quarterly, and yearly meetings. Susannah Lightfoot, née Hatton, who crossed the Atlantic as a traveling minister at seventeen, was praised after she died forty-four years later for telling her husband to leave her at her deathbed so that he could attend a quarterly meeting. The Quakers quoted her as saying before she expired, "There is nothing yields such comfort on a languishing bed as an evidence of having performed our religious duties."[93] Frequently ministers who traveled died away from their homes. Woolman's early ministerial companions Abraham Farrington and Peter Andrews were married men with children, and both of them died apart from their families on separate trips to England in the 1750s.[94]

Woolman started his own family in 1749, and for the duration of the marriage his wife Sarah would endure hardships as a consequence of his devotion to the ministry. The worst moment may have come in 1754, after the birth of their son William. In September, when William was three months old, John left home to attend a six-day session of the yearly meeting in Burlington.[95] It is impossible to know what happened next because John's journal is silent on the matter and the Quaker birth and death records are terse. What we know is that William died on September 30, ten days after the yearly meeting ended.[96] As we shall see in the next chapter, William's death inspired John to reconsider his entire way of living. He reallocated his time and energies in an effort to reconcile his responsibility to his family with his heartfelt sense of obligation toward God.

Chapter 4

The Road to Large Business: Family and Work

> I began with selling trimmings for garments and from thence
> proceeded to sell clothes and linens, and at length having got a
> considerable shop of goods, my trade increased every year and the
> road to large business appeared open.
> —John Woolman, *Journal*, chapter 3

FAMILIES OCCUPIED A central place in the eighteenth-century Quakers' vision of a moral social order. In his description of his parents' home at the beginning of his journal, Woolman vividly described what he thought a good Quaker family should do. The ideal family gave all its members security, instruction, and spiritual discipline. Without partiality, husbands and wives, parents and children, brothers and sisters lived together in one circle of love. In reality, however, the Quakers often failed to live up to this ideal. In such cases, the meetings frequently felt compelled to intervene. When Samuel Garwood "differed with his wife so far as to live separated from her," Burlington Monthly Meeting appointed Woolman to a committee charged with examining the situation and seeking a reconciliation.[1] In ordinary circumstances the Quakers conceived of marriage, parenthood, and filial responsibility as lifelong commitments. This belief made them cautious before sanctioning creation of families.

On September 4, 1749, Woolman and Sarah Ellis appeared before Burlington Monthly Meeting and the two of them "declared their intentions of marriage with each other." In accordance with its normal procedures the meeting responded by appointing two small committees, one composed of two men who were to speak to John, and another of two women to meet with Sarah. At separate conferences the committee members inquired into John's and Sarah's reasons for wishing to marry and their readiness to assume the responsibilities of life in a family.[2] One of the men assigned to speak with John was Josiah White. White had become a minister with him six years earlier, and the two men had served alongside each other at the Mount Holly meeting.[3] They knew each other well, and over the years their religious vocation would draw them closer together. White worked with John on at least six disciplinary committees investigating reports of drunkenness and other offenses committed by local Quakers and would eventually join him on Burlington Monthly Meeting's committee for visiting families.[4]

The committees that met with proposed marriage partners took their work seriously, and occasionally some couples were told not to wed. Everything went smoothly for John and Sarah, however. On October 2, 1749, after hearing reports from the two committees, Burlington Monthly Meeting found "no objection" to the match, and resolved that the couple was "at liberty to accomplish this marriage." John and Sarah accordingly married each other in the Mount Holly meetinghouse on Wednesday, October 18. The event, like all other Quaker weddings in the eighteenth century, resembled a meeting for worship. No scripted words were spoken other than John's and Sarah's brief vows. At the end of the hour, they signed their own wedding certificate, as did all the other Quakers in attendance, nineteen men and thirteen women. John's parents were present along with his brothers Asher, Abner, Uriah, and Jonah, and his sisters Sarah Elton, Patience Moore, Hannah Gaunt, Esther Woolman, and Rachel Woolman. Sarah's family was represented only by her maternal grandfather, John Abbott, and a cousin.[5]

Sarah Ellis, an only child, was born in Philadelphia in 1721, and her father died shortly after her birth. At two, she moved with her mother to Chesterfield, New Jersey, and her mother died when she was eighteen. In the years after her mother's death, she may have lived with her grandparents, but we have little evidence concerning her life before she met John.[6] John's account of his first encounter with Sarah leaves many questions unanswered. "Thinking seriously about a companion," he writes, "my heart was turned to the Lord with desires that he would give me wisdom to proceed therein agreeable to his will; and he was pleased to give me a well-inclined damsel, Sarah Ellis."[7] John had been "thinking seriously" about marriage for several years before he met Sarah, and he would continue to worry about the institution of marriage for the rest of his life. Within months of his marriage, he began serving on committees vetting other proposed matches, and in his ministerial career he would talk to at least fifteen men planning to enter into matrimony.[8] While he recognized the value of living in a loving, Quaker home, he also knew from his service as a minister that many families were neither righteous nor happy. It was therefore essential for him that both partners be "well-inclined."

Once during his travels Woolman visited Chesterfield Monthly Meeting with the reformer John Churchman. Churchman at the time was leading a campaign to more rigorously regulate marriage within the religious society, and he demanded strict enforcement of disciplinary rules forbidding pre-marital sex, incest, and marriages between Quakers and non-Quakers.[9] When Woolman and Churchman visited, the Chesterfield Quakers were engaged in several controversies concerning contested marriages, including one revolving around a woman named Amy Stockton who was reported to have married her first cousin, another involving John Harrison who was accused of fathering "a bastard child," a third concerning Elizabeth Nicholson who had married a non-Quaker, and a fourth centered on Marcy Poots who had occasioned a "public scandal" by having a child while she was still unmarried. Poots had allegedly compounded her offense by subsequently marrying a man who was not a member of the Society of Friends. As Churchman later described it, a "raw company" attended the meeting on that occasion. The Chesterfield Quakers did not abide by the "advice of the Yearly Meeting . . . which is against allowing such who are not members of our society to sit in our meetings for discipline unless they are nearly related to the parties concerned." Some of the non-Quakers in attendance, impatient to have cases resolved, pushed for decisions immediately. In effect, they took control of the agenda and demanded that the Quakers suspend their normal practice of investigating disciplinary cases for at least a month before reaching judgment. Perceiving that the meeting was veering out of control, Churchman and Woolman took the floor and reminded the Chesterfield Quakers of the value of convening "preparative meetings." Their advice was taken. The meeting delayed its decisions on all the contested cases for at least another month.[10]

The small committees that the meetings appointed to speak with men and women in advance of their marriages constituted only one of several disciplinary practices that the Friends pursued in order to promote good family life, but Quaker reformers considered those committees unusually important because they believed that bad marriages could do genuine evil. An ill-considered marriage could lead a man or a woman into a life of drunken idleness, cruelty, violence, and infidelity. In his ledger book Woolman copied out verses from a poem by Isaac Watts emphasizing the importance of marrying wisely and in accordance with divine will; otherwise the joys of matrimony would "transform to pain."[11] The Quaker reformers in the eighteenth century believed that bad marriages encouraged an array of evils. Woolman focused on one particular sin: greed.

Although keenly aware of the cost of raising a family, Woolman struggled to make sure that he did not organize his life around the pursuit of monetary gain. Observing the behavior of others, he believed that marriage could inspire worldly ambition and that the pursuit of high status and physical comfort could distract husbands, wives, and parents from their spiritual obligations, eroding their commitment to God. Woolman had difficulty thinking about family life without worrying about economics, and therefore, although he had thought about marrying for several years, the prospect of married life always troubled him. He had begun considering matrimony in the early 1740s, shortly after he took over the retail operations at his master's shop in Mount Holly. His employer lost interest in the business soon after Woolman arrived, and the young apprentice correctly guessed that the shop was about to close. This made him "thoughtful," as he described it, considering "what way I should take for a living in case I should settle" and marry. Woolman believed that his first responsibility was to serve God, but he also knew that in order to raise a family he would have to make money. After his arrival in Mount Holly he had "several offers of business that appeared profitable," but he turned them all down for fear that pursuing them would require too much "outward care and cumber." He feared that "with an increase in wealth the desire of wealth increased," and he did not want business concerns to distract him from his religious vocation.[12]

His sister Elizabeth provided a model for him. After leaving her parents' house on Rancocas Creek, she had moved to Haddonfield, New Jersey, a town four miles east of Philadelphia. Unmarried and working on her own, Elizabeth went into business as a tailor and made clothes for men and women. She quickly achieved some success at the trade, and by 1744 she had furnished her home with items that bespoke a modest prosperity. She owned a large looking glass, a walnut table, a tea service, silver spoons, and a collection of china. Her inventory as a tailor included fine gowns and gold buttons. Nonetheless, while she had done well economically, she retained her humility. John believed that his sister had received "the gracious visitations of God" after leaving her father's farm, and that the Lord had inspired her to lead a "self-denying, exemplary life." In the 1740s, Elizabeth wrote notes to God on small pieces of paper. On one she asked, "O Lord that I may enjoy thy presence, or else my time is lost and my life a snare to my soul." John loved her.[13]

Woolman decided to become a tailor like his sister, and he made arrangements to learn the trade from his master. He believed at the time that he was making the right decision, although he subsequently experienced some moments of inner conflict: "I felt at times a disposition that would have sought for something greater." For a while he divided his time between tailoring with his master and tending the shop, but when his master's wife died, the shop was finally closed, and Woolman was released. From that moment until the day of his marriage, he lived alone in Mount Holly and supported himself by making, altering, and repairing clothes.[14] Woolman kept records of his work, and his ledgers indicate that he had received extensive training. From the start he exhibited considerable versatility. He made gowns, waistcoats, greatcoats, jackets, cloaks, tunics, bonnets, stomachers, bodices, petticoats, stays, riding habits, knee breeches, trousers, and caps. He worked with leather, wool, imported Indian calico, and silk. In the first three years his business was almost exclusively clothing-related, though he also made bridles and reins.[15] But even then his plan was to diversify. In order to earn enough to make it possible to "settle" and raise a family he thought that he would have to supplement his income with "a little retailing of goods." The character of his business began to change sometime after 1746. As he described it, "I began with selling trimmings for garments and from thence proceeded to sell clothes and linens, and at length having got a considerable shop of goods, my trade increased every year and the road to large business appeared open."[16] In anticipation of raising a family he had purchased a house "at the upper end of Mount Holly" with space for his shop on the ground floor and bedrooms above.[17] His business was already expanding rapidly at the time of his marriage, and the birth of his daughter Mary in December 1750 increased his desire to earn more, to support a larger family in the future.[18]

He catered to a wide range of customers. He sold goods and performed services for wealthy slaveholders such as the prominent Quaker Thomas Shinn. He also supplied and serviced free blacks and bondsmen who appear in his ledgers without last names as "Negro Chap," "Negro Primus," "Negro Sam," and "Negro William." Several women are named in his account books as patrons of his shop, and it is likely that many more came and did business under their husbands' names. Working as a tailor and a shopkeeper, he had an opportunity to meet and converse with the full variety of Mount Holly residents.[19]

His customers seldom paid him cash. Instead they did work for him, gave him produce from their workshops, farms, and gardens, or offered him items they had bought elsewhere. For each of these transactions Woolman and his customers had to agree on the cash value of the things they exchanged, but their accounts rarely came into balance immediately. Most of his steady customers ran up debts. The stock of goods in his shop reflected the diversity of his clientele and the wide assortment of things they gave him in payment. In order to settle his accounts and dispose of his inventory he sold many things other than clothes. By the early 1750s, visitors to his shop could buy Delft china, ivory combs, pen knives, glass bottles, spoons, cups, mugs, paper, scissors, earthen pans, iron ladles, scythes, and fish hooks. They could also find a variety of locally produced and imported foodstuffs including veal, pork, sausage, spices, tea, coffee, chocolate, sugar, and rum.

Woolman lent books to at least fifty of his customers, including eleven women. The variety of titles he lent reveals the extent of Mount Holly's engagement with the wider world. He acquired and lent out a copy of John Locke's *Treatise on Education*, a collection of Britain's international treaties, and a synopsis of the laws of England. His customers borrowed practical guides including a manual on cider-making, another on navigation, and an advice book entitled *A Merchant's Pocketbook*. He had many volumes by Quaker authors, and it is hard to mistake the evangelical purpose behind some of his loans. He lent the Quaker theologian Robert Barclay's work to "Negro William," for example. At the same time, his books included spiritual and moral tracts written by non-Quakers whose arguments seemed to accord with the principles of the Society of Friends, such as Thomas à Kempis's *Imitation of Christ*, Sir Richard Blackmore's poem *Creation*, and an anonymous work entitled *The Oeconomy of Human Life*, which purported to be a piece of oriental wisdom discovered by an English merchant living in China.[20]

Woolman's work as a retailer brought him into intimate contact with Quakers and non-Quakers alike. In his pastoral work as a minister he had learned much about the lives of the members of his meeting, but as a shopkeeper he became aware of the habits and preferences of a broader segment of the population. He knew how his customers earned and handled money, what they ate and drank, and how they set their tables. His customers came to respect him as an educated man, and they demanded a wide range of services from him, taking advantage of his erudition. He drafted innumerable deeds and wills for them, and helped at least one customer start an account book. He found a dentist for another, and on at least two occasions he performed a surgical procedure himself, bleeding a man who was injured and a woman who felt ill.[21]

Through his work as a shopkeeper Woolman became engaged in the life of the community around him, assuming some responsibility for the wellbeing of his neighbors. It was difficult for him to maintain consistent principles as his business increased, but he sought to make it his "general practice" to buy and sell only "things really useful." Although he sold rum, he tried to make sure that his patrons drank it only "in moderation." He also warned his poorer customers not to buy anything too costly, and he thought that even his wealthy customers should respect the Quaker testimony in favor of plain living: "Things that served chiefly to please the vain mind in people I was not easy to trade in, and seldom did it, and when I did I found it weaken me as a Christian."[22] He always knew that his efforts to please his customers might tempt him to make compromises to the peril of his soul. On the inside front cover of the account book he started in 1753, he copied out the following lines from Proverbs: "The getting of treasures by a lying tongue is a vanity tossed to and fro of them that seek death. Labour not to be rich. Cease from thine own wisdom."[23] With these words he reminded himself of something he had sensed when he first moved to Mount Holly. Serving customers in a shop was spiritually dangerous. To succeed as a retailer, he had to satisfy those who came to the counter, or at least meet the demands of a large enough percentage of them to keep the business profitable. Yet he knew that in order to uphold his principles he would have to turn some of his customers away.

Woolman changed his mind about shop keeping in 1754. In his description of this event in his journal he does not directly mention his son, but instead observes in more general terms that by the end of that year he had come to recognize with new clarity that he "had but a small family." William had died and it is likely that Sarah was no longer able to bear children. It is clear that after William's death John did not expect his family to grow. Under these circumstances, he concluded that "Truth did not require me to engage in much cumbrous affairs." The "increase of business" had become a burden to him, and although he sensed that his "natural inclination was toward merchandise," he did not believe that he should follow his self-serving natural impulses. Thus, he began to steer some of his customers to other shops.[24] Woolman's account books reveal the extent of the change. After 1754 he did not handle coffee, molasses, tobacco, or snuff. By the end of 1755 he had given up selling indigo, rum, cordial, powder, and shot. He continued to work as a tailor, but even that side of his business changed. He had grown uneasy producing clothing "which pleased the proud mind in people" and he felt himself "strengthened to leave off that which was superfluous in my trade."[25] After 1755 he sometimes sold household items to his customers, and on rare occasions he even offered some of them spices, chocolate, sugar, and tea, but those transactions no longer constituted a significant part of his business. He described the event succinctly and accurately in his journal when he wrote that he "wholly laid down merchandise."[26]

By refocusing his retail operations, Woolman disengaged himself from several practices that had seemed to compromise his moral principles. It was no coincidence that he stopped selling snuff a few months before he joined other reformers at Philadelphia Yearly Meeting in condemning tobacco sniffing at worship. He had always been similarly uneasy about rum, and even fourteen years after he stopped selling the liquor he remained worried that he had not done enough to make sure that his customers never drank to excess. He interpreted his rum sales as part of a more general problem. If retailers catered to their customers' selfish impulses, they promoted wide-ranging bad behavior. Woolman believed that excessive drinking and "the custom of wearing too costly apparel" were linked. Striving to purchase extravagant finery led some of his customers to work excessively or make their servants work harder for them, "beyond what our Heavenly Father intends for us." When thus overworked, many who had never been drunkards before began to crave drink. Extrapolating from his own experience as a shopkeeper, Woolman interpreted the rising volume of rum sales across New Jersey as evidence of misdirected "immoderate labor."[27] He felt freer to speculate along these lines after he gave up large-scale "merchandise." Reducing his retail operations gave him greater confidence in pointing to his own life as a model for moral development. Shortly after he stopped selling luxuries and rum, he started writing his journal.[28]

There is no record of Sarah's immediate reaction to this change in her family's fortunes, but her later statements and behavior suggest that she came to see the wisdom of John's decision. In the only letter she wrote that has survived, she emphasized the importance of choosing a trade with an eye toward "spiritual advantage rather than worldly profit." Specifically, she indicated that she was struck with "sorrow" when she learned that a young man intended to become "a doctor or a lawyer." She asked, "What is this world and the pleasures here below, when compared with eternity?" She thought it was much better to be a farmer.[29]

The wives of other Quaker reformers adjusted similarly to their husbands' embrace of material simplicity. Margaret Churchman, the wife of John Churchman, supported his vocation with apparent "unity of spirit, harmony of conduct, and a concern to be exemplary to their offspring."[30] She understood his refusal to pursue the "opportunities he might have had to get outward riches."[31] John Churchman urged his son and grandchildren to follow his example: "choose husbandry," live "in the country," and disavow any ambition to acquire "great estates." He wanted his family to reject the "ways of merchandize."[32] Joyce Benezet, Anthony's wife, likewise supported her husband's disdain for material wealth. As a young man, Anthony was "brought up" to work in the "mercantile business," but he refused to pursue that career. According to the Friends' account of him, he tried several other potentially lucrative occupations, but discovered that each of them consumed "more of his time and attention than he found consistent with his peace of mind." Eventually he found contentment earning his living as a schoolteacher. Like Sarah Woolman and Margaret Churchman, Joyce Benezet was an active Quaker. The Friends remembered her as Anthony's "truly religious helpmeet."[33] Indeed both Joyce Benezet and Sarah Woolman became Quaker ministers. Joyce was a more accomplished speaker than Anthony, and while there is no record of Sarah giving vocal ministry, she assumed important administrative roles in Philadelphia Yearly Meeting. Sarah Woolman continued to serve as a delegate to the Yearly Meeting after John's death. Her service in that capacity ended only in 1777, when hostile armies faced each other in fields between Mount Holly and Philadelphia, making it impossible for her to attend.[34]

As the choices of John Churchman and Anthony Benezet suggest, John Woolman was hardly unique among the Quaker reformers of his era in seeking to distance himself from the world of pernicious commerce. More than a decade before Woolman scaled back operations at his shop, David Ferris, a Quaker retailer in Wilmington, made a similar decision. Ferris disliked selling rum. He also felt uneasy offering his customers "superfluous articles" of clothing such as "gay callicoes" and "flowered ribbands" which "we, as a society, did not allow our families to wear." In 1742 Ferris stopped selling such things and resolved to offer instead "such articles only, as were really useful."[35] Woolman distinguished himself among the reformers not by scaling back his retail operations, but rather by discussing his decision in the way that he did. In several essays and in the drafts of his journal, he drew upon his experience to develop a critique of economic life throughout the Delaware Valley and beyond. Like some of his commentary on other issues, his analysis of economics provoked controversy and sometimes reached beyond the boundary of acceptable

Quaker discourse. Therefore he withdrew some passages from his essays at the request of the Overseers of the Press and withheld other pieces from review altogether. He was persistent, however, and managed to gain approval for the publication of a considerable body of economic analysis.[36]

*   *   *

Economics played a central role in Woolman's understanding of history and his sense of God's plans for the world. Two years after he reduced his engagement with "merchandize," he spent a night in the woods of North Carolina without a fire, having gathered "some bushes under an oak" to sleep in. The ground was wet, he was uncomfortable, and the mosquitoes kept him awake. Looking at the stars, Woolman thought of humanity's first parents and their condition immediately after they had been expelled from the garden. Adam and Eve had had "no house, no tools for business, no garments but what their Creator gave them, no vessels for use, nor any fire to cook roots or herbs." Nonetheless God had provided them "means for their happy living in this world." Woolman concluded that "improving in things useful is a good gift and comes from the Father of Lights," but it was wrong to employ "creaturely cunning and self-exaltation" to make "inventions of men" that ran against divine wisdom. The faithful should "apply all the gifts of divine providence to the purposes for which they were intended."[37]

Woolman came to believe that "the least degree of luxury hath some connection with evil," and he asserted that it was the special responsibility of those who were looked upon as the "leaders of the people" to "stand separate from every wrong way."[38] He argued that "collecting of riches, covering the body with fine-wrought, costly apparel, and having magnificent furniture" impeded the operation of "universal love" and inspired self-serving desires of a kind that could not be found among "the children of light."[39] He asked himself, "Do I in all my proceedings keep to that use of things which is agreeable to universal righteousness?" He thought it would be wrong to exert effort or employ the labor of others to satisfy his own vanity.[40] He opposed those "branches of workmanship" that were "only ornamental," and insisted that decorative work was wasteful "in the building of our houses," in "hanging by our walls and partitions," and "in our furniture and apparel." He described "preparing carriages to ride in" as an evil superfluity, like adorning buildings with "curious engravings and paintings," and eating "delicious meats." He saw these things as markers of pretended superiority and unjust inequality.[41] In his assessment of his own life, he worried that if he owned things that were unavailable to a poor man, he might "lay a temptation in his way to steal," and he did not want to be responsible for luring men into the sin of thievery.[42]

Woolman stopped selling tea on a regular basis in 1755, and when he did so he joined a number of Quaker reformers who condemned tea drinking as the epitome of ostentation and waste. In 1742 the eccentric Quaker Benjamin Lay drew Benjamin Franklin's attention by staging a dramatic "public testimony" against tea drinking. According to Franklin's account, Lay went to the market in Philadelphia and set up a stall to display a box of china. After he had attracted an audience he began to shatter the pots, cups, and saucers with a hammer, until the crowd intervened, "overthrew him," spilled the box, and grabbed the unbroken pieces.[43] Years later, Joshua Evans resolved not to drink "East India tea" because he thought that home-grown herbal drinks would "suit our constitutions better than those herbs and shrubs which grow in so distant, and very different climates."[44] Evans was also concerned that importing tea was unnecessarily expensive, and he worried that the drink was habit-forming. He observed that tea drinking had become "universal even among those who know not where to get the next meal. So strong is custom some say they can not do without it twice a day."[45]

Like David Ferris before him, Woolman wanted to promote Quaker-style plain living among all his customers, not simply the Quakers. It was not enough, Woolman suggested, for members of the Society of Friends merely to live pragmatically and plainly only among themselves for the benefit of themselves. It was necessary for them to live well in the right spirit, and without any motivation toward self-aggrandizement. If the Quaker settlers in America considered their own interests "as distinct from others," and sought to "promote plain living in order to enrich our own country," they would be "living plain in a selfish spirit" and not following the lead of "true religion."[46] He believed that no one should seek to profit from "fetching or selling those things which they believe tend to alienate the minds of people from their true interest."[47] He decried the moral calculus which declared that it was evil to sell counterfeit and worthless goods, but acceptable to offer products such as rum which did positive harm to the purchaser.[48] His analysis extended well beyond liquor sales, however. He thought it was wrong to cater to any kind of self-indulgence.

The evolving Quaker critique of retailing focused not only on the products shopkeepers sold, but also on the way they behaved toward their clientele. When Ferris resolved to sell only useful things, he reconsidered the methods he used to set his prices. "I could not feel easy to sell my goods for as much as I could get for them, as was the practice with many." Instead Ferris sought to earn only "a moderate profit."[49] Woolman objected to the way persons engaged in trade spoke to each other. "There is a conversation necessary in trade," he wrote, that was similar to "one man pushing another with a warlike weapon."[50] This was a problem not only at local shop counters, but around the world. Woolman knew that greed sometimes led to violent conflict, and indeed he believed that "selfishness" was the "original cause" of all humanity's wars.[51]

In a late passage of his journal, Woolman launched into a rhythmic diatribe against avarice:

> In the love of money the voice of the stranger finds entrance.
> In the love of money the eye is not single to God
> In the love of money the understanding is closed up against the pure
>   example of truth, and thus becomes darkened.[52]

Woolman expressed similar sentiments in *Considerations on the True Harmony of Mankind*, where he quoted the words of Jesus, "Ye cannot serve God and mammon."[53]

Nonetheless, in that same essay he reaffirmed his belief in the redemptive power of love and argued that on occasion the rich could be good: "A person in outward prosperity may have the power of obtaining riches, but the same mind being in him which is in Christ Jesus, he may feel a tenderness of heart toward those of low degree, and instead of setting himself above them, may look upon it as an unmerited favor that his way through life is more easy than the way of many others." A good wealthy man could "employ his time in looking into the wants of the poor . . . and hold forth such a perfect example of humiliation, that the pure witness may be reached in many minds, and the way opened for a harmonious walking together."[54] Woolman never imagined that wealth could be evenly distributed. On the contrary, he believed that the "true order of kind Providence" had given men varying capacities for labor, and different needs. "Some who are tough and strong and their minds active choose ways of life requiring much labor to support them," he wrote. On the other hand, some men were "soon weary," less "apt for toil," and had "minds less sprightly." Those in this second category should rest quietly and "choose a life easy to support, being content with little."[55]

History also had an effect on the distribution of wealth. Woolman conceded that "by the agreements and contracts of our fathers and predeces-sors," as well as "by doings and proceedings of our own," some families had become richer than others. This was not going to change. Under these circum-stances, justice required that landlords and masters take "every opportunity of being acquainted with the hardships and fatigues of those who labor for their living." Woolman suggested that masters were more likely to be charitable to-ward their laborers if they experienced "hard labor" themselves.[56] He accepted the principle that "Man is born to labor" and that hard work could be instruc-tive and beneficial to the laborer. Nonetheless he expressed concern that this argument could be used to exploit men and limit their opportunities.[57]

In general terms, Woolman advocated reducing the hours that every la-borer worked in order to assure that toil and income were equitably and mod-erately distributed. He asked the question, "If 4 men, each working 8 hours a day, raise 200 bushel of rye in 60 days, how many hours must 5 men work to do the same business in the same time?" He provided calculations and gave an answer: 6 hours, 24 minutes, and he suggested that all the workers would be happier and healthier working only six and a half hours a day. As far as wages were concerned, he insisted that all God's creatures, so long as they lived "an-swerable to the design of our creation," were "so far entitled to a convenient subsistence that no man may justly deprive us of it." He urged landlords to "regulate their demands agreeable to universal love" by not charging excessive rents. Those who demanded "greater toil or application to business than is consistent with pure love" invaded their tenants' "rights as inhabitants of that world of which a good and gracious God is proprietor."[58]

Woolman felt sympathy for "those whose circumstance in life as free men required constant labor to answer the demands of their creditors." He argued that "if such who had great estates generally lived in that humility and plain-ness which belongs to a Christian life, and laid much easier rents and interests on their lands and moneys and thus led the way to a right use of things, so great a number of people might be employed in things useful," that labor would become simply "an agreeable employ." Those "branches of business" which "at present" seem "necessary to circulate the wealth which some gather, might in this way of pure wisdom be discontinued." He believed that many servants were worked too hard because of their masters' excessive devotion to luxury. "Did such who care for great estates attend with singleness of heart to [the Holy Spirit] which so opens and enlarges the mind that men love their neighbors as themselves, they would have wisdom given them to man-age without finding occasion to employ some people in the luxuries of life or to make it necessary for others to labor too hard."[59] "Were all superfluities and the desire of outward greatness laid aside and the right use of things universally attended to, such a number of people might be employed in things useful that moderate labor with the blessing of heaven would answer all good purposes relating to people and their animals, and a sufficient number have leisure to attend on the proper affairs of civil society."[60]

Woolman expressed the hope that in the future, God would lead some good people to be "patterns of deep self denial in things relating to trade and handicraft labor" and help those "who have plenty of the treasures of this world" to set an example by living a "plain and frugal life" and by paying better wages to "such whom they may hire."[61] But the wealthy could not effect this transition alone. The responsibility for establishing a righteous economic order lay with the laborers as well as with those who employed them. Woolman argued that "the pure principle of righteousness is the foundation whereon the men of God stand." Christian servants should obey their masters only if the orders they received were consistent with divine wisdom. "Such commands of men which cannot be performed without disobeying God are not sufficient authority for a servant of Christ to proceed upon," he asserted. "We ought to obey God, rather than men." Woolman felt sympathy for servants whose masters put them to work "to gratify the covetous, luxurious, or ambitious designs of others. If they comply not, they are liable to punishment, and if they do that which they believe is not right for them to do, they wound their own souls."[62]

While Woolman never advocated violent upheaval, he believed that the prevailing economic order created perpetual social tension: "Selfish worldly minded men may hold lands in the selfish spirit, and depending on the strength of the outward power, be perplexed with secret uneasiness, lest the injured should sometime overpower them, and that measure meted to them, which they measure to others." In the end, he believed, violent revolution would be unnecessary because God would make sure that justice prevailed. "Selfish men," he declared, "may possess the earth, but it is the meek who inherit it, and enjoy it as an inheritance from the Heavenly Father, free from all the defilements and perplexities of unrighteousness."[63]

Woolman's increasingly specific commentary on economic culture, combined with his desire to set an example for others, gave added significance to the occupational decisions he made after 1755. He never made a vow of poverty, but instead sought a way of living that would free him from distracting anxiety and make it easier for him to serve as a guide to others and to pursue his religious vocation. He had inherited land near Mount Holly in 1750, and after 1754 he had begun exploiting those fields more intensively.[64]

The Philadelphia merchant Thomas Clifford had been dealing with land-owners and growers in Mount Holly at least since 1750. Clifford bought timber and produce from farmers across the Delaware Valley, and exported pork to the Caribbean. In 1754 he acquired nearly 4,000 board-feet of timber from Woolman, and in 1756 he began purchasing salted pork, gammon, and lard from him.[65] Under Clifford's influence, Woolman's pig operations expanded rapidly. Clifford supplied Woolman with salt to cure his meat, and Woolman's salt orders appear to have doubled between 1756 and 1757.[66] As a consequence of his dealings with Clifford, almost immediately after he gave up "merchandize," Woolman saw a new "road to large business" open before him. In 1757 he sold Clifford at least 63 barrels of salted pork, 14 barrels of gammon, and substantial quantities of lard.[67] To maintain his pork business Woolman asked several of his neighbors and relations, including his brother Uriah, to carry letters, invoices, and cash between Mount Holly and Philadelphia.[68] He also hired his neighbors to haul his meat for him.[69] In his correspondence with Clifford, Woolman asked the merchant to calculate prices according to the rates prevailing in Philadelphia. He expected the prices to vary from day to day and he was ready to adjust his prices in accordance with changes in the market, but he refused to do any haggling himself.[70]

In late summer and early fall 1757, Woolman experienced considerable difficulty timing his shipments to Philadelphia. On one occasion his hauler departed unexpectedly quickly, leaving Woolman with "70 or 80 good gammons," unsold and locally unsalable, in Mount Holly. A few weeks later he had fat pigs ready for slaughter, perhaps enough for 10 or 15 barrels of pork, but the weather was so hot that he knew he could not safely process the meat. He asked Clifford to place an advance order, setting the price not at the prevailing rate but according to Clifford's estimate of what the pork was "likely to fetch three weeks hence delivered at Philadelphia."[71] Woolman continued to raise and sell pork until October 1758, and then his ledger books reveal an abrupt transition. He stopped working with Clifford, and from that date forward the only meat his sold in Mount Holly was beef or veal. It is possible that he stopped selling Clifford pork because he did not like raising provisions for the Caribbean islands. By 1758 Woolman was seeking to distance himself from slavery. But if that was the explanation for his decision, he never said so, at least not in any document that has survived in the historical record. It is equally possible that Woolman gave up the pork business because he disliked the awkwardness of conducting trade at a distance. After 1758, he worked with his customers almost exclusively face-to-face, and often served them in intimate ways.

For the rest of his life, Woolman grew grain on his land, and he hired laborers to help him at harvest time. Using his own scythe, he worked alongside his hired men.[72] He raised his own cattle, rented some meadows, and allowed neighboring farmers to graze their animals on his land for a fee. In 1755, with help from his neighbors, he established an orchard, planting 17 rows of approximately one hundred trees. He added 22 rows in 1756. The orchard produced several varieties of apples and some pears, and in 1759 Woolman began selling small trees.[73] His apples ripened at different times of year. Most were good for cider, but some, he noted in his ledger, were "very fine for drying."[74]

Still, a large portion of Woolman's income came from tailoring. While there may have been a shift in the quality of the apparel Woolman produced after 1755, there was no discernable decline in the volume of his business. He made garments on order and also repaired clothes. Contemporary descriptions of him suggest that he busied himself with sewing almost continuously, even when he did not have any immediate orders to fill.[75] Sewing was a solitary, contemplative activity, but Woolman's other tasks as a tailor were often very social. Mary Sill, a widow living near him in Mount Holly, spun yarn and thread for him, did his laundry, and sometimes sent her servant Polly to do the work.[76] Other neighbors supplied him with cloth dyes, fabrics, furs, and hides.

In 1762 Woolman visited the Quaker teacher Rebecca Jones at her school in Philadelphia.[77] Three years later, he started teaching his own classes in Mount Holly and would continue to teach children until 1769. His pupils included, according to Burlington Monthly Meeting, "poor Friends' children and others," although he rarely taught more than eight students at a time.[78] Woolman did not think that teachers should be distracted from their classroom work by any concern for the economic viability or success of their schools. The children would suffer, he warned, if their instructors' "thoughts and time" were "so much taken up in the more outward affairs of the school" that they could not "attend to the spirit and temper" of each child in their classes. The low wages generally offered teachers, Woolman argued, compounded this problem.

Woolman's advice to schoolteachers suggests that he thought that their lessons should resemble Quaker meetings for worship. "Christ our Shepherd being abundantly able and willing to instruct his family in all things proper for them to know, it remains to be our duty to wait patiently for his help. . . . It is therefore good for us in schools and in all parts of education to attend diligently to the principle of universal Light, and patiently wait" for the children to enter "the channel of true wisdom."[79] "It is a lovely sight to behold innocent children," he declared. "To labor for their help against that which would mar the beauty of their minds, is a debt we owe them."[80]

Woolman's *First Book for Children* appeared in 1769 and went through three printings. Joseph Crukshank, the printer, ran an advertisement in the *Pennsylvania Gazette* in December 1769 indicating that the third edition had been "enlarged." The price was 3 pence for a single copy, and 2 shillings for a dozen.[81] Woolman sold his primers in bundles, and in one instance he dispatched 100 copies at once.[82] The primers were small and cheaply made, and on the front covers Woolman indicated that he expected young children to deface the books. This was appropriate, he suggested, because the primers were designed to be expendable: "Much useful reading being sullied and torn by children in schools before they can read, this book is intended to save unnecessary expense." Woolman had the following notice printed on the front page: "Note: When the above alphabet is defaced, this leaf may be pasted upon the cover, and the Alphabet on the other side made use of."[83]

Through teaching their children, making and mending their clothes, and exchanging produce with them, Woolman learned much about his neighbors. His customers, in turn, became quite familiar with him, and this was particularly true among the Quakers who employed his services, some of whom already knew him as a prominent member of the Mount Holly Meeting. Josiah White, who in 1749 served on the committee that investigated the propriety of Woolman's marriage, became one of his customers in the 1760s. Woolman sewed breeches and gloves for White and his family and on various occasions sold them cedar boards, veal, apples, cider, saplings, and grafts of fruit trees. White, for his part, sold Woolman paper, books, honey, mead, limes, and an herbal medicine identified in Woolman's account books as "Calamus water." In 1765 Woolman schooled White's daughter Bathsheba and his son Jesse, and in 1769, White's daughter Mary attended Woolman's school.[84]

Just as Woolman served the children of Mount Holly in the early years of their lives, he also maintained a constant interest in the affairs of the dying and the dead, helping to compose wills and working as an executor on a succession of estates. This testamentary practice grew out of his general work as a draftsman. He had discovered early in his career that "writing is a profitable employ," and at the request of his customers he drew up a wide variety of documents including advertisements, bonds, leases, bills of sale, and deeds.[85] He also worked as a surveyor and made maps. In the early 1740s, he began helping old and infirm residents of Mount Holly make bequests, and he oversaw the settlement of several of his clients' estates.[86] By his own account, Woolman wrote wills for men and women when they were "sick, and expected soon to leave their families." Some of these dying men and women were poor, with "little to divide amongst their children."[87] At the other extreme, in 1753 he served as an executor of the estate of Thomas Shinn, who owned slaves and extensive landholdings. The process of settling the Shinn estate consumed several years.[88] Working as an executor, Woolman paid the doctors who attended to the dying in their final hours, purchased coffins for the deceased, and hired grave diggers.[89] He settled his clients' accounts with their servants, and as part of the process of disposing of their moveable property, scheduled auctions, posted advertisements for the events, oversaw the bidding, and finalized the sales. He negotiated the disposition of real estate, sometimes seeking to accommodate the interests of several parties at once, including tenants, potential purchasers, and the beneficiaries of the estates.

The Shinn properties were more complex than any other that Woolman handled. In that case he was one of two executors and worked alongside Shinn's son-in-law Henry Paxson. This was Woolman's first close engagement with Paxson, but the two men would meet in other contexts in the future. Paxson was a master at the Mount Holly ironworks. He was considered a gentleman, and later in life he would follow in his father-in-law's footsteps and represent Burlington County in the New Jersey Assembly.[90] Paxson and Woolman had several things in common. They knew each other as Quakers, and for a while they shared commercial interests. In the mid-1750s, both men engaged the services of Thomas Clifford, for example.[91]

In the process of settling the Shinn estate, and at several other times during his work as an executor, Woolman found himself, in league with others, rearranging features of the social structure of Mount Holly, not only distributing wealth within the community, but also determining the fundamental freedoms of its inhabitants. This experience profoundly informed his understanding of slavery. Responding to the needs, desires, and avarice of the beneficiaries also affected his analysis of family life.

Woolman was alert to the pernicious consequences of harboring ambitions for one's heirs. He believed that all people were born with a "natural desire of superiority," and this evil impulse often revealed itself as a perverse kind of parental concern for the next generation.[92] He saw first-hand how "a view to get riches and provide estates for children" had "entangled" many parents in the "spirit of oppression."[93] Woolman warned Quaker parents, not only when they wrote their wills, but more generally in the conduct of their lives, that their ambitions might do "sensible hurt to themselves," and also harm their children.[94] In *Considerations on the True Harmony of Mankind*, he emphasized the spiritual danger confronting parents who strove to "support their families in a way pleasant to the natural mind." Mothers and fathers who sought to achieve prosperity for their children often lost "that pure feeling of truth, which if faithfully attended to, would teach contentment in the divine will, even in a very low estate."[95] He expressed sorrow for "children who by their education are led on in unnecessary expenses."[96]

Woolman's commentary on family life reflects a profound ambivalence. He imagined that all good people after death entered into "that state of being where there is no possibility of our taking delight in any thing contrary to the pure principle of universal love." Specifically he believed that it would be impossible for a soul in heaven to take pleasure in partiality, or maintain a "selfish love" directed exclusively toward the members of his or her own family. Indeed, whenever the soul maintained such a "selfish love" there would be "an unpassable gulf between the soul and true felicity."[97] In his more earthbound discussions of family dynamics, Woolman declared that he had seen many corrupt families, with greedy, profane, self-important, and oppressive parents and children.

Nonetheless, he maintained his faith that families could serve as models for an ideal righteous order. Like other Quaker ministers, he believed that the Friends' good behavior at home should be made visible to the world. As spouses and parents, sometimes even as children, Quakers strove to be exemplary. Some respected Friends wrote advice to their sons and daughters with the tacit understanding that their words might be made public. Thus, after Abraham Farrington died, Woolman signed a memorial publicizing notes Farrington had written for his children.[98] Similarly, after his brother Abner died, John found Abner's journal in a "stitched book." Abner had addressed the work to his three sons and his daughter, and he began it by declaring that he had written "the chief part" of it "in the night, when you my dear children were asleep." Although Abner had apparently recounted his life story with domestic purposes in mind, John transcribed the work in order to send it to Philadelphia for review by the Overseers of the Press.[99]

John did not, by contrast, address his own journal to his daughter Mary. It is possible that he doubted whether he had ever been a model father. There is no surviving correspondence between John and Mary and little direct evidence concerning the tenor of their relationship. On one occasion, after a meeting for worship in Mount Holly, Mary was so excited by her father's vocal ministry that she took notes. John had called upon the young to take up the work of their elders, and on that morning, at least, Mary apparently sympathized with her father's religious convictions.[100] On the other hand, in John's general commentary on parenthood, it is easy to discern potential sources of tension between them. He joined other Quaker reformers in singling out young unmarried women as potentially frivolous, irresponsible consumers. He cited Isaiah's opposition to "the haughtiness of the daughters of Sion," and specifically repeated the prophet's objection to the "many ornaments" that young women wore, which Isaiah condemned as "vanity."[101] At Western Quarterly Meeting in 1767, John stood and spoke in a "singular and affecting" way, and asked "Friends in general, and in a particular manner the young women," to imitate Christ and give up the pursuit of "things delicate or superfluous, either in dress or furniture."[102]

While Woolman warned parents to avoid indulging their daughters, he seldom made comparable comments about relations between husbands and wives. The closest he ever came to such a statement was on Nantucket in 1760, where he was unusually impressed by the dangerous work of the whalers and the fragility of the island's economy. Since wood was scarce and the land was not fertile, the islanders were dependent on profits from whaling to purchase the necessities of life from the mainland. With this in mind, Woolman spoke to the women at Nantucket Monthly Meeting and admonished them to "educate their children in true humility and disuse of all superfluities" because of "the difficulties their husbands and sons were frequently exposed to at sea." The "more plain and simple their way of living was," he declared, "the less need of running great hazards to support them."[103] This comment was exceptional, however.

In general Woolman did not place any special blame on wives for making unnecessary household expenditures. Other Quaker ministers occasionally did so, but compared to most Christian groups in the eighteenth century, the Quakers exhibited an unusual respect for adult women and recognized their potential spiritual authority.[104] In John's essays, in his journal, and in the correspondence he exchanged with Sarah, there is no evidence that he ever thought that she corrupted him. To be sure, in the letters he wrote to his wife during his travels, he frequently confessed to what he called a "conflict in spirit." He was particularly pained during his visit to New England in 1760, when he left Sarah alone with Mary even though smallpox was sweeping New Jersey. "I feel a most tender concern for thee as knowing thy condition to be attended with difficulty, and find at times a disposition to hasten for thy sake." Nonetheless, he wrote, "such is the weight of the work I am engaged in . . . that I see the necessity for all nature to stand silent."[105] He told Sarah that when he felt sorry for himself and his family, he remembered others who suffered more, including the "widows," the "fatherless," those who had "poor tutors," and "many who have poor examples before them."[106] He believed that he had work to do, and he asked Sarah to place her trust in Providence.

Sarah's letters to John have not survived, but there is reason to believe that she shared his priorities. During John's 1760 journey to New England, she did indeed fall sick, but she did not mention that fact in her letters to her husband. John learned of her illness from other correspondents, and he suspected that Sarah maintained her silence so that he would not be distracted from his divinely appointed mission.[107] Overall, Sarah and Mary supported, or at least acquiesced, in John's decisions. When he scaled back his retail operations in 1755, for example, it was his birth family, not Sarah and Mary, who gave him difficulty.

John's ledger books reveal a lifetime of transactions with his parents and siblings. In general he treated the members of his birth family as he did his other customers. He charged his father for labor, for example, and demanded interest from his brothers on their debts.[108] Expecting to get paid at his regular rates, he made gowns for his sisters Rachel, Sarah, and Hannah, and hats, coats, jackets, breeches, stockings, gloves, and mittens for his brothers Abner, Abram, Asher, and Jonah.[109] His brothers, in exchange, supplied him with agricultural produce including wool, animal skins, cheese, potatoes, wheat, and substantial quantities of pork.[110] John traded books with his brothers and sisters, and the titles they exchanged suggest that he conversed with them about his evolving ideas. He lent his sister Rachel Locke's *Treatise on Education*, and he lent his brother Abram his manual on cider-making.[111] Not surprisingly, most of the books he lent to his brothers and sisters were religious titles, and they, in turn, supplied him with spiritually instructive texts. In 1766 John paid Uriah for a copy of George Fox's journal. Uriah sent the book from Philadelphia and arranged for Abner to deliver it.[112]

Although John's brothers and sisters adopted different ways of living, they all remained Quakers. Some of them, particularly John's brothers Abner and Asher, were active participants in meeting business. Nonetheless, with the exception of Abner, none of them fully shared John's convictions, and the ledger books reveal their differences. Even after John resolved to sell only practical

Figure 7. Silhouette portrait of
Uriah Woolman, from Amelia Mott
Gummere, ed., *The Journal and
Essays of John Woolman* (New York:
Macmillan, 1922), 535.

clothes, for example, Asher convinced him to make him an "underjacket" of silk.[113] He also managed to get John to sell him rum in 1755, sugar in 1763, and sugar, chocolate, and tea in 1764.[114] In 1762 John brought a large quantity of rum to his mother's house for distribution to a team of laborers working there.[115] He made compromises—for the most part, silently—to accommodate his immediate family members and is on record complaining only once, in response to Uriah.

Uriah was the fourth son in the Woolman family and eight years younger than John. Unlike his older brothers, he did not inherit any land, and he chose not to become a farmer. Instead, he took his modest cash inheritance to Philadelphia, where he opened a shop near the busy corner of Fifth and Market Streets, one block north of the Pennsylvania State House.[116] Uriah's business grew with the regional economy. He conducted trade with several prominent Quaker Philadelphia merchants, including Thomas Clifford and James Pemberton.[117] On occasion, he sold steel for Whitehead Humphreys, who operated a furnace two blocks west of his shop.[118] He also gradually expanded his long-distance operations, specializing in trade to the south, and eventually he invested in a ship that sailed monthly to Charlestown, South Carolina. Uriah's vessel carried passengers in accommodations that he advertised as "extraordinary" and "genteel."[119] Below deck the vessel carried an array of products to South Carolina, including farm equipment, household items, leather goods, livestock, seeds, beef, beer, bread, cheeses, cider, flour, potatoes, turnips, rum, and sugar.[120] On its return journeys, the ship brought hardwood, turpentine, indigo, and rice to Philadelphia.[121] Uriah also traded in wine.[122]

Uriah was just starting out in business when John became irritated with him. The trouble began in 1757, when Uriah learned that John was planning a ministerial visit to Quakers in the south. Uriah hoped to conduct "some business in North Carolina," and he asked to come along. John believed that Uriah's company would create "some difficulty," because John wanted to concentrate his energies on delivering a religious message to the Quakers, and he worried that he might be distracted by Uriah's interest in "outward affairs." The brothers talked the issue over several times before John relented and allowed Uriah to come.[123] Looking back on the trip years later, John reminded Uriah that it had been a time of "heavy labors" for both of them.[124] In 1757 John was only beginning to reform his economic life, but their experience together made it abundantly clear that Uriah, with his embrace of long-distance trade and his eagerness to supply the demands of wealthy landowners in the south, had chosen a divergent path. The brothers stayed together for the entire southbound leg of the journey, and they remained on good terms with each other even though Uriah's presence complicated John's effort to present himself as a model of practical-minded austerity. As we shall see in the next chapter, Uriah's company presented John with a challenge that he had to overcome during his protests against the exploitation of slaves.

In his journal and other writings, Woolman offered a sweeping prescription of how people should behave. Humanity's great goal, as he described it, should be harmony. In a symphony there are different parts to play, and life in that respect should resemble music. Obeying divine cues and accepting the roles that God has assigned to them, some people should marry, but others should not. Some couples should have many children, but others not. There will be schoolteachers, tradesmen, and laborers. Some families will hold more property than others. There will be landlords and tenants. Some men and women will be more inspired than their neighbors, cleverer, more industrious, and stronger. None of these distinctions should lead to disorder, however, because ideally everyone should follow God's directions, and even as they pursue their distinctive paths through life, they should care for one another as much as they care for themselves. Woolman's desire to promote "harmonious walking together" transformed his career as a Quaker minister. With increasing clarity, his vision of the perfect society informed his protests against slavery, warfare, the mistreatment of Indians, and unnecessary overseas trade. In the abstract, his project could be summed up easily. He wanted to see the world overtaken by "universal love."

Woolman may have considered his brother's company on that 1757 journey awkward, but it was also instructive, which is why he mentioned his brother in his journal. As a reformer, he never thought that it would be enough to pronounce abstract principles. The difficult work entailed grappling with the irritating details of his mundane existence, and negotiating with stubborn human beings.

Chapter 5

A Dark Gloominess Hanging over
the Land: Slavery

> I saw in these southern provinces so many vices and corruptions
> increased by this trade and this way of life that it appeared to me as
> a dark gloominess hanging over the land.
> —John Woolman, *Journal*, chapter 2

ELIZABETH WOOLMAN, JOHN's oldest sister, died at thirty-one on March 17, 1747.[1] This was a formative event for John, emotionally trying and instructive at the same time. Elizabeth had contracted smallpox, and during her waning days John had gathered reports from those who were with her and kept a record of the stages of her demise. He hoped to learn from Elizabeth's death, and years later when he wrote his journal he expected that his readers would gain from her example as well. Initially, Elizabeth responded to her illness with "sadness and dejection of mind," and she expressed regret for her "wanton and airy" conduct as a young girl. Eventually, however, she found comfort and tried to reassure her mother by telling her, "Weep not for me; I go to my God." On her last morning she told someone near, "I have had a hard night, but shall not have another such, for I shall die, and it will be well with my soul."[2] These were her last recorded words. They were precious to John and all Elizabeth's family, and it is quite likely they were spoken to a former slave.

Earlier in the decade John had served as a witness when his grandfather Henry Burr made his will, and he had watched as Burr appointed John's father Samuel to serve as an executor of the estate. Thomas Shinn was there as a witness alongside John. The beneficiaries included John's mother, six of his uncles and aunts, and someone without a last name whom Burr identified as "my Negro woman, Maria." Maria was fifty years old, and Burr had held her in slavery for many years. Township records indicate that she was living in his house as a slave in 1709.[3] Sometime before he wrote his will, Burr formally granted Maria and her daughters their freedom, and in his will he left her provisions and equipment that he believed she might need as she started a newly independent life. He bequeathed her a spinning wheel for linen, another for wool, an iron kettle, a pot, and "the bed whereon she generally lodges, with the bedstead and furniture thereto belonging." He left her a cow, a flock of chickens, and "all the provision that is left in the house . . . both the eatables and the drink," which in the end included wheat flour, cheese, pork, molasses, and rum.[4]

Although John does not mention her in his journal, Maria was intimately involved in the life of his family, both when she was a slave and after she was legally released. She was probably in the room when Elizabeth died. John and his brother Asher served as the executors of their sister's estate, and one of their first responsibilities was to settle accounts with Maria. On the day after Elizabeth's death, acting in his role as executor, John paid Maria eighteen shillings and nine pence.[5] Over the next decade, Maria worked as a weaver and lived with a man named Tony. She had two daughters, one named Isabella and the other sharing her name, Maria.[6] At the time of the older Maria's death in 1760, Isabella was living with John's mother, and during the 1760s both sisters would move into Asher's house. In 1771, Abner Woolman acknowledged these women's service to his extended family by remembering them in his will.[7] Similarly, in 1772 when John's mother drafted her will, she made bequests to "Negro Issabel" and "her sister Maria who lived with me."[8]

While there were no slaves living at the house on Rancocas Creek when Woolman was a boy, the older Maria and her daughters maintained close ties with the family, and this strongly suggests that even as a young man he was intimately familiar with slavery and its long-term implications. As an adult he never lived with black servants, but he employed former slaves and the children of slaves. He hired men he identified as "Negro Primus" and "Negro Sam" for a variety of tasks including cleaning ditches, helping with construction, beating and spinning flax fibers, and sawing and chopping wood. These were carefully negotiated, contractual arrangements. He employed the men only intermittently, but his relationship with Primus was a long one, spanning nineteen years. Woolman compensated his black workers with cash, molasses, and rum.[9] When he asked Primus and Sam to perform hard physical labor, he was almost certainly drawing on their training, experience, physical development, and skills. Quaker slaveholders in the vicinity of Mount Holly demanded similar work from their slaves. William Boen, a man held in slavery by a Quaker near Mount Holly in the 1750s, received an order one day to chop down a "great forest of woods" on his master's property, and he was sent out to accomplish the task alone.[10] Woolman's father never made any public protest against slavery, but in 1750, when the end of his life seemed near, he told his son, "I have all along been deeply affected with the oppression of the poor Negroes."[11] Woolman was similarly upset by his neighbor's treatment of slaves, and like his father he had difficulty expressing his views on slaveholding, but he found his voice earlier. He managed to issue his first mild protest in 1742.

In 1742 Woolman was an indentured servant, legally obligated under the terms of a year-long contract to work for the owner of the shop in Mount Holly. During that year the shopkeeper commanded obedience from three servants bound under very different terms: Woolman, another male servant gaining skills in tailoring, and an unidentifiable "Negro woman" held as a slave. Our only reliable record of these circumstances is Woolman's journal, which does not indicate whether the woman had belonged to the shopkeeper for a long time or whether she was a short-term speculative purchase like the Scottish indentured servants whose contracts he bought for the purpose of resale. We do know that in 1742 he decided to sell her. The shopkeeper came to Woolman and told him that he had found a buyer for the woman, and with the purchaser waiting outside the shop, he asked Woolman to write up a bill of sale. Woolman felt uneasy but obeyed the order. He felt obliged to do so under the terms of his contract, and he partially consoled himself with the thought that the woman was going to a good home. He knew and respected the purchaser, someone he describes in his journal as "an elderly man, a member of our Society." Still, the act of writing the bill disturbed Woolman, and he could not keep his silence. "I was so afflicted in my mind that I said before my master and the Friend that I believed slavekeeping to be a practice inconsistent with the Christian religion."[12]

Quakers had owned slaves since before the founding of New Jersey and Pennsylvania. In the seventeenth century, the Society of Friends missionaries found success among the planters of Barbados, and when George Fox visited the island in 1671, it was home to the largest Quaker community in the western hemisphere. At the time of the founding of Pennsylvania there were already hundreds of Quakers living on Barbados, and others on Nevis, Antigua, and Jamaica. At least fourteen Barbadian Quakers owned plantations worked by sixty or more slaves.[13] When the Friends came to settle West Jersey and Pennsylvania, they were familiar with the idea of slaveholding, and for the most part they were ready to accept the practice. Ships loaded with slaves began arriving in Philadelphia in 1684.[14] The demand for labor was high in the Delaware Valley, and the enslaved population grew rapidly.

Between 1681 and 1730, slaveholders and occasional slave traders occupied most of the positions of leadership within the Delaware Valley's Quaker meetings.[15] Thomas Chalkley is not widely known as a slaveholder, but he purchased and sold at least one slave.[16] Early in the eighteenth century, acknowledging fears that the Quakers were importing too many from Barbados and Africa, Philadelphia Yearly Meeting asked its members not to buy slaves from overseas, but it would not countenance any blanket attacks on slavery as an institution.[17]

During his visit to Barbados, Fox had told the enslaved workers there "to be sober and fear God, and to love their masters and mistresses, and to be faithful and diligent in their masters' service and business." Fox promised them that if they behaved well, "their masters and overseers will love them, and deal kindly and gently with them."[18] He spoke with authority, and his simple advice affected the practice of slaveholding among Quakers around the Atlantic World. While Quaker slaveholders in Burlington County may have worked their slaves hard, they reported with confidence that they kept them "generally well fed and clothed." Some slaves had been "taught to read and taken to meetings," though the meetings in the county admitted that they could have done more to provide their slaves schooling and guidance in their spiritual lives.[19] When Woolman told his master that he thought slavery was inconsistent with Christianity, he was declaring his opposition to a practice that had been common within his religious community for several decades. He was also objecting to the aspirations of some of his most well-respected neighbors. This was bold for a twenty-two-year-old, but Woolman was hardly the first Quaker to take such a stand. Compared to most of the early recorded antislavery protests among the Friends, his statement was meek.

A beleaguered minority of Quakers had begun protesting against slavery in the 1680s, and on several occasions they had expressed their views with disruptive vigor.[20] Burlington witnessed one of the most dramatic protests in 1738, when Benjamin Lay interrupted the Yearly Meeting by splattering Friends in the meetinghouse with fake blood. On another occasion, he reportedly dramatized his views by kidnapping the six-year-old son of a slaveholder so that that man and his wife could share the experience of losing a loved one to captivity.[21] Woolman, by contrast, merely spoke his sentiments briefly, and then acquiesced in writing up the bill of sale. Several earlier antislavery protestors had been denounced by their meetings. After Lay's outburst, the Yearly Meeting disowned him and arranged to publish an advertisement in the *Pennsylvania Gazette* declaring that he did not belong to the Quakers' "religious community."[22] It is quite possible that the fear of reprimand led some Quakers like Samuel Woolman to keep their opposition to slavery secret. John was hesitant about speaking because he did not want to violate his meeting's norms. But it is also clear from his account of his early statements against slavery that his thoughts were evolving. His ideas were always more complicated than Lay's, and in 1742 he was still discovering how he felt.

Woolman reports in his journal that he suffered remorse after obeying his master's orders and writing the enslaved woman's bill of sale. He told himself that he should have taken a firmer stance and refused to cooperate. Sometime later he had an opportunity to express himself less equivocally. The shopkeeper, in this case, was not involved. A Quaker acquaintance of Woolman's asked for his assistance in drafting a document that Woolman vaguely describes in his journal as an "instrument of slavery." The man had no authority over him, and therefore Woolman felt more comfortable declining the request. Woolman began the conversation by acknowledging that there were many Quakers who held slaves, but he went on to insist that the practice was "not right." The man responded by admitting that "keeping slaves was not altogether agreeable to his mind," but he explained that he felt he had no choice in this instance, because the slave had come into his household as "a gift to his wife from some of her friends."[23]

Woolman later had several similar conversations with neighbors who came to him for assistance in writing their wills. Perhaps remembering his grandfather, he acknowledged that some masters held slaves with good intentions, with "no other motives than the Negro's good," but such slaveholders were deluded, he warned, if they thought they could act as guardians of their slaves' interests and then bequeath them to the next generation. No father has "any assurance that his children will attain to that perfection in wisdom and goodness necessary in every absolute governor." Testators who left slaves to their offspring exposed the enslaved to a risk of abuse. Woolman records three episodes from the late 1740s and early 1750s involving slaveholders who wanted him to write their wills. In all these instances he refused to do the work requested unless the wills were altered to specify that the testator's slaves would be freed. The first time Woolman made this declaration, the man who had come to him left in silence. Woolman commented, "I thought he was displeased with me." The later two encounters had better outcomes. After extended periods of "friendly talk and "serious conference," he secured the slaves' freedom.[24]

Thomas Shinn's case was more complicated. Shinn had been served by slaves for his entire conscious life. A young man named Tabby had been held in trust for his "use" when Shinn was only two years old.[25] Fifty-four years later, in 1751, when Tabby was married, both he and his wife were working for Shinn as slaves. Shinn additionally held four younger persons enslaved in his household, possibly Tabby's children, three girls named Hannah, Jade, and Pleasant, and a boy named Jem. In 1743 Shinn had served as a witness when Burr made his will, and so he was aware that some Quakers were uneasy about keeping slaves and their offspring in bondage across generations. In his own will, he directed that Tabby and his wife should be freed, "immediately after my decease," and he left them five pounds' worth of goods, but he was not willing to liberate the children so quickly.[26] New Jersey law stipulated that anyone who freed a slave had to post a bond to support that person in the event of hardship, to make sure that no former slaves would ever claim poor relief.[27] Shinn did not want to saddle his heirs with this full obligation, and so he raised some of the necessary bond money by selling Hannah as a servant with a fixed term of service. To compensate his daughters for the liability they were assuming, he gave Jade as a bound servant to one of his daughters, and Pleasant to Martha Paxson, Henry's wife. Under the terms of these arrangements, all the young women would be freed when they reached thirty. Shinn retained Jem, who was only six years old in 1751, but he directed the executors of his estate to sell the boy after Shinn's death in the same way that Hannah had been sold, with the proceeds returned to the estate. Shinn died in April 1753, and Woolman and Henry Paxson sold Jem to a third party for £20. Years later Woolman wrote a note to himself in his ledger book indicating that Jem, whom he called "Negro James," would gain his freedom on January 2, 1775. He regretted that these arrangements had left Jem in bondage for so long.[28]

*   *   *

Woolman's early opposition to slavery grew out of his experience of life in western New Jersey, where slaves were ubiquitous. It was in conversation with his neighbors that he first expressed his view that slaveholding was inconsistent with Christianity. These were quiet comments, however. He began to consider

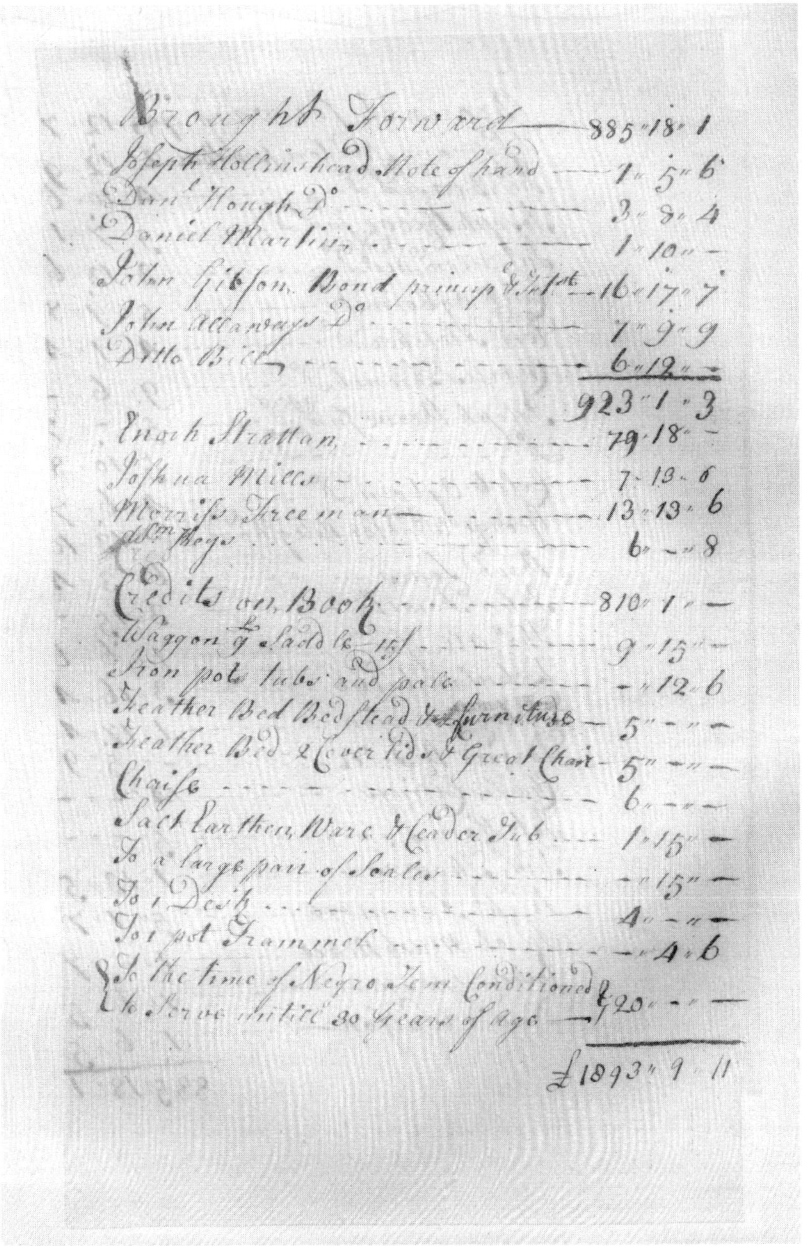

Figure 8. Woolman prepared the inventory of the Thomas Shinn estate, and ended it with this record of the proceeds from the sale of the services of Shinn's slave Jem. Courtesy New Jersey State Archives, Department of State.

making a public protest only after he traveled to the south. In the summer of 1746, during his "religious visit" to meetings in Maryland, Virginia, and North Carolina in the company of Isaac Andrews, Woolman was disturbed at the sight of "people who lived in ease on the hard labor of slaves."[29] He saw "white people and their children" pass their days "without much labor." Southern slaveholders generally "lived in a costly way and laid heavy burdens on their slaves." Woolman could see a difference between well-meaning masters and self-indulgent ones. He "felt more easy" in the company of slaveholders who lived frugally, performed "a good share" of the household labor, worked their slaves only moderately, and kept them "well provided for." By contrast he was so upset by the selfish slave masters that he disliked accepting their offers of drinks, meals, or lodging. Even in Maryland, Virginia, and North Carolina, he continued to believe, as he had in New Jersey, that it was possible for a master to hold a slave "with no other motives than the Negro's good." Nonetheless, after his travels in the south he began to think about slavery more systematically, weighing its impact not only on the inner workings of individual households but also paying attention to its pervasive influence on colonial society. He worried that the slaveholders of the south were encouraging each other to import increasing numbers of people from "Guinea," with the result that slavery was becoming a dominant and corrosive feature of the southern landscape. "I saw in these southern provinces so many vices and corruptions increased by this trade, and this way of life, that it appeared to me as a dark gloominess hanging over the land. . . . The consequence will be grievous to posterity!"[30]

Two years after his first journey south, Woolman appeared before Burlington Monthly Meeting and announced his intention to return to Maryland. One of those appointed to meet with him and discuss his plans was the future historian Samuel Smith. Woolman came back from that journey on December 5, bringing with him a certificate from the Quakers in Easton, on Maryland's eastern shore.[31] Recounting the trip in his journal, Woolman declared that once again that he had found it difficult to conduct a "religious visit" to Maryland. "Our Society in these parts appeared to me to be in a declining condition." He had traveled in the company of John Sykes, a sixty-five-year-old minister who like Woolman had found the work "heavy."[32] Woolman's comments on his 1748 trip are only brief, but it is noteworthy that Sykes would later join him as one of the Quakers' leading opponents of slaveholding.[33] This is one reminder among many that Woolman and the other antislavery Quakers of the 1750s had developed their critique of the institution together, on the basis of shared experiences and wide-ranging conversations.

After returning from his first trip south Woolman began working on an essay explaining the basis of his opposition to slavery. He showed an early draft of the work to his father, who read it over and made some suggestions for alterations. In general Samuel "appeared well satisfied" with the manuscript, and over the ensuing years he expressed impatience with his son for not getting the piece printed. In late autumn 1750, John's father caught a fever. John attended him during his illness, not only to monitor his physical health but also to his record his comments, anticipating that they might be unusually insightful last words. Samuel declined rapidly, and after a few days he was "so far spent that there was no expectation of his recovery." Nonetheless he remained lucid. As John described him, Samuel "had the perfect use of his understanding." One night as John sat by his father's bedside, his father asked him about the antislavery essay and whether he "expected soon to offer it to the Overseers of the Press." John made no record of his own reply. It was clear that Samuel wanted the essay published, but more than three years would pass before John submitted it for publication.[34]

Woolman's behavior in the early 1750s, and particularly his participation in the complex negotiations surrounding the Shinn estate, suggests that he may not have been ready to position himself as an uncompromising opponent of slaveholding. He was still wrestling with the implications of his early intuition that slavery violated the moral precepts of Christianity, and there were obvious tactical advantages to maintaining public silence on the issue. Slaveholders were more likely to ask him for help in writing their wills before he publicly declared that he was an opponent of slavery. Similarly, as the record shows, the slave owners who met with Woolman in the early 1750s were generally reluctant to give up their slaves immediately. Woolman had more success with them when he signaled that he was willing to compromise and asked them only to refrain from bequeathing slaves in perpetual bondage to the next generation.

It is also quite likely, as historian Jean Soderlund has suggested, that other Quakers advised Woolman to hold back.[35] Woolman made it a habit to consult trusted friends before submitting his writings to the Overseers of the Press. He asked respected Friends to read over his works, solicited their advice, and sometimes authorized them to edit his manuscripts in order to make sure that the review process went smoothly. In a letter to the prominent Philadelphia Quaker Israel Pemberton, he explained that he operated in this way to protect the oversight committee from unnecessary "labor."[36] In all likelihood, it would have required an enormous amount of work to get Woolman's essay published in 1746. In the previous half-century, debates over slavery had repeatedly disrupted the meetings, sometimes generating controversy so intense that the Quakers had found it difficult to deal with one another in a spirit of peace. In the most dramatic episodes, adamant opponents of slavery had taken the blame for stoking the hostilities. William Southeby had been warned to keep silent. Ralph Sandiford and Benjamin Lay had been disowned by Philadelphia Yearly Meeting. Woolman valued unity within the Yearly Meeting. Given a choice between generating discord and maintaining silence, he preferred to keep his ideas to himself.

In 1752 six new members were appointed to the meeting's Overseers of the Press, which had the effect of making the group, as a whole, more receptive to antislavery arguments.[37] In 1753 Woolman submitted his essay to the overseers, and the committee that reviewed the piece made only some "small alterations" before approving it for publication. The cost was covered by the Yearly Meeting. In his account of this event, Woolman indicates that the meeting produced the essay for distribution "amongst Friends," but as a pamphlet it was available to a much wider audience.[38] Its full title was *Some Considerations on the Keeping of Negroes, Recommended to the Professors of Christianity of Every Denomination*. It was advertised repeatedly in the *Pennsylvania Gazette*, and as early as February 1754 copies sold for a sixpence each at the Philadelphia premises of the printer, James Chattin.[39] The date is significant, because later in 1754 other Quaker reformers would publish their own antislavery writings. Woolman's essay came first.

In the seventeenth and eighteenth centuries, every writer who argued that slavery violated the precepts of Christianity faced a daunting problem: Jesus had never explicitly condemned the institution, and there were many passages in the Old and New Testaments that seemed to accord slaveholding spiritual sanction.[40] When he was addressing himself to a Quaker audience, for example in the pages of his journal, Woolman was willing to acknowledge this circumstance and present his antislavery stance as a new revelation. He declared that in "infinite love and goodness," God had "opened our understandings from one time to another concerning our duty" toward the slaves.[41] Such assertions held little persuasive power among non-Quakers, however, and when Woolman wrote for a general audience, he adopted the tactic taken by most other early antislavery writers. He argued from first principles. Ignoring those scattered passages in the Bible which seemed to authorize enslavement, he suggested that slavery violated the fundamental moral assumptions of Christianity.

Woolman addressed his essay not just to the Quakers, but to everyone who claimed to be a Christian.[42] In his characteristic fashion, he combined biblical exegesis with observations of the natural world to build an argument in favor of human equality. He took it on authority that all people were descended from Adam and Eve, and that therefore "all nations are of one blood." He cited illness, moral weakness, and mortality as proof of our common humanity. "We are subject to the like afflictions and infirmities of body, the like disorders and frailties in mind, the like temptations, the same death and the same judgment." He also saw an egalitarian message in the words of the resurrected Jesus: "Ye shall be witnesses to me not only in Jerusalem, Judea and Samaria, but to the uttermost parts of the Earth."[43] Once he had established the slaves' humanity, the rest of his argument was based on the Golden Rule. He quoted passages from Exodus, Leviticus, Deuteronomy, and Matthew to suggest that all people should treat strangers well, and he cited Ecclesiastes and First Chronicles in support of the proposition that slavery was a miserable condition.

Commenting specifically on the way slaves were treated in the British colonies of North America, he decried the slaveholders' general refusal to grant their slaves "a Christian education and suitable opportunity of improving the mind." In general, however, he did not openly concern himself with the details of the slaves' lives in America. He evinced much greater concern for the impact of slavery on the masters and their children. He argued that parents corrupted their sons and daughters by encouraging them to rely on the labor of slaves. The children of slave masters grew accustomed to "fullness, ease, and idleness," and became arrogant "by lording it over their fellow creatures and being masters of men in their childhood."[44] The habit of exploitation passed from one generation to the next, and quickly became self-perpetuating. "Customs generally approved and opinions received by youth from their superiors become like the produce of a soil." Woolman warned his readers against devoting themselves excessively to their children and holding others in slavery in order to serve the interests of their families. To underscore the importance of moderating parental devotion, he compared human beings to animals. The parental instinct was "good in the animal race" and even among humans, so long as it was "operating on us in a soft manner." It could kindle "desires of love and tenderness," but it should never be confused with "something higher." "Natural affection" encourages "inferior creatures" to "watchfully keep and orderly feed their helpless offspring," but it was dangerous for humans because it was "a branch of self-love."[45] Slaveholders who sought to advance the interests of their own families by holding Africans in perpetual bondage behaved like animals. They jeopardized their own salvation, and indeed they could place the future of colonial settlement in North America at risk. God had so far supported the colonists, but if they continued to "love self best," they would lose divine favor.

By the time Woolman's essay was approved for publication, there was a rising groundswell of opposition to slavery among the Quakers, especially in Philadelphia. Philadelphia Monthly Meeting began drafting a corporate statement against the slave trade just around the time that *Some Considerations on the Keeping of Negroes* appeared in print. Anthony Benezet, who had joined the Overseers of the Press in 1752, brought a draft of his own antislavery essay before the Philadelphia meeting on January 25, 1754. The meeting responded by appointing a committee to revise the piece for publication.[46] The revision and review process took several months. The monthly meeting sent a draft to Philadelphia Quarterly Meeting in August, which in turn resolved that the essay should be "recommended to the consideration of the Yearly Meeting," which was scheduled to convene in Burlington in September.[47] Woolman attended that session of the Yearly Meeting. There is no record of his participation in the discussions leading up to the publication of the meeting's *Epistle of Caution and Advice concerning the Buying and Keeping of Slaves*, but a memoir written many years later may give a hint of his demeanor during those debates. When Woolman rose to speak, he was "publicly opposed," and he responded by resuming his seat and weeping, "without attempting any justification."[48] Woolman was not always so inarticulate, but throughout his life a distinguishing feature of his ministry was his ability to personalize issues. Often he admitted to personal weakness, and when upset he telegraphed his distress. He often worried about offending other Quakers, and those anxieties could trigger tears.

In September 1754, Philadelphia Yearly Meeting approved the *Epistle of Caution and Advice* for publication, and directed that copies be distributed to all the quarterly meetings in the Delaware Valley.[49] Burlington Quarterly Meeting received 300 copies.[50] The epistle began by reminding the Quakers that the Yearly Meeting had for many years opposed the "importation" of slaves, and it cited that position as evidence that in general terms the Friends' disciplinary guidelines had long ago directed them to avoid "being in any respect concerned in promoting the bondage" of "Negroes and other slaves." The Yearly Meeting's statement emphasized the impact of the slave trade on Africa, identified newly captured slaves as "prisoners of war," and decried the practice of removing "parents from children, children from parents, and others who were in good circumstances in their native country."[51] Following the lead of earlier Quaker opponents of slavery, including the Germantown Quakers of 1688, John Hepburn in 1715, and Woolman more recently, the statement also invoked the Golden Rule, paraphrasing Jesus's admonition, "whatsoever ye would that men should do to you, do ye even so to them."[52] Accepting this principle as a premise, it followed logically that "To live in ease and plenty by the toil of those whom violence and cruelty have put in our power is neither consistent with Christianity, nor common justice."[53]

It has sometimes been asserted that Woolman had a hand in composing an early draft of the *Epistle of Caution and Advice*, but there is no evidence to support of this proposition.[54] Benezet initiated the composition process, and the essay was revised over a period of eight months, incorporating input from a widening circle of Quakers, first in Philadelphia, then in a broad part of southeastern Pennsylvania, and finally at the Yearly Meeting. An untold number of Friends participated. As a group, the authors were certainly aware of Woolman's earlier essay, and many of them would have spoken to him, but they took their argument in a direction that he had not pursued by emphasizing the impact of the slave trade on Africa. This emphasis made it easier to claim that the epistle was simply expanding upon the Yearly Meeting's long-standing opposition to slave imports. Africa also fascinated Benezet, and its prominence in the *Epistle of Caution and Advice* almost certainly reflects his influence as the author of the first draft.[55]

In later essays beginning in 1759, Benezet would mine travel narratives for evidence that slave trading destroyed stable, prosperous African communities, and in the process he provided the Quaker opponents of slavery some of their most compelling and effective arguments. In the short run, however, emphasizing the damage the slave traders inflicted on Africa served to highlight an ambiguity in the Yearly Meeting's stance toward slaveholding. Some Quaker slaveholders could rightly argue that the meeting reserved its harshest criticism for the commercial traffic in slaves, and that Friends could distance themselves from the worst evils of the slave trade merely by refusing to buy or sell people. The *Epistle* condemned the way masters generally treated slaves in North America, observing, "it's obvious that the future welfare of those poor slaves who are now in bondage is generally too much disregarded." But rather than opposing slaveholding categorically, the meeting only asked the Quakers to refrain from doing anything that would encourage the spread of the practice. Addressing "those dear Friends who by inheritance have slaves born in your families," the meeting asked those slaveholders to think of their enslaved servants as "souls committed to your trust," and to treat them well. It issued no immediate call for the masters to free all the people they held in slavery in their homes.[56]

The publication of *Some Considerations on the Keeping of Negroes* and the subsequent *Epistle of Caution and Advice* has long been recognized as a pivotal event in the spread of Quaker antislavery protest. Though its formal administrative reach extended only through the Delaware Valley, Philadelphia Yearly Meeting commanded respect from Friends across North America. By authorizing Woolman's essay, paying for its publication, and distributing it to Quaker meetings, the Philadelphia Quakers had lent their support to at least one unequivocal antislavery statement. The *Epistle of Caution and Advice* qualified its argument more than Woolman's pamphlet did, but it carried more authority as a letter from the meeting itself. Nonetheless, in 1754 there was no abrupt change in the behavior of the Friends as a group. Through the 1750s in Pennsylvania, 70 percent of Quaker masters refused to free their slaves.[57]

When Philadelphia Yearly Meeting reconvened in 1755, it returned to the issue of slavery and reaffirmed the compromise it had struck in drafting the *Epistle of Caution and Advice*. Woolman joined twelve other Friends in drafting queries which every monthly meeting reporting to Philadelphia would be required to answer. The tenth query read, "Are Friends clear of importing or buying Negroes and do they use those well which they are possessed of by inheritance or otherwise, endeavoring to train them up in the principles of the Christian religion?"[58] This question went further than earlier admonitions against participating in the import market, but it still reflected the consensus position.[59] Instead of categorically condemning perpetual bondage, as Woolman had done in *Some Considerations on the Keeping of Negroes*, the query only called on Quakers to desist from buying slaves and acknowledged that those Friends who already held individuals in slavery might continue to do so. Woolman supported the query, and indeed he participated in drafting it. Readers of his earlier pamphlet might conclude that he had moderated his stance, but procedurally he was adopting a stronger position by promoting formal disciplinary enforcement of a prohibition against slave trading. It is important to remember the procedural function of the queries. After 1755, at least four times a year, every meeting in the Delaware Valley was required to inquire into their members' participation in the slave market.

In May 1756 Woolman traveled to Flushing, New York, where he attended the Yearly Meeting of the Quakers on Long Island. John Scarborough, another opponent of slavery from Philadelphia Yearly Meeting, joined him there. Slaveholding was common among the New York Quakers, particularly within the "foremost rank" of Long Island Yearly Meeting, and in private conversations as well as at public gatherings, Woolman alerted the Long Islanders to "the inconsistency of the practice with the purity of the Christian religion." He did not receive a warm reception. Recounting the occasion afterward, he compared himself to Jeremiah, whose messages were "so disagreeable to the people and so reverse to the spirit they lived in that he became the object of their reproach."[60]

If Woolman felt isolated on Long Island, he felt much more so in 1757 in Maryland, Virginia, and North Carolina. Crossing the southern border of Pennsylvania had troubled him earlier, and referring to his 1757 entry into Maryland he wrote, "soon after I entered this province a deep and painful exercise came upon me." He resolved to distance himself from the amiable society of slaveholders, trying instead to "attend with singleness of heart to the voice of the True Shepherd and be so supported as to remain unmoved at the faces of men." As he described it, the effort almost made him crave death. He wrote in his journal that he "nearly" felt sympathy with Moses when he stood alone against the backsliding people of Israel. On one occasion Moses had pleaded with God, "If thou deal thus with me, kill me I pray thee." But like Moses, Woolman soon altered his outlook after determining that his despair stemmed from "the want of a full resignation" to God. When he recovered from his despondency, he thought of Psalm 131:2, "My soul is even as a weaned child."[61]

In his account of his travels in the South, Woolman commented on the lives of the slaves in much greater detail than he had earlier. He described gangs of men and women "followed at their business in the field by a man with a whip, hired for that purpose." He focused on the southern slaves' tattered and scanty clothing. "Men and woman have at many times scarce clothes enough to hide their nakedness, and boys and girls ten and twelve years old are often stark naked amongst their master's children." He noted that the slaves had "little else to eat but one peck of Indian corn and salt for one week and some few potatoes." He reported that southern masters paid little attention to their slaves' marriages. "Negroes marry after their own way," he observed, but southern slave owners "make so little account of those marriages that with views of outward interest they often part men from their wives by selling them far asunder." Woolman described the slaves as a "burden" on the "white people" of the South, and he predicted that the load would grow heavier until "times change in a way disagreeable to us." He warned that God might punish slaveholders by triggering some unspecified catastrophe. He emphasized that the slaves had "made no agreement to serve us."[62]

The southern landscape revealed to Woolman the stark connection between luxury and violence. "From small beginnings in error great buildings by degrees are raised and from one age to another are more and more strengthened by the general concurrence of the people." When "men of reputation" misbehave, "their virtues are mentioned in arguments in favor of general error." Writing about Virginia, he warned that "through the prevailing of the spirit of this world the minds of the many were brought to an inward desolation, and instead of a spirit of meekness, gentleness, and heavenly wisdom, which are the necessary companions of the true sheep of Christ, a spirit of fierceness and the love of dominion too generally prevailed."[63] Woolman was viscerally upset by the structure of southern society. He believed that the maintenance and protection of the slave system was becoming a dominant preoccupation of all the white people in the South. The local Quakers were hardly immune from this general trend, and Woolman worried that if the southern Friends continued to invest in slavery they would eventually abandon their religious society's distinctive commitment to peace. Given the depth of his sentiments on this issue, it is surprising how accommodating he was when he spoke about slavery at Virginia Yearly Meeting.

The Yearly Meeting was held in Nansemond, in the far south of Virginia, on May 28, 1757. Woolman was there to watch as the Virginia Quakers weighed the value of the "Pennsylvania queries," the questions he had helped revise two years earlier for Philadelphia Yearly Meeting's constituent quarterly, monthly, and smaller meetings. The Virginia Quakers intended to ask similar questions to their local groups, and they agreed on the utility of most of the listed questions, but they changed the wording of the query related to slavery and asked only for the meetings to report whether their members purchased slaves "to trade." By implication, the Yearly Meeting suggested that it was acceptable for Quakers to buy slaves to work in their own households or fields so long as they did not purchase those people for the purpose of immediately reselling them.[64] Woolman rose in objection and reminded the Virginia Quakers of another of the queries, one that asked the meetings to report whether any of their members bought or sold plunder taken in war. He declared that since "purchasing any merchandize taken by the sword was always allowed to be inconsistent with our principles, Negroes being captives of war or taken by stealth, those circumstances make it inconsistent with our testimony to buy them." This, in effect, had been one of the principal arguments advanced by Philadelphia Yearly Meeting's *Epistle of Caution and Advice*. Woolman was not suggesting that the Virginians should free everyone they owned as slaves as a consequence of accidents of birth. Instead, he was promoting the compromise that had been adopted in Philadelphia in 1754 and 1755, suggesting that Quakers should only desist from purchasing additional slaves. Nonetheless, as he described the discussion afterward, he did not "press" even this point, because the amended query that the Virginians were willing to accept took them "one step further than they had gone." Later, at a more exclusive gathering of ministers and elders, he told the men and women in attendance that their conduct would be "noticed by others" because they constituted "the first rank in the Society." He advised them that so long as they continued to hold slaves, they should make sure that they "divested" themselves of "all selfish views" and that they treated their enslaved servants well, taught them to read, and gave them access to the scriptures.[65]

Woolman was self-consciously politic when he addressed Virginia Yearly Meeting. He felt that in that setting, even more than in others, it was important not to stir up animosity. Friends gathered in such meetings to secure divine guidance, and they thought that they could receive it only if a spirit of love and unity prevailed. Woolman was less guarded when he spoke outside meetings, and in his journal he describes several conversations he had with southerners that were not so constrained. The friendliest exchange he recorded occurred in Port Royal, Virginia, where he met a colonel of the militia who struck him as a "thoughtful man." Woolman began by commenting on the contrast between people who "labor moderately for their living, training their children in frugality and business" and "those who live on the labor of slaves." He told the colonel that slaveholders were never as "happy" as those people who did their own work. The colonel agreed with him on that point, but he said the slaveholders' unhappiness stemmed from the indolence of the enslaved and suggested that "one of our laborers" could accomplish as much in a day as "two of their slaves." Woolman did not challenge that assertion but responded by suggesting that the slaves had no incentive to work hard. He told the colonel that "free men whose minds were properly on their business found a satisfaction in improving, cultivating, and providing for their families, but Negroes, laboring to support others who claim them as property, and expecting nothing but slavery during life, had not the like inducement to be industrious." Perhaps suspecting that he was losing the argument, the colonel changed tack and told Woolman that things were worse in Africa. "The lives of the Negroes were so wretched in their own country that many of them lived better here than there." Woolman chose not to pursue that line of inquiry, but instead admonished the colonel to consider the implications of any assertion that the slaves had been brought to North America for their own good.[66]

Later in his travels Woolman encountered that same argument regarding Africa from other white southerners, and he responded more forcefully. Some Virginians told him that Africa's internal wars had produced "wretchedness" for "the Negroes," and therefore "fetching them away for slaves" had only done them good. Woolman replied, "If compassion on the Africans in regard to their domestic troubles were the real motives of our purchasing them, that spirit of tenderness being attended to would incite us to use them kindly." Instead, he asserted, "we manifest by our conduct that our views in purchasing them are to advance ourselves." Furthermore, "our buying captives taken in war animates those parties to push on that war and increase desolations amongst them." Therefore "to say they live unhappy in Africa is far from being an argument in our favor." On another occasion during his travels Woolman met a man who asserted that the Africans were descended from Cain and carried his mark. His response to that assertion was simple: the man was wrong. All Cain's descendants had been killed in the flood. Not content with an attack on the man's biblical exegesis, he went on to assert that "The love of ease and gain are the motives in general for keeping slaves," and that the justifications that had been offered for the practice were "weak" and "unreasonable." That conversation ended abruptly.[67]

Woolman reports that he used "plainness of speech" when speaking to slaveholders in the South, and the phrase almost certainly carried a double meaning. He used the characteristic diction employed by Quakers and thereby identified himself as a member of the Society of Friends. He also avoided equivocation. When he spoke, he was blunt. But Woolman did not rely only on his words. Acting on the assumption that "conduct is more convincing than language," he resolved to do nothing that might be interpreted as lending support to the custom of slaveholding, and to dramatize his stance, he tried not to receive any benefit from the unpaid labor of slaves.[68]

Loosely modeling themselves on Jesus and his disciples, who traveled without money or baggage, Quaker traveling ministers in the eighteenth century customarily relied heavily on aid from their hosts to support them along their way.[69] To be sure, the ministers carried money and generally paid for their own transportation, but they lodged for free at the homes of local Quakers, received meals from them, and relied on them for a range of other services including the feeding and stabling of horses and the provision of guides. Woolman worried that it had become a mark of distinction and "civility" for wealthy Quakers in the South to host traveling ministers, and he did not want to flatter those who wanted to help him with a "regard to reputation." He was ready to accept hospitality when it was offered out of an apparent "inward unity of heart and spirit," but he believed that accepting such a gift generally "brings the receiver under obligations to the benefactor," and he did not want to be beholden to slave masters. Furthermore he thought that if he enjoyed any benefit or comfort derived from the uncompensated forced labor of slaves, he would in effect become a partner in their oppression.[70]

After suffering some torment over this issue, Woolman resolved to pay for his board and lodging as he traveled whenever failing to pay would obstruct "that work to which I believed he [God] had called me." He did not raise the issue until he was leaving a Quaker's house. Then, if his hosts were slave owners, host he would pay for his room and meals and ask his hosts to distribute the funds to "such of their Negroes as they believed would make the best use of them." Alternatively, Woolman would pay the slaves himself. Woolman traveled with a large quantity of small coins, and handing them over to wealthy homeowners for distribution to the slaves proved a "trial both to me and them." In general, however, Woolman found that this procedure was "easier than I expected." Most of his hosts allowed him to proceed in this manner, although it sometimes required "some talk" to convince them.[71]

We can only speculate about Uriah's posture during these negotiations. One can assume that he wanted to be sociable, because his motive for traveling south had been to find new suppliers and customers for his growing business as a merchant. John's account of his transactions with the slaveholders suggests that he took the initiative in settling accounts with them, and it is easy to imagine that Uriah stood silently nearby, not participating in the conversations. He, after all, was the younger brother, and unlike John he was not a revered minister. He had gained entry into most of these homes only as John's companion.

There was some tension between the brothers, however, and just beyond the border of North Carolina they parted ways. John turned north and started his long ride home.[72] Uriah, in all likelihood, proceeded to the western 'back settlement" of New Garden, North Carolina. The Woolmans had a cousin there named William Hunt who would soon become a prominent Quaker minister. He and Uriah established a friendship that lasted years.[73] For his part, John sent a letter to New Garden apologizing for his inability to visit in

person. In the letter he mentioned that he had heard there were "a large number of Friends in your parts that have no slaves." He told them "to keep clear
from purchasing any" so that they might be "preserved from those dangers
which attend such who are aiming at outward ease and greatness."[74]

It is tempting to see these two brothers traveling through the South simply as a pair of opposites, but it is important not to exaggerate the contrast
between them. Uriah was a devoted Quaker, and the letters he received from
Hunt suggest that he took counsel from his fellow Friends. Nothing he was
doing on that journey violated the norms of his religious society. Indeed, in
1757 Uriah took the trouble of securing official sanction for his journey south.
Both brothers obtained certificates before setting out. John's indicated that he
was undertaking a "religious visit," while Uriah's simply introduced him as a
"private Friend."[75] They started out together, although eventually they would
travel down different roads.

In 1763 John wrote to his brother to warn him of the "difficulties and
temptations which attends trade in the present condition of countries." John
acknowledged that even those "who eat the food which they raise and wear
garments of their own work" could be exposed to temptation, but earning a
livelihood through commerce was much more dangerous. John insisted that
"various kinds of traffic" were "connected with that spirit which works in disobedient children," and he felt particularly concerned for the souls of "those
who depend on merchandise for a living." John recognized that it was possible
for a rich man to enter heaven, but he made it clear to Uriah that he believed
his brother's path was a perilous one.[76] That was 1763, however. In 1757, John
was still in the pork business, raising meat for sugar-producing plantations
in the Caribbean, and his ideas were still evolving. He experienced some cre-
ative confusion during his journey south with his brother, especially when he
felt compelled to violate well-established Quaker customs and risk offending
his hosts.

In 1758 Philadelphia Monthly Meeting observed with disapproval that
despite its best efforts, "the unjust practice of purchasing and selling slaves"
seemed to be on the increase. The Philadelphia Quakers took the lead in addressing this issue, just as they had in 1754, and working through their Quarterly Meeting, they put slavery back on the Yearly Meeting's agenda. Making
it clear that their concerns extended beyond the slave market, they demanded
that Friends meetings throughout the Delaware Valley discourage "the practice
of buying selling *and keeping* slaves."[77] According to the Yearly Meeting's records, the proposal inspired extended discussions which took up "much time,"

and "the sentiments of many Friends" were aired.[78] Woolman was there, and according to his account no one dared to "openly justify the practice of slave-keeping in general." Instead the opponents of Philadelphia Monthly Meeting's motion recommended a more cautious approach lest the Yearly Meeting "give uneasiness" to Quaker slaveholders. Woolman's journal makes it clear that the argument reduced him to weeping. "I could say with David that tears were my meat day and night." But on this occasion, he found the strength to explicitly answer the contentions of those who disagreed with him. He acknowledged that the idea of freeing the slaves might be "difficult to some who have them," but he insisted that slave masters might see the matter differently if they were "weaned from the desire of getting estates."[79]

In the end, as Woolman described it, "the love of Truth in a good measure prevailed."[80] As one Philadelphia Quaker described it, the meeting renounced "the practice of keeping slaves for term of life . . . it being believed by the truly conscientious to be a great iniquity to keep them or their children, and children's children in perpetual captivity."[81] To give its resolution effect the Yearly Meeting appointed a committee of five ministers, John Churchman, John Scarborough, Daniel Stanton, John Sykes, and Woolman, to visit slavehold-ing families across the Delaware Valley and impress upon them the gravity of the decision. The Yearly Meeting had ruled that any Quakers who insisted on keeping slaves should be expelled from the Society of Friends. No expulsions would take place immediately, however. Woolman and the other committee members were expected to be patient, "to labor with" Quaker slaveholders and "inform their understandings," so that the Friends could "in time more universally" fulfill "the evangelical law of righteousness in this respect."[82]

In 1758 Woolman joined Scarborough and Stanton and visited Quaker slaveholders in Chester County, Pennsylvania, south of Philadelphia.[83] Later in that year Stanton came to Mount Holly and then traveled with Woolman to Crosswicks, New Jersey, where the two of them met Sykes. Stanton reports that the three men then traveled to "many places where they had slaves in bondage" and performed their appointed visits, "I hope in true love."[84] According to Woolman, some of the owners they met were already so "exercised" about slavery that they "appeared glad of our visit." At other homes, however, "our way was more difficult." Some slaveholders seemed "grievously entangled in the spirit of this world." In January 1759, Woolman joined Churchman in Philadelphia, and the two men spent a week together visiting Quaker slave-holders in the city. They concentrated their attention on the "more active" Friends. In March they met in Philadelphia again and visited slave masters they had not reached in January. Then a few months passed during which Woolman lost contact with the other members of the antislavery visiting committee. In July he decided that he could wait no longer, and he set out to visit some Quaker slaveholders on his own. Many of those visits were brief. On occasion Woolman would speak "in the fear of the Lord," tell the masters why he had come to visit them, and abruptly leave. "Thus sometimes by a few words I found myself discharged from a heavy burden."[85] The character of his visits changed later in the month after Churchman came to New Jersey to join him on his rounds. When the two ministers recounted the visits they undertook together, they used almost exactly the same words. They were "favored with peace" and "at times," at least, "divine love and a true sympathizing tenderness of heart prevailed."[86]

In November 1759, Woolman attended Quarterly Meeting in Bucks County, Pennsylvania, and a minister there asked for his help in visiting local Quaker slaveholders. Woolman agreed, but he needed time. He returned quickly home to Mount Holly and within a month was back in Bucks County. With his companion he went to see "the most active members" of the Quarterly Meeting who owned slaves. Woolman was apprehensive before this trip and he found the work physically difficult, or "hard to nature," as he described it. Nonetheless the sessions went better than he feared. "Tenderness of heart was often felt amongst us in our visits, and we parted with several families with greater satisfaction than expected." He visited "some noted Friends who had slaves" in Pennsylvania in the late spring of 1761, and other Quaker slaveholders at Manasquan, New Jersey, in August of that year. On those occasions he did not coordinate his actions with those of the other members of the antislavery visiting committee.[87]

Woolman, Churchman, Stanton and Scarborough reported back to the Yearly Meeting in 1759, and they declared that over the previous year they had made progress "in the visiting of such Friends who are possessed of Negro slaves." Their task was unfinished, however, and the meeting responded by telling them to continue "till they have discharged the service so far as may appear to them as their duty." Their assignment was renewed in 1760 and 1761, but in 1762 the committee asked to be disbanded, because antislavery sentiments had "spread among many brethren" in the local meetings who were already visiting slaveholders on their own. Woolman and his colleagues no longer felt that the Yearly Meeting needed a special committee to do the work.[88]

In 1761 in and around Haddonfield, New Jersey, Joshua Evans joined with "other exercised brethren" to travel "from house to house" visiting Quaker slave masters. Some of the slave owners dreaded the arrival of the delegation, because they did not know how their slaves would react. Therefore, Evans reported, the slave owners "would scarcely permit us to perform the visit." But he and his partners eventually found a way round the problem by employing an element of subterfuge. "I saw it was the Lord's work, and that in performing it we had to be 'wise as serpents, and harmless as doves.'" If the masters feared that the visit would "cause some uneasiness between them and their black servants" the antislavery committee would "first sit down in silence with the whole family" and make sure "not to let our communications give the blacks any knowledge of our business with those who held them." Only when they were alone with the "master and mistress" would they make their arguments.[89] The slaves, for the most part, did not participate in these discussions, because their presence would have been intimidating. It was generally assumed that their interests were well known and that therefore they would have little to add to the conversation. There was at least an element of truth in this assumption. In 1762 when William Boen's master asked him, "William, wouldn't thee like to be free?" Boen said nothing. "I didn't say any thing to it. I thought he might know I should like to be free."[90]

While the issue may have seemed simple to the reformers, slave masters did not always receive the antislavery message kindly. In his journal George Churchman described a difficult disciplinary session convened in Nottingham, Pennsylvania, during which a slaveholding woman "being more wealthy than some of her neighbors . . . could scarcely stoop to the strictness of discipline as it now stands amongst Friends."[91] Nonetheless, by the mid-1760s, the Friends' rule against slaveholding had secured its place alongside the meetings' other disciplinary strictures, and it was enforced in the context of routine business. In 1767, when a Quaker from Evesham, New Jersey, named Job Ridgeway applied for membership in Burlington Monthly Meeting, he confessed that he had recently "purchased a Negro." Woolman joined Henry Paxson on a committee of three local Quakers appointed "to make inquiry unto the case," assess the sincerity of Ridgeway's repentance, and determine whether he would be allowed to join the Monthly Meeting.[92]

Quakers outside the Delaware Valley noticed what Philadelphia Yearly Meeting was doing and took their own measures to discourage slaveholding. Writing on behalf of the Philadelphia meeting in 1762, Woolman praised the Friends of Long Island for their "laborious endeavors to discourage the practices of slave keeping."[93] He had been frustrated by their intransigence only six years earlier. One of the reformers' earliest and best publicized successes had come in 1758, when in a widely disseminated statement London Yearly Meeting admonished Quakers everywhere to avoid "reaping the unrighteous profits arising from that iniquitous practice of dealing in Negroes and other slaves." While the London Friends' statement did not explicitly call on masters to free the slaves they held, it ended by invoking the prophet Isaiah and his demand that the faithful spurn everything derived from evil commerce. "We . . . can do no less than with the greatest earnestness, impress it upon Friends everywhere that they endeavor to keep their hands clear of this unrighteous gain of oppression."[94] In 1759 Anthony Benezet reprinted the London Quakers' statement as an appendix to his first antislavery essay, and in 1760 when Woolman participated in the revision of New England Yearly Meeting's book of discipline, he watched approvingly as that meeting copied out the London meeting's warning verbatim and incorporated it into the New England Quakers' disciplinary code.[95]

The "gain of oppression" was a phrase that resonated in several ways. Some Quakers believed slaveholding itself was a "gain of oppression," and they used Isaiah's words simply to invoke the violent ways in which America's black slaves, or their ancestors, had been captured in Africa.[96] For others such as Woolman, however, Isaiah's words referred not only to the slaves themselves, but also to all the social and economic benefits that free people derived from slavery. Thus when he described his decision to refuse hospitality from slave owners in Virginia he declared that the comforts of the masters' homes constituted a "gain of oppression."[97] Eventually he would extend this line of thinking farther, and argue that sugar, rum, and all the other produce of the Caribbean were similarly tainted.

With their emphasis on monitoring their own personal behavior and setting a good example, their appeals to conscience, and their systematic efforts to confront wrong-doers, Woolman and his associates were deploying old methods of Quaker discipline in their campaign against slaveholding. But by applying those moral practices to a new range of social issues, they were on their way toward discovering a new approach to politics. Eventually they would come to believe that they could exert influence more pervasively and extensively than any government could, just by keeping an eye on the global implications of their daily conduct. As a transatlantic exchange, the slave trade almost literally brought the world home to the Quaker reformers, and it transformed their way of thinking. Nonetheless, it is not possible to understand the full import of their developing ideas without first examining the Delaware Valley Quakers' response to the Seven Years' War.

Chapter 6

Men in Military Posture:
The Seven Years' War

> There then appeared on a green plain a great multitude of men
> in military posture, some of whom I knew.
> —John Woolman, *Journal*, chapter 3

ON A NIGHT in February 1754 Woolman dreamed that while walking through an orchard he saw two lights in the sky resembling dull suns. Suddenly a storm of fire swept over the orchard from the east. Woolman was surprised, but not afraid. He noticed a friend standing nearby who was "greatly distressed in mind at this unusual appearance," and Woolman tried to be reassuring. He said, "We must all once die, and if it please the Lord that our death be in this way, it is good for us to be resigned." Woolman left the orchard and entered a house. He went upstairs and walked past a group of "sad and troubled" people. Crossing an attic room, he found a place to sit alone by a window where he could watch the firestorms pass outside. Then he saw "a great multitude of men in military posture" approaching from the east. He recognized some of them. As the men passed the house a few of them glanced up at Woolman and taunted him, but he held his silence. Finally a captain of the militia walked over to the ground beneath the window and explained to Woolman that "these men were assembled to improve in the discipline of war."[1]

In February 1754, nearly everyone in eastern North America was anticipating a war. In 1748, the Treaty of Aix-la-Chappelle had formally ended the last imperial conflict without satisfying the territorial ambitions of the expansionists in either the British or the French Empires. Ambitious imperialists on both sides had grown bold over the interim. French and British efforts to occupy disputed land had raised tensions on the border of Nova Scotia as well as in the Ohio Valley. Woolman's account of his dream indicates that he saw the Seven Years' War coming before it began, but that was hardly unusual for a well-read and politically engaged colonist. The dream was distinctive because it suggested that Woolman received his premonition in a vision and that he responded to the warning calmly, accepting the coming crisis as a test of his faith. When they met decades later to consider the publication of Woolman's journal, the Overseers of the Press may have detected a note of arrogance in the dream, and they removed it from the text.

In the 1740s during the most recent imperial war, Philadelphia Yearly Meeting had revised its discipline to emphasize that the Friends had been opposed to "bearing of arms and fighting" consistently "ever since we were a people." The meeting had cited the Sermon on the Mount, reminding the Quakers that "the Prince of Peace . . . hath commanded us to love our enemies, and to do good even to them that hate us."[2] In addition to making such moral arguments, Quaker ministers during that war had also advanced pragmatic, historical and legal arguments in favor of pacifism. They had cited William Penn and suggested that Penn's refusal to rely on military force had served the colonists in the region well. "How remarkably we have been preserved in peace and tranquility for more than fifty years," one Pennsylvania Quaker observed, "no invasion by foreign enemies, and the treaties of peace with the natives, wisely began by our proprietor William Penn, preserved inviolable to this day." Despite the ambivalent stance of the colonial government during various conflicts over the intervening years, some Friends asserted that Penn's policies had become an integral component of "the peaceable constitution" of Pennsylvania.[3] For his part, Woolman favored arguments founded on apparent logical and moral consistency. The Quakers' peace testimony seemed to accord with a simple principle that he would later pronounce to his students: "Take good measures to obtain good ends. Go not from goodness in pursuit of good."[4]

Nonetheless, adhering to the peace testimony had seldom been as simple in practice as the Quakers suggested. In the early years of their religious society, they did not articulate or pursue a consistently pacifist stance, and even after they made peace one of their defining, communal ideals, they continued to differ among themselves over its scope and meaning.[5] As a group they believed that government officials could legitimately use force to maintain order and give effect to the law. Therefore, they could support, when the occasion warranted, large-scale deployments to suppress insurrections. Many Quakers also believed that it was appropriate for the government to field soldiers to ward off or repel invasions. In general, the Friends paid their taxes in wartime, even though they were wary of impositions that were specifically tied to military action.[6]

Every tax had its own character, and over the decades various wartime revenue-raising devices had generated controversy among the Quakers in Pennsylvania. Delaware Valley Friends also squabbled among themselves over the arming of merchant vessels and the fortification of the Delaware River.[7] By 1754 the region's Quakers were already familiar with some of the complexity of the peace testimony, although most of them had experienced armed conflict only from a distance. Since 1674 the imperial wars had sidestepped New Jersey and Pennsylvania, sparing the Friends the dilemmas faced by pacifists living in combat zones. The Seven Years' War presented new challenges, and no thoughtful person living in the region found it easy to respond calmly.

The war began in the summer of 1754 on lands claimed by Pennsylvania in the upper reaches of the Ohio Valley, but it did not directly affect the lives of most people in the Delaware Valley until 1755, when General Edward Braddock arrived from Britain and marched an army with recruiting agents west from Maryland toward the Ohio. Following Braddock's defeat, Indian bands allied with the French attacked poorly-defended frontier settlements across hundreds of miles of Virginia and Pennsylvania.[8] Terrified, bereft, angry settlers fled east and demanded that the colonial governments launch a vigorous response. Woolman witnessed one of their earliest protests in fall 1755, when he was in Philadelphia doing work for the Yearly Meeting. "The calamities of war were now increasing," he remembered. "The frontier inhabitants of Pennsylvania were frequently surprised, some slain and many taken captive by the Indians." On a day that Woolman and his fellow ministers had set aside for drafting letters to distant meetings, protestors placed the body of a man killed by Indians onto a wagon and wheeled the corpse "through the streets of the city in his bloody garments to alarm the people and rouse them up to war."[9] The protestors succeeded in making colonists in the East aware of the suffering in the West. William Boen, who lived as a slave among the Quakers on Rancocas Creek, remembered, "When I went home, in the evenings, I often heard them talking about the Indians killing and scalping people; and sometimes, some of the neighbors would come in, and they and my master's family talked of the Indians killing such and such—nearer and nearer to us. And so, from time to time, I would hear them tell of the Indians killing, and scalping people, nearer and nearer, so that I began to think, like enough, by and by, they would kill me."[10]

In 1755 the Quaker-dominated Pennsylvania Assembly greeted the arrival of the British troops by helpfully allocating funds "for the King's use." The Penn-family proprietors of the colony were no longer Quakers, and the assemblymen understood that the money they raised would be used for military expenditures. Among other purposes, the revenues raised in Pennsylvania during the Seven Years' War would fund a volunteer militia. The militia was a novelty, but the colonial legislature had made other kinds of financial contributions during the previous two imperial wars. On those earlier occasions a few Quakers had protested against providing the government extra funds in wartime, but the counterargument had prevailed. The government needed money, and therefore revenue had to be raised. The assemblymen believed that they were following the advice of Jesus, endorsed by George Fox, to "render unto Caesar the things which are Caesar's." They came to the same conclusion in 1755, but the pacifists' protests were louder and more consequential.[11]

Almost immediately after the wartime appropriation was first proposed, a committee of Quaker ministers and elders, meeting in Philadelphia, issued a statement reaffirming their commitment to peace. Quoting the prophets and addressing themselves to all "Friends on the Continent of America," Woolman, John Churchman, and twelve others declared that God's cause would prevail "not by earthly might, nor power, but by my spirit, saith the Lord of hosts." North America's Quakers "had experience of that work which is carried on . . . by which operation that spiritual kingdom is set up, which is to subdue and break in pieces all kingdoms that oppose it, and shall stand forever." The ministers asserted that the "completion" of God's prophesies had begun. The time was coming when "nation shall not lift up sword against nation, nor learn war any more." All that was necessary was for the Quakers to behave "in all parts of our life as becomes our peaceable profession." If they did so, placing their trust in God "from one generation to another," they would see "the peaceable kingdom" gradually extend "from sea to sea, and from the river to the utmost ends of the earth."[12]

A few months later when the Pennsylvania Assembly was working out the financial details of its grant to the government, Churchman gathered a different group of approximately twenty pacifist Quakers. They drafted a petition and arranged to have the Quaker Speaker of the House read it aloud at a legislative session in the Pennsylvania State House. The petitioners invoked the founding of Pennsylvania and suggested that William Penn had set a precedent that carried binding legal force. By remaining peaceful and trusting in God, Penn had earned his colonists providential protection from the ravages of war. Churchman and his associates asked the assemblymen to remember their ancestors who "had left their native country and settled this then a wilderness" in order to obtain the "free enjoyment of liberty of conscience." If Pennsylvania revenues were now used to underwrite military expenditures, many Quakers would refuse to pay their taxes and suffer prosecution for following their consciences. Punishing Friends who refused to pay war-related duties would deprive the Quakers of the liberty they sought when they established the colony and therefore violate Pennsylvania's "constitution." The petitioners suggested that it would be better for the legislature to raise money for good purposes, "to support such of our fellow subjects, who are or may be in distress," or "to cultivate our friendship with our Indian neighbors."[13] This plea did not succeed in the Pennsylvania Assembly. There were a few assemblymen sympathetic to the petitioners, but they were outvoted, and in 1756 several of them resigned, in the process severely weakening the Quakers' influence in formal politics. The petition was more positively received in other circles, however, and in important ways it foreshadowed the course of pacifist Quaker activism for the duration of the Seven Years' War.

Unwilling to rely on the colonial governments "to support such of our fellow subjects who are or may be in distress," Woolman and his associates launched their own relief initiatives. When Philadelphia Yearly Meeting convened in Burlington in 1756, Woolman arrived as a member of a new ad hoc committee he had formed with Churchman and thirty other men. The committee drew the meeting's attention to the "distressed state of the frontier settlements of these provinces" and recommended that the Quakers raise a fund of at least £1,000 for the relief of two groups: Friends living in areas "immediately exposed to danger," and others who suffered from wartime deprivation and needed provisions in order to survive the winter. Woolman and the others proposed that a new standing committee of twelve Philadelphia Friends be appointed to consider appeals from Quakers in need, "especially such as suffer from the Indians or other enemies." In addition to providing relief, the proposed standing committee would be charged with sending reports on American affairs to their counterparts in London.[14] Philadelphia Yearly Meeting responded positively to this proposal, and the committee of twelve was established. Eventually its sessions became known as the "Meetings for Sufferings." The committee's agenda expanded, its term of service was extended indefinitely, and its work became a lasting feature of American Quakerism.

While the Meetings for Sufferings initially concentrated on the ordeals of the Quakers living in war zones, within a year the committee was seeking to ameliorate the suffering of other apparent victims of the conflict, including Delaware Indians and Acadian deportees. Interpreting its responsibilities broadly, the Sufferings committee also sponsored efforts to procure and distribute religious books in French and German, and to prohibit allegedly immoral theatrical performances in Philadelphia. The aim of these projects was to promote Quaker ideals and to convince all the people in the region to place their trust in God, in the hope that they might secure God's favor and lasting peace.[15]

In addition to the Sufferings committee, the reformers formed other organizations "to cultivate our friendship with our Indian neighbors." In Pennsylvania the "Friendly Association for the Gaining and Preserving Peace with the Indians by Pacific Measures" worked to revive the diplomatic tradition long associated with William Penn. The Friendly Association monitored the Pennsylvania government's conduct at treaty gatherings and gave publicity to the historical grievances of the Munsee and Lenape. While these activities strained the Friendly Association's relationship with Pennsylvania's proprietors, the group found many opportunities to cooperate with other colonial and imperial leaders. Eager to demonstrate the efficacy of its conciliatory program, the Friendly Association negotiated for the release of war captives and sought Indian acquiescence in the establishment of new schools, trading posts, and roads on western lands. In 1758 the group would labor unsuccessfully to secure safe passage for General John Forbes' road-building crews when Forbes was crossing Pennsylvania on his way to lay siege to Fort Duquesne.[16] Woolman did not participate in the activities of the Friendly Association during the 1750s, in part because he was distracted by other concerns, including one effort to bring peace to the Indians of New Jersey. In 1757 he became a founding member of the "New Jersey Association for Helping the Indians." The New Jersey Association was loosely modeled on the Friendly Association, but its program was designed in response to the circumstances of Indians living east of the Delaware River.

In contrast to most of their kindred groups living to the west, New Jersey's Indians generally avoided violence during the Seven Years' War, and they took care not to give offense to their neighbors. Despite their best efforts, however, racial animosities arose in wartime, and in fall 1755, fearing for their safety, a delegation of local Indians petitioned the Governor of New Jersey. They declared their "fidelity to His Majesty" and their "attachment to the English nation" and asked for protection. Governor Jonathan Belcher responded by establishing a registry designed to identify and protect "such Indians as are really friends." The government kept a list of those Indians' names, gave them certificates, and asked them to wear red ribbons to signal "their attachment to their brethren the English" and their status as "his Majesty's good subjects."[17] The ribbons, however, did not provide sufficient protection.

Across the Delaware River the following spring, the governor of Pennsylvania took advice from the commander of British forces in North America, William Shirley, and offered bounties for the scalps of "enemy" Indians, including men, women and children.[18] In April a New Jersey man, John Connolly, learned that the Pennsylvania government was about to offer these scalp bounties, and with help from three of his neighbors, he attacked a family of "friend Indians" in Somerset County, New Jersey. Connolly and his partners intended to remove the Indians' scalps "and carry them to Philadelphia, where they were to swear that they were enemy Indians, and they had killed them in the province of Pennsylvania." Armed with "guns, cutlasses, and an ax," Connolly and his partners arrived at midnight at a wigwam in Peapack, New Jersey. Their intended victims were a man named George, his wife Kate, and the couple's three children. George managed to escape after Kate wrestled a gun away from one of the attackers, but during the fight her head was cut "all to pieces" and she was shot in the stomach. She eventually died and her children were also killed, after being "wounded and mangled . . . in an inhuman manner." George survived as a living reminder of the fury generated by the war.[19]

In the spring of 1756 a party of Indian warriors allied with the French raided northern New Jersey near the Great Meadows. At least one family was killed, and two additional settlers disappeared. They either fled or were taken captive. Other families abandoned the area and over the next several months, their cleared fields began to revert to forest. The Quakers who remained suffered from deprivation, and they pleaded for assistance from Friends living farther south in the colony who were better protected.[20] After the raid, Belcher followed the lead of several other governors and offered a bounty for the scalp of any man, woman, or child who could be identified as belonging to an enemy Indian tribe. He specifically asserted that "the tribe of Indians distinguished by the name of Delawares" were "enemies, rebels and traitors" because they had committed outrages in concert with "divers other Indians enemies to his Majesty."[21] Read broadly, Belcher's proclamation imperiled the life of nearly every Indian living in the Delaware Valley. The "Delaware" nation brought together Munsee and Lenape speakers who before the onset of colonization had possessed the region. But Belcher knew that some of the Munsee and Lenape in New Jersey had kept their distance from the self-styled "Delaware" warriors who were fighting the British in the west. Kate and her children had belonged to a peaceful community, and Belcher issued his scalp-bounty proclamation just as outrage over their murder was rising. It had become clear even to the members of the governor's council that New Jersey needed a better system for protecting its Indian friends.[22]

In the aftermath of these events, Woolman became involved in the politics surrounding New Jersey's resident Indians. There were many proposals circulating at the time. Some colonists advocated expelling the Indians and forcibly resettling them in the west. Others, partly in an effort to counter the drive for removal, suggested setting aside land in New Jersey to be held in trust for "friendly" Indians. As early as 1754 the Presbyterian missionary John Brainerd, with support from his sponsors in the Scottish Society for Propagating Christian Knowledge, had proposed establishing a reservation in New Jersey. According to the terms of the Presbyterian scheme, missionaries and government agents would watch over the resident Indians and encourage them to live peacefully, establish family farms, and embrace Protestant Christianity.[23] In April 1757 Woolman joined eighteen other Quakers to form the New Jersey Association. Their group's aim was similar to that of the Presbyterians. They intended to promote peace in the colony by establishing a reservation which would provide a home for landless Indians, and eventually encourage them to take up farming. The founders of the New Jersey Association pledged to raise money by subscription in order to purchase 2,000 acres near the Pine Barrens where the Indians could "live comfortably together, and by hunting and fishing and what they could raise out of the earth, support themselves in a more convenient and reputable manner than they have hitherto done."[24]

Had the New Jersey Association's plan gone into effect, any of the colony's "native Indians" who did not already own land would have been entitled to settle and live rent-free on the reservation. Title to the property would have remained with the New Jersey Association, whose membership would have been restricted to the members of the Society of Friends. Six managers and one treasurer, all Quakers, would have had "oversight of the resident Indians" and responsibility for resolving any disputes that might have arisen among them. Once sufficient funds had become available, the Quaker overseers were to provide the Indians with houses, barns, fencing, stock and equipment, and eventually, if an endowment could be raised, to operate a school for the people under their charge. One of the project's aims was to put space between the Indians and the angry colonists in order to create a refuge from racial animosity and violence. The founders of the association also intended to discourage the resident Indians from traveling or consorting with travelers, because they believed that moving was inherently disruptive. They intended to "prevent as much as possible any communication of foreign Indians with the Indians residing on the [reservation] land," and bar any Indians from outside New Jersey from settling there. In the words of the association's charter, an overriding goal of the reservation proposal was to keep the Indians "out of the way of danger or of being seduced by rambling abroad."[25]

The debate over the future of New Jersey's Indians culminated in 1758 with the establishment of Brotherton, a tract of more than three thousand acres purchased by the colonial government and held in trust for resident "friendly Indians." Over two hundred Lenape- and Munsee-speakers came forward and moved onto the land. Many of them were the Presbyterian John Brainerd's parishioners, and in 1762 Brainerd became their official "superintendent and guardian." Although Brotherton was not run by Quakers, some Friends took an interest in the spiritual lives of the people who lived there. Before the Seven Years' War was over, the English traveling minister Elizabeth Wilkinson came to Brotherton. She convened a meeting for worship and sat with the Indians for nearly an hour in silence. "I did not expect I should have opened my mouth, but near the conclusion apprehended it my duty." Feeling obligated to speak, Wilkinson rose and warned the Indians that God would punish them for "sin of every kind" and that "there was no repentance after death." She made no record of the Indians' response to this message, but reported that she felt better after speaking. "I found much love in my heart towards them."[26]

Brotherton continued to operate until 1802, making its own small contribution to the intellectual and institutional development of reserve and reservation policies in the British Empire and the United States. Woolman's early support for the reservation was typical of his general response to the Seven Years' War. He was actively engaged in contemporary political debates, seeking to ease suffering and provide protection to people in immediate danger. He also believed that the war presented an opportunity for the Quakers over the long term. The Sufferings committee, the Friendly Association, and the New Jersey Association were all designed to promote amity between potentially competing groups. Woolman and the other founders of these organizations believed that they could draw support from all the Quakers in the Delaware Valley, and that in their efforts at outreach they would find common ground with Quakers and non-Quakers alike. The war was inherently divisive, however, and the reformers did not enjoy universal support even within the Society of Friends.

*   *   *

In the early weeks of the war, before the first of Braddock's troops arrived in North America, Burlington Monthly Meeting appointed Woolman and Abraham Farrington to discipline a Quaker named Joseph Lamb who had accepted a commission in the militia. New Jersey law required all free men between ages sixteen and fifty, with the exception of religious ministers, physicians, schoolmasters, millers, and officials of the government, to enlist in the militia, but it was possible to avoid serving by paying a series of fines. The government used the proceeds from these fines to purchase arms and ammunition for those militiamen who did not personally own the requisite musket, sword, powder horn, powder, and bullets. Lamb possessed these things, and he expressed no remorse for choosing the course he took. He wanted to perform his legal duty and did not consider it better to pay for someone else to shoulder a musket for him.[27]

During the first two years of the Seven Years' War, many Friends in Burlington County joined a collective and pooled their money in order to make sure that they would have enough money to pay their fines if they were summoned for militia duty. According to Joshua Evans, the Quaker members of this collective argued that they were simply taking an appropriate precaution, getting ready to follow "the doctrine of Christ in rendering Caesar his due." Evans was not convinced, however, and he refused to participate in the collective. He thought that it would be inconsistent "to hire men to do what I could not, for conscience sake, do myself." When issued his fine, he refused to pay, and a Sheriff came and seized goods from his farm to make up what was due as a penalty. According to Evans, the Sheriff took twice as much property as was necessary and sold it for "half value."[28] Others who refused to pay fines under similar circumstances tried to negotiate with the sheriffs to make sure that the property seized was just enough to cover the requisite sum. Some Quakers asked the sheriffs to give them change if the proceeds from the sale of their confiscated goods exceeded the amount of the fine set by statute. In 1755 Philadelphia Yearly Meeting intervened on that question and declared that paying the fine was the equivalent of employing a soldier and inconsistent with the peace testimony. Furthermore, the meeting warned, negotiating with a sheriff over the proceeds from the sale of confiscated goods was the equivalent of paying a fine. Those who sought to protect their property in this manner would be subject to Quaker discipline.[29] The Quakers had a long tradition of disobeying laws that seemed to require them to violate their principles. As Woolman explained, "Laws and customs are no further a standard for our proceedings than as their foundation is on universal righteousness."[30] The Yearly Meeting's warnings were not enough to stop men from paying fines to avoid militia duty, however, and there were a variety of other ways that a Quaker might respond inappropriately to demands from the army. In 1757, when recruiters came to Mount Holly and called out the militia to raise troops for the relief of Fort William Henry, Woolman saw some Friends enlist, others run away, and a few confront the recruiters, declaring their pacifist principles. He praised only the third group.[31]

In April 1758, an officer who lived in Mount Holly went door-to-door through the town seeking quarters for 100 soldiers. The men would be stationed in the town for approximately two weeks, and then proceed on a march toward French Canada. Later in the year, as part of an army of 16,000, they would take part in one of the worst defeats the British forces suffered during the war, at Ticonderoga.[32] That April when the officer came to Woolman's house and asked him to board two soldiers, Woolman was slow to respond. There were two subordinate men accompanying the officer and one of them declared that boarding soldiers did not violate Quaker principles. The officer also assured Woolman that he would be paid for the service. Woolman felt that he should give an answer and eventually said, "If the men are sent here for entertainment, I believe I shall not refuse to admit them into my house, but the nature of the case is such that I expect I cannot keep them on hire." Ultimately only one soldier was sent to Woolman's house. He stayed there two weeks and "behaved himself civilly." At the end of the period, the officer returned and tried to pay Woolman. Woolman refused the money, explaining that he had agreed to board the soldier only in "passive obedience to authority" and not for profit. Woolman recalled, "As I turned from him he said he was obliged to me, to which I said nothing." Almost immediately after the two men parted, Woolman worried that he had been rude, and he went to the officer's house to explain himself more fully.[33]

Later in the war Abner Woolman had a similar, if briefer, encounter with a body of soldiers, and Abner was able to handle the confrontation with greater self-confidence. He was standing by the door of his house in rural Burlington County when a company of soldiers marched past. Seeing him at the door, several of them approached him and asked if they could buy some cider. Unwilling to supply the army, Abner refused. He would not accept their money, nor would he give them any drink for free. Then the captain and the company's doctor walked up and asked to hire one of his wagons. Again Abner refused. "I told him that I looked upon the life of a man to be precious, and could not consistent with my religious principles do anything to forward them on their march." The captain drew out a press warrant signed by his superior officer and told Abner he could be forced to provide a wagon and a team of horses without compensation and that it would be better for Abner to lease the wagon and horses voluntarily. The captain preferred not to exploit his authority, take the wagon for free, and make Abner angry. Abner replied that if the company took his wagon and horses, it could only be by force and without payment. "I would not consent to hire them, and . . . I could not take pay for them as it was on a religious principle that I was against his having them." The captain initially seemed agitated at this, but then gradually grew pleasant. He told Abner that he was unique. According to Abner's account of the conversation, the officer told him that he "differed from all other men that ever he had conversed with, and as from a religious principle I was not easy to help them on their march, it was not easy to him to press my wagon and horses." The soldiers marched away without any cider, horses, or wagons from Abner's farm.[34]

Other evidence confirms the officer's observation that Abner was a rare Quaker in taking such an unequivocal stance against providing wagons to the army. When Philadelphia Yearly Meeting met in 1758, it received reports that Quakers in western Pennsylvania had leased General John Forbes wagons, horses, and drivers to convey "implements of war &c" westward in preparation for the siege of Fort Duquesne. The meeting condemned the practice of leasing wagons to the army, but indicated an openness to hear the Friends' opposing arguments, and appointed John Woolman to a committee consisting of thirty-four Friends to investigate the "circumstances of the cases." After discussing the matter with representatives from the western meetings, Woolman and his fellow committee members concluded that those Quakers who had provided the army with horses and wagons had done so under a misapprehension that they were not performing a military service. More education was necessary.[35]

The Quakers disagreed among themselves over how they should respond when ordered to serve in the militia, quarter soldiers in their homes, or deliver horses and wagons to the army. Woolman engaged in extended debates with other Friends on these questions. He did not like the controversy, but he could comfort himself with the knowledge that Philadelphia Yearly Meeting had explicitly addressed most of the relevant issues involved, and the positions he advocated conformed to the meeting's disciplinary guidelines. He had much greater difficulty with the problem of taxation.

In 1755 Woolman resolved not to pay any tax that was levied to finance the war effort. He preferred to remain passive, wait for a sheriff to come to his home, and "suffer patiently the distress of goods rather than pay actively." When he made this decision he thought that he was alone, but at Philadelphia Yearly Meeting in 1755 he encountered several like-minded Friends.[36] The Yearly Meeting appointed Woolman to a committee to consider the propriety of paying wartime taxes. Much discussion was necessary, because "Friends were not all of one mind in relation to the tax." In the weeks that followed Woolman heard from "upright-hearted men" and "noted Friends" who religiously paid their taxes and believed that it was wrong to withhold them. With reason, they warned him that tax resistance would "displease the rulers, not only here but in England." Nonetheless, after extended deliberations, in December 1755 Woolman's committee drew up an epistle advising Quakers not to pay a tax recently imposed on the inhabitants of Pennsylvania. The committee members were careful to express their loyalty to the government and their willingness to pay taxes for "such benevolent purposes as supporting our friendship with our Indian neighbors and relieving the distresses of our fellow subjects who have suffered in the present calamities," but the tax in question had clearly been imposed to fund the war. It was "principally intended for purposes inconsistent with our peaceable testimony."[37]

The December 1755 epistle was distributed widely in Pennsylvania but according to Woolman, many Quakers "openly spake against it." At the Yearly Meeting in 1756, some of the authors of the epistle challenged their critics to initiate disciplinary proceedings against them, but the meeting declined to take that step and the dispute simmered for another year.[38] In 1757 the Yearly Meeting appointed Woolman to yet another committee to reexamine the taxation issue. In doing so, the meeting took note of the "the diversity of sentiments" that had been expressed. The thirty committee members met and deliberated, but could agree only that the issue was so divisive that it would not be "proper to enter into a public discussion of the matter." The best they could do was issue a plea for all Quakers to have "charity towards one another" in the face of their ongoing disagreements.[39]

One point of contention in the taxation controversy was the importance of English precedent. Woolman conceded that "scrupling to pay a tax" to support military expenses was a new idea. He knew that even during the present war, the English Quakers paid their taxes in the full knowledge that much of the money would be used to fund military expenditures. He argued that the situation in the Delaware Valley was different, because the Quakers had never been an embattled minority in Pennsylvania or New Jersey. On the contrary, they held a measure of power in those colonies, and that circumstance placed a greater burden on them to behave in an exemplary manner, stand apart from others, and follow their consciences.[40] Woolman was cautious about advancing a more general argument against the payment of wartime taxes, in part because he did not want to antagonize English Quakers. In 1757 Philadelphia Yearly Meeting had pointedly directed his committee to consult with six traveling ministers who had arrived in Philadelphia from England.[41] Woolman was also wary of exacerbating and publicizing the divisions within his own yearly meeting, so much so that he directed the Overseers of the Press to delete several passages from his journal related to the taxation controversy.[42]

Abner Woolman, at home in Burlington County, felt less constrained. Like his brother he conceded that the Quakers had only recently discovered the evil of paying wartime taxes, but for Abner this discovery represented a startling new revelation. On an evening in 1758, after he had turned a tax collector away from his door, Abner felt glad.

> I remembered how of old time the Law was written on tables of Stone, but the substance of the new covenant was now fresh in my mind, that covenant in which the Lord immediately reveals his will in the hearts of his people, and it looked to me then and continues to look so, that the Lord in this our day is calling to some, and in tender love drawing their minds toward him to leave their acquaintance and kindred which they once took delight in, and follow the leadings of his unerring spirit, in some things which were not opened to our forefathers.[43]

John Churchman was similar to Abner in his assessment of the importance of not paying taxes in wartime. Churchman believed that the time had arrived when all Christians should be "clean handed," and he therefore concluded that he would never again "shake hands with that nature which would tear and devour, nor in any shape contribute to the price of blood." Churchman expressed regret that "a timorous disposition" had ever kept him from speaking out, "for fear of the frowns of elder brethren."[44] John Woolman may have agreed with Abner and Churchman, but in the conduct of meeting business he was frequently reminded of the need to seek reconciliation. Especially when he was discussing war-related problems, he listened carefully to the comments of others and responded with humility, even though he would never admit that he was willing to compromise his core principles.

One of the most extended disciplinary cases facing Woolman involved Samuel Busby, a Quaker from the vicinity of Rancocas Creek who enlisted on a privateer. Busby joined approximately 150 officers and crewmembers on the *Britannia*, a privately owned ship mounting sixteen cannons. They sailed from Philadelphia for the Caribbean on September 20, 1758, and over the next ten months captured at least ten other ships along with cargoes of dry goods, indigo, sugar, coffee, cocoa, oil, vinegar, and wine. They made prisoners of more than one hundred men and claimed title to sixteen captured slaves. On one of their prize ships, the crewmembers of the *Britannia* discovered a letter indicating that "a very large sloop, richly laden" was anchored in the harbor at Saint Vincent. The letter hinted that the French garrison on the island might be running out of gunpowder. Intent on taking advantage of the opportunity, the *Britannia* hastened to Saint Vincent and delivered an ultimatum to the French: surrender the sloop and four other vessels, or the privateers would "beat down their town." The French garrison, however, was adequately supplied, and the *Britannia* took fire not only from the fort, but also from "behind houses, rocks and trees." The fighting lasted from noon until nightfall, and at the end of the day the *Britannia* left without plunder. Its captain took consolation in the belief that he and his crew had inflicted pain on the island's "French, Indians and Negroes." He boasted that the *Britannia* had destroyed "half their town." Two of his crewmembers had been killed in the engagement, and eight were wounded, including Busby, who was "shot through the thigh." Busby came home to New Jersey in July.[45]

In November, 1759 Burlington Monthly Meeting asked Woolman and Henry Paxson to discipline Busby, and they met with him. After their first session Paxson reported that he saw "little hopeful" in the case, but Woolman declared that he was "willing to labor further" and asked for more time. Through the early spring of 1760 he and Paxson worked with Busby, seeking to convince him to recognize the error of his ways. The process continued until April when Woolman left on a ministerial journey to Rhode Island. In Woolman's absence, Burlington Monthly Meeting disowned Busby, declaring that he had shown no inclination "to offer any condemnation of his misconduct."[46]

Woolman's reluctance to pass judgment against Busby reflected his general uneasiness with the ways in which the war was dividing communities across the Delaware Valley. He knew that he had much in common with the privateer, and not just because of their shared religious affiliation. Woolman and Paxson had their own indirect ties to the violent world of Caribbean commerce. In 1757 their business associate Thomas Clifford had purchased a one-half stake in a brigantine he christened the *Sally*, a French ship that had been seized by the British navy and put up for sale. It is quite possible that Woolman's pork had been carried to Barbados, Antigua, and other Caribbean islands on board this prize vessel. Clifford had broken the Friends' rule against acquiring the spoils of war when he purchased his interest in the ship, but he respected the peace testimony in another important respect. He did not place guns on the deck of the *Sally*, and partly as a consequence he lost the vessel in 1761, when it was seized and repatriated by a French privateer.[47]

Since 1755 Woolman had participated in a series of debates that had seemed to follow a common pattern. They began by posing a stark dichotomy between engaging in warfare and maintaining a commitment to peace, but devolved into discussions that only served to identify shades of difference along an array of possible behaviors. The Quakers worried themselves over which taxes and fines they could pay, what kind of assistance they could give to the British army, and how they could do business in combat zones without taking forbidden plunder. When the deliberations revolved around such questions of detail, they had the potential of making nearly everyone in the meeting-house feel guilty, and the analysis was likely to frustrate those who wanted to make an uncomplicated statement in favor of peace. Woolman faced the same quandaries as everyone else, even though he yearned for simplicity. He wanted to behave in a way that sent an unequivocal and unqualified message to his neighbors, but in the context of the war he found it surprisingly difficult to do so. During his journey through Virginia in 1757, he heard of a group of young men who had been given an opportunity to perform in a way that Woolman could not. They had seized the occasion and found a way to embody the Quakers' pacifist message, and Woolman was deeply impressed.

In 1756, seven young Quaker men from New Kent County and Hanover County, Virginia, were drafted into the army under George Washington. They marched with their units and talked amicably with the men around them, including the officers and the common soldiers, but they defiantly refused to behave like soldiers themselves. They refused to eat their rations, and ostentatiously kept their mouths shut during roll calls. On one occasion, one of the men was stripped to the waist in preparation for a flogging, but by "the interposition of Divine Providence," it was said, he was "seized with an uncommon trembling to the astonishment of all the spectators," and "could scarce stand on his feet." The flogging was canceled. Eventually the men were imprisoned, but when their case reached Washington, he released them provisionally, and eventually, after an intervention from the Virginia Governor Robert Dinwiddie, their discharge was made permanent. The men had been with the army less than seven weeks, and they had never been obedient soldiers. Nonetheless, Washington signed a separate statement for each of the men, declaring that they had adequately "served in the Virginia regiment" for their allotted time. Commenting on the case, Dinwiddie declared that while he was ready to prosecute shirkers, he never wanted to punish men who resisted military service as a "matter of conscience."[48] Many Quakers interpreted this outcome as a triumph. Woolman passed through Hanover County on his way south in May 1757, lodging with the father of one of the men.[49] Two weeks later he heard more details about the episode at Virginia Yearly Meeting.[50] In September he wrote to the Quakers in Virginia on behalf of Philadelphia Yearly Meeting: "We are heartily glad that some of your young men were freely given up to endure affliction for the sake of that noble testimony which we are called to bear against wars and fightings, and it will be their joy and rejoicing that they were accounted worthy so to suffer . . . it is evident that the faithful suffering for the truth has ever had a tendency to promote the work of God in the earth."[51]

When he praised the seven Virginians in these terms, Woolman used language that would have been familiar to Quakers throughout the North American colonies. Since the spring of 1755, reform-minded American Friends had repeatedly described the war as a providential trial, suggesting that if the Quakers maintained their commitment to peace they might initiate a better era in human history.[52] This outlook was peculiarly American. The British Quakers generally responded to the Seven Years' War by thanking God for keeping them safe.[53] North America's Quakers, by contrast, knew that they were being tested, even if they sometimes had difficulty believing that the misery sweeping their continent could serve a good purpose. The most ardent pacifists among them were therefore vigilant, watching for signs of promise in the course of American events. They believed they found what they were looking for in 1760, when the Munsee prophet Papunhank came to Philadelphia and declared his devotion to Quaker principles. The worst of the war was over, and Friends were waiting for the better day to come.

Papunhank had been born early in the eighteenth century. His parents were reportedly Mahican, but as an adult he had joined the mixed population of displaced persons, former war captives, and others living among the Munsee in the northern Susquehanna Valley. Like many others who came of age in the region at that time, he had become a "drunken man," but in the 1750s he experienced a spiritual reawakening. In "a thoughtful melancholy" following the death of his father, he fled into the woods, where after five days alone he met God, who gave him "a sight not only of his own inward state, but also an acquaintance into the works of nature." Papunhank "was made sensible that Man stood in the nearest relation to God of any other part of the creation." This insight led him to reject the "folly and wickedness that prevailed" around him. He renounced alcohol and resolved never to engage in warfare. He began preaching, and eventually assembled a new religious community centered at a town called Wyalusing. In 1761 he reported that he had gathered 300 followers there.[54]

Only about half of the inhabitants of Wyalusing followed Papunhank's teachings, but those who did met every day before sunrise for worship and again every evening when the sun went down. They grew corn, kept livestock, and had "very good land." Papunhank was a hunter, and every year he left the town with other men to obtain skins and furs to sell to the British at Shamokin. Religious ceremonies were suspended during the hunt.[55] Well before Papunhank's arrival in Philadelphia, he and his followers had been identified as "Quaker, or religious Indians." They knew that they had been characterized in this way and were eager to emphasize the perceived affinity between their own beliefs and Quakerism. On their way to Philadelphia, Papunhank and his traveling companions said that it was their intention "to see the Friends chiefly, and to show that they really are Friends."[56]

After arriving in the city, Papunhank went to see Israel Pemberton, the leader of the Friendly Association, who helped him arrange three meetings with the Lieutenant Governor of Pennsylvania, James Hamilton. Papunhank came with three captives, a woman named Mary from Bedford, Massachusetts, a boy named Jacob from a southwestern settlement in Pennsylvania, and a girl of Dutch ancestry from a rural town in the colony of New York just across the border from New Jersey. These three had been taken prisoner in the recent fighting and had been assigned to the custody of families in Wyalusing. Papunhank delivered them to the governor, even though the young ones were frightened at the prospect of staying in Philadelphia. According to the scribe who recorded the event, "The children cried as if they would die when they were presented to us."[57]

Subsequently speaking to the governor with the help of a translator, Papunhank made no apologies on behalf of the people of Wyalusing, but instead declared that he had "never been concerned in war affairs." He announced that one "white man" remained in his town, a soldier named David Owen Frazier who had deserted his post in the Mohawk River Valley. Papunhank explained that Frazier was "tired with soldiering" and wanted to stay among the Indians. He asked the governor to intervene and secure Frazier a pardon. Papunhank also requested Pennsylvania's help in blocking the distribution of alcohol, and regulating the conduct of trade.[58] The Quakers were excited by his performance on that occasion, and at his second meeting with Hamilton, "a large audience of young and old persons attended." By the time of Papunhank's third session with the governor, "a large number of the people called Quakers" arrived with him when he entered the room. In addition to seeing Quakers in the council chamber, Papunhank attended their meetings for worship and, with the help of interpreters, conversed with Quaker ministers and elders.[59]

Papunhank returned to Philadelphia in 1761, by which time he had become an important figure among the Quakers. Anthony Benezet had assembled notes of Papunhank's meetings with the governor and an account of his religious experiences, which he distributed widely. Manuscripts of Benezet's essay, in English and in German translation, circulated among the colonists. When the piece reached England, the British Quakers had it printed. The Irish traveling minister Susannah Hatton joined another Quaker woman and went to Easton, Pennsylvania, to see Papunhank at a treaty gathering there. In total, perhaps as many as 80 Quakers saw Papunhank in Easton. A Quaker delegation accompanied Papunhank from that gathering to Philadelphia. Papunhank spent two weeks in the city in August 1761, and according to one Quaker witness he "attended most of our Meetings of Worship." He also had "solid opportunities of conversation" with "several Friends." It was at one of these meetings, at Benezet's home, that Woolman met Papunhank.[60]

The setting was conducive for talk, and the two men had the aid of an interpreter. The conversation revolved around "religious subjects," and "the cause of the frequent wars and bloodshed which so much prevailed in the world." Papunhank asserted that the creator had given men love in their hearts, but if they failed to "follow the leadings of this good spirit," evil spirits intruded, leading men to "dislike one another, grow angry with and endeavor to kill one another." Therefore, it was imperative for everyone to stay attentive to "that love which our maker had given us in our hearts," and to "look upon all mankind as one and so become as one family."[61]

Papunhank expressed a cautious reticence when asked to detail his religious beliefs. He said that he became afraid whenever he sensed that "he knew more than other people," because he did not want any pretense of personal superiority to interfere with the "love and affection" he felt for "all our fellow creatures." Furthermore he was wary of speaking too deliberately, because "it was not good to speak upon matters relating to the almighty only from the word of the tongue outward." It was better to stay silent until inspired. He told Woolman that when the "spirit of love" prevailed in his heart, "he was preserved to speak only that which was right." Woolman was pleased with what he heard, recognizing a close correspondence between Papunhank's message and the Quakers' beliefs. Other Quakers who saw Papunhank in 1760 and 1761 came to the same conclusion and suggested that he had recognized divine truth through immediate experience, without the intervention of missionaries.[62]

There are several reasons why Papunhank may have sounded like a Quaker. For decades Indian negotiators in the vicinity of Pennsylvania had been praising Quaker principles and invoking the memory of William Penn in order to plead for good treatment from Penn's successors. Thus Indians had long been complicit in elaborating upon and disseminating Pennsylvania's founding myth, suggesting that strong bonds of mutual sympathy and support had been established between the Quakers and the native peoples of the Delaware Valley. Papunhank carefully adhered to this diplomatic tradition. He told Governor Hamilton, for example, that he had "a sincere remembrance of the old friendship which subsisted between the Indians and your forefathers," and he vowed that he would "always observe it."[63]

Papunhank was one of several Indian prophets who acquired special insight based on visions they received in the 1750s. His claim to spiritual authority was based on his direct experience with God, and in 1760 and 1761 he continued to cite his personal encounters with the divine as a way of validating his teachings. Nonetheless, he also believed that the Quakers had something to teach him, and as he gained more familiarity with their way of expressing themselves, he increasingly described his own spiritual life in terms that invoked European and colonial religious traditions. Although the Quakers did not know it when they first met him, he had gone to a Moravian mission a few months before his visit to Philadelphia in 1760 and had already begun to adopt that group's spiritual vocabulary. By the time Papunhank met Woolman in 1761, he had also attended as many as a dozen Quaker meetings and so gained considerable familiarity with the teachings and practices of the Friends. There were significant differences between the Moravians and the Quakers, but there were also important rough similarities, particularly in the way the two groups described the power of heartfelt talk.[64]

Figure 9. Depiction, based on contemporary accounts, of the Delaware leader Teedyuscung. When Papunhank met Woolman in Philadelphia in 1761 he was probably dressed similarly, though perhaps not quite so flamboyantly.

Nearly all the Quakers who met with Papunhank were eager to hear him echo their testimonies, and once he began speaking, their excitement at sensing that he was close to Quakerism affected the way in which they described him and transcribed his answers to their questions. Benezet and Woolman may have exaggerated the correspondence between Papunhank's understanding of the operations of the spirit and their own beliefs, but there was a resonance between Papunhank's message and eighteenth-century Quakerism, reflected not only in what he said, but in the way that he spoke. Woolman was positively impressed by the manner in which Papunhank talked. "He appeared in much tenderness of spirit," Woolman observed, and "manifested the sense he was under the necessity and effect of divine love." He noted Papunhank's "sweetness of voice" and his expressive gestures, "often pressing his hand against his breast." Papunhank appeared inspired but also careful. Woolman indicated that he spoke "gravely." Papunhank wore a brightly colored coat and a ruffled shirt, but when he talked he resembled a Quaker minister.[65]

Papunhank's manner of expressing himself owed much to Native American traditions of oratory. Knowing the value of expressive gestures and persuasive performances, he sought to instill respect for the power of speech. When he talked to the Quakers in Philadelphia in 1760, he warned them more than once that spoken words should not be taken lightly and that serious matters should never be discussed outside their appropriate contexts. "I have a feeling sense in my own heart," he had said, "whereby I know when people speak from the head, or when they speak from the heart." When one Quaker asked him (through an interpreter) whether he would like to discuss "our Savior's words and good examples when on earth," he replied, "Such words as those are very good, and would be very acceptable at a fit time. Such things are awful, and should be spoken at a solemn time, for then the heart is soft, and they would go into it, and not be lost. But when the heart is hard, they will not go into it, but fall off from the heart, and so are lost." He gave a similar warning to Woolman, declaring that "it was not good to speak upon matters relating to the almighty only from the word of the tongue, but that in order that their words should be good they must come from the good or the heart." Just as it was important to speak in the right spirit, for words to be good and effective they had to be heard correctly. Papunhank told the Quakers, "whilst one is speaking, the other should hold his head down till the first has done."[66]

In 1761, after Papunhank's second visit to Philadelphia, Woolman joined Benezet and more than one hundred others in sending an epistle to London Yearly Meeting announcing that Papunhank's appearance among them was "a manifestation of the work of divine Grace." The London Quakers responded by celebrating "the present visitation of divine love and light extended to the Indians." In the draft of a letter he wrote in 1762, Pemberton suggested that Papunhank's arrival might have been a sign pointing toward the "fulfilling of the many glorious prophesies of the general spreading of the gospel of our Lord and Savior in the dark corners of the Earth, when the wilderness and the solitary places will be made to rejoice and become as the Garden of the Lord." Then, after writing those words, he had second thoughts. In all likelihood he thought his comments were excessively enthusiastic, and he struck them out.[67]

Years earlier, the founders of the New Jersey Association had expressed their gratitude toward the Munsee and Lenape. In the preamble to their charter, they had declared that it was "a truth fresh in the memory of several yet living" that "the native Indians of New Jersey were remarkably kind" to the first Quakers to arrive in the colony. The Indians had been cooperative "at a time when there were many hundreds of them to one white, and had they been disposed to have crushed the growing settlement, according to the natural appearance of things, nothing would have been easier." Nonetheless they had sold the Quakers land, allowed them to "sit down and improve their possessions quietly," and helped them in times of distress. Recognizing this history, the association gave thanks "to the natural and original proprietors of the soil whereon we reside, who treated our predecessors with such a distinguished regard."[68]

Woolman does not mention in his journal any personal encounters with Indians prior to his first meeting with Papunhank, but he indicates that for years prior to 1761 he had felt love in his heart "toward the natives of this land who dwell far back in the wilderness, whose ancestors were the owners and possessors of the land where we dwell, and who for a very small consideration assigned their inheritance to us."[69] Similarly in a private letter he wrote, "I often think on the fruitfulness of the soil where we live. The care that hath been taken to agree with the former owners the natives, and the conveniences this land affords for our use." These thoughts reminded him to make good use of the advantages he had received, to "take care that my cravings may be bounded, and that no wandering desire may lead me to so strengthen the hands of the wicked as to partake of their sins."[70] The Indians' meek response to the arrival of the first Quaker settlers in New Jersey served as a kind of reproach to Woolman, obliging him to behave with equal humility and kindness. He knew that in the intervening years many Indians had engaged in warfare, and as a group they were generally not a model for him, but in Papunhank he found a new exemplar, one who reminded him of God's power to touch a soul. Often it seemed that the Lord was particularly inclined toward the inhabitants of isolated places, and by all appearances Wyalusing was specially blessed. As soon as he met Papunhank, Woolman felt drawn to visit him in Wyalusing. He mentioned this idea to Sarah, but otherwise he kept the thought to himself.[71] There was reason to be cautious. London Yearly Meeting, for example, had celebrated Papunhank's apparent inspiration, but had also admonished the Delaware Valley Quakers to wait for "heavenly council" before venturing westward "to go in and out before that people." God sometimes worked through "visible means" to achieve his aims, but at other times he operated more mysteriously. Perhaps it would be better to leave Wyalusing alone.

Years earlier, Woolman had pledged money to underwrite the creation of a reservation in New Jersey as a way of repaying a debt that he insisted the colonists owed to the Indians. With the other founders of the New Jersey Association he had expressed his hope that a reservation would keep New Jersey's Indian and colonial populations stationary and separate, minimizing discord and competition for resources. The Association proposed rules for the reservation that were designed to promote the kind of peace and stillness that could lead to spiritual enlightenment. Woolman had the same aspirations for the Indians who lived "far back in the wilderness" where Papunhank came from, in the west. When he thought about the process of settlement in North America, Woolman emphasized the value of moving slowly, maintaining stability, and providing both the Indians and the settlers security and space. He supported the demarcation of clear geographical boundaries between the lands the Indians occupied and the settlers' farms. In 1757 the New Jersey Association had expressed its displeasure at seeing Indians "rambling abroad." Writing to North Carolina on behalf of Philadelphia Yearly Meeting in 1759, Woolman and Daniel Stanton similarly warned against "that unstable practice of Friends frequently moving with their families from place to place," particularly if the Quakers migrated with "views of worldly gain or to gratify an unsettled mind in seeking better land." There were many evils associated with transience, and the two writers mentioned several of them, but they particularly objected to the unlawful invasion of Indian territory. The Quakers in Philadelphia had received reports that some Friends in North Carolina had "not taken the proper caution with respect to settling on lands not fairly purchased of the Indians." Woolman and Stanton objected, asserting that no Quaker should go to live anywhere in the west without first making sure that the Indians had ceded title to the property.[72]

The Seven Years' War ended in February 1763, when under the terms of the Treaty of Paris, France ceded Britain formal sovereignty over Canada, the Great Lakes, the Ohio River Valley, and most of the rest of North America east of the Mississippi River. The news of the war's end arrived in the colonies a few weeks later, and it was difficult for anyone to interpret the outcome as anything other than a triumph of British arms. Pacifist Quakers, no matter how much they loved the British monarchy, must have greeted this development with ambivalence. Life would grow much more difficult for them in the ensuing months, once it had become clear that the Treaty of Paris had not brought peace to North America. No Indians had taken part in the negotiations in Paris, and in May an alliance of Native groups took up arms against the extension of British authority in the west, in a coordinated military campaign known to posterity as Pontiac's War.

In September 1763 Philadelphia Yearly Meeting learned that Quakers were leaving Western Pennsylvania to settle on contested land in North Carolina. In an effort to stop the migration, the meeting declared that "Friends should not purchase nor remove to settle such lands as have not been fairly and openly first purchased from the Indians by those persons who are or may be fully authorized by the government to make such purchases."[73] While the Quakers had much to worry about in 1763, they saw hope in the redirection of British policy. Two weeks after the Yearly Meeting made its statement, George III issued his proclamation creating a vast Indian reserve west of the Appalachian Mountains. The proclamation barred colonists from settling in the west unless they were moving onto land that the crown had purchased from the Indians. The Quakers were not the authors of the new policy, but they were ready to support it. Philadelphia Yearly Meeting withheld membership certificates from Friends who moved west in violation of the royal decree.[74]

In 1763 Woolman and John Pemberton (Israel's brother) were assigned the task of writing the Quakers on Long Island, and in their epistle they helped broadcast the "solid sense and judgment" of the Delaware Valley Friends. They told the Long Island Quakers that Philadelphia Yearly Meeting had expressed its unequivocal opposition to the uncompensated expropriation of Indian lands. But Woolman and John Pemberton did more than repeat the meeting's resolution. They declared that as part of the Quaker effort to protect the Indians' western territories, wealthy Friends should provide charity to the poor, "so that those in low circumstances amongst us, being treated with tenderness, may have less temptation to seek settlements on lands which have not been properly purchased of the natives."[75] In general, the Quakers were eager to do what they could to advance the apparently enlightened policy encapsulated by the Proclamation of 1763. Woolman, however, was more skeptical than others about the power of legislation and royal command. He was more interested in moral reform. The 1763 epistle to Long Island was typical of Woolman's writings in the 1760s in suggesting that peace could be maintained in the west only if the colonists showed greater charity toward each other in the zone of dense colonial settlement along the Atlantic coast.

Chapter 7

Not in Words Only:
Conspicuous Instructive Behavior

He said the cause why he appeared so, was that he believed it to be
his duty, to bear a testimony not in words only, but to be a sign to
the people.
  —Anonymous account of Woolman's travels in 1772

THE SEVEN YEARS' War made many Delaware Valley Quakers uneasy about
serving in government. In New Jersey and Pennsylvania, the war forced some
Quaker officer-holders into difficult dilemmas, because they were responsible
for punishing other Friends who had violated provincial laws on principle.
This problem was acute in Pennsylvania, where in some instances Quaker
sheriffs seized property from conscientious tax evaders in their own meetings. Woolman observed that when two Quakers confronted each other in
such a situation, the "difficulty was considerable."[1] In 1758 Philadelphia Yearly
Meeting decided that no Quakers should accept any office "in civil society or
government" that would require them to impose penalties on "their brethren
or others" for upholding the Quakers' ideals. Thus Friends were barred from
participating in military drafts and collecting fines or seizing property from
those who refused to join the militia. The meeting was vague about tax collection and it left open the possibility that Friends might still legitimately work as
sheriffs if they did not infringe on the Quakers' "liberty of conscience." Nonetheless, after 1758 Quakers who worked for the government faced heightened
disciplinary scrutiny. In some parts of Pennsylvania, local meetings sent dele-
gations to the homes of all the Quakers who held government commissions. If

an office-holder was found to have improperly punished a fellow Quaker, and if he remained unrepentant, he was prohibited from participating in meeting business.[2] Woolman worried for the souls of Quakers who were "active in civil society in putting laws in force which are not agreeable to the purity of righteousness." He observed that when Friends assumed such responsibilities, the performance of their duties had "a necessary tendency to bring dimness over their minds."[3]

The Quakers' discomfort with law enforcement had deep roots. Within their meetings they discouraged litigation, and they repeatedly expressed ambivalence about relying on the coercive power of government. As a shopkeeper, Woolman never wanted to sue his customers. He admitted that he once obtained a warrant to collect a debt from "an idle man" who was "about to run away," but that was the only time he ever "applied to the law to recover money." He suspected that other retailers resorted to the law more frequently. To confirm his suspicions, he asked the constable in Mount Holly how many warrants he served in a year. The constable gave Woolman his books and allowed him to count the cases. The man had served 267 warrants, delivered 103 summonses, and made arrests or seized property 79 times. The numbers troubled Woolman, because he thought Quakers should try to settle their disputes more gently.[4]

Since the earliest days of the religious society, Quaker ministers had cautioned against an excessive reliance on the formal mechanisms of law enforcement, but in the Delaware Valley the Seven Years' War deepened Friends' concerns. A turning point came in June 1756, when six Quaker members of the Pennsylvania Assembly gave up their seats. In explaining their decision, the assemblymen made it clear that they did not feel guilty about any votes they had cast, but they believed that they had abetted the evil actions of others by attending and providing the legislature a quorum. Their mere presence at the State House had made it easier for other legislators to pass pernicious wartime laws. Not all Pennsylvania Quaker assemblymen resigned in 1756, but the Friends who remained in the legislature found themselves outnumbered, and many Quakers began to think about the assembly in less sympathetic terms.[5]

Against this background in the late 1750s, reformers like Woolman increasingly doubted the wisdom of pursuing legislation as a strategy for effecting change. Many came to believe that they could advance their reform agenda without the aid of government. Woolman in particular began to argue that the civil authorities held far less power than most people pretended. Governments merely responded to pervasive evil tendencies in human societies. It was avarice, he insisted, that deadened souls and led to violence. Discussing the problem of warfare in sweeping historical terms, he described an aggregation of waste. "Numbers of people are hurried on, striving to collect treasures" of no intrinsic worth. Their misguided acquisitiveness eventually provoked them to contend with one another "even unto blood." In mobilization, "great numbers of men are often separated from tilling the earth and useful employ to defend what contending parties mutually claim as their interest." The prosecution of wars redirected the labors not only of the soldiers but also of those who provided "the food those armies eat, the garments they wear, their wages, vessels to transport them from place to place, and support for the maimed. . . . In the raising of great armies, and supporting them, much labor becomes necessary, and in the long continuation of these things, the yoke lies heavy on many poor people." Farmers and others were overworked "supporting those employed in military affairs," and in eighteenth-century North America the resulting labor shortage promoted an escalation in the slave trade. Thus warfare created "scenes of sorrow and distress" even far from the field of combat.[6] Woolman's analysis was informed by the Quakers' debates over various forms of civilian complicity in military action. He looked beyond government in assigning the blame for the Seven Years' War.

The war years from 1754 to 1763 were a time of transition for Woolman, as he examined his life with increasing comprehensiveness to determine whether he was implicitly contributing to organized violence. He came to believe that "selfishness" was the "original cause" of all humanity's wars, and that warfare affected nearly every aspect of life. Therefore peace could be achieved only after the structure of the economy changed. Woolman wanted to renounce all forms of selfishness and violence, and hoped that others would follow his example. He asked his fellow Quakers to "look upon our treasures and the furniture of our houses and the garments in which we array ourselves and try whether the seeds of war have any nourishments in these our possessions or not."[7]

*   *   *

Gunpowder and shot were never a large part of Woolman's business as a shopkeeper, but he gave up selling them abruptly in spring 1755. The last man to purchase powder or ammunition at Woolman's shop was a Quaker man named Daniel Gaskill, who purchased shot from him in April 1755. Gaskill also bought fishhooks on that occasion, and it is likely that he used his firearm, like his fishing tackle, to get food for his family.[8] Outside the context of the Seven Years' War, this might have seemed like an innocent activity, but after the conflict began Woolman grew cautious about selling lethal equipment even to pacifist customers. He did not want to supply the military directly or indirectly. It is possible also that he was reconsidering the propriety of hunting. The trauma of the war convinced Woolman's neighbor Joshua Evans that hunting, and meat-eating generally, violated the Quakers' peace testimony.[9] Woolman did not condemn meat-eating, but he never sold powder or shot again. In his only comment on hunting in his journal, he suggested that it was an indulgent, unnecessary activity, a "vain delight."[10]

In his writings, Woolman never explained why he stopped selling gunpowder. By contrast, he had much to say about his earlier decision to remove rum from his shelves. Rum may have merited more commentary because it was associated with several distinct kinds of violence, all of which Woolman unreservedly condemned. Rum sales may also have mattered more to him because they constituted a significant part of his business. Woolman had not opened his shop with the purpose of becoming a liquor purveyor, but local retailers were expected to offer rum by the gallon or more to keep their customers satisfied. "It was the practice of shop-keepers to sell rum," David Ferris remembered, "and I was told that if I did not conform to it, I need not expect to do any business of importance."[11] Figure 10 traces the monthly incidence of rum sales at Woolman's shop from February 1753 through November 1754.

Woolman stopped selling rum at the end of November 1754. His ledger books record only two subsequent sales, both in June 1755, one of them to his brother Asher.[12] The spike in Woolman's rum sales in November 1754 suggests that he stopped selling the liquor deliberately. Indeed, he may have briefly increased the volume of his sales in order to dispose of his stocks.

While it is clear that Woolman made a conscious decision to stop his rum sales, there is no single explanation why. Looking back on the decision in 1769, he indicated that his initial concern had been to discourage drunkenness. He grew more worried about the origins of the rum later in the 1750s and 1760s, after becoming "further informed" about the conditions of slaves' lives in the Caribbean.[13] The journals of other Quakers can help us reconstruct this chronology more precisely. Abner Woolman writes, "In the days of my youth I was in the practice of using sugar and other West India produce without thinking much on the manner of its being raised and made." This began to change for Abner in 1758, when he was "repeatedly and credibly informed that the labor" involved in the production of these goods was "chiefly performed

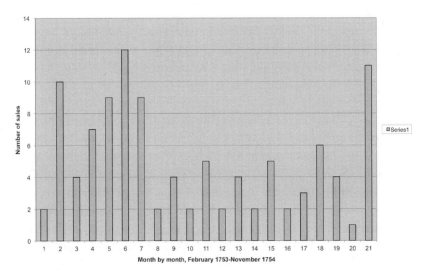

Figure 10. Rum sales in John Woolman's shop.

by slaves who are under oppression, many of whom were taken by violence from their native land, which with me is a sufficient reason to decline using the West India produce."[14] Joshua Evans indicates that he became acutely aware of the sufferings of the Caribbean slaves only in 1761, when he became deeply troubled by what he learned, and felt haunted "day and night" by the "cries of the slaves in the West-India Islands." It was then he resolved to refrain from using sugar, molasses, or rum.[15]

Woolman's first antislavery pamphlet in 1754 had maintained its focus on North America, but in subsequent months and years the Quakers' debate over slavery had expanded its geographical reach. The Philadelphia Yearly Meeting *Epistle of Caution and Advice* drew attention to the impact of the slave trade on Africa, and Woolman's account of his informal conversations in Virginia in 1757 suggest that the conditions of life in Africa had become a focus of the argument over slavery in many communities. The slaves' lives in the West Indies drew less attention in the 1750s, but the antislavery reformers' repeated invocation of the rules against acquiring the spoils of war tied their slavery argument to contemporary wartime violence in the Caribbean Sea. The plunder argument also invited Quakers to examine their behavior as consumers, and ask whether they were profiting from misery elsewhere.

As early as the seventeenth century, a few antislavery Quakers had argued that enslavement was a form of theft, and that those who benefited from
the slave trade were in effect receiving stolen goods and guilty of larceny.[16]
In 1737 Benjamin Lay had extended this argument by specifically associating
rum with slavery and suggesting that Pennsylvania should stop importing the
product from the West Indies.[17] Lay has been identified as "perhaps the earliest
abstainer from slave products," but in actuality he refrained from such a wide
variety of indulgences and comforts that the antislavery message implicit in
his behavior was subsumed within a wider call for moral reform.[18] Beginning
in the 1740s, in effect following Lay's advice, a few Quaker shopkeepers began
removing rum from their shelves. Ferris stopped selling rum in 1742, and he
would eventually become an ardent opponent of slavery, but by his own account he abandoned the rum trade primarily because he wanted to promote
sobriety, austerity, and righteousness.[19] Woolman, like Ferris, had multiple reasons for declining to sell rum, but by the 1760s he had come to believe that
he could express an uncompromising opposition to slavery by rejecting the
"fruits of the labor of slaves."[20] He explained his thinking in general terms in
his second published antislavery essay in 1762. "Seed sewn with the tears of a
confined oppressed people, harvest cut down by an overborne discontented
reaper, makes bread less sweet to an honest man."[21]

Woolman wanted to be an honest man, and his logic suggested that he
should avoid a wide array of products, including not just sugar, molasses,
and rum, but also tobacco, locally produced iron, and wheat grown using
slave labor in New Jersey, Pennsylvania, and Maryland. He never came close
to maintaining such a comprehensive boycott, however. Indeed, his ledger
books show that as late as 1764 he was still willing to accept sugar, molasses,
and rum from customers who offered to settle their debts to him in kind.[22]
Despite his resolution to abstain, he was still using those products. Evans had
similar difficulty, and drank rum occasionally as late as 1774.[23] Sugar, molasses,
and rum were so prominent in the diet and customs of the Delaware Valley
Quakers that even the most adamant opponents of slavery had trouble avoiding them. When Woolman's North Carolina cousin William Hunt attended
Philadelphia Yearly Meeting in 1761, he did not want to ingest the produce of
slave labor, but he discovered to his horror that he could "scarce eat or drink
anything lest I should partake of the gain of oppression."[24]

Woolman, Evans, and Hunt learned through experience how difficult
it could be to send a message through consumer behavior. As Hunt's comments indicate, a boycott of slave produce, if pursued with rigorous logical

consistency, would require a renunciation of many activities sponsored by Quaker meetings. Indeed the meetings themselves derived a significant part of their revenue from the "fruits of the labor of slaves." In 1758 Philadelphia Yearly Meeting banned slave traders from contributing to the meeting's coffers, but masters who were not "concerned in importing selling or purchasing slaves" continued to donate.[25] Therefore in 1762, when Woolman's second antislavery pamphlet appeared in print, he secured approval for the publication from the Overseers of the Press, but refused to allow Philadelphia Yearly Meeting to pay for the expense of printing and distributing the piece. Nor did he want any copies sent free to the local meetings. He knew that the meetings collected contributions from slave owners, and so he did not trust them to distribute his essay widely. He worried that some slave owners might think that since their donations had contributed to the cost of the essay, they could control its distribution. Masters might seize all the available copies to prevent their literate slaves from reading it. Woolman decided against the normal practice of having the pamphlet sent in bundles to Quaker meetings across the Delaware Valley, and instead used his own funds to employ the services of the printers Benjamin Franklin and David Hall. An advertisement for his work appeared in the *Pennsylvania Gazette* indicating that it was available to the general public at David Hall's shop in Philadelphia for seven pence.[26] The Overseers of the Press distributed their own advertisement indicating that if any meetings wanted copies of the essay they could get them in Philadelphia for a price at Hall's shop, another store owned by a Quaker on Market Street, or the home of the clerk of the meeting.[27]

Woolman's rejection of funds from the meeting reflected a shift in his thinking that had begun in 1757 when he refused the free hospitality of slave masters. He was growing skeptical of some of his religious society's standards of behavior. While visiting slaveholding Quakers in New Jeresey and Pennsylvania in the late 1750s and early 1760s, he was disturbed by the insidious power of conventionality, and he resolved to disentangle himself from those Quaker "customs" which were "distinguishable from pure wisdom."[28] In particular he reexamined his clothes. The traditional Quaker costume was austere, but it did have unnecessary decorative elements. It was made of dyed material and sported collars and cuffs.[29] Woolman decided to give up dyed clothing in June 1761, but nine months passed before he changed the way he dressed. He found the courage to do so after attending a meeting of ministers and elders in Philadelphia where several respected British and American Friends condemned "libertinism" among the Quakers.[30]

JOHN PEMBERTON.

HENRY DRINKER.

JAMES PEMBERTON.

JOHN PARRISH.

Figure 11. Four noted eighteenth-century Philadelphia Quakers in conventional Friends dress. From Amelia Mott Gummere, *The Quaker: A Study in Costume* (Philadelphia: Ferris & Leach, 1901), 72.

Woolman acquired his new costume in pieces, beginning with a hat that retained "the natural color of the fur." That hat worried him because in the early 1760s white beaver hats were popular among "some who were fond of following the changeable modes of dress," and he did not want to be fashionable. He would conform less and less to prevailing clothing styles over the next several months as he gradually wore out his remaining colored garments and replaced them with undyed, off-white clothes. Initially Woolman found it difficult to wear this new costume. He worried that other Quakers might interpret his clothing as an affectation, and for the first few weeks his self-consciousness made it difficult for him to wear his clothes in public and speak. Eventually, however, he "felt an inward consolation," and by the end of 1762 he had become confident enough to tell any Quakers who asked him that he wore white garments in obedience to God's will.[31]

Woolman designed and chose his clothes with expense and "serviceability" in mind. To keep costs down, he rejected useless appendages such as cuffs, ruffles, and collars. He objected to cloth dyes because he thought that they damaged cotton, linen, and wool.[32] According to one description,

> His shoes were of uncured leather, tied with leather strings, his stockings of white yarn, his coat, waistcoat, and breeches of a strong kind of cloth undyed, the natural color of the wool, the buttons of wood with brass shanks; his shirt of cotton unbleached, about 14d. per yard, fastened at the neck with three large buttons of the same stuff, without either cravat or handkerchief about his neck; his hat a very good one was white.

Many of those who met him were fascinated by his outfit, and their descriptions of his clothing were meticulous, even if they varied slightly. One witness asserted Woolman's hat was "drab"; another claimed that the buttons on his coat were made of wool. One writer indicated that his shirt was "coarse raw linen," and his "coat, waistcoat and breeches" were made from a "white coarse woolen cloth." All agreed he had "no cuffs to his coat." Two witnesses were struck by Woolman's failure to wear a "neck-cloth"; another was impressed by the absence of buckles on his shoes. Nonetheless, every surviving description of his clothing agrees on one point: "he was all white."[33]

Woolman saw his clothing as a manifestation of his lowliness, his willingness to distance himself from those around him, and his ultimate devotion to God. Since the mid-seventeenth century Quaker ministers had occasionally concluded that God required them to violate social norms, sometimes to the point of embarrassment. Early in his career as a minister, George Fox had walked through Litchfield with stockings on his feet but no shoes, pronouncing, "woe unto the bloody city of Litchfield."[34] Other early Quakers, imbued with millenarian enthusiasm, had worn sackcloth and ashes, or preached in so little clothing that they were described by contemporaries as naked.[35] Strangely dressed prophetic figures continued to arise from among Quaker meetings in the eighteenth century. In the 1750s, an itinerant Quaker preacher named Joseph Rule tried to enter Buckingham Palace dressed in white robes that resembled, it was said, the clothing worn by the "patriarchs" and "old phi-losophers."[36] Woolman differed from these earlier figures in that he wanted his costume to be emulated. When Fox preached barefoot he had not expected his listeners to give up their shoes, and Rule had never advocated general use of togas. Woolman, by contrast, condemned the practices of the textile industry and the currents of contemporary fashion. He wanted others to dress like him, or at least to stop using dyes.

Woolman associated colorful clothing with self-aggrandizement, compet-itiveness, injustice, impoverishment, triviality, and impiety, a catalog of evils he identified as "the unquiet spirit in which wars are generally carried on."[37] While he insisted that fashionable clothing promoted violence and greed, he wore his stark, practical outfit as a sign of commitment to an alternative ap-proach to life. Woolman associated white clothing with moral purity; he also valued whiteness because it accentuated stains.[38] His avoidance of dyed cloth was the principal reason his clothes were so white, but he was also conscien-tious about keeping himself clean.[39] He believed that white garments kept a person honest because they required constant cleanliness, while colored or patterned textiles disguised dirt.[40] Woolman's clothing demanded the kind of meticulousness he sought to maintain in all aspects of life. He believed that if others followed his example, not only in his clothing but in his entire manner of living, the global economy could be rebuilt on new foundations, satisfying humanity's material needs without exploitation, warfare, or slavery.

As with the boycott of rum, there were North American precedents for Woolman's effort to promote simple clothes. In the late seventeenth century, antislavery activist Thomas Tryon had advised the Quaker colonists in Penn-sylvania and New Jersey to dress only in locally made textiles, with natural, locally produced colors, as part of his broad scheme to promote a just and sim-ple economy.[41] Similarly in the 1730s, two of the most prominent opponents of slavery in the Delaware Valley had expressed their convictions by wearing coarse and unadorned costumes. Ralph Sandiford insisted on wearing cloth-ing "of the natural color of the material," while Benjamin Lay went barefoot and wore "tow trousers and a tow coat, very much darned."[42]

Woolman discussed his objections to colored clothing in an essay entitled "A Plea for the Poor."[43] The essay was not published in his lifetime, but he showed it to others in manuscript form, and on a few occasions he discussed his objections to cloth dyes with his fellow Quakers. For the most part, how-ever, he let his clothes speak for themselves. As he explained his strategy to someone who challenged him, he believed he had a duty to "bear testimony not in words only, but to be a sign to the people."[44] Some of his associates understood and embraced his message. His brother Abner, for example, responded enthusiastically, declaring "the Most High at this time is calling to some and moving upon their hearts, to forsake some of their acquaintance and the use of costly apparel and died colors, which once they delighted in. The ways of the Most High are wonderful."[45]

Around the same time that Woolman decided to avoid cloth dyes, Joshua Evans came to a similar resolution and began wearing clothing "of domestic fabrication, altogether in its natural color, and clear of superfluous appendages."[46] By dressing this way Evans demonstrated, as he put it, that he was "willing to be accounted a fool." His clothing dramatized his self-deprecation, serving as a declaration of his rejection of trivial fashion and his wholehearted devotion to God. But like Woolman, Evans did not merely want to stand apart. He advanced general arguments against patterned and colored clothes. He argued that colorful garments were deceitful because they hid dirt, and that cloth dyes damaged linen and wool. More generally, he thought that dying cloth was a wasteful diversion of economic resources. Wearing undyed clothing became an element in Evans's broad project for economic and spiritual reform, his vision of a future without exploitation or slavery. His inexpensive, utilitarian, unfashionable clothing humbled him. Evans advocated humility not only as an intrinsic virtue but also with the conviction that, if everyone avoided self-indulgence, the "hungry would be fed, and the naked, clothed."[47]

Woolman's clothing distinguished him from other Quakers, and his costume signaled a shift in his ministerial career in the early 1760s. From 1761 forward, he sought to promote peace, humility, and compassion not only through his economic activity, his spoken and published words, and his social interactions, but more immediately and instantaneously through his unusual appearance. He believed he was answering the charge Fox had given to Quaker ministers a century earlier, to make their "carriage and life . . . preach among all sorts of people, and to them."[48] Woolman's clothes, however, did not always preach effectively. They confused many Friends who could not comprehend why he dressed the way that he did. Some found his clothing distracting and even ridiculous. When George Churchman saw Woolman give ministry in rural Pennsylvania in 1767, he judged that "The authority of truth came over in some degree, though a wrong spirit was not altogether quashed in some unredeemed members." With "so much stupidity" in the meetinghouse, "it seemed a trying season to the upright hearted."[49]

Woolman remained a faithful Quaker, but his pursuit of moral consistency and his resolution to stand out as a "sign" sometimes interfered with his ability to cooperate with other Friends. This problem surfaced, for example, in 1763, when Woolman went to see Papunhank. The Friendly Association had wanted to send an emissary to Wyalusing for some time, in part because they had received indications that Papunhank might not be able to answer their expectations of him. Woolman was willing to take the trip, but he had his own reasons for going, and his performance on that occasion did not satisfy the Friendly Association's needs. He did not gather much useful intelligence. In order to understand the political context for Woolman's trip, and the idiosyncrasy of his behavior on that occasion, it is necessary to review the shifts in Papunhank's relationship to the Quakers between 1761 and 1763.

When Papunhank first visited Philadelphia in 1760, the Quakers who met him were excited by the ways in which his beliefs seemed to mirror their own. Over the next few years, when they recounted their meetings with him and assembled collections of his sayings, they emphasized the ways in which he resembled them, while neglecting possible differences. Their eagerness to project their own beliefs onto Papunhank was obvious. London Yearly Meeting responded to Delaware Valley Quakers' reports of Papunhank's visits by warning them that there was much about the Indians they did not know and specifically much about the Indians' religious experience that was beyond their comprehension or influence. The Quakers who saw Papunhank outside Philadelphia had reason to take this advice seriously. In places where Indians outnumbered Quakers, Papunhank behaved much less like a member of the Society of Friends.

Israel Pemberton visited one of Papunhank's religious ceremonies during the 1761 treaty gathering at Easton. He described the event in a letter to his wife, a letter that served as the basis for an account of the event in the official reports of the Friendly Association and was republished much later by a Quaker missionary organization. In the letter, Pemberton recounted Papunhank's oral performance in dramatic terms. He strained to find a way to describe what Papunhank did with his hands, indicating that "He sat all the time, but with his hands exposed as much as could be well done that way." He also reported that Papunhank preached so loudly that he could be heard not only in the cabin where he sat, but in several others nearby where women and children waited to hear his words. Pemberton was intrigued by the apparently exotic elements in this performance. The account he sent to his wife circulated widely, but only in a heavily edited form. The redacted versions omitted the peculiar details, not mentioning Papunhank's hands and leaving the impression that he spoke with all the worshippers gathered together in one room. Quaker ministers rarely reached Papunhank's decibels, and they did not have his way of speaking with his hands. Thus, the Friendly Association and later missionary groups made Papunhank's mode of worship seem more like the meetings for worship commonly held by Quakers.[50]

Something similar happened in connection with Papunhank's stance on gift-giving and trade. At his first two appearances before the governor of Pennsylvania, in Philadelphia in 1760 and again at Easton in 1761, Papunhank had refused to receive the governor's gifts, declaring that the prospect frightened him because he was unworthy of the honor. He was not a powerful leader and did not want anyone to think that he sought to become one. Papunhank was not opposed to receiving presents in other contexts, however. Indeed, in his dealings with the Friendly Association, he insisted that exchange of gifts was an essential component of good relations.[51] He left Philadelphia in 1760 with an assortment of fancy items the Friendly Association had given him, including fine garments and gilt boxes.[52] In 1761 he surprised the Quakers at Easton by offering them more than 50 beaver skins and several other pelts. After an awkward period of consultation, the Quaker delegation accepted the gifts and at the end of the gathering gave "Papunhank's Company" a bundle of items including blue cloth, shirts, and some cash.[53]

Over the long term, Papunhank wanted to encourage an expansion of trade as a way to advance the interests of the people of Wyalusing. In 1761 he actively solicited fur traders, hoping to find someone willing to establish a permanent post in his town.[54] The Quakers, as a group, were divided in their attitudes toward commerce, but the published accounts of Papunhank's views were drafted by austere proponents of simplicity like Anthony Benezet, who wanted to hear Papunhank oppose acquisitiveness. When they recounted his statements on gift-giving, they repeated only Papunhank's cautionary words, and left the impression that he feared the corrupting influence of all worldly goods.[55] When Nathaniel Holland, a Quaker trader living in Shamokin, learned that Papunhank was encouraging fur traders to come to Wyalusing, he sent a warning to Benezet. He also spoke through an interpreter to Papunhank, advising him that it would be a mistake for the inhabitants of Wyalusing to "suffer men of bad practices to come among them as they professed to be a religious people."[56]

Holland was worried that Papunhank might be vulnerable to corrupting influences, but he also knew Wyalusing was a complex and divided community. Even if Papunhank maintained fidelity to his principles, he had to adjust to social and political pressures to survive. On at least one occasion he had disappointed the Quakers. In advance of the gathering at Easton, the governor had asked him to locate and return all the colonial-born captives living among the Munsee. The Friendly Association had touted its ability to facilitate return of captives as one its most valuable services to Pennsylvania.[57] At Easton Papunhank told the governor that "some of the prisoners" were still at Wyalusing, but he would not return any of them until he was certain that he could bring back them all.[58] The process of repatriating captives had become difficult because many of the children adopted into Indian families preferred to stay in their new homes. At the close of the treaty gathering, a young girl who had been given up by another Indian group was assigned to the temporary custody of Susannah Hatton, but escaped and fled with her adoptive Indian mother. Papunhank joined a search party and set out after the girl but could not find her. In their official report on the incident, the directors of the Friendly Association admitted that "most of the children" who had been returned to colonial society were unhappy and preferred "to live with the Indians."[59]

Later that year, Papunhank confronted several heads of households in Wyalusing and demanded that they give up the colonial-born captives living in their families. After the masters refused to give the captives up, Papunhank demanded that they leave the town. Tensions were rising in Wyalusing, and Papunhank's troubles increased after an Indian man who had attended the Easton conference was killed by hostile settlers on his way home. Delaware war parties sought retribution by raiding the nearby colonists' farms, seizing horses, and threatening more severe violence. Papunhank opposed them and sent the Friendly Association and the governor of Pennsylvania reports of the warriors' activities. Then, in the late autumn of 1761, Papunhank was attacked. He received a gash to his neck and a nearly crippling wound to his arm. For a while the Quakers believed his wounds would kill him, but Papunhank recovered slowly, and spent much of that winter in Shamokin, dependent for a season on Quaker protection and support. He returned to Wyalusing in the spring of 1762, and the Quakers had heard very little of him since.[60]

The Friendly Association wanted information on Papunhank, and as a group they were greatly relieved late in the autumn of 1762 when Woolman began seeking approval to visit Wyalusing. Burlington Monthly Meeting endorsed his plans, and in March 1763 the ministers and elders of Philadelphia Yearly Meeting gave their support, declaring that Woolman, dressed in white, should go as a "minister of our Lord Jesus Christ." The meeting drafted a document for him to use like the traveling certificates normally issued to Quaker ministers planning to visit other meetings. It was a special minute addressed to "Papahounoal and other religiously inclined Indians at or near Wyhaousin." Though Papunhank was not a Quaker, and there was no formal meeting at Wyalusing, the Philadelphia Quakers gave Woolman a copy of their minute so that he could present it to his hosts upon his arrival.[61]

In May 1763, when Woolman learned that three Indian women and one man from near Wyalusing were in Philadelphia and preparing to return home, he met with them. Discerning that they were "sober people," he asked them to guide him to the town. His intentions at that time were simple. "Love was the first motion," he remembered, "and then a concern arose to spend some time with the Indians, that I might feel and understand their life, and the spirit they live in." He thought that he might "receive some instruction from them" and that they in turn could be "helped forward by my following the leadings of truth amongst them."[62]

Woolman's motivations became more complicated in the days leading up to his trip. Tensions were rising along the Pennsylvania frontier, and "traveling appeared perilous." The thought of going west started to frighten Woolman, and even before he left home the journey became a test of his faith. He decided that he should demonstrate his obedience to God's will. On his last Sunday afternoon at the Mount Holly meetinghouse he rose and quoted a Psalm, declaring to those around him that although he was facing danger, he took comfort from the knowledge that the "the angel of the Lord encampeth round about them that fear him." On the day before he left, reports arrived in Philadelphia of widespread combat in the west. This was the start of Pontiac's War. Some of the Quakers who had previously approved of Woolman's journey reassessed the wisdom of his trip, and they went to Mount Holly to warn him not to go. They summoned him out of his bed and took him to a public house, where they told him that "the Indians had taken a fort from the English westward, and slain and scalped English people in divers places." Woolman returned home to bed, and waited until the next morning before mentioning the warning to Sarah. She felt "deeply concerned about it," and the two of them considered the matter for a "few hours." In the end, John became "settled in a belief" that it was his duty to proceed. Sarah "bore it with a good degree of resignation," and later that day he left.[63]

It is not clear whether the leaders of the Friendly Association were among those who favored a postponement, but once Woolman had resolved to continue with his journey, the group took a particular interest in his progress. Israel Pemberton traveled with him for a day at the start of his trip, and another member of the Friendly Association, William Lightfoot, accompanied him as far as Bethlehem, as did Pemberton's brother John. Another Quaker, Benjamin Parvin, remained by Woolman's side the rest of the way. Woolman's four Indian guides stayed with them for the entire journey, and Woolman was also joined along the path by Job Chillaway, who spoke both Munsee and English and who had experience negotiating encounters between colonists and Indians. Chillaway stayed with Woolman's party until it reached Wyalusing, but then left, expressing regret but pleading he had to hurry to warn "the inhabitants to the westward" of the danger of attack. With Chillaway gone, Woolman and his companions were left without the aid of an experienced translator.[64]

It took Woolman eleven days to reach Wyalusing. After his first night in the woods, he arose feeling muddy and unwell. It rained for several days, and one day the weather was so unpleasant that he and his companions never left their tents. When they could, they rode horses, following a well-traveled path, but they found the way "much grown up with bushes and interrupted by abundance of trees lying across it." They led their horses through swamps, confronted rattlesnakes, and crossed ridges where "the roughness of the stones and the cavities between them and the steepness of the hills" made the passage seem dangerous. More discouraging still were the stories they heard. Three days before they reached Wyalusing they were told "of the Indians taking an English fort westward and destroying the people." It was said that the warriors were planning more attacks. One party had arrived not far from Wyalusing displaying "two English scalps" and announcing that "it was war with the English."[65]

Woolman did not witness any bloodshed. By his own account, the closest he came to the fighting was an awkward moment when he startled an Indian man who reached for his hatchet, but that episode ended amicably. The man had "no other intent than to be in readiness in case any violence was offered to him," and after the two men looked at each other more closely, they relaxed. Nonetheless, although he successfully negotiated that encounter, Woolman remained apprehensive until he reached Wyalusing. The thought of falling captive to the Indians was "grievous" to him. He feared that "they, being strong and hardy, might demand service of me beyond what I could bear." On good days he felt that his "will and desires" were "broken." He achieved "a state of perfect resignation" and was ready to follow God's directions "wheresoever" they might lead. At other times, though, he wavered. On the day before he reached Wyalusing, he learned that three warriors had recently come into the area announcing their intention to attack the English in Juniata. The shock of hearing this news, he conceded, was a "fresh trial of my faith."[66]

On his way to Wyalusing, Woolman saw pictographs on the sides of trees, "mostly in red but some with black" which he interpreted as "representations of men going to and returning from the wars, and of some killed in battle." He saw these images as "Indian histories," and the sight of them led him to think on

> the innumerable afflictions which the proud, fierce spirit produceth in the world—thinking on the toils and fatigues of warriors traveling over mountains and deserts, thinking on their miseries and distresses when wounded far from home by their enemies, and of their bruises and great weariness in chasing one another over the rocks and mountains, and of their restless, unquiet state of mind who live in this spirit, and of the hatred which mutually grows up in the minds of the children of those nations engaged in war with each other.

His analysis of the lives of the Indians in the mountains paralleled his interpretation of the slaveholding society of the American south. In both contexts he placed great emphasis on the pernicious influence of bad behavior, which over the course of generations established evil customs that were difficult to break.[67]

Woolman's discomfort and apprehension led him to think expansively about the experience of those around him. He knew that many of the older people he met, or their parents, grandparents, or more distant ancestors, had lived by streams rich with fish on the fertile coastal plains of the Atlantic. They had moved west only after the arrival of European settlers, and their endeavor to survive on "barren hills" had reordered their way of life. He lamented the dubious practices of colonial fur traders and land dealers who had encouraged men to abandon their families in the pursuit of game, distributed liquor, and repeatedly convinced Indian communities to make overhasty and ill-advised retreats. The Indians had fled, but it seemed that they had found no refuge in the mountains. On a hillside five days away from Wyalusing, Woolman imagined he saw the continent before him. "I had a prospect of the English along the coast for upward of nine hundred miles where I have traveled. And the favorable situation of the English and the difficulties attending the natives in many places, and the Negroes, were open before me. And a weighty and heavenly care came over my mind, and love filled my heart toward all mankind."[68]

Woolman hoped that the Quakers, by setting a good example, could alter the lives of those who met them. He had specific ideas about how the Indians' lives might be changed for the better. Having given up their best lands for "trifling considerations," they had been lured into trading practices that harmed them. Woolman observed that their "manner of clothing themselves" was "altered from what it once was," and they were compelled to exert themselves in damaging ways in order to acquire clothes. Their hunters had to "pass over mountains, swamps, and barren deserts, where traveling is very troublesome, in bringing their skins and furs to trade with us." Still greater damage was done to them when they exchanged their skins for rum, which deprived them of their reason and resulted in violent outbursts and resentments that were "frequently of long continuance." Indian men were induced to "waste their skins and furs in purchasing a liquor which tends to the ruin of them and their families." After exhausting journeys in the pursuit of game, they were left without the "necessities of life," and became "angry with those who for the sake of gain took the advantage of their weakness."[69]

Woolman and Parvin were overtaken on their way to Wyalusing by a Moravian missionary, David Zeisberger. Zeisberger spoke German, but with the aid of German-speaking Indian interpreters he could speak to the local Indians with much more facility than the Quakers could. By the time Woolman's party arrived at Wyalusing, Zeisberger had already moved into Papunhank's large house at the center of the town and had declared that he was ready to stay as long as he remained welcome.[70] Woolman felt weak when he came to Wyalusing, and he sensed that he "appeared inferior to many amongst the Indians." Nonetheless, he was relieved to have arrived, and felt "inwardly joyful" because God had preserved him.[71]

Woolman described Wyalusing as a compact settlement of approximately forty wooden houses with bark roofs.[72] As he approached, he was greeted by a woman carrying a baby who had heard he was coming. She spoke briefly with his guides to confirm his identity. Then Woolman sat down on a log next to Parvin "in a deep inward stillness," and the woman came over and sat near them. According to Woolman's journal, the three of them felt a "great awfulness coming over us." They "rejoiced in a sense of God's love manifested to our poor souls." They did not speak to each other. Woolman's guides had gone into the town; they had no interpreter and no common language.[73]

During his stay at Wyalusing, Woolman worshipped with the Indians alongside Zeisberger. Some of the inhabitants worried that the two men might tussle, but publicly at least, they did not interfere with one another.[74] At the first meeting for worship, Woolman spoke a "few short sentences" to introduce himself, and some of those who heard him understood what he said and translated for the others. On the next evening, however, he felt moved by the presence of "pure gospel love," and "the interpreters, endeavoring to acquaint the people" with what he said, "found some difficulty." Woolman tried to cooperate in the translation process, slowly pronouncing one sentence at a time, but eventually gave up and continued speaking without interruption in English, confident that God, at least, would understand him. After he finished, he saw Papunhank say something unintelligible to one of the interpreters. Later that evening Woolman was told that Papunhank had said, "I love to feel where words come from."[75]

Papunhank seemed to be reiterating what he had said years earlier in Philadelphia, that he had "a feeling sense in my own heart whereby I know when people speak from the head, or when they speak from the heart."[76] His comment in Wyalusing had additional significance for Woolman, however. In Philadelphia, Papunhank had had the aid of translators. Now he was saying that he could sense where Woolman's words came from without knowing specifically what he had said. Papunhank was responding to his physical, spiritually charged presence without comprehending any specific words. This was what Woolman wanted to accomplish by becoming a "sign." He felt reassured that Papunhank had been "helped forward" by seeing him follow "the leadings of truth" in Wyalusing.

Zeisberger was present throughout Woolman's visit. The Moravian's journal presents a skeptical view of the Quakers' interactions with the people of Wyalusing. Woolman acknowledged that his first efforts at communication with the assembled Indians had been awkward, but he insisted that things had gotten better after he asked those who spoke a little English to give up their efforts at translation. Zeisberger, by contrast, did not notice or record the presence of "divine love" on that occasion. On the contrary, he observed that when Woolman spoke to the congregation uninterruptedly in English, the effort seemed "to the Indians to be not very important." Zeisberger also recorded a series of conversations that Woolman did not mention in his journal. He indicated that Papunhank, in Zeisberger's presence and presumably with the help of at least two who could translate, told Woolman and his companion that he intended to join the Moravians. The Quakers reportedly responded that doing so would have no effect, that becoming a Moravian would neither "improve" Papunhank nor do him much harm, "for there were people among all religions who sought and loved God." Papunhank interpreted this comment as suggesting that he and his followers could be Quaker and Moravian simultaneously, and he rejected that option: "If they should adhere to two parties they would only be more confused than before." The conversation, in effect, ended at that point. "The Quakers wished them luck."[77]

The next day, according to Zeisberger's journal, Woolman and Parvin spoke with the Moravian missionary without any Indians present. They told him that they had originally planned to stay in Wyalusing longer, but "the time had grown long for them" and they intended to return home. The Quakers acknowledged that Zeisberger had "taken on a heavy burden," but they questioned the wisdom of offering the Indians baptism. As Zeisberger described it in his journal, "They spoke again with me about baptism, and said we baptized the Indians, but they did not think it important but rather depended upon the inner activity of the spirit." The three men debated this issue among themselves for a few minutes, and later that day the two Quakers left. Five days later, Papunhank received baptism. He formally became a Moravian and remained one for the rest of his life.[78]

Woolman would have liked to have brought the people of Wyalusing closer to Quakerism. In September 1763, after he reported to Philadelphia Yearly Meeting about his visit, that meeting sent the news to London that Woolman had been "affectionately received" by Papunhank and his followers, and that "in the short time he stayed" at the town he had had "several satisfactory meetings with them." But earlier that summer, when Woolman first told the leaders of the Friendly Association about his time in Wyalusing, they were frustrated that he had so little to say. Shortly after leaving the town, Woolman had sent Israel Pemberton a letter that contained little more than the brief assurance that he had seen nothing "in that place which to me appeared like disaffection to the English." On returning to New Jersey, he gave John Pemberton a fuller report, but the Pembertons were disappointed he had spoken so little to the Indians. Woolman had been, as John Pemberton phrased it, "closely engaged to attend to the concern he was engaged in," and he was therefore less interested than he might have been in "questioning the Indians."[79]

From the moment he first learned that his journey might be dangerous, Woolman's principal concern had been to demonstrate the "all sufficiency of God," and God's "care in providing for those that fear him." As he explained it in a letter to Sarah, it had been his "daily labor" during his travels to achieve "full resignedness" to God's will, because he felt certain that if he did so all would "end well." Woolman wanted his journey to demonstrate the efficacy of peace and love. He hoped to show through his own trials and experiences that God would protect and support faithful Christians. After his return he told the ministers and elders in Philadelphia that he had survived "a time of great exercise," but he had "performed his intended visit" and had been "preserved to return without damage." This might have seemed like a small achievement, but it carried special significance in 1763. Woolman had relied on God's protection, and in effect he had performed a practical demonstration of the efficacy of trusting Providence. He believed that through his actions he had reasserted a truth that had been demonstrated before, by the first Quaker settlers in New Jersey and Pennsylvania.[80]

In an epistle he drafted for Philadelphia Yearly Meeting in 1759, Woolman had maintained that God sheltered and strengthened the original Quaker colonists in the Delaware Valley, not only by sustaining them "through the difficulties attending the improvement of a wilderness," but also by finding a place for them "in the hearts of the natives." "It was by the gracious influence of the Holy Spirit," he suggested, that the Quakers had found a way to "work righteously and walk uprightly one toward another and toward the natives, and in life and conversation manifest the excellency of the principles and doctrines of the Christian religion." The assertion that God would touch the hearts of belligerents in order to protect pacifist Quakers carried great political significance during the Seven Years' War, and again in 1763 when warfare tore through western Pennsylvania. While the Society of Friends was divided over the meaning of its peace testimony, many non-Quakers passionately objected to the Quakers' refusal to take up arms. Anglican William Smith was among the most incredulous. Referring to the Quaker pacifists, he fulminated, "Infatuated Enthusiasts! Who made them more righteous or holy than others? Who separated them from the *Men of the Earth*, or set them apart as the CHOSEN OF GOD, to be defended by Miracles, without the ordinary Means? *My soul rises at such horrid Doctrine! I cannot swallow it!*" Smith's rhetoric was heated, but he correctly identified a current within American Quaker pacifism.[81]

The immediate prospects for advancing the cause of peace and Quaker spirituality on Pennsylvania's frontiers deteriorated rapidly after Woolman's visit to Wyalusing. On his way home from the town he passed through Wyoming. He had met Indians from Wyoming on his way out, but when he reached the town on his return he discovered that "the Indians were mostly gone." Delaware leader Teedyuscung had lived there, but had died a few days earlier. It was reported that someone, possibly Iroquois warriors or newly arrived settlers from Connecticut, had set fire to Teedyunscung's cabin while he lay inside asleep, unconscious with his wife in an alcoholic stupor, as their home burned. Following Teedyuscung's death Wyoming's Indian community had abandoned the place, joining a stream of refugees fleeing from the violence associated with Pontiac's War.[82]

Approximately six months later, along with the other residents of Wyalusing, Papunhank was evacuated and taken to an island in the Delaware River near Philadelphia, ostensibly for his own protection. He survived a long subsequent ordeal, as he and his fellow internees were removed from the island, marched northward through New Jersey, and then brought back to Philadelphia and confined in the city barracks after hundreds of angry settlers, known to posterity as the "Paxton Boys," threatened to kill them.[83] After his release Papunhank returned to Wyalusing, and in 1767 the inhabitants sent a message to Philadelphia Yearly Meeting inviting a delegation from the Society of Friends to visit and reaffirm old bonds of friendship. Israel Pemberton summoned some Quaker elders to prepare a response, but the group could not identify anyone "suitable" who was willing to go. Similarly in 1771, another community of Delaware Indians asked the Friendly Association to send them a schoolteacher. By that time the Association had virtually ceased operations, but Pemberton assembled its old directors and asked them if they could identify any "sober" and "religious" teachers ready to live among the Delaware. No names came forward. Woolman took notice of these events. No one formally asked him to answer the call, and he was busy with other matters, but he was convinced the Indians wanted instruction from the Quakers.[84] In 1772 Papunhank left Wyalusing and moved west to help establish a new Moravian mission beyond the Ohio River. Even after he moved to the Ohio Valley he maintained an intermittent correspondence with Quakers in Philadelphia. He professed friendship, but Pennsylvania had become a difficult place for any Indians to live.[85]

The Paxton Boys had threatened Quakers as well as Indians, accusing pacifists within the Society of Friends of exerting excessive political influence and leaving Pennsylvania defenseless. In February 1764, with the rioters massed just north of Philadelphia, several Quakers took up arms to defend themselves from the mob. This episode deeply unsettled the religious community, foreshadowing more controversies to come, as the Quakers struggled to adjust to new, potentially violent forms of political mobilization in New

Jersey and Pennsylvania.[86] Woolman did not comment directly on these events in his journal, but in one entry about an incident in 1764 he discussed both his dismay and his stubborn resolution in the face of worsening conditions in the west. In the fall of that year he hired a man who had been earlier captured by Indians. The man had seen two other captives tortured to death. One of the captives had been pierced with wooden splinters that were subsequently set on fire, and the other had been forced to run around a tree dragging his entrails behind him. Hearing these stories saddened Woolman, but in his journal he wrote that after a good night's sleep, he awoke the next day "with a fresh and living sense of divine love." Warfare, he reminded himself, began when "pride" led to "vanity," which in turn prompted "men to exert their power in requiring that of others" which they themselves would "rather be excused from." He wrote a note to himself, asking whether coercion generated "hard thoughts." Do "hard thoughts when ripe become malice? Does malice when ripe become revengeful," and in the end lead men to "inflict terrible pains on their fellow creatures and spread desolations through the world?" The solution, he concluded, was to remember that "the Prince of Peace is the Lord, that he communicates his unmixed wisdom to his family that they, living in perfect simplicity, may give no offence to any creatures, but may walk as he walked."[87]

Like Woolman, many Quaker reformers retained a millenarian sense of optimism despite the setbacks of the 1760s, but their moralistic understanding of the process of historical change may have ironically undermined their ability to reach out to distant Indians during the later years of that decade. Anxious to retain God's favor in the face of an escalating series of crises, many Quakers who had once been engaged in Indian affairs turned their attention to questions they thought were more closely related to their own personal morality. Some protested against theatrical performances and horse races.[88] Others concentrated on the regulation of marriage, and a few like Woolman devoted most of their energy to the controversies that continued to divide Quaker communities over the slave trade, slaveholding, and the meaning of emancipation.[89]

Woolman appeared before Burlington Monthly Meeting in March 1766 and announced that he "had had an exercise on his mind to visit Friends meetings in the lower counties of Pennsylvania and on the eastern shores of Maryland."[90] The meeting's minutes do not mention Woolman's intention to proceed on foot, but his account of the episode in his journal suggests that he had been thinking about traveling in this way for "several years," and that he had recently revealed his plans to at least some other Quakers. "I believed the Lord moved me to travel on foot amongst them, that by so travelling I might have a more lively feeling of the condition of the oppressed slaves, set an example of lowliness before the eyes of their masters, and be more out of the way of temptation to unprofitable familiarities." One of those he spoke to was his neighbor John Sleeper, who responded by telling Woolman that "he was under a concern to travel the same way."[91] Woolman returned to the Monthly Meeting in April and announced that his trip would be slightly delayed. Sleeper would come with him. The meeting approved of the new plan, and in May the two men set off together. Sleeper's readiness to come along, and his insistence that he had been contemplating such an undertaking before Woolman made his announcement, should serve as a reminder that there were many passionate opponents of slavery among the Quakers in the 1760s, and that a growing number of them were coming to believe that they could help effect change by performing demonstrative gestures.

On the eastern shore of Maryland Woolman and Sleeper met a religious group led by a man named Joseph Nichols, who was not a Quaker but according to Woolman's assessment seemed to profess "nearly the same principles as our Society." In his journal Woolman notes that Nichols's followers were "sober, well-behaved men and women," but he gives no hint of the extent to which their behavior resembled his own.[92] It is possible that they changed their way of living after Woolman left them, for it was only around that time that they began renouncing slaveholding. Soon some of them would make it a policy to refuse hospitality from slave owners and reject "any goods either produced or procured through slave labor."[93] After meeting Woolman the "Nicholites" also started to dress like him. They made it their policy to "keep from making or buying any dyed, striped, flowered, corded or mixed stuff," and to avoid "all needless cuts and fashions" in their clothes.[94] According to a man who visited the Nicholites in 1780, they dressed only in white, strove to "take everything from nature," and refused to listen to anyone who did not conform to these rules. "If a man were to speak like an archangel . . . and wore a black, or colored coat, he would not be received by these people."[95]

Woolman did not claim credit for inspiring the Nicholites. On the contrary, he was excited by the idea that the group had received its own divine inspiration. Nonetheless, it is very likely that the Nicholites were influenced by Woolman, and it is noteworthy that they emulated him only by adopting behaviors that he wanted to promote. They distanced themselves from the slave economy, and they rejected cloth dyes, but they did not begin traveling long distances on foot. Woolman hiked for miles that summer as an experiment and a way to stage a dramatic protest, but he did not consider long-distance walking a sensible mode of transportation under ordinary circumstances. The experience caused him physical pain, and he did not recommend it to others. He believed that God had called on him to make a statement against slavery in this way. He thought of Jesus and his sufferings, and returned to walk through Maryland alone in 1767, and again in 1768.[96]

Just as he had hoped to learn about the Indians by going to Wyalusing, Woolman believed that walking through Maryland would teach him about the lives of the slaves. It is not clear, however, how many slaves he met on those walks. His journal does not mention any. Rather than acquiring knowledge through conversation, he was seeking to gain direct experience by grappling with a practical problem slaves confronted. Just by walking he was trying to educate himself, and at the same time make a better-informed and more effective protest against slavery. To be sure, he knew that it was difficult for a free person to understand the perspective of a slave, especially the views of those who were born overseas. In an unpublished essay he declared that he had found it almost impossible to speak with men and women from Africa. "These poor Africans were people of a strange language and not easy to converse with, and their situation as slaves too generally destroyed that brotherly freedom which frequently subsides between us and inoffensive strangers."[97] He found it easier to speak with individuals who had spent their entire lives in New Jersey. Walking through Maryland was an evocative action, but in the late 1760s Woolman's most instructive encounters with slaves and former slaves occurred at home in Mount Holly.

A few weeks before Woolman left for Wyalusing, William Boen came to him with the news that he had entered into an agreement with his master to secure his freedom. He was preparing to embark on life as a free man, and he wanted to marry a black woman named Dido who lived in Mount Holly. Boen professed sympathy with Quaker principles and indicated that he did not want to live with Dido unless they were married. Woolman in all likelihood knew Dido, because she worked as a servant for his cousin Joseph Burr. He agreed to help and convened a meeting for worship at Burr's home to solemnize the marriage.

John and Sarah Woolman attended the event along with Burr and a few other local Quakers. Dido's parents Catherine and London were there, as were other blacks from the area including Primus, the man Woolman employed to do manual work, and Jem, Thomas Shinn's former slave, whose name appears on the wedding certificate as "Jeams." The blacks present at the event signed their names to the document, or had others write their names for them; this was important because it indicated that they were full participants in the solemnization of the marriage. In validating the match, they were assuming a responsibility usually reserved for religious ministers or members of the Society of Friends.[98] Shortly after the wedding, Boen asked the Mount Holly Meeting to accept him as a Friend and allow him to participate fully in Quaker business, but he was refused. According to the meeting's account of its decision, the "way" was not opened in "Friends' minds" to receive Boen as a member. Instead, the Mount Holly Quakers simply encouraged him to "continue faithful," and by all accounts, he did.[99]

The gathering that Woolman organized to recognize Boen's marriage resembled special meetings for worship that Quakers in Philadelphia had been convening for blacks four times a year since 1756.[100] Such meetings were rarely held in New Jersey, and when blacks attended Friends' ordinary meetings they were assigned a subordinate status. At large meetings they were expected to sit apart. In 1756 the Philadelphia Quakers added a special section for black worshipers in their Second Street meetinghouse.[101] In 1763 Woolman did not insist that blacks receive equal treatment within the Society of Friends, but the help he gave Boen in arranging his marriage represented an important step. Woolman was gaining a more intimate understanding of the problems confronting slaves and freed people. The difficulties they faced in getting married and maintaining stable families had concerned him for years, but in working through the logistics of Boen's wedding he paid attention to details he had never noticed before. Later in the decade he would concentrate on other aspects of the blacks' physical experience in the meetinghouse.

Even though the Mount Holly meeting kept blacks from participating in its decision-making process, slaves and former slaves often came on Sundays for worship. One of those who attended regularly was Jem, the young man whom Woolman, as an executor of the Shinn estate, had sold as a servant bound to labor until age thirty. In spring 1769 Woolman made calculations in his ledger book to determine how long it would take for Jem to gain his freedom. Jem was twenty-four and had at least five more years to serve. On a Sunday in June Woolman sat in the "uppermost seat" in the meetinghouse, looked across the room at Jem, and tried to imagine how the scene appeared from the perspective of God, "that awful being that respecteth not persons nor colors." Underage white servants customarily gained their freedom at twenty-one, and as early as 1754 Woolman had publicly rejected the logic that had been used to justify Jem's extended term of service.[102] Seeing Jem at worship, Woolman perceived that "all was not clear," and he decided that he needed to "make some restitution."[103]

Woolman felt that he owed a personal debt to Jem, and he wanted to pay back precisely what was due. Since there had been two executors working on the Shinn estate, and Jem had been unjustly bound to serve an extra nine years, Woolman decided to pay for half of that extra service. He purchased a bond guaranteeing Jem compensation for four years and six months of labor, to be paid when he gained his freedom.[104] There is no record of Henry Paxson's response to these arrangements. Paxson was the other executor, and Woolman may well have intended to shame him into paying the remaining half of what was due. Woolman's purpose was not merely to settle his own accounts but to set an example for others, and indeed in the long run he hoped to provoke a general discussion of societal reparations.

In the mid-1760s Woolman tried to calculate the debt that might be owed to the heirs of a hypothetical male slave who had been "violently taken from Guinea" at forty and "labored hard till old age." If the man's labor had been worth 50 pounds, his heirs would deserve that sum with interest. Adding 3 percent annual interest and compounding every ten years, Woolman calculated that on the enslaved man's death, his children should receive 141 pounds. "Where persons have been injured as to their outward substance and died without recompense, so that their children are kept out of that which was equitably due to their parents, here such children appear to be justly entitled to receive recompense from that civil society under which their parents suffered."[105] Abner became concerned about the outstanding debts the Quakers owed their former slaves in the late winter of 1768. "I became settled in my mind that if those whose estates were advanced by the labor of slaves would give up freely to have the case examined . . . it would be pleasing to providence and add to their happiness even in this life" to have "equity put in practice." "At this present time," Abner wrote, "there is negroes amongst us who have monies justly due to them from members of our Monthly Meeting."[106] Abner may or may not have had Jem in mind, but John knew that in Jem's case he had behaved like a slave master.

Woolman's conscience often caused him pain, and never more so than in 1769. Even before he calculated his debt to Jem, he was looking back on his life, paying attention to his conduct during the early 1750s, and among his sins he remembered the profits he had made selling sugar, molasses, and rum.

Recognizing that he had indirectly profited from slave labor, he decided that "the small gain I got by this branch of trade should be applied in promoting righteousness in the earth."[107] He knew that "no sum may properly be mentioned as an equal reward for the total deprivation of liberty," but he sensed that he had a debt to settle with the slaves of the Caribbean.[108] Therefore, even though he did not know what he would do when he got there, he decided to sail to Barbados.

Chapter 8

The Deep: Crossing the Sea

> While we were out, the wind rising high, the waves several times
> beat over us, that to me it appeared dangerous, but my mind was at
> that time turned to him who made and governs the deep, and my
> life was resigned to him.
> —John Woolman, *Journal*, chapter 7

WOOLMAN'S VIEW OF travel across the ocean darkened over the course of his life. With his boyhood home near the Delaware River and the port of Burlington only a few miles away, he grew up familiar with long-distance sailing ships. His first experience on the open seas came when he traveled to New England at age twenty-six. He recounted that trip in his journal with a precision that reflected an element of excitement. He took sailing vessels from Long Island to Connecticut, from Rhode Island to Nantucket and back, and then from New London to Long Island. He calculated that in total he sailed 150 miles.[1] His account of those voyages contains no hint of apprehension or regret. He was more disturbed, and had more to say, after his second passage to New England in 1760. The difference reflects the expansion of his concerns and the redirection of his attention since 1747, as well as the specific incidents during the trip.

In late April 1760, on his way to New London, Woolman survived a rough passage across Long Island Sound in a "large open boat." The wind tossed the vessel, on occasion (it seemed to Woolman) nearly swamping it. "The waves several times beat over us," he wrote. "To me it appeared dangerous." Although frightened, he "turned to him who made and governs the deep" and resigned himself. "I had fresh occasion to consider every day as a day lent to me and felt a renewed engagement to devote my time, and all I had, to him who gave it."[2]

His response to the storm was influenced by Quaker tradition.[3] The Quakers' way of talking and writing about the sea was informed by their reading of the Bible, which, beginning with the first chapter of Genesis and continuing through the story of the flood, the destruction of the Pharaoh's army, Job's description of Leviathan, Jonah's ordeals, the ministry of Jesus on the Sea of Galilee, and the adventures of Paul, repeatedly depicted the open water as a place of incomprehensible power, beyond the capacity of humans to master or control. Furthermore, Quaker ministers knew from experience that sailing could be dangerous, and they insisted that no one should tempt Providence by setting sail at cross-purposes with God. Praying aloud on the decks of ships, traveling ministers proclaimed this principle to everyone within earshot.[4]

Later on that same trip in 1760, Woolman made a slow sail from Rhode Island to Nantucket. The ship captain was hesitant about embarking, and he told his passengers that they would leave only "if the wind be fair and way open to sail."[5] Nonetheless they went and, sailing into slack wind, they barely got away from the mainland. They camped for the night on Naushon Island, on the opposite side of Buzzards Bay. Unable to find adequate lodging on the island, a few of the travelers took beds in a public house, and the rest slept on the floor. Returning to their ship early the next morning, they sailed for Nantucket and nearly got there, but had to row into the harbor in two small boats at the end of the day.[6]

During his five days on Nantucket, Woolman was repeatedly reminded of how unpredictable the weather was, and how risky it could be for the islanders to embark in ships: "I observed many shoals in their bay, which makes sailing more dangerous, especially in stormy nights. I observed also a great shoal which encloses their harbor and prevents their going in with sloops except when the tide is up. Waiting without this shoal for the rising of the tide is sometimes hazardous in storms, and waiting within they sometimes miss a fair wind." When he left the island, Woolman was part of a group of approximately fifty who boarded a ship and then disembarked; the voyage was canceled because of changeable winds. He managed to sail away the next day, on his second attempt.[7]

After he returned to his home to Mount Holly, Woolman continued to think about the time he had spent that summer sailing, and he believed his experiences had been instructive. In the fall he met an English traveling minister named Jane Crosfield, who was planning to take a wintertime trip to New

England. He warned her about the "wide waters" and "high winds usual in the winter." He advised her to consider the example of the Apostle Paul, who was stranded on an island as a consequence of storms and responded by pausing in his travels and doing good where he was. He told her to remember "him who made and commands the winds and the waters," and to be ready to wait if the conditions were bad for traveling. If "high winds or storms sometimes prevent thy going forward so fast as thou could desire, it may be thou may find a service in tarrying."[8] High winds and waves might be manifestations of God's will. Sometimes, paradoxically, the Lord might summon a person *not* to travel, in effect sending someone on a mission by asking the person to stay still. Woolman advised Crosfield to consider the possibility.

Woolman became increasingly apprehensive about sailing just as he was learning more about the evils of transatlantic commerce, beginning with the activities of slave traders at sea. In this regard, his visit to Rhode Island in 1760 was a revelation. With their heavy investments in the slave trade, the Rhode Islanders upset him nearly as much as the Virginians had. While in Rhode Island he struggled to make sure he was never seduced by the slave traders' "affability," "kindness," "superficial friendship," and "smooth conduct." He spent hours with Quaker slave masters, and looking back on his time in Newport he wrote, the "great number of slaves in these parts and the continuance of that trade from there to Guinea made a deep impression on me, and my cries were often put up to my Father in secret that he would enable me to discharge my duty faithfully."[9]

Woolman wrote his second antislavery essay after returning from that New England trip. He finished a draft in November 1761 and sent copies to John Churchman and Israel Pemberton. He also gave the piece to the Overseers of the Press, who sent it to Anthony Benezet for comments.[10] The essay differed markedly from Woolman's first antislavery pamphlet, beginning with the way it framed the issue. Whereas his first antislavery essay had focused on slaveholders in North America, the 1762 essay identified the point of contention as "importing and purchasing the inhabitants of Africa as slaves," and concentrated much of its discussion on the slave trade.[11]

Quoting travelers' accounts, Woolman described the interior of Africa as peaceful and prosperous. He indicated that the Africans "with a little labor raise grain, roots, and pulse to eat, spin and weave cotton, and fasten together the large feathers of fowls to cover their nakedness, many of whom in much simplicity live inoffensive in their cottages and take great comfort in raising up children." This bucolic world was under attack, he suggested, as a consequence of the transatlantic slave trade. Slaving vessels were sites of violence and dehumanizing cruelty. Woolman provided his readers with the description of a ship in which men were transported "standing in the hold, fastened one to another with stakes for fear they should rise and kill the whites." The women were held "between the decks, and those that were with child in the great cabin, the children in the steerage pressed together like herrings in a barrel." He relayed an account of a group of enslaved men who starved themselves during their passage across the ocean, and he retold the story of an African man who leaped from the deck only to drown in the sea.[12] In thus shifting the focus of his analysis of slavery, Woolman was following the lead of Benezet, whose *Observations on the Inslaving, Importing and Purchasing of Negroes*, published in 1759, quoted accounts of ship captains lingering near the African shore and instigating warfare from a distance in order to collect large numbers of slaves.[13] In 1762 Benezet produced a second pamphlet with more detailed accounts of the slave trade.[14]

As Benezet drew Woolman's attention to the dismal role of transatlantic shipping in the operations of the slave trade, so John Churchman dramatically alerted him to the dual function of ships as commercial vehicles and instruments of war. Since the 1740s Churchman had protested against arming merchant vessels, and in the 1750s he became a leading Quaker opponent of slavery. Early in the 1760s Woolman was a witness as these two concerns of Churchman collided. In September 1761 Woolman was attending a meeting of ministers and elders in Philadelphia when Churchman arrived and asked for a certificate authorizing him to visit "Barbados and probably some of the neighboring islands." The ministers and elders supported the idea, and Woolman joined the others in signing a certificate declaring that Churchman would be advancing God's purposes by traveling to the West Indies.[15]

Churchman subsequently fell ill, but recovered and returned to Philadelphia later that autumn to "inquire for a passage."[16] He brought along his wife, his son, his daughter-in-law, and some more distant relatives, all of whom intended to see him off on his trip.[17] After arriving in town and making the necessary inquiries, he was told that there were five ships in the river preparing to leave for the Caribbean, three of which were "near ready to sail." He learned also, however, that all five vessels were "prepared with guns for defense," and he felt a "secret exercise" in his mind against going to inspect them. He thought the matter over for a few days, and then went to a meeting of local Quaker elders where he felt a "singular freedom" to express his views. Churchman told them, "I came to town in order to take my passage for Barbados, but found myself not at liberty to go in any of those vessels, because they carried arms for defense; for as my motive in going was to publish the glad tidings of the Gospel, which teacheth love to all men, I could not go with those who were prepared to destroy men." The elders backed Churchman's judgment, and he pressed the issue further, generalizing from his experience by asking whether it was right for Quakers to own, charter, ship freight on, or insure any ships that mounted guns. He did not receive an immediate reply to this query, but afterward remembered returning to his lodgings with "so much peace of mind in thus bearing my testimony, that I thought if all my concern ended therein, it was worth all my trouble."[18] A few months later, in March 1762, Churchman returned to the larger Meeting that had originally endorsed his itinerary. Woolman was in attendance on that occasion when Churchman "acquainted the meeting with the reasons of his not having yet proceeded on a visit to the West Indies."[19]

Over the next few years Woolman wrote a series of essays examining the bad effects of oceangoing trade and transportation.[20] Most of these pieces were not published in his lifetime. In one instance the Overseers of the Press cautioned him against publication, because he was trying to address too many issues at once.[21] Woolman's concerns were expanding dramatically. By mid-decade he was objecting not only to the operations of armed merchantmen and slaving vessels, but more generally to the voyages of nearly all the ships that sailed the ocean. He maintained that maritime commerce exacerbated pernicious social distinctions, increased poverty and exploitation, and by introducing foodstuffs inappropriate to local climates, imperiled health.[22] He complained that rich men, to pay for "expensive articles, brought from beyond the sea," sent "a great deal of flour and grain abroad out of our country." This had the consequence of making bread and animal feed scarce, and impoverishing "laboring people."[23] He warned that God would punish the colonists of New Jersey and Pennsylvania if they continued to violate his "gracious design" by sending his gifts "abroad in a way of trade."[24] Oceangoing trade also wasted the lives of laborers and sailors. By "giving way to a desire for delicacies, and things fetched far, many men appear to be employed unnecessarily; many ships built by much labor are lost; many people brought to an untimely end; much good produce buried in the seas; many people busied in that which serves chiefly to please a wandering desire, who might better be employed in those affairs which are of real service."[25] Woolman acknowledged the usefulness of some transatlantic shipping. "Laying aside all superfluities and luxuries, while people are so much thicker settled in some parts than in others, a trade in some serviceable articles may be to mutual advantage."[26] Nonetheless he insisted that Christians should engage in "trade and traffic no farther than justice and equity evidently accompanies." Otherwise they might "give offence" to their trading partners, including unconverted peoples in distant lands who were "unable to plead their own cause."[27]

Woolman's displeasure with sailing intensified his opposition to the slave trade. This was dramatically evident in his response to Benezet's 1766 essay *A Caution and a Warning to Great Britain and her Colonies*. While in many ways similar to Benezet's earlier works, the *Caution* was more ambitious in the variety of arguments it advanced, the volume of evidence it presented, and the audience it was intended to reach. Working together, Philadelphia Yearly Meeting and its London counterpart printed thousands of copies of the 1766 pamphlet, delivered one to every sitting Member of Parliament, and sent others in bundles to Quakers on both sides of the Atlantic.[28] Woolman's Meeting in Burlington received forty.[29] The *Caution* cited Christian principles, but in explaining his opposition to slavery Benezet also employed the language of contemporary politics. He asked why "those who distinguish themselves as the Advocates of Liberty" remained "insensible to the treatment of thousands and tens of thousands of our fellow-men." Slaveholding, he asserted, was "inconsistent with every idea of liberty and justice."[30] Benezet objected to slavery in general terms, but in the body of his pamphlet, drawing on travelers' accounts, he concentrated on the circumstances of the slaves in the Caribbean, and on the operations of slave traders off the coast of Africa.

Woolman read the pamphlet closely, copying out long quotations and interspersing them with his own observations based on personal experience, conversations he had had with slaves and masters, and imaginative leaps stemming from his effort to attend to the subject "with a compassionate heart." For example, remembering how difficult it could be to part from one's family to travel by sea, Woolman remarked, "If we consider them [the enslaved Africans] as violently separated from their homes, and from all their most intimate acquaintance, their case appears sorrowful." Slaving vessels, he observed, frequently carried hundreds of slaves. "Even free passengers would meet with difficulty on a long voyage." Imagine what it would be like, he suggested, if the number of passengers on a ship were "equal to a freight of slaves." That would be bad, "but how much greater is the difficulty of these poor sufferers? For this being a scene of violence, the whites in providing against the Negroes rising tie the men to posts in the hold, where they are but poorly accommodated as to bodily nourishment." Woolman thought of ships as places of nausea. "People

not used to the sea are often so sick in rough weather that the operation is frequently as strong as physic." It would be worse for the slaves because "a freight
of slaves" was only "slightly attended." "Through distress of mind, through
the breathing of so many in a close place, and want of necessary accommodations to keep the place sweet and clean, mortal distempers frequently break
out amongst them." Sick people, he observed, need comfort. "In sickness we
have need of help from sympathizing friends, but how calamitous is the case
of these people when sickness thus breaks out amongst them."[31] Woolman
described the suffering of the slaves in transit in very physical terms, and he
was able to do so in part because he imagined them suffering through an ag-
gravated form of an ordeal he had personally endured. He thought of them
riding in a ship.[32]

Woolman's embrace of austerity, love of country life, pacifism, and opposition to slavery all contributed to his disdain for ocean travel and commerce.
Nonetheless, he felt repeatedly drawn to visit places overseas. In summer 1764
he dreamed of going on a "religious visit" to a country "beyond the sea" that
was preparing for a war. In his dream he successfully took the trip and made a
small gesture in favor of peace.[33] Undoubtedly he hoped to perform a similar
service when he resolved to go to the Caribbean in 1769, but first he would
have to get there.

*   *   *

Sarah Woolman became an elder of Philadelphia Yearly Meeting in 1766, and
over the next several years she served in that capacity alongside John.[34] In
March 1769 she was present at the spring meeting of ministers and elders
when John appeared before the gathering and announced that "the pointings
of the Divine finger" had directed him to sail to the Caribbean. The ministers
and elders listened, deliberated among themselves, and then issued a certificate authorizing John to travel as a minister to the "West India Islands."[35] John
began looking for a vessel sailing for the West Indies, but eight days later he
changed his mind and decided he should let the matter rest for a while.[36] He
and Sarah may have discussed the matter privately. "The time of leaving my
family hath not appeared clear to me," he explained.[37] In October he resumed
his search for a ship. He had special bread baked in preparation for his voyage,
and declared optimistically, "I know nothing against going out pretty soon if
way open."[38]

The clerk of Philadelphia Yearly Meeting in 1769 was James Pemberton, a merchant heavily invested in West Indian trade. Pemberton financed and coordinated commercial transactions in widely dispersed ports. He deployed vessels and cargoes on trade routes between the Caribbean islands, imported sugar, rum, and other products into Philadelphia, and facilitated export of rum to more distant markets.[39] Pemberton and Woolman traveled in the same circles. Pemberton's two brothers Israel and John had worked closely with Woolman over the years. Pemberton also knew Uriah Woolman well, and when he heard that John Woolman wanted to go to the Caribbean, he sent him a message using Uriah as courier.[40] In partnership with John Smith, a prominent Quaker merchant in Burlington, Pemberton owned a half inter-est in the brigantine *Rachel*, which was preparing to sail for Barbados.[41] John Smith was the brother of the historian Samuel, and Woolman had known the Smiths for more than twenty years.[42] Woolman responded to Pemberton's message by visiting John Smith twice, first in Burlington and then in Philadel-phia. Smith wanted to take Woolman to see Pemberton on that second occa-sion, but Woolman refused. Instead he went home to Mount Holly, composed a letter, and on a second trip to Philadelphia handed it in person to both Pem-berton and Smith. The letter set forth his reasons for wanting to travel to the West Indies and his concerns about going as a paying passenger on their ship.

In his letter Woolman explained that he had decided to go to the Carib-bean after reading Benezet's *Caution* and learning "of the oppression the slaves in the West Indies lie under." He felt drawn to visit the islands, but he was uneasy about booking passage in a "vessel employed in the West India trade." Seeking a way to make it clear that he would not countenance iniquitous traffic and did not want to profit from it, he had briefly considered hiring an empty ship to take him to the islands. He rejected that option, though, because he did not want to behave in a way that suggested that he opposed all trade. After all, he explained, if there were a total embargo on commerce in the Caribbean, "many there would suffer for want of bread." A better option, he concluded, was to sail on the *Rachel* and pay a premium for his passage. He reasoned that if the merchants had been operating in a manner that was "con-sistent with pure wisdom . . . the passage money would for good reasons be higher than it is now." If he paid only the low charge that the ship owners were demanding, his passage in effect would be subsidized by profits derived from slavery. Paying extra, he explained, would demonstrate his refusal to benefit from the labor of slaves. Woolman remained uneasy, however. Asked whether he would like to inspect the *Rachel*, he refused.[43] Instead, he left Philadelphia for New Jersey and stayed there until after the vessel had sailed.[44]

Through his conduct, Woolman was issuing a rebuke to his close associates and two of the most prominent Quakers in the Delaware Valley. James
Pemberton presided over the annual gatherings of the region's Friends, and
John Smith was a prominent figure in Burlington. In 1755 Smith had served
alongside Woolman on the Philadelphia Yearly Meeting committee for visiting families, and beginning in 1756 the two men had worked closely together
on administrative and disciplinary tasks for Burlington Monthly Meeting.[45]
By 1760 they knew each other well, and Woolman respected Smith's judgment. On one occasion he had told Smith that he dreamed "I was in a room
with thee, and thou drawing thy chair nigh toward mine, did, in a friendly
way, tell me of sundry particular failings thou had observed in me, and expressed some desire that I might do better." When Woolman awoke he forgot
the details of what Smith had said in the dream, and so he wrote to him and
asked for the "particulars."[46] Woolman trusted Smith then, but several years
later when he refused to board Smith's vessel for the Caribbean, he implicitly
challenged his old friend's moral authority and discernment.

Woolman's decision to cancel his Caribbean trip in 1769 bears some re-
semblance to the choice Churchman had made eight years earlier. Churchman, however, had found an occasion to explain his thinking publicly, and
had used the opportunity to chastise Philadelphia's Quakers for investing in
armed ships. Woolman, by contrast, left Philadelphia almost furtively, speaking to no one. The only written statement he made was his letter to Smith
and Pemberton. Eventually he would arrange to have that letter printed in his
journal, but rather than simply explaining his refusal to go to Barbados, the
letter muddied the issue by raising the alternative possibility of Woolman's
paying a premium and sailing. In their journals both men declared that they
felt relief after canceling their trips, but Churchman rode home happily accompanied by his family, exuding "peace of mind."[47] Woolman, on the other
hand, went home alone. His wife and daughter greeted him when he reached
Mount Holly, but he recorded in his journal that he felt out of place among
them, like a "sojourner" in his own home.[48] He tried to conquer his restlessness, but within a few days he fell sick, and he interpreted his illness as a
warning from God.

According to one witness who visited Woolman in Mount Holly in January, he was lying in his bed "like a man dying." He told those around him that
"he had very great horrors on his mind for departing from the purity of his
testimony in relation to the West India traffic. . . . Under this anguish of soul,
evident to all about him, he stood up on his feet, though weak, and with a

lamentable voice cried mightily to God that he would have mercy upon him, a miserable sinner, for that he had lately, under extreme weakness, given up the purity of his testimony against the West India trade." Woolman explained that he had partaken "freely" of "rum and molasses." Some have speculated that he may have taken rum as a medicine, or that he might have drunk a toast after the wedding of his brother Asher, who had been married a month earlier, but it is equally possible that he was speaking figuratively and referring to his offer to pay for a berth on Pemberton's and Smith's ship.[49]

Though the cause may be uncertain, there can be no doubt that Woolman collapsed. On one morning during his illness, perhaps fearing that he might not recover, a circle of friends including Henry Paxson and his wife gathered at Woolman's bedside for worship.[50] It is not clear whether Woolman spoke on that occasion, but before he regained his physical strength he reported receiving a succession of spectacular visions, and a Quaker man named Caleb Carr recorded two of them in the back pages of Woolman's account book. On the third of January, 1770, Woolman guessed that "death was upon me." He told Carr afterward, "I . . . closed my eyes and waited to know if I might now be relieved out of this body, but I looked at the Church and I was moved for her, and I was held fast." He sensed that he "might remain some longer in the body . . . speaking some words to the Church." Before dawn the next day, he heard words that "commanded" him to "open the vision." The voice told him that "the day is approaching when the man that is most wise in human policies shall be the greatest fool, and the arm that is mighty to support injustice shall be broken to pieces, the enemies of righteousness shall make a terrible rattle, and shall mightily torment one another, for he that is omnipotent is rising up to judgment."[51]

Woolman's most spectacular vision came two weeks later, on the night of January 19, when he came "so near to the gates of death" that he forgot his name. In a dream, he set out to discover who he was, and he found "a mass of matter of a dark gloomy color" stretching out before him "between the south and the east." Someone informed him that this murky aggregation was composed of "human beings in as great misery as they could be and live." He was told further that he was part of that company, and that he should no longer consider himself "as a distinct or separate being." Woolman remained with the mass for "several hours," and then he heard "a soft, melodious voice, more pure and harmonious than any voice I had heard with my ears before." He believed it was "the voice of an angel who spake to other angels." The voice was chanting, "John Woolman is dead." At least until he heard the angel's song, those hours may have been the loneliest of Woolman's life. Isolated from others by illness, floating in the private world of his dreams, he felt himself dissolving. No living person could reach him, and he no longer had a name. But his sense of alienation did not last. On the contrary, that moment away from living human company served to inspire in him an expansive new sense of global social engagement. He came to realize that the statement "John Woolman is dead" referred not to his physical existence, but rather to "the death of my own will."[52] As he explained in an essay he wrote two years later, the Holy Spirit could "mortify the deeds of the body in us," and once that had happened it was possible to say, in the words of Saint Paul, "it is no more I that live, but Christ that liveth in me."[53]

In the second part of Woolman's dream, angels carried him "in spirit" to see mines where "heathens" worked for Christian masters. The miners complained that if Christianity had authorized their oppression, then Christ was "a cruel tyrant." Woolman awoke and began to cough up blood, which he took as a sign not to drink from silver cups, because "people getting silver vessels to set off their tables at entertainments were often stained with worldly glory."[54] Responding to stories that had also alarmed Benezet, Woolman expressed concern about the methods the Spanish used to extract silver from Peru.[55] In a letter some time after his dream, he lamented the "manner of taking of the silver mines southwestward, the conduct of the conquerors toward the natives, and the miserable toil" of the workers in the mines. He admitted, "I sometimes handle silver and gold as a currency," but he felt misgivings about it, and he remained receptive to the possibility that God might instruct him to reject gold and silver coins.[56]

The day he awoke, Woolman tore a page out of his ledger book and wrote out a statement against "the customary use of silver vessels about houses." He did not describe his dream, but declared simply that "this morning" his "understanding" had been "opened in pure wisdom" and he had received "the counsel of the Lord." Echoing Jesus he pronounced, "He that can receive it, let him receive it." He condemned the use of silver teapots, cups, trays, and other implements as "a manifest conformity to outward show and greatness." "There is idolatry committed in the use of these things," he wrote, warning that if anyone sold their silver vessels to others, their action would encourage the spread of idolatry. There was only one proper course to take: put the offending items away, and follow the example of Jacob, who hid his household's idols under an oak.[57]

There is no record of what Woolman did with that piece of paper. Initially at least, he may have kept it to himself. He refused to use silverware from that morning onward, and he expected to be called on to explain his behavior. He may have kept the note as a reminder, so that he would know what to say when someone tried to serve him food or drink using silver utensils. In his journal he reports that soon after he recovered his health he dined at a Friend's house in Burlington, and during the meal drinks were served only in "silver vessels." Woolman was thirsty but resolute. "I, wanting some drink, told him my case with weeping, and he ordered some drink for me in another vessel." Over the next two years he had similar experiences "in several Friends' houses."[58]

Woolman's insistence that silver items should be discarded complicated his work both as a minister and as a testamentary advisor. Between 1751 and 1769 Woolman helped to settle at least 28 estates, and in that capacity he had frequently distributed silver items as well as other pieces of furniture and clothing that were not merely utilitarian but also manifested "outward show and greatness."[59] His workload slowed after 1769, however. From 1770 to 1772 his name appeared on the records of only three estates, all involving relatively humble farmers who did not have any ostentatious possessions.[60] In spring 1772 he made a marginal note in his journal that strongly suggests he may have steered away other customers. He wrote that at "sundry times" he felt his "mind opened in true brotherly love to converse freely and largely with some who were entrusted with plentiful estates, in regard to an application of the profits of them consistent with pure wisdom."[61] If Woolman was maintaining his professed principles, he told these men and women to bury their silver.

He had similarly blunt conversations with ailing and elderly Quakers whom he visited as a minister. In 1771 Woolman saw Peter Harvey a few months before Harvey died. Woolman "had some loving conversation with him in regard to sundry things in his possession . . . which appeared to be conformable to the [evil] spirit of this world." The inappropriate objects were decorative, exhibiting "sundry sorts of superfluities in workmanship." According to Woolman, Harvey "appeared to take my visit very kind, and though he was not fully settled in his mind as to what he should do with them, yet he told me that he was inwardly united to a plain way of living." After Harvey's health deteriorated Woolman returned, and Harvey confessed that he had made some bad purchases in his youth. Even at the moment when he bought those items he had sensed that he was moving into darkness. Harvey could not yet see clearly "what to do with them," though they had become "a burden to his mind." Woolman's last visit with Harvey was more cheerful. Harvey told Woolman that "in this his sickness" he "had tasted of that joy which is the everlasting portion of them who are sanctified, and that the thoughts of death were not terrible to him." Woolman reported that Harvey "appeared in a meek and loving frame of spirit," which seemed to suggest that he had found his way out of his darkness, though Woolman did not record what he had done with his frivolously decorated possessions.[62]

Some Quakers reduced Woolman to tears when he discussed with them why they should never acquire ostentatious utensils or furniture, but others accepted his advice solemnly. Besides Harvey, other Quakers who met Woolman during this uncompromising period of his life were pleased and positively impressed.[63] An Irish traveling minister who visited Mount Holly in 1771 singled out Woolman's avoidance of silver as one of his most admirable characteristics: "His concern is to lead a life of self-denial. Pomp and splendor he avoids. Does not use silver or useless vessels that savor of the pomp of this world. His house is very plain, his living also, and yet [he] enjoys plenty of the good things that are necessary for Christian accommodation. We dined with him, and were kindly entertained."[64]

Like his decision to wear unfashionable clothes, Woolman's opposition to silver and ornamentation distinguished him from most of his Quaker neighbors. Although he was able to maintain a comfortable home, he was increasingly finding the wider community of Mount Holly and western New Jersey less congenial. Thus it is not surprising that he continued to dream of travel. In April 1770, when he appeared before Burlington Monthly Meeting to announce the cancellation of his Caribbean trip, he declared that he wanted to go somewhere else, and he proposed conducting "a religious visit as far southwest as Carolina." Woolman's close friends Henry Paxson and Josiah White were assigned to discuss this proposal with him. The discussions, as it turned out, consumed an unusually long time. Paxson and White returned to the meeting in June to ask for a continuance, and in July Woolman came to the meeting to say that "he felt his mind resigned in relation to the visit southwestward," and he "believed at present he might have peace in staying at home."[65] His peace did not last, however. By the autumn of 1771, he was dreaming of sailing for England.

In general, the American colonists' relationship to England had grown more fraught since the end of the Seven Years' War. Woolman maintained his loyalty to the British government, and he never explicitly took a side in the debates at the center of the imperial crises of the 1760s and early 1770s. He had other concerns. Woolman avoided tea during the Patriots' boycott not because it was taxed, but rather because the beverage was customarily sweetened with slave-produced sugar.[66] In 1769, in his capacity as a correspondent between the Delaware Valley Quakers and the Yearly Meeting in London, Woolman had reassured the British Quakers that Philadelphia Yearly Meeting would direct its members to behave "as becomes good and faithful subjects, both in word and conduct," "to promote the like sentiments of duty and affection" among others, and "to prevent any among us from dealing with such as are suspected to be guilty of fraudulent practices respecting the revenue." He promised the British Friends that despite the "late afflicting occurrences," the Delaware Valley Quakers would discourage any "practices inconsistent with our peaceable profession and principles."[67] Woolman was aware of the controversy surrounding Parliamentary taxation in the colonies, but nothing that happened in those tumultuous years diminished his love for the English.

During his lifetime Woolman had met at least twenty-one Quaker ministers from England, and two from Ireland, who had sailed to North America to visit Friends Meetings. Two of his closest ministerial colleagues, Abraham Farrington and Peter Andrews, had died on trips to Britain, and he additionally heard reports from at least six others who had gone to England or Ireland, survived, and returned.[68] Woolman had learned much from these acquaintances, and he also knew a great deal about England from his reading. Furthermore he felt that his knowledge was enhanced by inspiration. In the winter of 1771, he dreamed that he had been carried across the ocean, and standing in the fields where the founders of Quakerism had preached, he felt the "spring of the gospel" open in him. When he described this vision to Burlington Monthly Meeting, he said that England "looked like home to me."[69] Woolman asked for a traveling certificate, and the meeting gave him one "directed to the Quarterly and Monthly Meetings of Friends in Yorkshire" and further afield in Great Britain, Ireland, and Holland if Woolman felt moved to travel so far.[70] In February 1772 Burlington Quarterly Meeting expressed its approval, and in March Sarah Woolman was present and participating when John received a third certificate from Philadelphia Yearly Meeting's ministers and elders.[71] All the available evidence indicates that Sarah approved of John's plans. She had heard him speak of England, and it seems that she had confidence she could manage without him temporarily. But other members of his family had their own reasons to object.

Abner Woolman became physically weak in the late 1760s, and in 1768 his daughter Sarah moved into John's household.[72] John would later take custody of Abner's son Samuel as well.[73] When Abner died in November 1771, John assumed greater responsibility for all four of Abner's children.[74] He told them,

Woolman House, near Mount Holly.

Figure 12. House Woolman built for John and Mary Comfort. Courtesy Quaker and Special Collections, Haverford College.

"The deep trials of thy father, and his inward care for you are often in my re-membrance, with some concern that you his children may be acquainted with that inward life to which his mind whilst amongst you was often gathered." John warned them to maintain "a watchful frame of mind, and know that which supports innocent young people against the snares of the wicked."[75] Abner had died at a critical juncture in his children's lives. None of them had reached the age of majority, and they relied on John's support. John wanted to help, but he felt certain the Lord was calling him to England. His family ties were not going to stop him.

He was also departing from his daughter Mary at a difficult time. In April 1771, at a modest gathering in the Mount Holly Meetinghouse, Mary married a Quaker man from Pennsylvania named John Comfort.[76] Over the next few months, Woolman oversaw the construction of a house for his daughter and her new husband. It was an elaborate operation. Woolman negotiated with at least seven suppliers to acquire the requisite timber, nails, bricks, stone, lime, and hardware. He employed at least ten craftsmen and laborers to erect and finish the house. His younger brother Jonah worked on the project, as did Pri-mus, the black man who worked for him intermittently over many years. The Comforts' house was two stories high with an attic above and a paved cellar below the stairs. There was a brick chimney in the corner of the house and a large fireplace on the ground floor. The house had four casement windows in the front, and four smaller windows in the back. One can assume Woolman avoided "superfluous" decoration, but the house was not unusually Spartan in appearance. It was a conventional family home.[77] Woolman and his crew completed their work in August. The Comforts moved in immediately, and within a few weeks Mary was pregnant.[78]

John and Mary Comfort were facing challenges. In a fragment of a letter Woolman wrote to them the day before he left Mount Holly, there is a hint that they might have been having difficulty supporting themselves. Mary was expecting her baby in June, and it is possible that both she and her husband were ill. Woolman wrote, "My leaving you, under the trying circumstances now attending you, is not without close exercise, and I feel a living concern that under these cares of business, and under bodily affliction, your minds may be brought to a humble waiting on him who is the great preserver of his people."[79]

It was customary for Quaker ministers to settle their "outward affairs" prior to crossing the ocean. As part of that process Woolman made provision for the support of his family in the event that he did not survive the journey. Before leaving Mount Holly, he deeded his house and property to John Comfort's father Stephen, who would hold the land in trust for the benefit of Sarah during her lifetime.[80] Woolman also arranged for his brother Asher to pay some of his outstanding debts, and on his last day at home, in a final gift to his daughter, he hired a neighbor to build the Comforts a small cart with springs.[81]

The Comforts may have asked Woolman to delay or cancel his trip, but if they did so it is unlikely that they had support from Sarah. There is no evidence that she voiced any objections, even though John made a decision prior to his departure that made his absence more difficult to bear for those he left behind. After hearing reports about the English post office and how it overworked and abused postboys and their horses, he responded passionately. To avoid giving the postal service business, he asked his family, his neighbors, and the ministers and elders in Philadelphia, not to send him letters by post. He knew, as he made this request, that it would make it more difficult for him to hear back from America. Even so, he knew also he was acting "for righteousness sake," and though he had some misgivings, "through divine favor" he was "made content."[82]

John was also making other awkward requests. On the day before he left Mount Holly, he gave Sarah a letter he had written to the Quaker minister Elizabeth Smith, who had intended to take a trip to Britain a year earlier. In

April 1771 Sarah and John had joined 91 others in signing Smith's traveling certificate.[83] Smith had subsequently contracted an illness that prevented her from sailing, but over the intervening year John had felt increasingly uneasy about having endorsed her certificate. In the brief letter he asked his wife to deliver, he told Smith he had signed the travelling certificate "expressing thee to be exemplary" even though he had known at that time that there were "things amongst thy furniture which are against the purity of our principles."[84] According to Smith's descendants, Woolman was objecting to a set of wooden side chairs he had seen in Smith's home with shells carved on their backs and knees.[85]

Elizabeth Smith was the sister of historian Samuel and Woolman's friend John. Forty-eight and unmarried, she had devoted her life to the Society of Friends. The women of Philadelphia Yearly Meeting declared that "the dealings of the Lord" had been "with her from the early time of youth."[86] She had been recognized as a minster at twenty one.[87] One contemporary observer described her as "a pattern of modest virtue."[88] Others praised her as "deep in council, sound in Judgment, awful [in] her manners, refined [in] her sentiments, and graceful [in] her deportment."[89] Noted Quaker minister John Hunt began his own journal by citing Smith's ministry.[90] On at least two occasions in the 1760s, Woolman had traveled with Smith visiting Quaker families in New Jersey.[91] It is not clear whether Sarah actually delivered John's letter. Smith died in October 1772, and during her last weeks she wrote an epistle to Friends in New Jersey which was read after her death in the Monthly, Quarterly, and Yearly Meetings "to the tendering of many hearts."[92] Her final words were recorded and memorable. She expired proclaiming that she was passing "into joy unspeakable and full of glory."[93]

Woolman may have had specific objections to the shell imagery on Smith's chairs because scallops were fertility symbols, but in other contexts during this period he expressed opposition more generally to workmanship that was "only ornamental."[94] In protesting against carved and decorated furniture he was distancing himself from almost all his neighbors, including members of his own birth family. The Woolmans' wooden furniture may not have had shells carved into it, but it sported decorative lathe work.[95] Woolman's message to Smith fit a broad pattern. He was feeling increasingly alienated from those around him in New Jersey, and this was reflected in his eagerness to travel.

On the day he left, according to various versions of his journal, Woolman "parted with" or "took leave of" his family early in the morning.[96] Years later, however, Sarah reported that John had left that day without waking

Figure 13. Table that once belonged to Asher Woolman. Courtesy Dallas Museum of Art.

her. According to her account, he had gone to bed in the previous evening "as usual," but in the morning she "missed him, and supposing he was making ready to depart went down stairs, but finding him gone she went into the road in search of him, and ascertained from one of the neighbors that he had seen him about daylight with a bundle under his arm going on foot towards Philadelphia."[97] John felt ready to go. Over the previous two weeks, writing letters and making intermittent trips to Philadelphia, he had made detailed arrangements for his voyage.[98] It had not been easy, but this time, in contrast to 1769, he believed that he had found an appropriate berth.

Woolman had booked a passage for London on the *Mary and Elizabeth*, a 180–ton brig. He had chosen the ship without seeing it, feeling confident it would be right for him. The *Mary and Elizabeth* was owned by a Quaker, and it frequently carried American Friends to London. In spring 1772 several other American Quakers had reserved cabins, including John Bispham, a twelve-year-old "modest orderly lad" from Mount Holly who had attended Woolman's school.[99] The ship crossed the Atlantic four times each year, arriving in Philadelphia in the spring and departing again for London in less than a month. It returned to Philadelphia every fall and sailed back to England before the onset of winter. The vessel took passengers in both directions and brought a wide assortment of consumer goods to Pennsylvania. According to advertisements in the *Pennsylvania Gazette*, it carried "a large assortment of European, with some India goods." Its cargos included tea, glass, china, silk, lace, calicoes, other fabrics, tablecloths, handkerchiefs, gloves, fancy shoes, hats for men, women, and children, including "ladies' hats with feathers, or gold and silver bands," dolls, clothing for dolls, earrings, and other jewelry. One advertisement identified a consignment carried on the *Mary and Elizabeth* as being entirely composed of items "in the newest and gentilest taste." The passengers also traveled in style. Advertisements touted the ship's "excellent accommodations"; some labeled the cabins "extraordinary."[100]

When Woolman first saw the *Mary and Elizabeth*, he was appalled and asked if he could travel in steerage. Explaining himself to the owner, he indicated that the carved woodwork and "imagery" on the upper deck made him uncomfortable. They manifested, he said, "superfluity of workmanship," and since part of the price he would pay for a cabin would defray the cost of those decorations, he felt a scruple against taking an ordinary passenger's accommodation.[101] Woolman's decision became "a little known in town," and at least three Quakers met with him and tried to talk him out of bunking with the sailors below decks, but he maintained his resolution. He believed that he had found a new way to make a statement through his unusual behavior. Still, he barely grasped the full implications of his decision. The voyage would be an education for him.

Oceangoing vessels in the eighteenth century were dramatically hierarchical in their architecture, and by asking to sleep with the sailors below deck Woolman seemed to be making an egalitarian gesture. But when Woolman explained his choice, he never suggested that he wanted to spend time with the sailors, learn about their lives, or express solidarity with them. Nonetheless, once the ship had departed, sleeping below decks gave him an unplanned opportunity to educate himself about the maritime workforce. Nearly every aspect of that experience, from the time he first boarded the *Mary and Elizabeth* until he disembarked in London, disturbed him. As his objections mounted, he developed a more comprehensive and detailed critique of the maritime world.

From the outset it was hard sailing. High winds and rain battered the ship for nearly a week after it rounded the southern tip of New Jersey.[102] Woolman watched the sailors work almost continuously to keep the vessel on course through the storm. They took shifts day and night, and in their intervals below decks they slept crowded in close quarters. Exhausted men left wet clothes in heaps on the floor, and when they awoke they put on whatever grimy pants and shirts they could find. Years earlier Woolman had argued that laborers should never be required to put in eight-hour days. He had made this argument without thinking about sailors. Now that he was among them, he worried about the discomfort and danger they endured. After their exertions, the men sought liquor for comfort.[103] Woolman understood, but did not approve.[104]

The weather on the sea reminded Woolman of the power of Providence. During a violent storm he told the Quakers on board that "he had been contemplating that which is more worthy to be depended on than the skill of the mariners or the firmness of the ship."[105] The other Friends were thinking along similar lines. Indeed, while the *Mary and Elizabeth* was still at the wharf in Philadelphia, Samuel Emlen, his wife, and another Quaker woman had solemnly gathered with the captain in the cabin, and the captain was reminded of the following words: "The Lord on high is mightier than the noise of many waters, even than the mighty waves of the sea." Emlen and the other Quaker passengers remembered those words after the storm rose. They all placed their trust in the "Preserver of men."[106]

Woolman spent most of the voyage yearning for dry land. Feeling vulnerable and out of place on the water, he sympathized with some "dunghill fowls" the others had brought on board.[107] He commented on the birds' "pining condition," and noticed that the roosters stopped crowing a few days after the vessel sailed from the mouth of the Delaware. They stayed silent until the ship had reached the coast of England. "Then," he wrote, "I observed them crow a little."[108] The poultry suffered in the voyage. Some were slaughtered for their meat, and approximately 14 were drowned or otherwise killed by breaking waves. A number of others succumbed to disease and died on the trip. Watching these animals, Woolman reminded himself that God was the "Fountain of Goodness who gave being to all creatures" and that his love extended "to caring for the sparrows." God had intended "the animal creation" to be "under our government," and for humans to maintain "a tenderness toward all creatures made subject to us." Therefore, people should avoid doing anything that might lessen the animals' "sweetness of life." More specifically Woolman concluded that it would have been better to carry "a less number" of poultry "to eat at sea."[109]

Woolman took a principled stance against paying for well-decorated accommodations, but he never promised to stay away from the other passengers in their berths.[110] After the weather worsened, he discovered that his presence below decks interfered with the sailors' work, and from that time he retreated for hours at a time to the cabins. The sailors were difficult company for him. He described them as a people apart, marked by an "almost universal depravity." He was distressed by the sailors' lack of religious feeling, and he spoke with them about it, one at a time, seeking "to turn their minds toward the fear of the Lord." In this manner he conversed with the men repeatedly, and he found that they were "mostly respectful to me, and more and more so the longer as I was with them."[111]

There were five boys in the crew training to be sailors, two of whom had been raised in Quaker families. Woolman convinced these boys, along with most of the other crew members, to attend Sunday Quaker meetings with the other passengers on the ship. Bringing the men to worship did not, however, change them. It seemed as if nothing would. After two weeks at sea Woolman concluded that no Quaker father could, with a clear conscience, allow his son to train to be a sailor: "A pious father whose mind is exercised for the everlasting welfare of his child may not with a peaceful mind place him out to an employment amongst a people whose common course of life is manifestly corrupt and profane."[112]

Woolman was disgusted with the sailors even before he heard them telling stories about "voyages to Africa" and "the manner of bringing deeply oppressed slaves into our islands."[113] The men on the *Mary and Elizabeth* were not at that time working in the slave trade, but sailors cycled on and off slaving vessels. After crossing the ocean from Africa, ships routinely discharged part of their crews before returning to Britain in preparation for another voyage south. The sailors left in colonial port cities looked for work on other ships.[114] Thus, it was common for sailing vessels to have crewmembers with experience in the transatlantic slave trade, even if the ship itself had never been to the African coast. Woolman listened to the sailors' talk and responded by lamenting the moral condition of British maritime culture generally. Describing his reaction in his journal, he adopted an expressive style close to speech:

A great trade to the coast of Africa for slaves, of which I now heard frequent conversation amongst the sailors!

A great trade in that which is raised and prepared through grievous oppression!

A great trade in superfluity of workmanship, formed to please the pride and vanity of peoples' mind!

Great and extensive is that depravity which prevails amongst the poor sailors![115]

Woolman's complaint brought together several of his objections to maritime commerce, including the slave trade, the proliferation of woodcarving, and the poor morals of the mariners. He was reacting emotionally, and at that moment he was unable to articulate with any clear internal logic how his ideas were linked. Nonetheless he was convinced that the evils he listed fed off one another and combined to make the merchant fleet pernicious. In condemning maritime trade so emphatically and comprehensively, he may have overstepped the bounds of what some of his contemporaries considered acceptable Quaker discourse. After he died his journal was submitted to Philadelphia Yearly Meeting and London Yearly Meeting for publication. The Philadelphia Quakers printed his lament in full, but when the English published their own edition of Woolman's journal they deleted this passage from the text.[116]

At the end of his voyage, Woolman saw London and the largest collection of sailing vessels he had ever seen. Once again his words nearly failed him, and some of his commentary was suppressed by the English Quakers.[117] From the deck of the *Mary and Elizabeth* he "saw many ships passing and some at anchor near," and he sensed "the spirit in which the poor bewildered sailors too generally live." Overall they suffered from a "lamentable degeneracy." The "seafaring life," he wrote, was "full of corruption and alienation from God."[118]

Woolman would never board a ship again. During his four months in England, he campaigned against slavery, but he also elaborated more generally on the ill effects of maritime commerce. He wrote six essays during this period, four of which, "On Loving Our Neighbors as Ourselves," "On the Slave Trade," "On Trading in Superfluities," and "On a Sailor's Life," were apparently written as a series. They were published together and discussed related themes, expanding on Woolman's objections to ocean-going trade.[119]

In the first essay, "On Loving Our Neighbors as Ourselves," Woolman discussed poverty in England. He recommended higher wages and shorter working hours, suggesting that the rich had failed to give the poor their due and had strayed from their Christian duty. England's economic problems, he asserted, were caused by a failure of altruism, blindness on the part of the rich stemming from "self-love." His second essay, "On the Slave Trade," emphasized the suffering of slaves on shipboard and was similar to his 1762 antislavery pamphlet, except that in this piece he indicated that he had collected information about the slave trade from individuals with experience in the business, including enslaved Africans and men who had been employed on slaving vessels. The third essay, "On Trading in Superfluities," condemned England's manufactories because they produced goods traded on the coast of

Africa for slaves. More generally he suggested that the English undertook unnecessary labor, and he recommended "self-denial in things relating to trade
and handicraft labor." Returning to the theme of his first essay, he suggested
that those who lived a "plain frugal life" were more likely to offer better wages
to their laborers.[120]

The fourth essay, "On a Sailor's Life," presented the climax of Woolman's
argument. He began by discussing the slave trade and its corrupting influence
on young men who sought employment at sea. He indicated that he had had
"many opportunities" to "feel and understand the general state of seafaring
amongst us" and had concluded that there were too many people working
on ships. The problem, in the end, seemed simple, and Woolman tried to
point the way to a better world. If there were fewer sailors, the "channels of
trade would be more free from defilement" and "heathen nations" would be
presented with better examples of "righteousness." "Fewer people would be
employed in vanities and superfluities," and there would be fewer cities in the
world. More people would adopt the "sweet employment" of caring for animals, and wealthy landowners would care for the poor.[121] Woolman advocated
a "country life" for everyone. The rich should be humble in their aspirations
and care for their neighbors. Animal husbandry was a good vocation, but even
shepherds should be able to spare time for the community's needs. If different
populations were far from each other, they should live independently and not
rely on trade. When a "large hazardous ocean" separated different branches of
the human family, "the inhabitants of each place" should "live on the produce
of their own land."[122]

This analysis led Woolman into a conundrum at the center of his understanding of history and his place in the world. From childhood he had been
raised to celebrate his colonial ancestors, and he had been taught to believe
that they had come to North America to advance a mission initiated by the
English Quakers in the seventeenth century. Friends had crossed the Atlantic
not merely for their own safety and comfort, but to promote God's cause on
a global scale. After Woolman reached maturity and became a minister, his
frequent contact with traveling Quakers reminded him that he belonged to an
ocean-spanning religious movement, one that could maintain its unity only
by sending messages and passengers across the Atlantic.

Unfortunately, the ships the Quakers used were part of the infrastructure
of the British Empire. Riding on those vessels, the Quakers took advantage
of a technology developed and refined by men engaged in the most exploit-
ative and domineering practices of the eighteenth century. Oceangoing ships

were indispensible tools for the operation of the slave trade and the projection of military power overseas. Woolman and his fellow traveling ministers, it seemed, had fallen into a trap. They were seeking to advance their mission by relying on the services of the worst of their neighbors. Furthermore, by paying for their berths, they encouraged investors, merchants, ship captains, and mariners to continue to engage in their pernicious activities. These thoughts upset Woolman and had a pervasive effect on his response to Britain. He had initially wanted to come to the country because he saw it as his ancestral and spiritual home. But after his arrival he found himself among Quakers who were "mixed with the world in various sorts of business and traffic carried on in impure channels."[123] England had witnessed something glorious when George Fox preached there, but it seemed that in the intervening century many things had gone wrong.

Chapter 9

A Messenger Sent from the Almighty:
England and Death

> I have looked at the smallpox as a messenger sent from the Almighty
> to be an assistant in the cause of virtue, and to incite us to consider
> whether we employ our time only in such things as are consistent
> with perfect wisdom and goodness.
> —John Woolman, *Journal*, chapter 6

WOOLMAN MONITORED HIS health closely and in the late 1760s, to ward
off illness, he started to avoid many foods.[1] Under ordinary circumstances, his
diet was "plain, chiefly consisting of bread and milk or butter &c."[2] During
his voyage across the Atlantic in 1772, he was reduced almost entirely to eating bread, though he sometimes indulged in a wayward snack. Samuel Emlen
sailed with him and reported that he "kept I think much within his usual [di-
etary] restrictions on board, though [he was] not so confined as to be unwilling to partake of some parts of our stores."[3] During the storm in the first week
of the voyage, at least five of the Quaker passengers became nauseous, but
Woolman's stomach remained calm. He recorded in his journal that "through
the tender mercies of my Heavenly father I have been preserved" from seasick-
ness, but he also noted ominously that he suffered from afflictions "of another kind." Woolman felt trapped in the cabins and below deck by the "rainy
weather and high winds." Being "shut up in a close, unhealthy air" weakened
him. He found breathing so difficult that he stood through the nights near a
crack by the hatchway door to catch what he could of a fresh breeze. His ap-
petite failed him. He struggled to be patient, and after several miserable nights

the weather broke. "A clear pleasant morning," he wrote, "and as I sat on the deck I felt a reviving in my nature." He interpreted this experience as a lesson, "bringing me to feel that which many thousands of my fellow creatures often suffer."[4] The physical strain of the voyage made it easier for him to identify with sailors and slaves. Although eager to disembark, Woolman stayed on board the *Mary and Elizabeth* after most of the Quaker passengers landed at Dover. The others intended to proceed to London by stage coach, but Woolman had resolved not to travel that way out of concern for the welfare of the horses.[5] Crossing the ocean had taken a toll on his health, but those who knew him well were neither surprised nor alarmed by his appearance when he arrived in London. He had been prone to mild illness for many years, and when his cousin William Hunt saw him he gave this vaguely ambiguous assessment of his health: Woolman was "as well as usual."[6]

Sensing that he had been "mercifully helped to bear the difficulties of the sea," Woolman went "strait from the waterside" to Devonshire House, the gathering place for London Yearly Meeting. The ministers and elders had already assembled there for a morning session when he arrived.[7] Woolman reported that his heart was "enlarged" when he entered the meeting, and his mind was "united in true love to the laborers . . . gathered from the several parts" of Britain.[8] Forty Quarterly Meetings had sent approximately 140 representatives to the sessions. Along with the British delegates there were a number of American Quakers in attendance. Some observers thought that it was the largest group of American traveling Friends ever assembled in London.[9] With several adjournments, the meeting would last nearly a week. From the start, the event captivated Woolman. It was only after a full day of worship and business that he set out in search of the lodgings that had been prepared for him.

An unusually frank letter of introduction had crossed the ocean with Woolman on the *Mary and Elizabeth.* Woolman himself might have carried it, though given its contents it is possible that he knew nothing about it.[10] In the letter, John Pemberton warned a Quaker in London named Joseph Row that Woolman would appear "singular" when he met him. Woolman followed "a straighter path than some other good folks are led or do travel in." Pemberton advised Row that it would be "safest for Friends . . . to leave him much to his own feelings," and avoid "arguments or persuasion" with him, because Woolman would "do nothing knowingly against the Truth." For accommodation he wanted "simplicity and plainness." "Little will content him," Pemberton wrote, "and the poorer the fare the more acceptable." Specifically, Pemberton suggested that the London Quakers lodge Woolman at Row's house or else with another austere Quaker, a pewterer named John Townsend.[11] In accordance with Pemberton's advice, Woolman was sent to stay with Townsend. He made few overt demands on his host, and Townsend later reported that Woolman's "self-denying example" was "truly profitable to me and my family."[12] Woolman was at Townsend's house once when "a large company of Friends" came to visit, but that moment was unusual.[13] Except when he went to meetings, Woolman did not venture far outside and for the most part kept to himself. When asked why he did not socialize more, he explained that he was vulnerable to smallpox.[14]

In 1759, when smallpox swept the Delaware Valley, Woolman had seriously considered being inoculated against the disease. At that time many of his neighbors acquired immunity by cutting themselves and rubbing a small quantity of infected tissue into their wounds. This procedure was usually effective, but Woolman noted that "a few died" after exposing themselves to smallpox. Those deaths convinced him that inoculation was unwise. He was ready to take measures to "hinder the force of this disease by innocent means," but he would not approve of any treatment that could be "mortal" or "hurtful to our bodies."[15]

Woolman's response to other ailments illustrates the array of treatments he was willing to take. He had adopted his restricted diet after noticing a lump growing on his nose.[16] He bought medicinal herbs from at least two suppliers, including his neighbor and fellow minister Josiah White, who considered himself an expert of the curative power of local plants.[17] Woolman relied on White's services in part because he wanted to avoid ingesting foreign medicines.[18] He believed that his body was adapted to the climate and produce of New Jersey, and so he avoided imported cures. For similar reasons he worried about the adverse health effects of travel.

Trusting Providence, Woolman took to the road if he felt called to do so by God. He told Townsend that he was willing to fall ill if he did so "in going to meetings and in the way of his duty," but he did not want to risk his health unnecessarily.[19] Nonetheless when he traveled after 1759 he was often preoccupied by disease. By his own account, he was "a little cautious" about visiting houses in Philadelphia when there were cases of smallpox in the city.[20] He grew steadily more fearful as he ventured farther from his home. During his long journey through the northern colonies in 1760, he gathered reports of disease. From Massachusetts he wrote to Sarah in Mount Holly, "I have heard very little of the smallpox since I came off Long Island."[21]

Woolman opposed smallpox inoculation because he thought that it was uniquely God's prerogative to spread disease. He viewed the contagion as an instrument of Providence like famine, earthquake, and war. God used these traumas to humble humanity, chastise the wicked, and instruct. "I have looked at the smallpox," he wrote, "as a messenger sent from the Almighty to be an assistant in the cause of virtue." Specifically, the disease was a divine warning to refrain from unnecessary business, frivolous visits, and "any assembling of people together but such as were consistent with pure wisdom."[22] In London, Woolman met Sophia Hume, a seventy-one-year-old Quaker reformer who had her own forceful objections to smallpox inoculation. In a pamphlet *Remarks on the Practice of Inoculation for the Small Pox* Hume likened the procedure to gambling, and condemned it unequivocally. "It appears a manifest inconsistency, nay I was going to say no less than mere mockery, to give ourselves a distemper, and then pretend to pray to God to be carried safely through it."[23] On this question, and on many others, Woolman and Hume agreed. Hume had grown up in South Carolina, but she had moved to London in the 1740s. The British Quakers counted her as one of their own, though they were conscious of her American origins.[24] Her writings were widely published in Britain and America, and she corresponded regularly with Anthony Benezet.[25] When Woolman and Hume met in London, they recognized each other as kindred spirits. Though the fear of disease kept Woolman from socializing with other English Quakers, he did see her. Before he left London, he gave her a copy of the latest chapter of his journal, and authorized her to revise it.[26]

Woolman had not crossed the ocean to see London. He wanted to stand in the rural fields he associated with the origins of Quakerism, and he expected to find those places in the north of England. His goal was Yorkshire, and indeed in Philadelphia he had been so focused on that region that when he started looking for a ship he searched in vain for a vessel that would sail directly to a northern port and skip London altogether.[27] Thus he may have felt some relief when on June 15 he began his long walk to York.

The sea voyage had already weakened him, and after he left London his insistence on walking, his busy itinerary, and his restricted diet exhausted him further. Woolman was "apprehensive of taking the small pox" in Oxfordshire. Samuel Emlen saw him there and believed that he was still "pretty well," but worried that Woolman was damaging his health by living "abstemiously to a great degree to the hurt or weakening of his health, at times unnecessarily." After two weeks on the road Woolman was "poorly with a very troublesome cough," even though he insisted that he was recovering.[28] When he reached the border of Yorkshire four weeks later, he maintained that he was "middling well in health."[29]

He was working hard. As he traveled north he attended nearly every Quaker meeting along the way. In addition to small local meetings, monthly meetings, and quarterly meetings, he asked for special permission to visit women's assemblies and sessions for youth. He also helped organize impromptu gatherings for worship in private homes, and these events often attracted large numbers of curious non-Quakers. At Nottingham approximately 130 people came to see him. According to one observer it was "more than the house (which was not small) could hold." The meeting Woolman attended at Sheffield was similarly "much crowded, and many went away and stood out of doors."[30] Emlen wrote that there was "much flocking to meetings" when Woolman was present.[31] The young American Quaker Deborah Morris worked alongside Woolman during some of his time in the north, and she reported, "Wherever we go there is such thronging there is not time but when in bed for retirement."[32]

While others may have been excited by his visits, Woolman himself did not find the experience invigorating. On the contrary, by August 16 he was suffering from a condition which he described as "inward poverty." He was in a "watchful, tender state," waiting for divine guidance. He wrote that he had felt a "great distress of mind since I came on this island" because so many English Friends were implicated in the slave trade. Even though Quakers as a group had renounced slave trading, they continued to participate indirectly in that commerce. He lamented, "Great is the trade to Africa for slaves! And in loading these ships abundance of people are employed in the factories, amongst whom are many of our Society!" Woolman worried that the Quakers in England had lost their earlier ways. They indulged in "superfluity" in their clothing and in "the furniture of their houses." During his travels he was "entertained at the houses of Friends who had sundry things about them which had the appearance of outward greatness." Initially he had been silent about this, but eventually he found a way to speak privately with the ostentatious Quakers.[33]

Woolman was also taking detailed notes, recording the price of rye, wheat, oatmeal, mutton, bacon, cheese, butter, house rents for the poor, and coal. Along with his record of prices, he gathered information on working conditions and wages of poor laborers, taking note of the distinctive arrangements employers made in different parts of the country to provide food and drink

Figure 14. This chair, with its finely shaped legs and colored upholstery, graced the home of one of Woolman's Quaker hosts in the north of England. Despite whatever misgivings he may have had, Woolman reportedly sat in it. Author's photograph.

for their workers. He made a record of the wages paid female spinners. He observed that in much of the country, "many poor children learn not to read." He noticed that firewood was "very scarce and dear." At the end of his list of observations he made exclamations of dismay: "Oh, may the wealthy consider the poor!" and "May those who have plenty lay these things to heart!"[34]

Woolman had arrived in England with a certain wariness about the country as far as its treatment of horses was concerned. After he had spent time there his uneasiness increased. He was told that stagecoaches often traveled 100 miles in 24 hours and that horses were killed through hard driving or made blind.[35] Stagecoaches occasionally collided with pedestrians in the dark. Woolman also heard about postboys who froze to death in the night. He concluded from these stories that there was too much "hurry in the spirit of this world that is aiming to do business quick and to gain wealth."[36] England's mistreatment of animals was symptomatic of a more fundamental problem with its economy.

On his way to York Woolman walked "in wet weather through narrow streets in towns and villages," and the "dirtiness under foot and scent arising from the filth" sickened him.

> Near large towns there are many beasts slain to supply the market, and from their blood, etc., ariseth that which mixeth in the air. This, with the cleaning of the stables and other scents, the air in cities in a calm, wettish time is so opposite to the clear pure country air that I believe even the minds of people are in some degree hindered from the pure operation of the Holy Spirit.[37]

The vapors rising from the accumulation of manure, blood, and other waste from carcasses made walking through the towns an ordeal. It was even worse in the textile-producing regions, where Woolman's shoes were stained by run-off from the dyeing of cloth. The dyes were a useless and dangerous indulgence. After Woolman lodged with a cloth-dyer in Kendal, he wrote to tell him "I had a sense of the pride of people being gratified in some of the business thou followest, and I feel a concern in pure love to endeavor to inform thee of it. Christ our leader is worthy of being followed in his leadings at all times. The enemy gets many on his side. O that we may not be divided between the two, but may be wholly on the side of Christ!"[38] Woolman was particularly exercised by the English textile industry, but he was more generally upset with the country's urban culture. In the north of England, he prayed for God's assistance in directing town dwellers who were "sincere in heart" to leave and "live a country life."[39]

Recently in his writings he had expressed a general concern for "the condition of many who dwell in cities." He expressed hope that they might be inspired to choose a "country life" or find "some change of employ." Under the "refining hand of the Lord," he declared, he had "seen that the inhabitants of some cities are greatly increased through some branches of business" contrary to the leading of the Holy Spirit. Being "entangled in these things tends to bring a cloud over the minds of people" and impedes "the coming of the kingdom of Christ on earth as it is in heaven."[40] Woolman had already expressed these views in America. His encounter with England only strengthened his convictions.

The longer he stayed in England, the more upset he became, and partly as a consequence, his thoughts returned repeatedly to America. He managed to write home on occasion without relying on the post office. In August he gave Emlen a letter for John Comfort and asked him to arrange to have it sent to America.[41] Using other couriers he wrote John and Mary Comfort again in September.[42] He also found a way to write to Sarah on at least one occasion. That letter opened with a poignant declaration of how much he missed his family. "Though I feel in a good degree resigned on being absent from you," he wrote, "my heart is often tenderly abjected toward you, and even to weeping this morning while I am about to write."[43] In London Townsend received mail for Woolman from America. Woolman told him to open and read every letter and forward the mail north only if the message was "of a nature greatly requiring haste."[44] During his time in the north, Woolman gave travelers headed to London letters to carry for him to Townsend.[45] At least once, when he was approaching Yorkshire, he received news of his family from his host.[46] Nonetheless, Woolman felt cut off. On the night of August 22, at Preston Patrick, after he had finally reached the heart of the country where the young George Fox preached, he dreamed of his mother.[47]

As Woolman grew weary, he found comfort in the company of Americans and British Quakers who had been to North America. He lodged with several Quakers who knew the colonies, including Jane Crosfield, whom he had met during her visit to the Delaware Valley in 1760.[48] At the outset of his walk, he traveled alongside William Hunt and another American Friend. Although they did not walk with him, they joined him at Hertford Quarterly Meeting and later at a village in Bedfordshire.[49] Two other American Quakers, Sarah Morris and her niece Deborah, similarly joined Woolman for an extended

period when he was in the north. Sarah Morris, an experienced traveling minister, had undertaken one extended journey through the northern colonies
in the company of Elizabeth Smith and Joyce Benezet.[50] She was a respected
Philadelphia Friend who had originally planned to come to England with
Smith. The uncertainty surrounding Smith's illness had delayed her journey,
but with Deborah as her companion she had managed to arrive in England
three months ahead of Woolman. Her itinerary tracked his over the last part
of the way to York.

Several of the American ministers traveling through England at the time
of Woolman's visit echoed his statements and pleaded with the English to
adopt a more simple life.[51] An English Quaker, William Forster, saw Sarah and
Deborah Morris alongside Woolman. He was positively impressed with all
three of them, and particularly admired the austere example Woolman seemed
to set. Generalizing from the encounter, he compared Woolman to Sophia
Hume, and suggested that North America produced better Quaker leaders.
Addressing himself to an American Friend he wrote, "I think your ministers
in general far exceed ours, though we are favored with several eminent ones."[52]

The dynamics of transatlantic travel invited such invidious comparisons, because in general those who crossed the ocean to perform ministerial
work were unusually devout, committed, and principled Friends. Woolman's
longstanding affection for England had been nurtured by his close contact in
North America with English traveling ministers, but those visitors may have
given him too lofty an impression of the country and left him vulnerable to
disappointment when he arrived and encountered the ordinariness of most
Quakers there. A similar dynamic operated when the English came to visit
America. Elizabeth Wilkinson, an English minister, was disillusioned after
meeting the American Friends. In 1762, in vocal ministry at Burlington Quarterly Meeting, she upbraided Woolman's neighbors for the way they dressed
their children. She complained that the young ones at the meeting "appeared
with cross pockets and other marks of the world's fashions about them." They
were too young to have chosen their own clothing and therefore could not
be held accountable for "such disobedience." The transgression could only be
"charged to the parents' account."[53] Wilkinson's indictment of the American
Quakers closely resembles the complaints that Woolman lodged against the
English, and this similarity should make us cautious about using such commentary to draw too stark a contrast between English and American Quakerism. The commentary of American traveling ministers, and the English
response to their lessons and conduct, do not by themselves provide sufficient

evidence to support any sweeping conclusion that American Quakerism was more austere. Nonetheless, there were indeed distinctly American features to Woolman's appearance, his manner of speaking, his conception of politics, and his program for reform.

*   *   *

Woolman belonged to a contingent of American Friends who became disillusioned with formal politics during the Seven Years' War. That war had divided North America's Quakers, and when it was over there were still many American Friends who remained inclined to address political questions one issue at a time, identifying discrete problems which could be remedied through judicial or parliamentary channels. But Woolman adopted a more spontaneous and comprehensive strategy for reform. Since the founding of Pennsylvania, a millenarian tradition had arisen among the Quakers suggesting that the Society of Friends, with God's assistance, could change the world starting with the Delaware Valley. Quakers like Woolman promoted this vision even after they backed away from participation in government. Seeking a way to effect change without resorting to governmental action, they resolved to apply an axe "to the root of corruption" and make the world better by living well, trusting God, and serving as examples to others.[54]

London Yearly Meeting had participated in the Delaware Valley Quakers' debate over government service during the Seven Years War, even going so far as to encourage those Friends serving in the Pennsylvania assembly to withdraw from the chamber for the duration of the conflict. Nonetheless, that controversy had never engaged the Quakers in Britain with anything like the same intensity as it did the Americans.[55] British Friends lived farther from the theaters of conflict, and since they exerted considerably less political influence in their own country than did Quakers in Pennsylvania and New Jersey, they were far less likely to feel guilty about the conduct of the war. Stung by their wartime experiences, many American Quakers distanced themselves from formal politics in the 1760s, but the conflict had no comparable effect on Quakers in Britain.

In 1772 Woolman was present and watched as London Yearly Meeting devoted hours to a discussion of how best to influence Members of Parliament. British Quakers were seeking ways to convince the government to alter its procedures for collecting tithes.[56] That issue had engaged their attention for decades. Woolman referred to the extraordinary lobbying skills the Yearly

Meeting had acquired during this long campaign in his last recorded vocal ministry in York. He told the Quarterly Meeting there that since "Friends had been solicitous for, and obtained relief from, many of their sufferings," so they should work "in an individual capacity, as way may open" to convince "those in authority, especially the legislative power in this kingdom" to relieve the "hardships and sufferings of the slaves."[57]

In that statement at least, Woolman was unfairly critical of the London Quakers. After all, the "way" had never opened for him to work "in an individual capacity" to reach out to any Members of Parliament. Furthermore, London Yearly Meeting had already demonstrated that it was ready to assist American antislavery advocates like Anthony Benezet who wanted to present their arguments to men in authority. In 1766 the London Quakers helped Benezet send pamphlets to hundreds of MPs.[58] With help from British Quakers, Benezet also corresponded with leaders in the Church of England and with Granville Sharp, the self-taught lawyer who in the early 1770s became Britain's most accomplished antislavery campaigner.[59]

In contrast to Benezet, Woolman never corresponded with prominent British antislavery activists, or with any religious or political leaders outside the Society of Friends. He was almost entirely oblivious to the currents of contemporary British politics as related to slavery or the slave trade. There is no evidence that Woolman was aware of the case of *Somerset v. Stewart*, for example, which was decided in 1772 while he was traveling in England. Slaveholders and opponents of slavery alike interpreted the *Somerset* ruling as effectively freeing all the slaves in the country.[60] Granville Sharp was the lead advocate in the *Somerset* case, and in November 1772 Benezet wrote Sharp to draw his attention to Woolman and his writings.[61] Before that time, Benezet had never done much to publicize Woolman's work outside Quaker circles. In his own pamphlets he had cited Woolman only twice, once without attribution in 1760 and a second time naming him in 1771.[62] In both instances he quoted passages in Woolman's essays that did not explicitly address the issue of slavery, but instead discussed in general terms the pernicious long-term effects of maintaining bad customs. Perhaps in 1772 Benezet hoped to give Woolman wider publicity and draw him into a more diverse community of antislavery activists in Britain. Unfortunately, by the time Benezet wrote Sharp, Woolman was already dead.[63]

In Woolman's era it was increasingly common for politically minded Americans to emphasize the global impact of social customs and private behavior. The expansion of consumer markets, transatlantic trade, and the proliferation of newspapers gave many colonists an exaggerated sense of the role they played in the economic life of the empire.[64] This new perception of influence instilled a sense of empowerment and responsibility among the Americans that affected their response to several transatlantic controversies. Those who protested against parliamentary taxation placed great faith in the efficacy of boycotts. As part of their protests, many of them dressed only in domestically produced clothing.[65]

American antislavery campaigners like Woolman were even more ambitious than the Patriots. Woolman and other like-minded American Quakers believed that abolition would affect more than the status of the enslaved. It would require and inevitably entail a change in the fundamental premises of economic and social life. Because of the prevalence of slaveholding in North America, they were more likely than their British counterparts to think of slave labor as an integral part of the imperial economy and to associate emancipation with profound social change. This was the message Woolman sought to convey dramatically through his clothes.

For years Woolman had tried to make a statement through his clothing, but he could do so effectively only if those around him noticed how he dressed and thought about it. In the 1760s his costume had generated some controversy among his neighbors when he first adopted it, but over the intervening years the people who met Woolman regularly had grown used to his eccentricity. Furthermore, he was hardly the only oddly dressed reformer among them. When John Cox was a boy in Mount Holly he knew Woolman well, and looking back after many years he declared, "My memory of John Woolman is so distinct it seems as though I could see him now before me. He was about my size, dressed in light clothes and a white hat."[66] That was all Cox had to say about Woolman's clothing. The English, by contrast, had had little time to adjust to Woolman's appearance. Some were startled, others were amused, and many were disturbed. When he arrived at Quaker meetings in England children pointed at him and he attracted crowds.[67] Adults complained that he was making himself "singular" and unnecessarily disrupting the decorum of their gatherings.[68] Some interpreted his clothing as a symbol of moral purity and suggested that he was presumptuous in assuming such a mantle.[69] Others were impressed by Woolman's willingness to humble himself, but even if they admired his discipline, they insisted that they would never dress like him.[70]

An unidentifiable witness who saw Woolman at Sheffield reported that "He was remarkable for the singularity of his dress." Although initially surprised by his outfit, this person warmed to Woolman after watching him.

"Though many might think him whimsical from the odd appearance he made, he was a man of great understanding and had very good natural abilities, [and] a mild and benevolent disposition, as might be easily discovered by the natural unaffected simplicity of his manners, which never failed of procuring respect from all who were acquainted with him." This witness quoted Woolman telling the gathering at Sheffield that his clothing served as a statement against the "pride and extravagancy" of his day. The times, he said, "greatly abounded with superfluities."[71] These comments were recorded and preserved by a woman named Mary Andrews. Women as a group may have been more willing than men to find a message in Woolman's clothing. Tabitha Hoyland, for example, saw Woolman in Sheffield and noted that the meetings he attended were "exceedingly crowded." She speculated that the crowd gathered in part "through curiosity to see John's particular dress, and [in] part I hope from a better motive." Those with the better motives "went away well satisfied," but she noted that Woolman's "uncouth appearance will be likely to prejudice many." She went on to speculate on why Woolman dressed as he did.

> I can't but think Providence hath some wise end in what seems difficult to reconcile with man's wisdom. Perhaps it may be intended as a means to wean many from the things which outwardly adorn the body, and likewise other luxuries and delicacies, too much prevailing amongst those in exalted stations.[72]

When Hume commented on Wolman's costume, she declared that she felt "great unity" with him but also suggested that her reaction was rare. She indicated that most of the other Quakers she met praised Woolman but then went on to say, "If he has this faith to himself, they can be easy with him, but [they] desire to be excused if he is proposed as an example."[73]

In contrast to these women, the men whose comments are recorded almost uniformly declared that Woolman's costume was a distraction, even though they valued his ministry after they had adjusted to his appearance and began to hear him speak. Morris Birkbeck described Woolman as "singular in his conduct and conversation, as well as dress, amongst men." Although Woolman had "a path to walk in peculiar to himself," Birkbeck was ready to listen to what he had to say, because he "advanced nothing that he could not maintain with propriety of argument founded on Scripture and Christian principles."[74] Elihu Robinson reported that Woolman's appearance at London Yearly Meeting drew "the attention of the youth" and caused "a change of countenance in some," but Robinson thought that "the simplicity, solidity and clearness of many of his remarks made all these vanish as mists at the sun's rising."[75] William Forster, who also saw Woolman in London, declared that his "remarkable appearance" attracted "the notice of many." Nonetheless Forster concluded that Woolman's "steady uniform deportment, his meekness and unaffected humility, his solidity no less in conversation than in his ministry, which is instructing and edifying, creates much esteem and well corresponds with his appearance."[76] John Fothergill saw Woolman at London Yearly Meeting and judged that he was "solid and weighty in his remarks," but went on to suggest that Woolman would be able to serve the meeting better if he were "cured" of his "singularities."[77] Watching Woolman interact with the British Quakers, William Hunt concluded, "The singularity of his appearance is not only strange, but very exercising to many valuable Friends who have had several opportunities of conference with him." Hunt added, however, that the "purity" of Woolman's ministry won "universal approbation."[78] Emlen's verdict was similar, but harsher. He expressed concern that Woolman's "singularity in white garb gets sometimes into his way with those who do not know him worthy."[79]

If they were just responding to his appearance, the men had more reason than the women to feel challenged by Wolman's clothing, for the simple reason that it was their costume that he was rejecting. Nonetheless, if the English Quakers heard what Woolman had to say about clothing, they knew that his opposition to frills and cloth dyes applied to male and female fashion alike. Indeed, in objecting to dyed cloth, Woolman condemned nearly every suit of clothes in England. The English wore clothing made from standardized, commercially produced textiles. Whether they bought their garments ready-made or sewed them at home, the cloth they wore was nearly always dyed.[80] Woolman considered this wrong, and as he walked toward York he became increasingly disgusted with the English practice of dyeing cloth. The prevalence of dyeing was emblematic of larger problems he observed in the English economy. It was wasteful, deceitful, damaging, and a misallocation of resources. Nonetheless, its very irrationality suggested the possibility of easy reform. Unhappy as he was in the cloth-producing towns, Woolman ruminated optimistically about what might be accomplished "if the value of dyestuffs, the expense of dying, and the damage done to cloth were all added together and the expense applied to keep all sweet and clean."[81]

Woolman's spirits rose slightly toward the end of his journey. It had been a common pattern in his experience as a traveler that almost everywhere he went, even if he was uneasy with most of the people he encountered, he eventually found a community that seemed to agree with him. As a young minister in North Carolina, for example, he saw a "hopeful appearance" among the youth he worshipped with near Albemarle Sound. In New England he met another small group of young people who seemed to have spontaneously discovered Quakerism. Later in life he encountered heroic pacifists in Virginia and a non-Quaker group of worshippers in Maryland who opposed slavery, rejected colored cloth, and in general held beliefs close to his own. Woolman's account of his travels in England was cut short by his illness and death, but there is ample evidence from his abbreviated journal and other sources to suggest that he met an unusually sympathetic circle of Quakers in York.

On September 21, 1772, the Quaker meeting at York sent Henry Tuke, the seventeen-year-old son of a local elder, to serve as Woolman's "guide and companion from his previous stopping place into the city." Tuke would remember "the indescribable sweetness of this walk" for the rest of his life. Traveling Quaker ministers who came to York usually stayed with the Tuke family in the city, but Woolman asked if he could stay somewhere outside the walls, and so Tuke took him to the home of Thomas Priestman. Priestman's house was not far from the city walls, but by lodging there Woolman escaped from "the bustle and noise" of York. He slept in a back room which was "very quiet and retired, there being no thoroughfare at the back of the house except a footpath." As one nineteenth-century visitor described it, Priestman's house was "a little out of the town in the clean country."[82] Its location mattered enormously to Woolman.

Woolman's three-month walk had increased his lifelong sense of the importance of the countryside. In defiance of nearly everything he had seen in the towns of England, he continued to associate peaceful, rural pastures with the future. His concern for the welfare of animals, his uneasiness with urban life, his opposition to slavery, and his general critique of acquisitive commerce had led him to embrace a millenarian alternative. Woolman was "under the weight of this exercise" as he passed through the north of England. He caught a glimpse of God's promise to the prophet Isaiah among the sheep in the fields.[83] He saw a cosmic drama playing itself out in the landscape of Yorkshire. Summarizing his testimony after his death, York Quarterly Meeting reported that Woolman "was fully persuaded that as the Life of Christ comes to reign in the Earth all abuse and unnecessary oppression, both of the human and brute creation, will come to an end."[84]

According to York Quarterly Meeting's retrospective testimony, Woolman was "much out of health" during its sessions. He told his hosts that he had been "poorly in health for some time," but that this was nothing unusual. He often felt feverish in the late summer and early fall, and he still felt "so well in health as to continue traveling." The gathering in York began on Tuesday, September 22, and continued for three days. Woolman participated fully until Thursday afternoon, when he had to excuse himself. From that time forward he confined himself to the Priestman house, and on the following Saturday spots began to appear on his face. By Sunday it was clear that he had smallpox. Some of those who came to see him that weekend thought that his austere diet might protect him. They speculated that the disease might have less of an effect on him because "he had seldom eaten flesh for some time." Soon, however, there were sores all over his body.[85]

From the moment he received the diagnosis of smallpox, Woolman began to anticipate death. He had been contemplating the prospect of dying for many years, and he had done his best to prepare himself. He had long insisted that every death served a purpose. In his pastoral work he declared that when "the righteous" were "removed" by death, "their change is happy," and when "the wicked" were "taken away in their wickedness," God's object was "clear."[86] The moment of death was telling. Woolman assumed that each person's spiritual state at that instant would all but determine his or her fate in the afterlife. In his *First Book for Children* he had directed his young pupils to copy out the following warning: "when one that is wicked dies in his sins, his soul finds no rest in the other world."[87]

The first time Woolman ever witnessed death, the process went badly. In the early 1740s, when he was working as an apprentice in the shop at Mount Holly, his master purchased some "Scotch men servants" from "on board a vessel" to sell their contracts of indenture. The shopkeeper found buyers for the labor of several of the men immediately, but left the remainder with Woolman at the shop. One of those men was ill, and Woolman watched him through the night as he died. The man cursed and swore. He died angrily, unrepentant, and, from Woolman's perspective, unprepared. Woolman was frightened by this experience, and for a short time thereafter he was uneasy about staying at the shop, as if the cursing man had left some evil presence behind.[88]

In general, Woolman's later encounters with death had proven less disturbing, and indeed on several subsequent occasions he had been inspired by good deaths. In 1747, when his sister Elizabeth died, he had consulted with her bedside attendant in order to obtain a full narrative of the event. He cherished his sister's final words and judged that she had "retained a hope which was an anchor to her." He was similarly inspired by his father's passing. He recorded in his journal that when Samuel Woolman died "he had no doubt but that in leaving this life he should enter into one more happy."[89]

John was even more attentive during his brother Abner's demise. In the three months before Abner died on November 4, 1771, John visited him several times and talked to his brother about his spiritual condition, watching carefully as Abner "gathered bodily strength a little," and "soon grew weaker again." During one of the visits, Abner told John that he wanted to be with him alone on his last day. When it appeared that death was imminent, John came to see him and then stayed with Abner for five hours before the end. He observed that Abner "appeared in a quiet state of mind, and was glad to see me." After he asked his wife and children to leave the room, Abner told his brother that he felt confident of his own salvation. He also declared that he felt a "a lively concern that the active members in our Society might keep to the Spirit of Truth in their living and outward concerns." Abner was "much exercised in an inward Sympathy with the oppressed," and even in his final hours he "felt that concern still to live in his mind." Using John as his messenger, he had advice for the Quakers in general. He also wanted John to know what the experience of death was like. John believed that Abner's final statement was particularly significant, and he transcribed it verbatim. Abner said, "I have greatly desired a support that I may bear these heavy pains with patience . . . but these pains are different from any that I ever felt before." Abner's wife and children came into the room for the final moment. Abner's speech "failed, under the pangs of death, and at length he did not appear to have much pain, but to outward appearance breathed quiet and easy for half an hour or more, and departed like one going to sleep."[90]

After Abner died, John transcribed his writings, including several statements concerning death. Throughout his adult life Abner had worried about dying unexpectedly, because he wanted an opportunity to ready himself. "When death comes, if we are not prepared, O how shall we feel then! If we have time to think we shall then have mournful thought! . . . Death sometimes comes suddenly and may not be put by. My mind hath been deeply affected with the thoughts of it." Abner maintained that ideally, the moment of death should be the culmination of a lifelong renunciation of the "things of this world." He wrote, "Remember that this world is not thy proper home. Thou ought to be a stranger in it. Thy business is to do good with what divine providence hath entrusted thee with, and above all things to strive daily to be prepared for thy last change."[91]

It was common for eighteenth-century Quakers to believe that their lives could be enriched and their consciences honed, if they maintained a constant awareness of impending death. They paid particular attention to each other's last moments, in the belief that the experience of dying could be instructive. When revered ministers fell dangerously ill, Friends gathered around their bedsides to hear what they had to say. The British Quakers published multivolume collections of the final words of the pious, and the Americans produced a similar stream of literature in memorial testimonials and in the appendices of published journals. John Churchman had two collections of deathbed ministry published, because he approached death twice. He recovered from a nearly fatal illness in 1761 and then succumbed to a fever in 1775. On both occasions, Friends gathered to hear him speak. They compiled detailed accounts of his statements and behavior in the expectation that his last sayings would be worth printing after his death. In 1761 and again in 1775, Churchman recommended a pious resignation to God's will, but he also gave very specific advice on a variety of contemporary issues. On one evening in 1761, with four visiting Quakers present, he found the strength to express his views on paying provincial taxes in wartime. Later, with a different set of visitors standing around his bed, he discussed the social dynamics of decision-making within Quaker meetings. He protested against "the custom of drinking drams, or strong spirits mixed" and complained that the Quakers of the Delaware Valley were abandoning their commitment to a simple material life. In 1775 he promoted mid-week meetings for worship.[92] Churchman was slightly unusual in getting the opportunity to perform this service twice, but Quakers on both sides of the Atlantic assumed that the last days of life were a time of acute insight, and were eager to take advice from the dying.

Woolman fell ill at a propitious moment, shortly after two other well-regarded pious Quakers had set good examples in the way they had parted from the world. Samuel Fothergill, an English champion of reform, had died earlier that summer, while London Yearly Meeting was still in session. In anticipation of his death his relations had made a collection of Fothergill's deathbed statements and arranged to have them read aloud in London.[93] By all accounts, Fothergill's words affected the Yearly Meeting's deliberations, and the knowledge of his imminent death gave the gathering an unusual spiritual gravity. Later that summer, only a few days before Woolman's arrival in York, Woolman learned that William Hunt had died in Newcastle of smallpox. Hunt's death received considerable attention because he had given edifying ministry at the end. His last statements were distributed widely by word of mouth, in private correspondence, and eventually in print. After hearing what his cousin had said, Woolman helped broadcast at least one of the messages. He wrote back to America that Hunt's last words were, "The Truth is over all."[94]

Woolman responded to the news that his own death might be near by working urgently on his journal. Before embarking on his trip to England, he had left manuscripts of his first ten chapters with the Overseers of the Press in Philadelphia, but since that time he had written two more chapters.[95] During his week in London, he had revised his account of his sea voyage and he had left manuscripts of that chapter with Sophia Hume and John Townsend.[96] His final chapter, describing his travels in England, remained unfinished. On September 27 he wrote a letter to John Eliot, a member of London Yearly Meeting's Committee on Friends' Books, asking him to retrieve his draft of Chapter Eleven from Hume and Townsend, assemble, edit (if necessary), and copy over the manuscripts of both final chapters, and send them to America to join the manuscripts he had left behind.[97] He wrote this letter before he had finished Chapter Twelve.

On September 28, unable to write and declaring himself "so weak in body that I know not how my sickness may end," Woolman dictated his journal's last entry. He wanted to complete an item of unfinished business by telling the story of "an honest-hearted Friend in America, who departed this life less than a year ago." This man, "some months before his departure," had described a dream to Woolman. It was a vision of people walking backward and forward in a fog, in blood-stained garments, and it represented, according to Woolman, the spiritual state of those whose actions supported the slave trade. A few months later, apprehending the approach of death, the man summoned Woolman to sit alone with him at his bedside. Woolman was there for approximately five hours, and an hour before the man's death he called the man's family into the room. Woolman thought that the man seemed "calm and quiet" at his last moment.

Now approaching his own death, Woolman was worried that he had never written that man's dream down, and he wanted to rectify the problem. He recited this last entry to Priestman, and together they worked on it for two days. Priestman could not have fully understood why the episode mattered so much to Woolman, because Woolman did not name the dying dreamer in the entry. It was Abner. John had wanted to get Abner's works published, but had not been able to see any of them printed before he sailed for England. In the end, of all his brother's visions and words of wisdom, this dream was the only fragment that would ever appear in print. On the evening of September 30, after giving Priestman a final note concerning the entry, he said, "I believe the Lord will now excuse me from exercises of this kind." He announced that he had only one more task to perform, which was to die well, but "it must be in the Lord's time, which I am waiting for."[98]

Ironically, the news of Woolman's illness had reminded some English Quakers of the value of smallpox inoculation.[99] Woolman wanted those around him to derive other lessons from his last days. Like Churchman, he had had some practice with the ritual. In January 1770 he had come "nigh unto death," or so it had seemed. Eminent Quakers had gathered around his bedside to sit with him then, and they had taken notes with the intention of recording his final words.[100] Woolman kept that experience in mind in 1772 as he composed his thoughts for his dying day.

Like Abner and Churchman, he used much of his remaining energy re-iterating longstanding concerns, knowing that the approach of death would give his statements greater authority. Recounting an earlier vision, he told the Yorkshire Quakers that he cherished the legacy of George Fox, and that that was one reason why he had felt drawn toward the "northern parts" of England.[101] But he also reminded them that many things had gone wrong in the eighteenth century. He expressed horror and remorse for the fate await-ing those who lived "separated from the divine harmony," and when he pro-nounced these words he was careful to make sure Priestman wrote them down.[102] On another occasion he announced that he had foreseen "the great calamity that is coming upon this disobedient nation."[103] Toward the end of his illness, when his words were "in general difficult to be understood," he managed to pronounce this sharp lament: "How many are spending their time and money in vanity and superfluities, while thousands want the necessaries of life, who might be relieved of them, and their distresses at such a time as this, in some degree softened by the administering of suitable things."[104]

Along with these pronouncements, Woolman provided more self-referential, revealing commentary on his physical condition and state of mind. He was thinking about Mount Holly. "In the beginning of his illness" he asked the Quakers in York to track down his former pupil John Bispham, who had crossed the ocean with him on the *Mary and Elizabeth* and was now somewhere in England. They found a way to send a message to the boy, and Bispham came to York and sat quietly in Woolman's room for two days before he died.[105] As far as his "wife and family" were concerned, Woolman said that he had inwardly "taken leave" of them, yet sensed that they were somehow close. "I feel them near to me at this time," he said, "yet I freely give them up." Acknowledging that he could never return to New Jersey, he professed his faith that his family would be sheltered, if it pleased God, by "divine protection."[106]

Remembering a critical moment in his life, early one morning Woolman "broke forth in supplication," and thanked God for afflicting him with illness during his youth. He believed that in that instance and in all the subsequent times when God had chastised him, he had eventually been healed. Remembering those episodes he asked God to stay with him now, as "a father and a friend."[107] One morning, one of Woolman's attendants asked him how he felt, and he replied, "I don't know that I have slept this night. I feel the disorder making its progress, but my mind is mercifully preserved in stillness and peace."[108] Later he acknowledged that "the pains of death must be hard to bear," but they were unavoidable and he had done his best to prepare himself.[109] Continuing on the same theme, he said, "This trial is easier than I could have thought, by my will being wholly taken away." He suspected that if he had been worried about the outcome, the illness would have been more difficult to endure, but he felt serene. "My mind enjoys a perfect calm."[110] At other times, however, he conceded that staying calm required labor. "The disorder was strong at times," and it would come over his mind "like a whirlwind."[111] The first episode of that sort occurred on September 28. Those who saw him reported that "he could think little and but as a child."[112] That moment passed, however, and within a few hours he regained his composure and intelligibility.

One of the more noteworthy features of Woolman's last week was his ability to give attention to each of the new acquaintances who spent time with him. After he died, York Quarterly Meeting observed that Woolman had an unusual gift that allowed him to "communicate freely to the several states of the people where his lot was cast."[113] This had never been more obvious. He developed an effective working relationship with Priestman, and even as he was dying he came to know the various members of the Tuke family well.

Initially Woolman had protested that he did not want to give "needless trouble" to anyone, but his condition deteriorated rapidly, and eventually he relented and asked Esther Tuke, Henry's stepmother, to watch over him. Esther was relieved that Woolman was asking for help. She had already concluded that "constant attendance" would be necessary. In order to be with Woolman, she moved temporarily into the Priestman house. There was a second bed in Woolman's room, and she rested there. Esther found it "exceedingly trying" to watch Woolman in pain, knowing she could offer him "little relief." Nonetheless, after the ordeal was over she was thankful for the experience. Woolman had amazed her. "I never beheld the like fortitude, patience, and steady resignation. His hope and confidence was so strong and firmly fixed, that the greatest storms of affliction were not able to move him, or make him to utter an impatient word."[114]

Woolman asked Esther to take care of some "little matters" after his death. She promised to follow his directions, but added that she hoped he would live and sort through the tasks himself. Woolman latched onto the word hope, and replied, "My hope is in Christ, and though I may now seem a little better, a change in the disorder may soon happen, and my little strength be dissolved." He insisted that he was content with that possibility, because "if it so happen, I shall be gathered to my everlasting rest." Esther, however, continued to argue gently with him. She reminded him of the deaths of Fothergill and Hunt, and said that that she "could not help mourning to see so many faithful servants removed at so low a time."[115]

One of the tasks that still preoccupied Woolman was "wrapping his corpse." He told Esther and her husband William that he wanted the Quakers to sell his clothes and use the proceeds to cover the inevitable burial expenses: wages for the grave diggers plus the cost of an ash coffin and a piece of "cheap flannel" to serve as a shroud. Woolman explained that he was "not willing to have the coffin made of oak, because it is a wood more useful than ash for some other purposes." When Esther heard these instructions she began to cry, and he told her to stop. "I had rather thou wouldst guard against weeping or sorrowing for me," he said. "I have had some painful conflicts, but now they seem over, and matters are settled, and I look at the face of my dear redeemer."[116]

Henry Tuke's sixteen-year-old sister Sarah served as an attendant at Woolman's bedside. One night, when she offered Woolman a drink, he said, "My child, thou seemest very kind to me, a poor creature. The Lord will reward thee for it."[117] That same night, however, he told her that he was unsure whether he should eat, because he felt "nearly arrived" at the point where his soul would have rest.[118] Sarah Tuke saw glory in Woolman's death. His "faith and patience, with the sweet savor of his pure spirit, made a deep and profitable impression on her mind." Years later she declared that she had seen in him "the power and goodness of the divine hand, which she felt secretly at work in her own heart, calling her to newness of life and holiness before the Lord."[119]

Although Woolman did not send for a doctor, a young Quaker apothecary came to his bedside on hearing that he was ill. A few days later a second apothecary who was not a Quaker joined the first. Of the two, the non-Quaker developed the more complex relationship with Woolman. He was "very anxious to assist," and convinced Woolman to take a "cordial" to soothe his throat. Woolman also agreed to accept another of the apothecary's concoctions "with a view to settle his stomach." That second medicine went down "without effect," and after watching Woolman vomit repeatedly the apothecary asked, "What shall I do now?" Woolman answered, "Rejoice evermore, and in everything give thanks." This comment did not apparently comfort his exasperated non-Quaker helper, and so Woolman eventually added, "This is sometimes hard to come at."[120]

While Woolman agreed to take some medicine, he told the apothecary that he would not ingest anything that had "come through defiled channels or oppressive hands." He explained that he had "a testimony to bear against those things, which he hoped to bear to the last." Woolman consulted the apothecary closely about his condition, and he offered his own advice on a range of acceptable treatments. At times he appeared to be getting better, but Esther Tuke "scarcely ever expected his recovery during his sickness." She thought that there were only two possible outcomes for Woolman: either he would compromise his principles and take all the proffered medicine, or he would die. She assumed that given this choice he would die. Woolman had another way of describing the dilemma. He said that he chose to depend on God, who could either cure him or let him die easily. In the end, the apothecary believed that Woolman had known what was best. He said that as a patient, Woolman could not have been "better ordered than he ordered himself."[121]

After approximately one week in bed Woolman lost his eyesight and the ability to speak, but continued to communicate through writing. His final words were not uttered but scrawled on a note. "I believe my being here is in the Wisdom of Christ," he wrote, "I know not as to Life or Death."[122] At approximately 5:45 a.m. on October 7, 1772, he "seemed to fall into an easy sleep." He slept for "about half an hour" and then "seeming to awake, he breathed a few times with more difficulty, and so expired without sigh, groan, or struggle."[123]

Morris Birkbeck, who saw Woolman at the Yearly Meeting in London, corrected himself when he later reported that Woolman had "died." It would have been better, he said, "to use his own words" and say that he had "departed this life." Woolman had addressed this semantic question at the Yearly Meeting, and he had maintained that the latter phrase was "more expressive, or better adapted to the nature of the change, it being only a removal or passing of the soul which can never die, from this state of probation to an abiding place forever."[124] In their account of Woolman's death, the Quakers in York declared that he had "entered into the mansions of everlasting rest."[125] Abner had described the process of dying in similar terms. He expected to enter "mansions of glory." In that "glorious kingdom," Abner wrote, "the wicked cease from troubling . . . all tears shall be wiped away and . . . the Soul shall continually rejoice and sing praise to the redeemer, world with out end."[126] John harbored the same hopes. He believed that an angel would appear before him and guide him to that kingdom. He described the process in an effort to reassure Sarah Tuke. "The messenger will come," he told her, and "release me from all these troubles."[127]

Epilogue

On October 9, 1772, Woolman's body was buried in York. William Tuke made the arrangements, doing his best to follow the deceased's instructions. Woolman had wanted his clothing traded away to defray the costs, and although Tuke had tried to exchange Woolman's hat, shirt, and trousers for a coffin and a shroud, there had been little time. The carpenter and the clothier he approached made it clear that they preferred money, so at that point Woolman's former student John Bispham intervened. Bispham paid the two tradesmen cash and arranged to have Woolman's peculiar costume shipped back to America. The gravedigger agreed to work in exchange for Woolman's shoes.[1]

The grave was left unmarked because the Quakers associated tombstones with idolatry. As a matter of principle they would not build monuments to themselves. Nonetheless, many of those who came to the Friends burial ground that Friday afternoon felt no qualms about exalting Woolman. A Methodist preacher attended, and to the surprise of the Quakers he spoke at the graveside.[2] The non-Quaker apothecary was also there. He kept silent through the burial, but after returning home he wrote a poem proclaiming that Woolman was more worthy of celebration than many "kings and heroes" who had been honored in verse. It would be wrong, the apothecary thought, for Woolman to "die in oblivion." Referring obliquely to the patch of ground where the body lay buried, he called on the muses to provide a "protectress" for Woolman's "hallowed shrine." He declared that in his lifetime Woolman had exhibited "unbounded love" embracing "all sects, all nations." There were "thousands" who could testify that "his words were powerful and divinely sweet."[3]

Within days of the burial the apothecary's poem joined a stream of laudatory pieces circulating in manuscript form around England. Thomas Priestman and Esther Tuke wrote extended accounts of Woolman's final week. A woman named Mary Barnard wrote a poem emphasizing his Christ-like habit of self-denial and suggesting that his travels on foot had reenacted the last walks of Jesus. Enclosed with private correspondence, preserved and recopied, these writings passed from household to household. William Tuke sent a copy of Priestman's report to John Elliot in London.[4]

At that time, the English had only fragmentary information about Woolman. None of his essays had ever been published in England, although individual copies of a few pieces, including his pamphlets *Considerations on Pure Wisdom* and *Considerations on the True Harmony of Mankind*, had made their way across the ocean. Less than a month after Woolman's death the printer Mary Hinde, who regularly published pamphlets and books for London Yearly Meeting, took those two essays to the Overseers of the Press and requested permission to print them "at her own risk." Four days later she received a copy of Woolman's *Epistle to the Quarterly and Monthly Meetings*, which John Pemberton in Philadelphia had sent Joseph Row. Hinde asked if she could add that essay to her booklet, and the Overseers approved. On his deathbed Woolman had made arrangements for Eliot to receive unpublished manuscripts of essays he had written on "two or three different subjects" since his arrival in England. Woolman expected those essays, on the Golden Rule, the slave trade, unnecessary commerce, the sailors' life and silent worship, to be forwarded to Philadelphia along with the last chapters of his journal. There is no evidence that Elliot sent those manuscripts to America. Instead, he showed them to several Quakers in London including Hinde, who brought them to the Overseers of the Press. In November they agreed that she should include them in her ever-expanding collection of essays. Finally, in December, she obtained permission to add an edited version of Priestman's account of Woolman's death. Her booklet was now 137 pages long. It appeared in spring 1773 as *Serious Considerations on Various Subjects of Importance*.[5] In June 1773, London Yearly Meeting received a copy of Woolman's essay on spoken ministry, and responded by subsidizing a second publication. The meeting authorized Hinde to produce 1,500 copies of that essay, which were then distributed free of charge to all the Quaker Meetings in England, Wales, Scotland, and Ireland.[6]

Over the winter of 1772, Thomas Priestman, William Tuke, and three other Quakers in York drafted a statement about Woolman that was read at London Yearly Meeting the following June. Their statement briefly mentioned Woolman's travels through North America and emphasized his opposition to slaveholding, but it also revealed that none of the Quakers in York had ever seen any of his antislavery essays. "We understand," they reported, that he

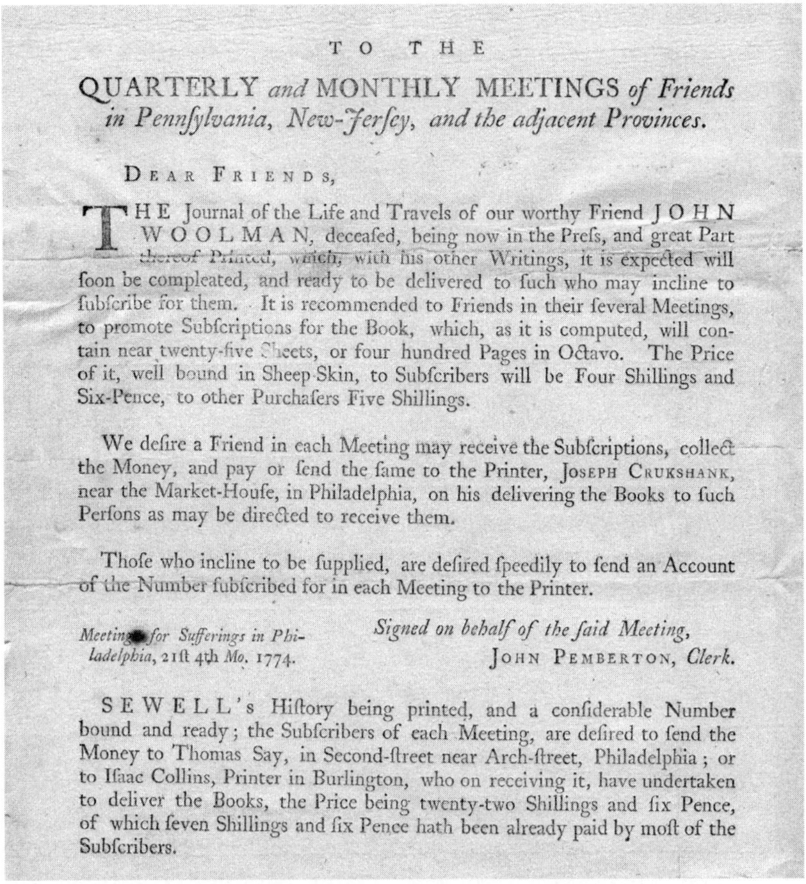

TO THE

QUARTERLY *and* MONTHLY MEETINGS *of Friends in Pennsylvania, New-Jersey, and the adjacent Provinces.*

DEAR FRIENDS,

THE Journal of the Life and Travels of our worthy Friend J O H N WOOLMAN, deceafed, being now in the Prefs, and great Part thereof Printed, which, with his other Writings, it is expected will foon be compleated, and ready to be delivered to fuch who may incline to fubfcribe for them. It is recommended to Friends in their feveral Meetings, to promote Subfcriptions for the Book, which, as it is computed, will contain near twenty-five Sheets, or four hundred Pages in Octavo. The Price of it, well bound in Sheep-Skin, to Subfcribers will be Four Shillings and Six-Pence, to other Purchafers Five Shillings.

We defire a Friend in each Meeting may receive the Subfcriptions, collect the Money, and pay or fend the fame to the Printer, JOSEPH CRUKSHANK, near the Market-Houfe, in Philadelphia, on his delivering the Books to fuch Perfons as may be directed to receive them.

Thofe who incline to be fupplied, are defired fpeedily to fend an Account of the Number fubfcribed for in each Meeting to the Printer.

Meeting for Sufferings in Phi-   *Signed on behalf of the faid Meeting,*
ladelphia, 21ft 4th Mo. 1774.   JOHN PEMBERTON, *Clerk.*

SEWELL's Hiftory being printed, and a confiderable Number bound and ready; the Subfcribers of each Meeting, are defired to fend the Money to Thomas Say, in Second-ftreet near Arch-ftreet, Philadelphia; or to Ifaac Collins, Printer in Burlington, who on receiving it, have undertaken to deliver the Books, the Price being twenty-two Shillings and fix Pence, of which feven Shillings and fix Pence hath been already paid by moft of the Subfcribers.

Figure 15. A fund-raising advertisement for the first publication of Woolman's journal. Courtesy Quaker and Special Collections, Haverford College.

"wrote some books" against slavery.[7] English perceptions of Woolman would change radically in the following winter when the first copies of the North American edition of his journal arrived.

The Quakers in Philadelphia had begun "inspecting" the first ten chapters of Woolman's journal in the summer and early fall of 1772, and later that winter, after they received the news of Woolman's death and drafts of his last two chapters, they entered into an extended, painstaking editorial process. A committee was appointed to revise the journal, and spent months going over the text. The editors deleted dozens of short passages they judged factually inaccurate, wrong-headed, or superfluous. The process took more than a year.

In the winter of 1773, the editors were meeting once a week, and in January 1774 they reported that the journal was "nearly ready for the press." A standing committee of the Yearly Meeting authorized the publication of 1,200 copies. Still more months would pass before the volume appeared, however, because the meeting chose to raise the necessary funds by subscription.[8] The editors took advantage of the delay by adding to the text.

By April they had already decided to publish Woolman's essays along with the journal.[9] They included every major piece that had been approved for publication in America as well as the essays Woolman had written in England, as edited under the direction of Hinde. Accepting the word of the London Quakers, they placed Woolman's essay on vocal ministry at the conclusion of the journal as if it were his final entry. They eventually inserted Hinde's edited account of Woolman's dying statements and York Quarterly Meeting's memorial testimony concerning Woolman. In August 1774, just before publication, they received a similar memorial statement from Burlington Monthly Meeting, which they placed alongside the testimony from York. The final volume was 436 pages long.[10] Compared to the English Quakers who would subsequently reedit the journal, the editorial committee in Philadelphia was more receptive to the full range of Woolman's commentary. The committee included men like John Pemberton and Anthony Benezet who had worked with Woolman for years. While they may not have agreed with every element of Woolman's program for reform, they sympathized with the broad outline of his critique of the contemporary world and his aspirations.

When confronted with the full body of Woolman's work, the English were more selective in their response. On the one hand, there was a contingent in England who had at best only a rough sense of the content of Woolman's spiritual message, but understood that the abolition of slavery was central to his project. The author of the death notice that appeared in the *Leeds Mercury* asserted that Woolman's decision to wear undyed clothing stemmed from the "exquisite" feelings he felt for the "bondage and oppression of the poor enslaved negroes." The short newspaper piece suggested that Woolman's manner of dress fit into a coherent pattern because he "refused every accommodation, both in diet and apparel, which was produced by [slave] labour."[11] This may have seemed a plausible explanation for Woolman's costume, but it bore no relation to his actual commentary on deluded grandeur, waste, and the corrupting influence of fashion. For this writer, and for some others, Woolman was best understood simply as an opponent of slavery.

On the other hand, for many Quakers in England, Woolman's antislavery position was incidental to his hallowed status as a pious and faithful man. When they praised him, they concentrated on his religious convictions. The essays that Hinde published contained antislavery arguments, but the issue did not arise in the accounts of Woolman's illness and death, the laudatory poems that were written during the period of mourning, or the most widely-disseminated piece, Woolman's essay on vocal ministry.

Thomas Wagstaffe was one of the first in England to read Woolman's journal. Like most later readers, he was moved by the early chapters and saw Woolman's entire life work prefigured in his youthful experiences. Wagstaffe composed an essay on Woolman for an anthology of memorial tracts that emphasized deathbed experiences. He began his account of Woolman's life with that moment on the hillside when as a six-year-old boy Woolman hid from his schoolmates to read from the last chapter of Revelation. In the rest of the essay, Wagstaffe concentrated almost entirely on Woolman's spirituality and his renunciation of worldly concerns, but on his fourth page he did insert one sentence on Woolman's visit to Wyalusing, and on the next page he included one sentence on Woolman's opposition to slavery. Wagstaffe's piece concluded with six pages drawn from the collection of dying sayings Hinde had published, praising the edifying example Woolman had set by the way he met his end.[12]

Another early English reader of the journal was Thomas Letchworth. On February 13, 1775, the Quaker Overseers of the Press in London appointed Letchworth to a special committee charged with producing an "abbreviation" of Woolman's journal. Letchworth took charge of the publication process. He was a poet and magazine publisher who in the past had criticized the British for their destructive material extravagance. In a poem published in 1766, Letchworth wrote, "Pride sends us o'er the globe from pole to pole / To rake the mines of Peru—to import / The tinsels of the Indies—'Tis our pride / That swells enormously the heart's desires / For mere terrestrial superfluities."[13] For the most part Letchworth was a sympathetic reader of the journal. He agreed with Woolman on many things, but saw passages in the American edition that he thought never should have appeared in print.

Letchworth's committee convened immediately, and its first order of business was to identify sections to omit. Within three days the committee had identified "various passages" to cut from the British edition of Woolman's journal, entries which, the committee members asserted, related only to the concerns of Americans.[14] When Letchworth received authorization to proceed with publication on February 27, he sent out a circular letter asking for subscribers.[15] In his effort to generate interest, he announced that Woolman's writings contained "the noblest and most rational Christian doctrines, expressed in good language." "In religion he was of no party, nor a lover of party spirit, but the friend of all mankind." Woolman was, Letchwroth wrote, a "Christian Socrates."[16] Even though he praised Woolman extravagantly, he also mentioned that the journal would be abridged.

Letchworth sent this letter to prominent Friends across the country. In an effort to raise funds in Yorkshire, he sent the letter to William Tuke.[17] Tuke had already seen the American edition of the journal, and he perceived no need to shorten it. In March 1775 Tuke brought Letchworth's letter to the Quarterly Meeting at York, which responded by sending an epistle to London requesting republication of the American edition "whole."[18] Despite this request, in the early summer of 1775 Letchworth produced an edition of the journal with several extended passages excised that had been published in America, including descriptions of two of Woolman's supernatural visions,[19] his discussion of his misgivings about paying taxes in wartime,[20] his commentary on smallpox inoculation,[21] his refusal to drink from silver cups,[22] some of his harshest criticisms of British maritime culture,[23] his objections to dyed cloth,[24] his comments on low wages and the high cost of living in England, and his complaints about the accumulation of filth in English towns and the abuse of horses on England's roads.[25]

The new edition of the journal began with an "Advertisement to the Reader" explaining why it had been necessary to shorten it. Concentrating almost entirely on the last two chapters, Letchworth cited Woolman's letter to Eliot in which the author had asked Eliot to assemble and copy over his manuscripts, granting him permission to "leave out such [material] as he should think proper." "Notwithstanding" these instructions, Letchworth declared, Eliot had sent the two chapters "entire, without any alteration" to America, though some of their contents may have been intended as "private memorandums only," and others were "not expedient to be preserved on record in this nation."[26]

It is not clear when the first copies of the abridged edition reached York, but on June 29, declaring their unanimity on the issue, the Yorkshire Quakers repeated their earlier statement. They expressed their wish that the "whole works of John Woolman" be published, "as printed in America, unless some small parts appear upon further examination exceptionable."[27] This second epistle led to several more discussions in London. Letchworth's editorial committee was reassembled and asked to justify its actions in shortening the journal.[28] Eliot, who had not participated in the abridgement process, was now asked to join in the deliberations as the editors drafted their answer to the Quakers in York.[29] After talking the matter over, the London Quakers concluded that they had done nothing wrong. They declared that their edition contained "the most important parts of the journal." Some of the excised passages were "of a private nature," while others "did not relate so particularly to the state of things in this nation as they did to some other places." Furthermore, some of Woolman's observations seemed "to proceed from want of better information."[30] After receiving this response, the Yorkshire Quakers fell silent.[31]

Although it was published in different forms in Britain and America, Woolman's journal was an immediate success on both sides of the Atlantic. Before the end of 1775, two editions of the American version had been printed in Philadelphia, and three editions of the British abridgement had been published in London. The American edition was reprinted in Ireland in 1776, but the next several English imprints would be abridged.[32] The London Quakers' abridgement of the journal fit a pattern. In her earlier editorial efforts, Hinde had similarly dampened or excised Woolman's harshest criticism of Britain. With support from the Overseers of the Press, she had rearranged and consolidated Woolman's last essays, removing Woolman's criticism of the English economy from the prominent position he had given it.[33] Her collection of Woolman's last words also omitted his proclamation that a "great calamity" was "coming upon this disobedient nation."[34]

The London edition of Woolman's journal cut several passages that would speak to the concerns of future generations. In the late nineteenth century, Fabians and other socialists drew on Woolman's comments on the plight of the laboring poor in an effort to build support for wide-ranging economic reform.[35] In the twentieth century, animal rights activists and vegetarians, citing entries that had been omitted from the original English edition of the journal, would celebrate Woolman as one of their own.[36] Nonetheless, while the editors in London cut potentially significant passages, they gave the work a sharper focus, retaining those entries that they considered most "important." According to Letchworth's "Advertisement," one of the great contributions of the journal was the "many weighty and pertinent advices" it contained "relative to slavery and the oppression of the Negroes in the plantations." Woolman's account of his life was so persuasive, Letchworth insisted, that there was no need to include his antislavery essays in the appendix, as had been done in America. The British abridgement of the journal functioned well by itself as an antislavery tract.[37]

Intermittently since the seventeenth century, antislavery activists had been seeking to advance their cause with a compelling personal narrative. Some had adopted a tactic that scholars have called "ventriloquism," creating fictional characters to tell the story of the slave trade from the slaves' perspective.[38] It would not be not until the late 1780s, however, with the publication of Olaudah Equiano's *Interesting Narrative*, that the antislavery movement found an extended, compelling, apparently authentic, and popularly effective life story written by a former slave.[39] Similarly, the antislavery movement had not yet discovered an affecting personal account written by a thoroughly repentant former slave master or slave-trader.[40] Woolman's story, with its insistent expressions of personal guilt for his participation in an economy based on slavery, satisfied a rhetorical need.

The London Quakers were hardly the last group to edit down Woolman's journal in order to highlight his opposition to slavery. The journal's terse prose and concrete language gave even brief excerpts emotive power. In the nineteenth century, abolitionists streamlined the text. They recounted the episode at the shop in Mount Holly when Woolman felt uneasy about assisting in the sale of a slave. They recalled how he hesitated before challenging the views of slaveholding testators and Quaker elders. It was clear to see, however, that once he had found the courage to express himself he had done so dramatically. Eventually he had decided to travel like a slave, on foot.[41] In a poem posthumously addressed to Woolman, an abolitionist writer described the effect of these abridgements in the simplest possible terms:

> . . . the wrongs and sufferings of the slave,
> Stirred the deep foundations of thy pitying heart,
> And still thy hand was stretch'd to aid and save,
> Until it seem'd that thou hadst taken a part
> In their existence, and couldst hold no more
> A separate life from them . . .[42]

Some antislavery activists began to describe Woolman as the founder of their movement. His story seemed to explain the origins of abolitionism in an emotionally satisfying way. As Whittier described him, Woolman was "one of the weak and poor of this world," yet as abolitionism spread, "the little one" had "become a thousand."[43] Assigning Woolman primacy, some writers all but ignored the contributions of other early opponents of slaveholding. An abolitionist poet in 1790, for example, suggested that "Europe" had been unaware of the suffering of slaves until Woolman appeared on the scene.[44] Singling him out gave added drama to the history of abolitionism, and it carried an empowering message. Woolman's life seemed to demonstrate the latent power of humble human beings.

On January 1, 1808, a black pastor named Peter Williams, Jr., gave a sermon in New York City celebrating the end of the transatlantic slave trade. He declared that Woolman had established a "pattern of piety and brotherly kindness" that had been adopted by "the humane of every denomination." The results had been momentous. The abolitionists after Woolman had "assailed the dark dungeons of slavery; shattered its rugged wall, and enlarging thousands of captives, bestowed on them the blessings of civil society."[45] Williams took advantage of Woolman's reputation for piety and kindness to suggest that opposing slavery had become a necessary element of the Christian life. He implicitly shamed those who disagreed with him by claiming that Woolman's perspective had been adopted by all good Christians regardless of the details of their creeds. As Williams's sermon indicates, the abolitionists' invocation of Woolman often gained persuasive power by invoking his reputation for holiness.

Just as Letchworth's abridgement of the journal had foreshadowed later, more rigorous efforts to simplify his life as an antislavery tale, so the literature that appeared in Britain immediately after Woolman's death anticipated another stream of literature celebrating Woolman as the "Quaker saint."[46] A poem by "B. Barton," dated December 8, 1823, and repeatedly republished, praised Woolman but failed to mention his opposition to slavery. Barton suggested that Woolman would be part of the chorus singing with the angels when Christ returned to raise the dead. Woolman was immortal, Barton insisted, and would stand in that small circle of saints "Whose spiritual garments are pure by lavation / In the cleansing blood of THE LAMB!" Christ's glory alone had been his aim.[47] Woolman's life acquired multiple meanings in the century after his death, but all the writers who celebrated him shared one characteristic. They kept the spotlight on the man himself and left the people he encountered in the shadows.

When the Mount Holly Meeting's testimony concerning William Boen's life appeared in print in 1829, Woolman's admirers gained access to a new story recounting his momentary partnership with a black man.[48] Nonetheless, for the next hundred years the arrangements that Woolman made to facilitate Boen's marriage were never mentioned in the laudatory literature on the "Quaker saint." Initially this silence may have stemmed in part from racial prejudice and discomfort with the egalitarian implications of the tale. After Boen's death, one Mount Holly Quaker made a point of declaring that his case was exceptional. "Rare, indeed, are the instances we meet with, in which we feel called upon to record the virtues of any of this afflicted race of people."[49] The initial silence lingered, however, and even today Boen's marriage and his subsequent efforts to join the Mount Holly Meeting are not hinted at in most accounts of Woolman's life.[50] Papunhank, by contrast, figures prominently in the Woolman literature, because the story of Woolman's journey to Wyalusing has had a powerful appeal for those writers who praise Woolman for his perseverance, piety, and zeal. But even today, when those writers tell that story, their treatment of Papunhank almost invariably omits a great deal. Papunhank was famous in Woolman's lifetime, and he remained well known into the nineteenth century. His visits to Philadelphia and his subsequent work with the Moravians were recounted repeatedly to inspire and encourage Christian missionaries.[51] But the literature focusing on Papunhank never mentions Woolman, and writers interested in Woolman almost uniformly ignore Papunhank's time in Philadelphia. Instead, Papunhank appears in accounts of Woolman's trip to Wyalusing only as a mysterious man dwelling in the wilderness. Writers repeat his translated comment "I love to feel where words come from" and analyze the statement at length, because without knowing more about Papunhank it seems like a miracle that an Indian could have gained so much from what Woolman said in English.[52]

At various times over the past two centuries, there have been rhetorical advantages to ignoring Boen and implying that Papunhank never left the woods, but there is another, simpler explanation for why most discussions of Woolman's life and career have provided little or no information about these men. Until the publication of Amelia Mott Gummere's 1922 annotated edition of Woolman's journal and essays, nearly everything that anyone knew or said about Woolman was derived from one source: the 1774 Philadelphia edition of the journal, with Woolman's essays, dying words, and the testimonies of the York and Burlington Quakers annexed.[53] Even now it is the journal, and not the supplementary material that scholars have gathered over the years, that shapes most discussions of Woolman. He wrote that journal with a particular purpose in mind, and there was no space in it for Boen's struggles or for background information on Papunhank.

Woolman began writing his journal in 1755 or 1756 with the expressed purpose of sharing his experience of the divine. He wanted to serve as a model to others and help them hear and heed God's call. As he explained at the outset of the work, "I have often felt a motion of love to leave some hints in writing of my experience of the goodness of God."[54] Woolman's constant introspection in the pages of the journal, his insistence on concentrating on his own spiritual condition, was central to his purpose. When he started writing the work, he could not have known that his life would be so adventurous, but as the years passed his journal changed unexpectedly in character. It became not only a conventional spiritual autobiography but also an unusually rich chronicle of Woolman's torment during the Seven Years' War, his confrontation with the problem of slavery, and more generally his ambivalent relationship with the economy of the British Empire.

The journal's appeal has always stemmed in part from how well it was written. The English essayist Charles Lamb declared that it was the only American book that he had ever read twice.[55] His contemporary Henry Crabb Robinson wrote that the work was a "gem," and labeled Woolman a "beautiful soul." Robinson was impressed by Woolman's skill with prose. "An illiterate tailor, he writes in a style of the most exquisite purity and grace. His moral qualities are transferred to his writings."[56] Decades later another British critic came to a similar assessment. "Here is a lack of adjectives, an entire absence of emphasis, a systematic habit of under-statement that, in the climax of a paragraph or the crisis of an emotion, seems at times almost ludicrous." Nonetheless, this writer liked the effect, declaring that for "the reader of severer taste," Woolman's "unfaltering reticence" was "the choicest grace" of his style.[57] Samuel Taylor Coleridge came close to declaring that reading Woolman's journal would benefit anyone. "I should almost despair of that man who could peruse the life of John Woolman without an amelioration of the heart."[58] The journal struck a chord with European as well as American audiences, but it resonated especially well with the inhabitants of Woolman's home country, because it belonged to a developing American genre. It was the story of an exemplary man whose life seemed to encapsulate the history of his people. Woolman's journal has sometimes been compared to Benjamin Franklin's autobiography, and while the two works were written with very different purposes in mind, they both retain a peculiar appeal to the pretensions of Americans.[59]

From the moment it was published, Woolman's journal has been read by Quakers and non-Quakers alike. It has gained power from each reader's ability to identify with the author in spite of his extreme singularity. Ironically, Woolman's life and message may have a special poignancy for those who do not share his specific religious convictions. For the vast proportion of Woolman's readers who do not maintain his trust in providence, his program for reform can seem commonsensical and at the same time wonderfully, refreshingly, almost comically naïve. There can be no doubt that if we all lived carefully and behaved well in every instance, in every detail, we could change the world. But who could place any faith in a program like that? Woolman worked for the establishment of a perfect world where people could live together without selfishness, stupidity, or aggression. He expected that all creatures would eventually adopt a new pattern of behavior, leaving their base instincts behind. He recognized the enormity of this endeavor, and he never thought that mere mortals, on their own, could muster or maintain the strength to accomplish it. Indeed the impracticality of the project demonstrated its transcendence. He remained hopeful only because he expected intervention from God.

Abbreviations

JW	John Woolman
1753 Ledger	1753 Ledger Book, Woolman Collection, Box 1, Historical Society of Pennsylvania
1769 Ledger	1769 Ledger Book, Woolman Collection, Box 2, Historical Society of Pennsylvania
Book of Executorship	Book of Executorship to the Last Wills of Various Persons, 1746–1765, and Daybook of work done as a tailor, 1743–1746, Woolman Collection, Box 1, Historical Society of Pennsylvania
Friends House	Friends House Library, London
Haverford	Special Collections, Haverford College Library
HSP	Historical Society of Pennsylvania
Huntington	Huntington Library
Leeds	Special Collections, Leeds University Library
NJSA	New Jersey State Archives
Swarthmore	Friends Historical Library, Swarthmore College
BMM	Burlington Monthly Meeting
BQM	Burlington Quarterly Meeting
CMM	Chesterfield Monthly Meeting
LYM	London Yearly Meeting
NEYM	New England Yearly Meeting
PQM	Philadelphia Quarterly Meeting
PYM	Philadelphia Yearly Meeting
VYM	Virginia Yearly Meeting
WQM	Western Quarterly Meeting
YQM	York Quarterly Meeting

Notes

1. John Greenleaf Whittier, "Quaker Slaveholding, and How It Was Abolished," *National Era*, April 8, 1847, 1:14, 2; see also April 15, 22, 1847, 1:15, 2, 1:16, 3.

2. John Woolman, *Some Considerations on the Keeping of Negroes Recommended to the Professors of Christianity of Every Denomination* (Philadelphia, 1754).

3. *An Epistle of Caution and Advice concerning the Buying and Keeping of Slaves* (Philadelphia, 1754).

4. For an overview of the literature on Woolman, see the Epilogue.

5. Jean R. Soderlund, *Quakers and Slavery: A Divided Spirit* (Princeton, N.J.: Princeton University Press, 1985); Gary B. Nash and Jean R. Soderlund, *Freedom by Degrees: Emancipation in Pennsylvania and Its Aftermath* (New York: Oxford University Press, 1991). While highlighting the variety of Quakers who participated in the debate over slavery in the eighteenth century, Soderlund and Nash also emphasize Quaker resistance to abolition, and their work provides an important corrective to earlier, more celebratory works such as Thomas E. Drake, *Quakers and Slavery in America* (New Haven, Conn.: Yale University Press, 1950).

6. Whittier also promised Garrison that he would remind the Quakers of Anthony Benezet's antislavery work, but in subsequent years he would cite Woolman's labors much more emphatically. Whittier to William Lloyd Garrison, November 12, 1833, in John B. Pickard, ed., *The Letters of John Greenleaf Whittier*, 2 vols. (Cambridge, Mass.: Belknap Press of Harvard University Press, 1975), 1:133. For the start of his campaign see Whittier ("A Friend") "To the Members of the Society of Friends," April 16, 1834, in Pickard, ed., *Letters*, 1:148. On Whittier's becoming an abolitionist see Charles A. Jarvis, "Admission to Abolitionism: The Case of John Greenleaf Whittier," *Journal of the Early Republic* 4 (1984): 161–76. Although most nineteenth-century American Quakers celebrated Woolman's holiness, they were not equally active in their opposition to slavery. See Elizabeth Buffum Chace, *Anti-Slavery Reminiscences* (Central Falls, R.I.: Freeman, 1891); Drake, *Quakers and Slavery in America*, 133–66; Ryan P. Jordan, *Slavery and the Meetinghouse: The Quakers and the Abolitionist Dilemma, 1820–1865* (Bloomington: Indiana University Press, 2007). Thomas D. Hamm, *The Transformation of American Quakerism: Orthodox Friends, 1800–1907* (Bloomington: Indiana University Press, 1992) provides a good introduction to the divisions within the American Society of Friends in the nineteenth century.

7. John Greenleaf Whittier, ed., *The Journal of John Woolman* (Boston: Osgood, 1872), 2, 31.

8. Andrew Smellie's introduction to John Woolman, *The Journal of John Woolman* (London, 1902, reprint of 1898 edition), xiv. Smellie prefaced his assessment with an elaborate qualifier. Individually or in groups, abolitionists had been compared to Napoleon before. See Louis Taylor Merrill, "The English Campaign for Abolition of the Slave Trade," *Journal of Negro History* 30 (1945): 382–99, 397; Christopher Leslie Brown, *Moral Capital: Foundations of British Abolitionism* (Chapel Hill: University of North Carolina Press, 2006), 7–8.

9. Rosemary Moore, *The Light of Their Consciences: The Early Quakers in Britain, 1646–1666* (University Park: Pennsylvania State University Press, 2000) provides a good introduction to the founding principles of early modern Quakerism. See also Richard Bauman, *Let Your Words Be Few: Symbolism of Speaking and Silence Among Seventeenth-Century Quakers* (New York: Cambridge University Press, 1983). For Quaker belief and practice in America, see Meredith Baldwin Weddle, *Walking in the Way of Peace: Quaker Pacifism in the Seventeenth Century* (Oxford: Oxford University Press, 2001); Carla Pestana, *Quakers and Baptists in Colonial Massachusetts* (New York: Cambridge University Press, 1991); Barry Levy, *Quakers and the American Family: British Settlement in the Delaware Valley* (Oxford: Oxford University Press, 1992); J. William Frost, *The Quaker Family in Colonial America* (New York: St. Martin's, 1973). Rebecca Larsen, *Daughters of Light: Quaker Women Preaching and Prophesying in the Colonies and Abroad, 1700–1775* (New York: Knopf, 1999); and Carla Gerona, *Night Journeys: The Power of Dreams in Transatlantic Quaker Culture* (Charlottesville: University of Virginia Press, 2004) are important works that span the ocean.

10. Thomas P. Slaughter, *The Beautiful Soul of John Woolman, Apostle of Abolition* (New York: Hill and Wang, 2008). I have several detailed disagreements with Slaughter's work; for those I refer the reader to Chapter 2 nn19, 93, Chapter 4 n33, Chapter 5 nn42, 54, Chapter 8 nn20, 42, 77, Epilogue nn9, 50. See also my review in *Christian Century*, September 9, 2008, 42–44.

11. See Jack D. Marietta, *The Reformation of American Quakerism, 1748–1783* (Philadelphia: University of Pennsylvania Press, 1984). With its emphasis on issues that divided the Quakers, Marietta's work is corrective in much the same way that Nash's and Soderlund's altered our earlier view of Quaker antislavery. For a sense of the earlier perspective on reform, see Sydney V. James, *A People Among Peoples: Quaker Benevolence in Eighteenth-Century America* (Cambridge, Mass.: Harvard University Press, 1963).

12. John J. McCusker and Russell R. Menard, *The Economy of British America, 1607–1789* (Chapel Hill: University of North Carolina Press, 1991), 203.

13. Thomas M. Doerflinger, *A Vigorous Spirit of Enterprise: Merchants and Economic Development in Revolutionary Philadelphia* (Chapel Hill: University of North Carolina Press, 1986) is a good introduction to the economic history of the eighteenth-century Delaware Valley. For a sense of the transformation of material culture, see Jack L. Lindsey, ed., *Worldly Goods: The Arts of Early Pennsylvania, 1680–1758* (Philadelphia: Philadelphia Museum of Art, 1999); J. William Frost, "From Plainness to Simplicity: Changing Quaker Ideals for Material Culture," in Emma Jones Lapsansky and Anne A. Verplanck, eds., *Quaker*

Aesthetics: Reflections on a Quaker Ethic in American Design and Consumption (Philadelphia: University of Pennsylvania Press, 2003), 16–40. It is difficult to measure the rate of economic growth precisely, because many of the changes in living standards that are obvious to historians are difficult to quantify. See generally Russell R. Menard, "Colonial America's Mestizo Agriculture," in Cathy Matson, ed., *The Economy of Early America: Historical Perspectives and New Directions* (University Park: Pennsylvania State University Press, 2006), 107–23.

14. See Albert O. Hirschman, *The Passions and the Interests: Political Arguments for Capitalism Before Its Triumph* (Princeton, N.J.: Princeton University Press, 1977); Joyce Appleby, *Economic Thought and Ideology in Seventeenth-Century England* (Princeton, N.J.: Princeton University Press, 1978). The slow death of the moral economy has generated a vast scholarly literature. For an overview of its importance for early American history see Daniel Vickers, "Competency and Competition: Economic Culture in Early America," *William and Mary Quarterly* 3rd ser. 47 (1990): 3–29.

15. The Seven Years' War and Pontiac's War created a crisis for American Quakerism, and have generated a rich and expanding literature. See Kevin Kenny, *Peaceable Kingdom Lost: The Paxton Boys and the Destruction of William Penn's Holy Experiment* (Oxford: Oxford University Press, 2009); Peter Silver, *Our Savage Neighbors: How Indian War Transformed Early America* (New York: Norton, 2008); Nicole Eustace, "The Sentimental Paradox: Humanity and Violence on the Pennsylvania Frontier," *William and Mary Quarterly* 65 (2008): 29–64; David Sloan, "'A Time of Sifting and Winnowing': The Paxton Riots and Quaker Non-Violence in Pennsylvania," *Quaker History* 66 (1977): 3–22.; Jack D. Marietta, "Conscience, the Quaker Community, and the French and Indian War," *Pennsylvania Magazine of History and Biography* 95 (1971): 3–27; Ralph L. Ketcham, "Conscience, War and Politics in Pennsylvania, 1755–1757," *William and Mary Quarterly* 20 (1963): 416–39.

16. Christopher Brown, "Empire Without Slaves: British Concepts of Emancipation in the Age of the American Revolution," *William and Mary Quarterly* 56 (1999): 273–306.

17. See T. H. Breen, *The Marketplace of Revolution: How Consumer Politics Shaped American Independence* (New York: Oxford University Press, 2004); for a comment on the ways in which the study of Quaker reformers might augment Breen's analysis, see David Waldstreicher's review of Breen, *Journal of American History* 91 (2005): 1416–17.

18. There is an old strand of scholarly literature that dismisses the early abolitionists as inconsequential and suggests, for example, that the British campaign against the slave trade started abruptly in the 1780s. Marcus Rediker's narrative in *The Slave Ship: A Human History* (London: Penguin, 2007), 308–42 implicitly perpetuates this view. See also Adam Hochschild, *Bury the Chains: Prophets and Rebels in the Fight to Free an Empire's Slaves* (Boston: Houghton Mifflin, 2005). Brown's *Moral Capital*, by contrast, traces the growth of the antislavery movement from its beginnings in colonial America, through the American Revolutionary era into the early nineteenth century. Other recent works including Vincent Carretta, *Equiano the African: Biography of a Self-Made Man* (Athens: University of Georgia Press, 2005) and Maurice Jackson, *Let This Voice Be Heard: Anthony Benezet, Father of Atlantic Abolitionism* (Philadelphia: University of Pennsylvania Press, 2009) adopt this deeper chronological perspective, which allows us to assess the full contribution of the Quakers.

CHAPTER I. PAST AGES: HISTORY

1. Phillips P. Moulton, ed., *The Journal and Major Essays of John Woolman* (Richmond, Ind.: Friends United Press, 1971), 23; Revelation 22:1–2.

2. Moulton, ed., *Journal*, 118; see also 29; Marjorie Freund, "Introduction," in Elizabeth M. Perinchief, ed., *The Woolman Family* (Mount Holly, N.J.: John Woolman Memorial Association, 1991); John Woolman's will, March 26, 1711, in ibid., 5–6; Samuel Woolman's will, August 11, 1750, Recorded Wills, West Jersey, Book 6, 391–94, 391; Samuel Woolman's estate inventory, 4761–4766C, NJSA.

3. Freund, "Introduction," in Perinchief, ed., *Woolman Family*. See also ibid, 1–2; Burlington Monthly Meeting Records of Births and Deaths, 1677–1805, f. 108, Swarthmore.

4. Abner Woolman, Journal, Chapter III, Haverford. For an overview of sibling relations in colonial America see C. Dallet Hemphill, "Sibling Relations in Early American Childhoods: A Cross-Cultural Analysis," in *Children in Colonial America*, ed. James Marten (New York: New York University Press, 2007), 77–89.

5. Barry J. Levy, " 'Tender Plants': Quaker Farmers and Children in the Delaware Valley, 1681–1735," *Journal of Family History* 3 (1978): 116–35; Levy, *Quakers and the American Family*, 148–49, 243–44.

6. *New Jersey Archives*, first ser. (1880–1928) 30:547; Samuel Woolman's will, August 11, 1750, Recorded Wills, West Jersey, Book 6, 391–94, NJSA.

7. Moulton, ed., *Journal*, 29.

8. Moulton, ed., *Journal*, 118. See also John Woolman, *Considerations on Pure Wisdom and Human Policy* (Philadelphia, 1768), 12.

9. Moulton, ed., *Journal*, 44.

10. Moulton, ed., *Journal*, 23, 25.

11. Moulton, ed., *Journal*, 39.

12. See John Woolman, "A Plea for the Poor, or A Word of Remembrance and Caution to the Rich," in Moulton, ed., *Journal*, 238–72, 264; John Woolman, *An Epistle to the Quarterly and Monthly Meetings of Friends* (Burlington, N.J., 1772), 5.

13. Woolman, "Plea for the Poor," 267.

14. Moulton, ed., *Journal*, 23, 29; *New Jersey Archives*, first ser. 30:547; Inventory of Samuel Woolman's estate, August 25, 1750, NJSA.

15. Gabrielle M. Lanier, *The Delaware Valley in the Early Republic: Architecture, Landscape, and Regional Identity* (Baltimore: Johns Hopkins University Press, 2005), 112; George DeCou, *Burlington: A Provincial Capital* (Philadelphia: Harris and Partridge, 1945), 47–48.

16. Perinchief, ed., *Woolman Family*, 7b.

17. Samuel Smith, *History of Nova Caesarea* (Burlington, N.J., 1765), 496. See also Carl Raymond Woodward, ed., *Ploughs and Politics: Charles R. Read of New Jersey and his Notes on Agriculture, 1715–1774* (New Brunswick, N.J.: Rutgers University Press, 1941); DeCou, *Burlington*, 50–52.

18. Uriah Woolman, Bills of Lading, 1772–1775, Am. 917, HSP; *Pennsylvania Packet*, July 20, December 7, 1772, December 2, 1773, March 7, 1774, February 6, 1775;

Pennsylvania Gazette, July 21, July 28, October 27, December 22, 1773, June 8, 1774, and March 1, 1775.

19. Abner Woolman, Journal, Chapter VII.

20. *A Century of Population Growth* (Washington, D.C., 1909), 184.

21. Smith, *History of Nova Caesarea*, 496.

22. *Pennsylvania Gazettte*, August 24, 1738, October 5, 1749, May 16, 1751, October 26, 1752, March 27, 1753, October 2, 1755, December 19, 1765.

23. According to a census conducted in 1745, slaves constituted 6.3 percent of the county's population. See Jean R. Soderlund, "African Americans and Native Americans in John Woolman's World," in Mike Heller, ed., *The Tendering Presence: Essays on John Woolman* (Wallingford, Pa.: Pendle Hill Publications, 2003), 148–66, 152.

24. *Pennsylvania Gazette*, April 25, September 30, 1754, April 26, 1764.

25. Doerflinger, *Vigorous Spirit*, 70–134.

26. Lindsey, ed., *Worldly Goods*.

27. Moulton, ed., *Journal*, 24.

28. Testimony of Burlington Monthly Meeting, August 1, 1774, in Amelia Mott Gummere, ed., *The Journal and Essays of John Woolman* (New York: Macmillan, 1922), 332.

29. Moulton, ed., *Journal*, 24.

30. Moulton, ed., *Journal*, 93; Abner Woolman, Journal, Chapter IX, Haverford.

31. Moulton, ed., *Journal*, 36, 72–73, 98–99.

32. Woolman, "Plea for the Poor," 258.

33. Journal manuscript, Woolman Collection, Box 2, p. 280 and back p. 1, HSP; Gummere, ed., *Journal*, 397–8; Moulton, ed., *Journal*, 146–47.

34. Soderlund, "African Americans and Native Americans," in Heller, ed., *Tendering Presence*, 150–51, 157.

35. *Pennsylvania Gazette*, February 14, April 4, 1765.

36. Smith, *History of Nova Caesarea*, 502, on rattlesnakes 503–10.

37. Woolman, *Some Considerations*, 19.

38. Moulton, ed., *Journal*, 28, 97–98; Woolman, *Some Considerations*, 6.

39. Moulton, ed., *Journal*, 98–99. See Proverbs 14:34.

40. Gummere, ed., *Journal*, 7 n3, 25–26.

41. Moulton, ed., *Journal*, 139–40; *A Collection of Memorials Concerning Divers Deceased Ministers* (Philadelphia, 1787), 254; Weddle, *Walking in the Way of Peace*, 254; George Churchman, Journal, 1:79, 2:1, Haverford; Samuel Comfort's 1800 copy of Woolman's journal, with notes, marginalia p. 188, Swarthmore.

42. Moulton, ed., *Journal*, 146–47.

43. Moulton, ed., *Journal*, 118.

44. 1753 Ledger, 220; Moulton, ed., *Journal*, 167; William Sewel, *History of the Rise, Increase, and Progress of the Christian People called Quakers*, 3rd ed. (Philadelphia, 1728).

45. 1753 Ledger, 219–20; John Woolman, *Considerations on the True Harmony of Mankind, and How it is to be Maintained* (Philadelphia, 1770), 28; Woolman, *Epistle*, 4, 12.

46. Woolman, *Epistle*, 3, 10.

47. Moulton, ed., *Journal*, 188.

48. Testimony of Burlington Monthly Meeting, August 1, 1774 in Gummere, ed., *Journal*, 330.

49. Woolman, *Epistle*, 9.

50. Moulton, ed., *Journal*, 188.

51. Woolman, *Epistle*, 9.

52. *An Epistle from our Yearly Meeting* (Philadelphia, 1746). For Woolman's attendance at this meeting see PYM Minutes, 1681–1746, 447, Swarthmore.

53. Hermann Wellenreuther, "The Political Dilemma of the Quakers in Pennsylvania, 1681–1748," *Pennsylvania Magazine of History and Biography* 94 (1970): 135–72.

54. Account of Woolman's illness and death, in Moulton, ed., *Journal*, 304.

55. Woolman, *Considerations on True Harmony*, 12–13, 27–28.

56. Moulton, ed., *Journal*, 76, 147.

57. Moulton, ed., *Journal*, 75–6; 1753 Ledger, 219–20.

58. John Woolman, *Considerations on Keeping Negroes, Recommended to the Professors of Christianity, of Every Denomination, Part Second* (Philadelphia), 1762), 4.

59. Woolman, *Epistle*, 8–9.

60. Woolman, *Considerations Part Second*, 4.

61. Moulton, ed., *Journal*, 77 n9; Woolman, "Plea for the Poor," 252; Woolman, *Considerations on True Harmony*, 5–6

62. William Cave, *Primitive Christianity: or, The Religion of the Ancient Christians in the First Ages of the Gospel* (London, 1702).

63. Woolman, *Considerations on True Harmony*, 5, 27–28; Woolman, "Plea for the Poor," 254.

64. Woolman, *Considerations on True Harmony*, 12; Woolman, "Plea for the Poor," 253, 255.

65. See, for example, Moulton, ed., *Journal*, 62–63; Woolman, *Considerations on True Harmony*, 2, 10–11.

66. Moulton, ed., *Journal*, 32, 52, 60.

67. 1753 Ledger, unpaginated eighth page. In their preference for biblical names, the colonial Quakers equaled, and may have surpassed, the seventeenth-century New England Puritans. Biblical names did not predominate in other religious communities nearly as much. In early modern England, approximately half of the male population carried such names. See Gloria L. Main, "Naming Children in Early New England," *Journal of Interdisciplinary History* 27 (1996): 1–27, 16; Daniel Scott Smith, "Continuity and Discontinuity in Puritan Naming: Massachusetts, 1771," *William and Mary Quarterly* 51 (1994): 67–91, 67.

68. Perinchief, ed., *Woolman Family*, 8.

69. Quoted in Michael L. Birkel, "Preparing the Heart for Sympathy: John Woolman Reading Scripture," in Heller, ed., *Tendering Presence*, 88–104, 89.

70. See Lisa M. Gordis, "Spirit and Substance: John Woolman and 'The Language of the Holy One'," in Heller, ed., *Tendering Presence*, 67–87, 70–71.

71. Woolman, *Considerations on True Harmony*, 10–11. See Revelation 18:4.

72. Moulton, ed., *Journal*, 23.

73. Moulton, ed., *Journal*, 72–73.

74. Abner Woolman, Journal, Chapter XXXII (transcribed and edited by John Woolman in 1771), Haverford.

75. Woolman, *Considerations Part Second*, 25.

76. John Woolman, "Conversations on the True Harmony of Mankind, and How it May be Promoted," in John and Isaac Comly, eds., *Friends' Miscellany* (Philadelphia, 1831–39), 1:337–55, 339.

77. *An Epistle from our General Spring Meeting of Ministers and Elders* (Philadelphia, 1755), 1–2.

78. Moulton, ed., *Journal*, 185.

79. Isaiah 11:6–7.

80. Moulton, ed., *Journal*, 28.

81. John Woolman, *A First Book for Children*, 3rd ed. (Philadelphia, 1769); Anthony Benezet to George Dillwyn, July 1778, in George S. Brookes, *Friend Anthony Benezet* (Philadelphia: University of Pennsylvania Press, 1937), 327–28.

82. 1769 Ledger, loose page.

83. Woolman, "Plea for the Poor," 238.

84. Journal manuscript, Woolman Collection, Box 2, back p. 17, HSP.

85. Woolman, "Conversations," in Comly and Comly, eds., *Friends' Miscellany*, 1:340.

86. *Memoirs of the Lives of Benjamin Lay and Ralph Sandiford* (Philadelphia, 1815), 24, 48; John Hunt, "Notices of Benjamin Lay," in Comly and Comly, eds., *Friends' Miscellany*, 4:275; "Memoirs of Joshua Evans," ibid., 1:299–312, 302–3; Joshua Evans, Journal., ibid.,10:1–212, 27–30; Benezet to John Smith, December 9, 1757, Vaux Family Papers, 638 5/26, HSP. I would like to thank Jonathan Sassi for this reference. See also Donald Brooks Kelley, "'A Tender Regard to the Whole Creation': Anthony Benezet and the Emergence of an Eighteenth-Century Quaker Ecology," *Pennsylvania Magazine of History and Biography* 106 (1982): 69–88; Geoffrey Plank, "'The Flame of Life was Kindled in All Animal and Sensitive Creatures': One Quaker Colonist's View of Animal Life," *Church History* 76 (2007): 569–90.

87. Abner Woolman, Journal, Chapters VII, XVIII, XXXII, Haverford.

88. Undated letter from Abner Woolman, bound with his journal, 14, see also Abner Woolman, Journal, Chapter XXXII, Haverford.

89. Abner Woolman, Journal, Chapter XXVIII, Haverford.

90. Abner Woolman, Journal, Chapters XXII, XXXVI, Haverford.

91. Joan Gilbert, "John Woolman (1720–1772): Abolitionist and Animal Defender," *Animals' Agenda* 11 (1991): 24; 1753 Ledger; 1769 Ledger, see esp. 10.

CHAPTER 2. DESERTS AND LONELY PLACES: SOCIAL DIVERSION
AND SOLITARY MEDITATION

1. Moulton, ed., *Journal*, 24–25. See Proverbs 12:10.

2. Woolman, *Considerations Part Second*, 25; see Woolman, "Plea for the Poor," 258–59.

3. Moulton, ed., *Journal*, 29.

4. See Bauman, *Let Your Words Be Few*.

5. Moulton, ed., *Journal*, 58. For a discussion of the origins of the Quaker understanding of spiritual insight see Moore, *Light of Their Consciences*.

6. John Wooolman, *An Extract from John Woolman's Journal in Manuscript, Concerning the Ministry* (London, 1773), 4.

7. John Cox, "Sketches and Recollections," 1, Dillwyn Parrish Recollections and Sketches, HSP.

8. Woolman, *Considerations on True Harmony*, 29–30; see Joel 2:25.

9. Cave, *Primitive Christianity*, 65.

10. See Woolman, "Plea for the Poor," 250, 259; Woolman, *Considerations on True Harmony*, 5, 15.

11. Woolman, *Considerations on True Harmony*, 30–31.

12. Moulton, ed., *Journal*, 27, 28, 70–71, 74, 155, 159.

13. Abner Woolman, Journal, Chapter I, Haverford.

14. Joshua Evans, journal manuscript, RG 5/190, 7, Swarthmore.

15. Woolman, *Considerations on True Harmony*, 9. See also Woolman, "Plea for the Poor," 255.

16. Woolman, *Considerations on True Harmony*, 23.

17. 1769 Ledger, loose page.

18. Moulton, ed., *Journal*, 24, 47, 185–86. For Woolman's use of the phrase "night vision" see 191.

19. 1753 Ledger, 26; Isaac Watts, *A Wonderful Dream* (Boston: Zachariah Fowle, n.d. 1765?). Slaughter's assertion that Woolman "rejected" poetry regardless of its spiritual content is misinformed. Woolman copied out passages from two poems attributed to Isaac Watts, and he valued the work of Sir Richard Blackmore, for example. Woolman owned Blackmore's poetic work *Creation*, and lent it out to customers in his shop. See 1753 Ledger, 21 contra, 219–20; Isaac Watts, *Horae Lyrica: Poems Chiefly of the Lyric Kind*, 6th ed. (London, 1731), 209–12; Richard Blackmore, *Creation: A Philosophical Poem* (London, 1718); Slaughter, Beautiful Soul, 84.

20. See Moulton, ed., *Journal*, 161–62, 191–92.

21. Elizabeth Wilkinson, Journal, 91–92, Haverford.

22. For an overview of Quaker beliefs concerning dreams see Gerona, *Night Journeys*. For a broader discussion of early American dream culture, see Mechel Sobel, *Teach Me Dreams: The Search for Self in the Revolutionary Era* (Princeton, N.J.: Princeton University Press, 2000).

23. Moulton, ed., *Journal*, 24n6.

24. PYM Epistle to Friends on Long Island, September/October 1762, PYM Miscellaneous Papers, 1748–1762, 1762, f. 13, Swarthmore; for Woolman's joint authorship of this epistle see PYM Minutes, 1747–1779, 167, Haverford. See also Woolman, *Some Considerations*, 15; Woolman, *Epistle*, 5. William Forster to William Birkbeck, Jr., July 1772, Mss. vol. 77, f. 1, Friends House. For eighteenth-century American Quaker views on education see Barry J. Levy, "Tender Plants"; Frost, *Quaker Family*, 64–92.

25. Woolman, "Plea for the Poor," 263–64.

26. Moulton, ed., *Journal*, 25–26. See also ibid, 183; Woolman, *Considerations on Pure Wisdom*, 14; JW to ?, July 9, 1769, Journal manuscript, Box 2, p. 281, HSP.

27. Moulton, ed., *Journal*, 24–26.

28. See, for example, PYM Minutes, 1747–1779, 71, Swarthmore.

29. PYM Epistle to Friends in Rhode Island, September 1761, PYM Miscellaneous Papers, 1748–1762, 1761, f. 14, Swarthmore; for Woolman's joint authorship of this epistle see PYM Minutes, 1747–1779, 155, Haverford.

30. William J. Allison, ed., *Memorials of Rebecca Jones*, 2nd ed. (Philadelphia, 1849), 35–36.

31. Moulton, ed., *Journal*, 26.

32. For Woolman's use of these terms see Moulton, ed., *Journal*, 174, 191.

33. Woolman, *Considerations Part Second*, 8.

34. Woolman, "Plea for the Poor," 258–59.

35. 1769 Ledger, loose page.

36. Moulton, ed., *Journal*, 26n16.

37. Moulton, ed., *Journal*, 26.

38. Account of Woolman's illness and death, in Moulton, ed., *Journal*, 304.

39. Moulton, ed., *Journal*, 120, 155, 173; see also ibid., 56.

40. For a dramatic literary presentation of this outlook, which was common among English Protestants regardless whether they were Quakers, see Daniel Defoe, *The Life and Strange Adventures of Robinson Crusoe, or York, Mariner* (London, 1719), 101–6.

41. Andreas Rivetus, quoted in William Penn, *No Cross, No Crown: A Discourse Shewing the Nature and Discipline of the Holy Cross of Christ*, 6th ed. (London, 1702), 2:150–51. See also Sophia Hume, *Remarks on the Practice of Inoculation for the Small Pox*, 2nd ed. (London, 1767), 34 n; Abner Woolman, Journal, Chapter XXII, Haverford.

42. Moulton, ed., *Journal*, 26.

43. Moulton, ed., *Journal*, 28–30.

44. Moulton, ed., *Journal*, 32.

45. Moulton, ed., *Journal*, 32.

46. George Fox, *Journal* 2 vols. (London, 1709), 1:28–29.

47. Peter Thompson, *Rum Punch and Revolution: Taverngoing and Public Life in Eighteenth-Century Philadelphia* (Philadelphia: University of Pennsylvania Press, 1999), 21–26.

48. Gabriel Thomas, "An Historical Description of the Province and Country of West New Jersey in America," 1698, reprinted in Albert Cook Myers, ed., *Narratives of Early Pennsylvania, West New Jersey and Delaware 1630–1707* (New York: Scribner's, 1912), 338–52, 349; [Anthony Benezet], *The Mighty Destroyer Displayed* (Philadelphia, 1774), 10, 21.

49. *An Epistle of the Yearly Meeting of Friends held at Burlington . . . 1726* (Philadelphia, 1727), 3.

50. PYM Minutes, 1747–1779, 13, 18, 71, 230, Swarthmore.

51. According to Woolman's records as a retailer in Mount Holly, the purchasers of large quantities of rum included Edward Andrews, Samuel Andrews, Joseph Burr, James Southwick, and Josiah Southwick. See 1753 Ledger.

52. 1753 Ledger, 29 contra and 30.

53. [Benezet], *Mighty Destroyer*, 6–7, 18–24.

54. Evans, Journal, Comly and Comly, eds., *Friends' Miscellany*, 10:33–36.

55. Moulton, ed., *Journal*, 55.

56. Woolman, "Plea for the Poor," 244.

57. The two Delaware Valley Quakers who first advanced medical arguments against drinking were Joshua Evans and Anthony Benezet, both of whom, through reading and personal discovery, came to believe that liquor was more deleterious than water in the early 1770s, after Woolman's death. See Evans, Journal; [Benezet], *Mighty Destroyer*.

58. Woolman, "Plea for the Poor," 247. These comments echo some made by John Churchman in 1761. See John Churchman, *Account of the Gospel Labours and Christian Experiences of a Faithful Minister of Christ, John Churchman* (Philadelphia, 1779), 211.

59. Moulton, ed., *Journal*, 54, 55; Woolman, "Plea for the Poor," 245.

60. Abner Woolman, letter, 1770, in, Journal, 12, see also ibid., Chapter XII, Haverford.

61. [Benezet], *Mighty Destroyer*, 15.

62. John Miller, "'A Suffering People': English Quakers and Their Neighbours, c. 1650–1700," *Past and Present* 188 (2005): 71–103, 96–97.

63. Sophia Hume, *A Caution to Such as Observe Days and Times* (London, 1766), 5–6. See Amos 5:22.

64. James, *People Among Peoples*.

65. For a full discussion of the implications of this impulse see Marietta, *Reformation*.

66. For an indication of this see photostat manuscript of Woolman's sea journal, 18, Friends House.

67. Moore, *Light of their Consciences*, 118–19, 177; Bauman, *Let your Words Be Few*, 46–51.

68. Moulton, ed., *Journal*, 23, 25.

69. PYM Minutes, 1747–1779, 71, Swarthmore.

70. PYM Epistle to Friends in Rhode Island, PYM Miscellaneous Papers, 1748–1762, 1761, f. 14, Swarthmore.

71. On Woolman's effort to control his anger see Moulton, ed., *Journal*, 110–11.

72. Moulton, ed., *Journal*, 138–39.

73. Moulton, ed., *Journal*, 34–35, 57, 112; Woolman, "Plea for the Poor," 247. See Proverbs 29:25.

74. Moulton, ed., *Journal*, 110–11; NEYM Minutes, 1683–1787, 251; PYM Minutes, 1747–1779, 71–2, Swarthmore; PYM Ministers and Elders Minutes, 1735–1774, 453, Haverford.

75. PQM Minutes, 1723–1772, 292, Haverford.

76. PYM Epistle to Friends in Rhode Island, PYM Miscellaneous Papers, 1748–1762, 1761, f. 14, Swarthmore.

77. PYM Epistle to Friends on Long Island, Miscellaneous Papers of Philadelphia Yearly Meeting, 1748–1762, 1751, f. 15; for Woolman's joint authorship of this epistle see PYM Minutes, 1747–1779, 24, Swarthmore.

78. Robert Barclay, *An Apology for the True Christian Divinity* (London, 1703), 512.

79. *Epistles from the Yearly Meeting of Friends* (London, 1818), 397, citing Romans 8:13.

80. George Churchman, Journal, 1:43; PYM Minutes, 1747–1779, 164, Haverford.

81. JW to ?, July 9, 1769, Journal manuscript, Box 2, p. 281, HSP.

82. George Churchman, Journal, 1:32; PYM Ministers and Elders Minutes, 1735–1774, 427–30, Haverford.

83. Woolman, *Considerations on Pure Wisdom.* 3.

84. Woolman, *Considerations on True Harmony*, 3–4, 5, 17–18, 25–26. See Isaiah 66:18; Psalms 2:8.

85. JW to Israel Pemberton, January 1771, Pemberton Papers, 22:86b, 87, HSP.

86. PYM Sufferings Minutes, 1756–1775, 367–68, Swarthmore.

87. 1769 Ledger, loose page.

88. Moulton, ed., *Journal*, 61. See Psalm 119:19.

89. See for example Moulton, ed., *Journal*, 62–63.

90. See especially the early pages of Woolman's 1753 Ledger, and the pages following his journal manuscript in Woolman Collection, Box 2, HSP. See also, for example, Manuscript M, Manuscript P, and John Woolman, Essay on Silver Vessels, January 20, 1770, Woolman Manuscripts, Swarthmore.

91. See, for example, Fragment of John Woolman's journal, addressed to Israel Pemberton, Woolman Collections, Swarthmore.

92. The footnotes in Moulton, ed., *Journal*, detail this editorial process precisely.

93. John Woolman, *The Works of John Woolman, in Two Parts* (Philadelphia, 1774), 52–53, 233–36; Moulton, ed., *Journal*, 58, 185–86. Slaughter's assertion that the editorial committee of the Overseers of the Press "eliminated all" of Woolman's dreams is mistaken. See Slaughter, *Beautiful Soul*, 304.

CHAPTER 3. MORE THAN WAS REQUIRED: QUAKER MEETINGS

1. Perinchief, ed., *Woolman Family*, 8; Moulton, ed., *Journal*, 29, 31, 39n22, 312.

2. Moulton, ed., *Journal*, 29–30, 35.

3. Moulton, ed., *Journal*, 29–30.

4. Moulton, ed., *Journal*, 30.

5. This is an estimate based on Woolman's count of 47 adult male members. See 1753 Ledger, unpaginated eighth page.

6. Moulton, ed., *Journal*, 31.

7. *Collection of Memorials Concerning Divers Deceased Ministers* (Philadelphia, 1787), 401.

8. Evans, Journal, Comly and Comly, eds., *Friends' Miscellany*, 10:26.

9. *Collection of Memorials*, 392; see Martha Paxson Grundy, ed., *Resistance and Obedience to God: Memoirs of David Ferris (1707–1779)* (Philadelphia: Friends General Conference, 2001).

10. Evans, Journal, Comly and Comly, eds., *Friends' Miscellany*, 10:14, 16–17.

11. Elizabeth Wilkinson, Journal, 1761–1763, 72–73, 75, Haverford.

12. George Churchman, Journal, 1:73, Haverford.

13. LYM Minutes, 15:247–49, Friends House.

14. Moulton, ed., *Journal*, 31.

15. BMM Minutes, 1737–1756, 79, 95; BQM Minutes, 1686–1767, 142, Swarthmore.

16. Moulton, ed., *Journal*, 42.

17. Edith K. Livesay, "John Woolman: Persona and Person" (Ph.D. dissertation, University of Delaware, 1976), 173–75.

18. John Cox, "Sketches and Recollections," 25, Dillwyn Parrish Recollections and Sketches, HSP.

19. Testimony of York Quarterly Meeting, Gummere, ed., *Journal*, 327.

20. Woolman, *Extract*, 2–3.

21. Deborah Morris, Journal, quoted in Henry J. Cadbury, *John Woolman in England: A Documentary Supplement* (London: Friends Historical Society, 1971), 93, 97; Minutes of Oxfordshire Women's Quarterly Meeting, quoted in ibid, 79; Moulton, ed., *Journal*, 90, 123, 182.

22. Diary of Elihu Robinson, Diary, 1768–1772, June 14, 1772, MS R3/2, Friends House.

23. Thomas Priestman, Diary, quoted in Cadbury, *John Woolman in England*, 115, See Matthew 15:13.

24. John Cox, "Sketches and Recollections," 24, Dillwyn Parrish Recollections and Sketches, HSP.

25. Evans, Journal, 10:14.

26. Moulton, ed. *Journal*, 152n57.

27. For a description of Woolman's quieting effect on a meeting for worship see Deborah Morris, Journal, quoted in Cadbury, *John Woolman in England*, 91.

28. Abner Woolman, Journal, Chapters XX, and XXXV, Haverford.

29. Elihu Robinson, Diary, 1768–1772, June 11, 1772, MS R3/2, Friends House.

30. Evans, Journal, 10:14.

31. BMM Minutes, 1737–1756, 275–76, Swarthmore.

32. *Collection of Memorials*, 168.

33. *Collection of Memorials*, 190.

34. Moulton, ed., *Journal*, 103.

35. BMM Minutes, 1737–1756, 180, 264, 289, 294, 308, BMM Minutes, 1757–1770, 16, 19, 42, 180, BQM Minutes, 1686–1767, 185, Swarthmore; BMM Women's Minutes, 1747–1799, 56, Haverford. For a discussion of the roles taken by women within the meetings, see Larsen, *Daughters of Light*; Mary Maples Dunn, "Saints and Sisters: Congregational and Quaker Women in the Early Colonial Period," *American Quarterly* 30 (1978): 582–601.

36. 1769 Ledger, loose page.

37. JW to ?, July 9, 1769, Journal manuscript, Woolman Collection, Box 2, 281, HSP.

38. BMM Minutes, 1737–1756, 97, 112, 115, BMM Minutes, 1757–1770, 234–36, Swarthmore.

39. BMM Minutes, 1737–1756, 102–4, Swarthmore.

40. BMM Minutes, 1737–1756, 205, Swarthmore. For an overview of Quaker disciplinary process see Marietta, *Reformation*, 3–31.

41. BMM Minutes, 1737–1756, 228, Swarthmore.

42. *Collection of Memorials*, 275.

43. PYM Epistle to Friends on Long Island, 1756, PYM Miscellaneous Papers, 1748–1762, 1756 f. 13a, Swarthmore. For the authorship of this statement see PYM Minutes, 1747–1779, 84, Haverford.

44. BMM Minutes, 1737–1756, 240–43, 266, 198; 1757–1770, 124–25, 129–30, Swarthmore.

45. BMM Minutes, 1737–1756, 240–43, Swarthmore.

46. BMM Minutes, 1737–1756, 266, Swarthmore.

47. PYM Minutes, 1747–1779, 71–72, Haverford.

48. BQM Minutes, 1686–1767, 143, Swarthmore.

49. BMM Minutes, 1737–1756, 259, Swarthmore.

50. BMM Minutes, 1737–1756, 295–96. See Moulton, ed., *Journal*, 55.

51. PYM Minutes, 1747–1779, 123, Haverford; BMM Minutes, 1757–1770, 28, 99, 143–44, Swarthmore.

52. Marietta, *Reformation*.

53. Moulton, ed., *Journal*, 47, 89.

54. Abner Woolman, Journal, Chapter VII, Haverford.

55. PYM Minutes, 1747–1779, 71–72, Haverford.

56. PYM Minutes, 1747–1779, 76–77, 123, 142, Haverford.

57. PYM Minutes, 1747–1779, 117, Haverford.

58. Moulton, ed., *Journal*, 94–95. See also Daniel Stanton, *A Journal of the Life, Travels, and Gospel Labours of a Faithful Minister of Jesus Christ, Daniel Stanton* (Philadelphia, 1772), 112.

59. George Churchman, Journal, 1:19, Haverford; WQM Minutes, 1758–1798, 62, Swarthmore.

60. See Janet Whitney, *John Woolman: American Quaker* (Boston: Little Brown, 1942), 474–47; Moulton, ed., *Journal*, 4–5.

61. *Collection of Memorials*, 105; Thomas Chalkley, *A Collection of the Works of Thomas Chalkley* (Philadelphia, 1749), 299.

62. BMM Minutes, 1737–1756, 180, Swarthmore. See George J. Willauer, Jr., "Editorial Practices in Eighteenth-Century Philadelphia: The Journal of Thomas Chalkey in Manuscript and Print," *Pennsylvania Magazine of History and Biography* 107 (1983): 217–34.

63. Moulton, ed., *Journal*, 34.

64. *Pennsylvania Gazette*, February 19, 1754; 1753 Ledger, 218.

65. *Collection of Memorials*, 186–91.

66. "Memoirs of Joshua Evans," Comly and Comly, eds., *Friends' Miscellany*, 1:304, 306.

67. Moulton, ed., *Journal*, 34.

68. For a vivid account of the pressures of travel in the ministry, see Elizabeth Wilkinson, Journal, Haverford.

69. *Collection of Memorials*, 171.

70. Moulton, ed., *Journal*, 34.

71. Moulton, ed., *Journal*, 307; Gummere, ed., Journal, 534.

72. Moulton, ed., *Journal*, 38.

73. Moulton, ed., *Journal*, 36, 37.

74. Moulton, ed., *Journal*, 37.

75. BQM Minutes, 1686–1767, 183–85, Swarthmore; Moulton, ed., *Journal*, 45.

76. BQM Minutes, 1686–1767, 243, Swarthmore; *Pennsylvania Gazette*, June 3, 1756. By 1756 "Great Meadows" had been renamed "Hardwick."

77. Moulton, ed., *Journal*, 41–42.

78. 1753 Ledger, 224.

79. Moulton, ed., *Journal*, 66–67.

80. VYM Minutes, 1702–1836, 94–96, Haverford.

81. PYM Minutes, 1747–1779, 71–72, Haverford.

82. NEYM Minutes, 1683–1787, 247–48, 250, Swarthmore.

83. George Churchman, Journal, 1:41, Haverford.

84. Moulton, ed., *Journal*, 66–67.

85. Moulton, ed., *Journal*, 110–11.

86. PYM Minutes, 1747–1779, 16, 24, 29, 45, 65, 84, 101, 114, 129, 139, 155, 167, 180, Haverford.

87. PYM Minutes, 1747–1779, 194, 209, 228, 238, 248, 257, 267, 277, Haverford. Hunt and Mason were British. On Hunt, see Gummere, ed., *Journal*, 511–12; on Mason, of the Meeting of PYM Ministers and Elders, 1735–1774, 415, Haverford. On Churchman's travels to Britain, see Churchman, *Account*, 82–166; on Horne's travels, see William Horne to John Pemberton, September 15, 1763, Pemberton Papers, 16:139, HSP. On White's travels, see PYM Ministers and Elders Minutes, 1735–1774, 423, 430, Haverford.

88. Elihu Robinson. Diary, 1768–1772, June 11, 1772, MS R3/2, Friends House.

89. John Fothergill to Samuel Fothergill, London, June 9, 1772, Port. 22, f. 126, Friends House.

90. JW to Rachel Wilson, August 30, 1772, Port. 6/34, Friends House; Moulton, ed., Journal, 188.

91. Woolman, *Epistle*; Woolman, *Extract*. Although for many years this second piece was published as part of Woolman's journal, there is reason to believe that he wrote it as a free-standing essay. See Gummere, ed., *Journal*, 313 n2.

92. Woolman, *Epistle*, 2. See Galatians 2:20.

93. *Collection of Memorials*, 406

94. *Collection of Memorials*, 74–75, 190, 193–94.

95. PYM Minutes, 1747–1779, 43, Swarthmore.

96. BMM Records of Births and Deaths, 1677–1805, 104, Swarthmore.

CHAPTER 4. THE ROAD TO LARGE BUSINESS: FAMILY AND WORK

1. BMM Minutes, 1757–1770, 70, Swarthmore.

2. BMM Minutes, 1737–1756, 182–83, Swarthmore.

3. BMM Minutes, 1737–1756, 95, 168, Swarthmore; 1753 Ledger, unpaginated eighth page.

4. BMM Minutes, 1737–1756, 95, 168, 205, BMM Minutes, 1757–1770, 6, 14, 28, 57, 63, 99, 125, Swarthmore; 1753 Ledger, unpaginated eighth page.

5. BMM Minutes, 1737–1756, 183, Swarthmore; Marriage certificate, Woolman Collection, Box 1, f. 3, HSP.

6. Gummere, ed., *Journal*, 37–38.

7. Moulton, ed., *Journal*, 44.

8. BMM Minutes, 1737–1756, 191, 198–99, 201–2, 210, 220, 222, 233, 261, 270–72, 273, 299, BMM Minutes, 1757–1770, 206–7, 220–21, 273, Swarthmore.

9. See Marietta, *Reformation*, 32–39.

10. CMM Minutes, 1884–1827, 246–47, Swarthmore; Churchman, *Account*, 196.

11. 1753 Ledger, f. 21 contra. See Watts, *Horae Lyrica*, 209–12.

12. Moulton, ed., *Journal*, 35.

13. Moulton, ed., *Journal*, 39–40; Whitney, *John Woolman*, 471–72; Book of Executorship, 2.

14. Moulton, ed., *Journal*, 35–36.

15. Book of Executorship.

16. Moulton, ed., *Journal*, 35, 53.

17. Moulton, ed., *Journal*, 29, n. 31; *Pennsylvania Gazette*, September 26, 1776.

18. Burlington Monthly Meeting Records of Births and Deaths, 1677–1805, 104, Swarthmore.

19. 1753 Ledger, 1769 Ledger; on Shinn see 1753 Ledger, 5; Gummere, ed., *Journal*, 46–47; *Documents Relating to the Colonial History of the State of New Jersey* 16 (Trenton, N.J., 1891), 89; *Collections of the New Jersey Historical Society* 9 (Newark, N.J., 1916): 190–91.

20. 1753 Ledger, 219–20; see [Robert Dodsley], *The Oeconomy of Human Life* (Philadelphia, 1751).

21. 1753 Ledger, 18 contra, 40 contra, 203, 210; Moulton, ed., *Journal*, 51.

22. Moulton, ed., *Journal*, 53, 54, 156.

23. 1753 Ledger, inside front cover; see Proverbs 21:6, 23:4.

24. Moulton, ed., *Journal*, 53–54.

25. JW to John Wilson, September 22, 1772, Port. 6/34, Friends House.

26. Moulton, ed., *Journal*, 53–54.

27. Moulton, ed., *Journal*, 54, 156.

28. Woolman indicates that he was thirty-five when he began his work, which places the date between October 19, 1755 and October 19, 1756. See Moulton, ed., *Journal*, 23.

29. Sarah Woolman to ?, January 1776, in Gummere, ed., *Journal*, 40.

30. Churchman, *Account*, 15; see also 224–25.

31. *Collection of Memorials*, 325.

32. Churchman, *Account*, 212.

33. *Collection of Memorials*, 412. See also Jackson, *Let This Voice Be Heard*, 18–20. Slaughter incorrectly suggests that Anthony Benezet disapproved of women ministers. See Slaughter, *Beautiful Soul*, 188.

34. BQM Women's Minutes, 1686–1845, 123; PYM Women's Minutes, 1681–1814, 180.

35. Grundy, ed., *Resistance and Obedience*, 44–45.

36. On Woolman's withdrawal of some commentary, see Journal manuscript, Woolman Collection, Box 2, back p. 1, HSP.

37. Moulton, ed., *Journal*, 55, 72–73.

38. Moulton, ed., *Journal*, 54–55.

39. Woolman, "Plea for the Poor," 250.

40. Moulton, ed., *Journal*, 119–20.

41. Woolman, "Plea for the Poor," 261, 266.

42. Journal manuscript, Woolman collection, Box 2, back p. 279, HSP.

43. *Pennsylvania Gazette*, March 25, 1742.

44. Evans, Journal, Comly and Comly, eds., *Friends' Miscellany*, 10:25.

45. Joshua Evans, Journal, RG 5/190, f. 15, Swarthmore.

46. Woolman, "Plea for the Poor," 259.

47. Journal manuscript, Woolman Collection, Box 2, back page 2, HSP.

48. Moulton, ed., *Journal*, 125.

49. Grundy, ed., *Resistance and Obedience*, 45.

50. Woolman, *Considerations on True Harmony*, 19, citing Proverbs 12:18.

51. Woolman, "Plea for the Poor," in Moulton, ed., *Journal*, 252.

52. Moulton, ed., *Journal*, 174, n. 57; Journal manuscript, Luke Howard Collection, f. 27, p. 7, Friends House. See Matthew 6:24, Luke 16:13.

53. Woolman, *Considerations on True Harmony*, 13.

54. Woolman, *Considerations on True Harmony*, 13, 14.

55. Woolman, *Considerations Part Second*, 25–26.

56. Woolman, "Plea for the Poor," 241–44.

57. Woolman, *Some Considerations*, 15–16.

58. Woolman, "Plea for the Poor," 239–40, 245.

59. Moulton, ed., *Journal*, 55, 118–19.

60. Woolman, "Plea for the Poor," 240.

61. Moulton, ed., *Journal*, 184.

62. Woolman, "Plea for the Poor," 267–68.

63. Woolman, *Epistle*, 14.

64. Samuel Woolman's will, Recorded Wills, West Jersey, Book 6, 391, Samuel Woolman's estate inventory 4761–4766C, NJSA.

65. Grace Hutchison Larsen, "Profile of a Colonial Merchant: Thomas Clifford of Pre-Revolutionary Philadelphia" (Ph.D. dissertation, Columbia University, 1955), 292; 1753 Ledger, 23 contra, 213 contra.

66. JW to Thomas Clifford, November 7, 1756, August 4 and 19, 1757, Clifford-Pemberton Papers, 1:179, 273, 277, HSP.

67. JW to Clifford, January 14 and October 13, 1757, Clifford-Pemberton Papers, 1:205, 2:7, 1753 Ledger, 213 contra.

68. JW to Clifford, November 7, 1756, January 14, August 4, 1757, Clifford-Pemberton Papers, 1:179, 205, 273, HSP.

69. See, for example, 1753 Ledger, 213.

70. See JW to Clifford, November 7, 1756, August 4, 1757, Clifford-Pemberton Papers, 1:179, 273, HSP.

71. JW to Clifford, August 6 and September 27, 1757, Clifford-Pemberton Papers, 1:274, 294, HSP.

72. John Cox, "Sketches and Recollections," 1, Dillwyn Parrish Recollections and Sketches, HSP.

73. 1753 Ledger, 208, 218.

74. 1769 Ledger, 32.

75. See, for example, Samuel Emlen to Sarah Emlen, June 6, 1772, Letters of Samuel Emlen, 1772–1797, 23, HSP.

76. 1753 Ledger, 233 and 233 contra; *New Jersey Archives*, first ser. 32:123.

77. JW to Rebecca Jones, April 20, 1762, Woolman Manuscripts, Swarthmore. See. Allison, ed., *Memorials of Rebecca Jones*, 36.

78. Testimony of Burlington Monthly Meeting, August 1, 1774, in Gummere, ed., *Journal*, 331; 1753 Ledger; 1769 Ledger.

79. Woolman, "Plea for the Poor," 263–65.

80. Testimony of Burlington Monthly Meeting, August 1, 1774, in Gummere, ed., *Journal*, 331.

81. *Pennsylvania Gazette*, December 21, 1769.

82. 1769 Ledger, 40 contra.

83. Woolman, *First Book.*

84. 1753 Ledger, 242 and contra, 1769 Ledger, 28–29; see *Pennsylvania Gazette*, April 4, 1765.

85. Moulton, ed., *Journal*, 46.

86. Book of Executorship; *New Jersey Archives*, first ser. 30:77, 142, 171, 210, 364, 462, 547.

87. Journal manuscript, Woolman Collection, Box 2, 279, HSP.

88. *Pennsylvania Gazette*, May 24, 1753; Thomas Shinn's will, 5325–5334C, NJSA; Book of Executorship, 3–6.

89. Book of Executorship, 1, 2 contra, 9.

90. *Pennsylvania Gazette*, March 30, 1758, June 16, 1768, March 26, 1772.

91. Larsen, "Profile of a Colonial Merchant," 303.

92. Woolman, "Plea for the Poor," 249.

93. Moulton, ed., *Journal*, 164–65.

94. William Forster to William Birkbeck, Jr., July 1772, Mss. vol. 77, f. 1, Friends House.

95. Woolman, *Considerations on True Harmony*, 5.

96. Journal manuscript, Woolman Collection, Box 2, 280, HSP.

97. Woolman, "Plea for the Poor," 249–50.

98. *Collection of Memorials*, 186; BMM Minutes, 1757–1770, 87, Swarthmore.

99. Abner Woolman, Journal, Introduction, Preface and Chapter III, Haverford.

100. 1753 Ledger, 178.

101. Woolman, *Considerations on True Harmony*, 7.

102. WQM Minutes, 1758–1798, 62, Swarthmore.

103. Moulton, ed., *Journal*, 114.

104. For the views of some other ministers see PYM Women's Minutes, 1681–1814, 100, BQM Women's Minutes, 1686–1845, 117, Swarthmore.

105. JW to Sarah Woolman, June 14, 1760, Woolman Collection, Box 1, f. 5, HSP.

106. JW to Sarah Woolman, April 24, 1760, quoted in Moulton, ed., *Journal*, 107.

107. JW to Sarah Woolman, June 14, 1760, Woolman Collection, Box 1, f. 5, HSP.

108. Book of Executorship, 14 and back pages, 1753 Ledger, 225.

109. Book of Executorship; 1753 Ledger, 210 contra, 225, 234; 1769 Ledger, 4 contra, 7, 24 contra, 30.

110. 1753 Ledger, 225 contra, 234 contra, 239, 1769 Ledger, 30.

111. 1753 Ledger, 219–20.

112. 1753 Ledger, 234 contra.

113. 1753 Ledger, 225.

114. 1753 Ledger, 211, 238–39.

115. 1753 Ledger, 231.

116. Samuel Woolman's will, Recorded Wills, West Jersey, Book 6, p. 391, NJSA. For the location of Uriah's shop see *Pennsylvania Packet*, February 6, 1775, November 9, 1789.

117. See JW to Clifford, November 7, 1756, Clifford-Pemberton Papers, 1:179, JW to Israel Pemberton, November 11, 1769, Pemberton Papers 21:85, HSP.

118. *Pennsylvania Packet*, February 6, 1775; J. Thomas Sharf and Thomas Westcott, *History of Philadelphia, 1609–1884* (Philadelphia: Everts, 1884), 3:2250.

119. *Pennsylvania Packet*, July 20, December 7, 1772, December 2, 1773, March 7, 1774.

120. Uriah Woolman, Bills of Lading, 1772–1775, Am. 917, HSP.

121. *Pennsylvania Packet*, March 7, 1774; *Pennsylvania Gazette*, July 21, July 28, October 27, December 22, 1773, June 8, 1774, March 1, 1775.

122. Joshua Hart to Aaron Lopez, February 8, 1773, *Collections of the Massachusetts Historical Society* 7th ser., vol. 9 (Boston, 1914), 425–26.

123. Moulton, ed., *Journal*, 58.

124. JW to Uriah Woolman, June 4, 1763, Gratz Mss., case 8, box 25, HSP.

CHAPTER 5. A DARK GLOOMINESS HANGING OVER THE LAND: SLAVERY

1. Book of Executorship, opening page.

2. Moulton, ed., *Journal*, 39–40.

3. Soderlund, "African Americans and Native Americans," in Heller, ed., *Tendering Presence*, 152–53.

4. Will of Henry Burr, 3593–3596C, NJSA.

5. Book of Executorship, 1.

6. While none of the surviving documents explicitly identify Isabella and Maria as the

older Maria's daughters, Woolman's records of the older Maria's estate indicate that he arranged for transportation to allow the decedent's "two children" to attend her funeral, and on the same page he makes provision for the care of Woolman's mother's house in Isabella's absence. Book of Executorship, 15 and contra.

7. Abner Woolman's will, 9309–9315C, NJSA.

8. Elizabeth Woolman's will, in Gummere, ed., *Journal*, 602.

9. 1753 Ledger, 21 contra, 35; 1769 Ledger, 43.

10. "Memoirs and Anecdotes of William Boen," Comly and Comly, eds., *Friends' Miscellany*, 5:269–80, 270–72.

11. Moulton, ed., *Journal*, 45.

12. Moulton, ed., *Journal*, 32–33.

13. See Larry Gragg, *The Quaker Community on Barbados: Challenging the Culture of the Planter Class* (Jefferson City: University of Missouri Press, 2009), 64.

14. Nash and Soderlund, *Freedom by Degrees*, 10.

15. Soderlund, *Quakers and Slavery*, 34

16. Donald D. Wax, "Quaker Merchants and the Slave Trade in Colonial Pennsylvania," *Pennsylvania Magazine of History and Biography* 86 (1962): 143–59, 155 n40.

17. Soderlund, *Quakers and Slavery*, 20–21, 25; J. William Frost, ed., *The Quaker Origins of Antislavery* (Norwood, Pa.: Norwood Editions, 1980), doc. 7.

18. Quoted in Brycchan Carey, "The Barbadian Origins of Quaker Antislavery," *Ariel: A Review of International English Literature* 38 (2007): 27–47, 37.

19. BQM Minutes, 1686–1767, 246, Swarthmore.

20. Soderlund's *Quakers and Slavery* contains the best comprehensive overview of early Quaker antislavery action. Though not a Quaker, Thomas Tryon was close to Friends; for a full grasp of the early debate, scholars should consider Philippe Rosenberg, "Thomas Tryon and the Seventeenth-Century Dimensions of Antislavery, *William and Mary Quarterly* 61 (2004): 609–42.

21. Robert Vaux, *Memoirs of the Lives of Benjamin Lay and Ralph Sandiford* (Philadelphia: Conrad, 1815), 25–29. For background on Lay see Andreas Mielke, " 'What's Here to Do?' An Inquiry Concerning Benjamin and Sarah Lay, Abolitionists," *Quaker History* 86 (1997): 22–44.

22. *Pennsylvania Gazette*, November 9, 1738. See PYM Minutes, September 16–20, 1738, Haverford.

23. Moulton, ed., *Journal*, 33n48.

24. Moulton, ed., *Journal*, 46, 50–51.

25. *New York Geneological and Biographical Record* (New York, 1898), 9:139.

26. Thomas Shinn's will, 5325–5334C, NJSA.

27. Soderlund, *Quakers and Slavery*, 42.

28. Thomas Shinn's will, 5325–5334C, NJSA; 1769 Ledger, loose page; Moulton, ed., *Journal*, 152–53.

29. BMM Minutes, 1737–1756, 150, Swarthmore; Moulton, ed., *Journal*, 36–8.

30. Moulton, ed., *Journal*, 38.

31. BMM Minutes, 1737–1756, 171, 173, Swarthmore.

32. Moulton, ed., *Journal*, 42–43, 312.

33. See PYM Minutes, 1747–1779, 121, Haverford.

34. Moulton, ed., *Journal*, 44–45.

35. Soderlund, *Quakers and Slavery*, 27.

36. JW to Israel Pemberton, 1761, Pemberton Papers 15:111, HSP.

37. Jonathan D. Sassi, "With a Little Help from the Friends: The Quaker and Tactical Contexts of Anthony Benezet's Abolitionist Publishing," *Pennsylvania Magazine of History and Biography* 135 (2011): 33–71, 39.

38. Moulton, ed., *Journal*, 47.

39. *Pennsylvania Gazette*, February 26, 1754; Woolman, *Some Considerations*.

40. See, for example, Genesis 9:25–27; Levitcus 25:45; Ephesians 6:5.

41. Moulton, ed., *Journal*, 93.

42. Slaughter is incorrect in suggesting that Woolman addressed his 1754 essay to "Quakers," in contrast to his 1762 antislavery essay which he addressed to "Christians." Both pieces carried the subtitle "Recommended to the Professors of Christianity of Every Denomination." and neither one of them relied heavily on distinctly Quaker texts. The only Quaker work Woolman cited in his 1754 anti-slavery essay was an apology for Christianity written by the London Quaker Alexander Arscott, and Arscott wrote for a general Christian audience. See Moulton, ed., *Journal*, 203 n3; Slaughter, *Beautiful Soul*, 244.

43. Woolman, *Some Considerations*, 2, 5.

44. Woolman, *Some Considerations*, 5, 15.

45. Woolman, *Some Considerations*, introduction, 5, 15.

46. Soderlund, *Quakers and Slavery*, 27n28.

47. PQM Minutes, 1723–1772, 178–80, Haverford; PYM Minutes, 1747–1779, 43–45, Swarthmore; Soderlund, *Quakers and Slavery*, 149.

48. John Cox, "Sketches and Recollections," 1, Dillwyn Parrish Recollections and Sketches, HSP.

49. PYM Minutes, 1747–1779, 45, 66, Swarthmore.

50. BQM Minutes, 1686–1767, 220, Swarthmore.

51. *Epistle of Caution and Advice*, 1–3.

52. Matthew 7:12. See also Luke 7:31; Frost, ed., *Quaker Origins*, doc. 3; John Hepburn, *The American Defense of the Golden Rule* (1715); Woolman, *Some Considerations*, 9.

53. *Epistle of Caution and Advice*, 2.

54. Despite repeated claims to the contrary, there is no evidence that Woolman was directly involved in drafting the *Epistle of Caution and Advice*, nor did the pamphlet quote any of Woolman's published or unpublished work. Janet Whitney was the first to make these claims, but the document she cites as evidence, the epistle to Friends in Virginia that Woolman wrote with Benezet, makes no mention of slavery and does not contain any language similar to the Yearly Meeting's published antislavery statement. See PYM Miscellaneous Papers, 1748–1762, 1754, f. 22, PYM Minutes, 1747–1779, 45, Swarthmore; J. William Frost, "The Origins of the Quaker Crusade Against Slavery: A Review of Recent Literature," *Quaker History* 67, 1 (1978): 42–58, 50n20. For the ongoing misapprehension

see Whitney, *John Woolman*, 193–94; Thomas E. Drake, *Quakers and Slavery in America* (New Haven, Conn.: Yale University Press, 1950), 56; James, *People Among Peoples*, 137; Edwin H. Cady, *John Woolman: The Mind of the Quaker Saint* (New York: Washington Square Press, 1966), 79n7. To his credit, David Sox avoided this mistake in *John Woolman, 1720–1772: Quintessential Quaker* (Richmond, Ind.: Friends United Press, 1999), but the error has resurfaced in Slaughter, *Beautiful Soul*, 159, 414n8, and Jackson, *Let This Voice be Heard*, 53, 244.

55. For Benezet's interest in Africa see Jonathan D. Sassi, "Africans in the Quaker Image: Anthony Benezet, African Travel Narratives, and Revolutionary-Era Antislavery," *Journal of Early Modern History* 10 (2006): 95–130.

56. *Epistle of Caution and Advice*, 5, 6.

57. Nash and Soderlund, *Freedom by Degrees*, 65.

58. PYM Minutes, 1747–1779, 72, Swarthmore.

59. For Philadelphia Yearly Meeting's 1743 query warning against buying imported slaves, see Brycchan Carey, *From Peace to Freedom: Quaker Rhetoric and the Birth of American Antislavery, 1658–1761* (forthcoming, Yale University Press), chap. 4.

60. Moulton, ed., *Journal*, 52. See Jeremiah 20:9.

61. Moulton, ed., *Journal*, 59, 60. See Numbers 11:15.

62. Moulton, ed., *Journal*, 62, 65, 66.

63. Moulton, ed., *Journal*, 64.

64. VYM Minutes, 1702–1836, 96, Haverford.

65. Moulton, ed., *Journal*, 66–67.

66. Moulton, ed., *Journal*, 61.

67. Moulton, ed., *Journal*, 62–63.

68. Moulton, ed., *Journal*, 60, 61, 67.

69. See Luke 10:4.

70. Moulton, ed., *Journal*, 59–60.

71. Moulton, ed., *Journal*, 60, 61.

72. Moulton, ed., *Journal*, 71; See also BMM Minutes, 1757–1770, 7, Swarthmore.

73. *Memoirs of William and Nathan Hunt* (Philadelphia, 1858), 83–91.

74. Moulton, ed., *Journal*, 69.

75. VYM Minutes, 1702–1836, 101, Haverford.

76. JW to Uriah Woolman, June 4, 1763, Gratz Mss., Case 8, Box 25, HSP.

77. PYM Minutes, 1747–1779, 112, emphasis added. See PQM Minutes, 1723–1772, 246, 250, 254, Haverford.

78. PYM Minutes, 1747–1779, 121, Haverford.

79. Moulton, ed., *Journal*, 92. See Psalm 42:3.

80. Moulton, ed., *Journal*, 93.

81. Stanton, *Journal*, 111.

82. PYM Minutes, 1747–1779, 121–22, 148, Haverrford.

83. Stanton, *Journal*, 111; Moulton, ed., *Journal*, 94.

84. Stanton, *Journal*, 113.

85. Moulton, ed., *Journal*, 95–96.

86. Churchman, *Account*, 199–200; Moulton, ed., *Journal*, 96.

87. Moulton, ed., *Journal*, 102, 117.

88. PYM Minutes, 1747–1779, 130, 141, 160, 172–73, Haverford.

89. Evans, Journal, Comly and Comly, eds., *Friends' Miscellany*, 10:17–18. See Matthew 10:16.

90. "Memoirs and Anecdotes of William Boen," Comly and Comly, eds., *Friends' Miscellany*, 5:269–80, 272–73. See also "A Testimony from Friends of Mount Holly, New Jersey, concerning William Boen," ibid, 1:388–92, 389.

91. George Churchman, Journal, 1759–1766, 1:38, Haverford; but see also 1:6.

92. BMM Minutes, 1757–1770, 285.

93. PYM Epistle to Friends on Long Island, September 25, 1762, PYM Miscellaneous Papers, 1748–1762, 1762 f. 13, Swarthmore.

94. *Epistles from the Yearly Meeting*, 330–31. See Isaiah 33:15.

95. [Anthony Benezet], *Observations on the Inslaving, Importing and Purchasing of Negroes* (Germantown, 1759), 8; NEYM Minutes, 1683–1787, 250, Swarthmore.

96. See, for example, *Collection of Memorials*, 288.

97. Moulton, ed., *Journal*, 59. For a similar early use of this phrase, see William Hunt, Journal, 81, Haverford; *Memoirs of William and Nathan Hunt*, 47–48.

CHAPTER 6. MEN IN MILITARY POSTURE: THE SEVEN YEARS' WAR

1. Moulton, ed., *Journal*, 47.

2. Manuscript Discipline from Alloways Creek and Greenwich, 1762, 316–17, Swarthmore. See Matthew 5:44.

3. Moulton, ed., *Journal*, 80. See Churchman, *Account*, 72.

4. 1769 Ledger, loose page.

5. Weddle, *Walking in the Way of Peace*, 39–54; Moore, *Light of their Consciences*, 122–24, 180–83; Christopher Hill, *The Experience of Defeat: Milton and Some Contemporaries* (New York: Viking, 1984), 129–69.

6. See, for example, the advice of London Yearly Meeting in VYM Minutes, 1702–1836, 98–99, Haverford. See also NEYM Minutes, 1683–1787, 249–50, Swarthmore.

7. Wellenreuther, "Political Dilemma"; Carl E. Swanson, *Predators and Prizes: American Privateering and Imperial Warfare, 1739–1748* (Columbia: University of South Carolina Press, 1991), 160–61; Peter Brock, *The Quaker Peace Testimony, 1660 to 1914* (York: Sessions Book Trust, 1990), 106–11.

8. Matthew C. Ward, *Breaking the Backcountry: The Seven Years War in Virginia and Pennsylvania, 1754–1765* (Pittsburgh: University of Pittsburgh Press, 2003), 60–68; Kenny, *Peaceable Kingdom Lost*, 71–75.

9. Moulton, ed., *Journal*, 84. See Silver, *Our Savage Neighbors*, 77–78.

10. Memoirs and Anecdotes of William Boen," Comly and Comly, eds., *Friends' Miscellany*, 5:270.

11. See generally, Marietta, "Conscience, the Quaker Community, and the French and

Indian War." See Matthew 22:21. For an overview of the politics surrounding the appropriation, see Kenny, *Peaceable Kingdom Lost*, 76–82.

12. *Epistle from our General Spring Meeting*; Moulton, ed., *Journal*, 47–50. See Psalm 72:8. For the political context of this statement see Ketchan, "Conscience, War and Politics," 418.

13. Churchman, *Account*, 169–71.

14. PYM Minutes, 1747–1779, 85–90, Haverford; PYM Sufferings Minutes, 1756–1775, 27–29, Swarthmore.

15. James, *People Among Peoples*, 172–74.

16. Theodore Thayer, "The Friendly Association," *Pennsylvania Magazine of History and Biography* 67 (1943): 356–76; James, *People Among Peoples*, 178–92. See also Theodore Thayer, *Israel Pemberton: King of the Quakers* (Philadelphia: Historical Society of Pennsylvania, 1943), 97–112.

17. Proclamation of Jonathan Belcher, December 3, 1755, *New Jersey Archives* 16:571–73.

18. Geoffrey Plank, *Rebellion and Savagery: The Jacobite Rising of 1745 and the British Empire* (Philadelphia: University of Pennsylvania Press, 2006), 160–62.

19. *Pennsylvania Gazette*, July 1, 1756; Council Minutes, June 30, 1756, *New Jersey Archives* 17:38–40; Silver, *Our Savage Neighbors*, 162.

20. *Pennsylvania Gazette*, June 3, 1756; BQM Minutes, 1686–1767, 243, Swarthmore; C. A. Weslager, *The Delaware Indians: A History* (New Brunswick, N.J.: Rutgers University Press, 1972), 264.

21. Proclamation of Jonathan Belcher dated June 2, 1756, *New Jersey Archives* 17:29–31; Weslager, *Delaware Indians*, 264.

22. Weslager, *Delaware Indians*, 261–81; Proclamation of Jonathan Belcher; Council Minutes, June 30, 1756; Edward McM. Larrabee, "Recurrent Themes and Sequences in North American Indian-European Culture Contact," *Transactions of the American Philosophical Society* N.S. 66, 7 (1976): 1–52, 7–8.

23. *New Jersey Archives* 1st ser. 0:355–58; Larrabee, "Recurrent Themes," 4–18; Jean Soderlund, "The Delaware Indians and Poverty in Colonial New Jersey," in Billy G. Smith, ed., *Down and Out in Early America* (University Park: Pennsylvania State University Press, 2004), 289–311; Margaret Connell Szasz, *Scottish Highlanders and Native Americans: Indigenous Education in the Eighteenth-Century Atlantic World* (Norman: University of Oklahoma Press, 2007), 131–33; Weslager, *Delaware Indians*, 263–75; James Axtell, *The Invasion Within: The Contest of Cultures in Colonial North America* (New York: Oxford University Press, 1985), 264, 275.

24. Articles of the New Jersey Association for Helping the Indians, 975B, 1–2, Haverford.

25. Ibid., 2–3, Haverford.

26. Elizabeth Wilkinson, Journal, 1761–1763, 141, Haverford.

27. See BMM Minutes, 1737–1756, 281, Swarthmore; *The Votes and Proceedings of the General Assembly of the Province of New-Jersey, Held at Burlington on Thursday the Fourth of October 1744* (Philadelphia, 1744), 82–100.

28. Joshua Evans, Journal, RG 5/190, 11–12, Swarthmore. See also Evans, Journal, Comly and Comly, eds., *Friends' Miscellany*, 10:19–20.

29. PYM Minutes, 1747–1779, 77–78, Swarthmore.

30. Woolman, "Plea for the Poor," in Moulton, ed., *Journal,* 240.

31. Moulton, ed., *Journal,* 87–88.

32. For an account of the Battle of Ticonderoga see Fred Anderson, *Crucible of War: The Seven Years' War and the Fate of Empire in British North America, 1754–1766* (New York: Knopf, 2000), 240–49.

33. Moulton, ed., *Journal,* 89.

34. Abner Woolman, Journal, Chapter VI, Haverford.

35. PYM Minutes, 1747–1779, 112, 118–20, Haverford.

36. Moulton, ed., *Journal,* 76–77. See generally Marietta, "Conscience, the Quaker Community, and the French and Indian War."

37. Moulton, ed., *Journal,* 75–77, 84–86.

38. Moulton, ed., *Journal,* 86.

39. PYM Minutes, 1747–1779, 105, 107, Haverford; Moulton, ed., *Journal,* 87.

40. Moulton, ed., *Journal,* 83–84.

41. See Marietta, "Conscience, the Quaker Community, and the French and Indian War," 19–21.

42. Moulton, ed., *Journal,* 77 n9, 83 n22, 85 n27, 87 n28, 90 n33.

43. Abner Woolman, Journal, Chapter IX, Haverford.

44. Churchman, *Account,* 209–11.

45. *Pennsylvania Gazette,* May 10, 1759. Information on the 1758–59 campaigns of the Britannia can be found in *Pennsylvania Gazette,* August 10, 17, September 21, November 16, 23, 1758; January 11, February 15, March 8, April 5, 19, May 10, 31, July 12, 1759. For a sense of the make-up of Saint-Vincent's population see Bernard Marshall, "The Black Caribs: Native Resistance to British Penetration into the Windward Side of St. Vincent, 1763–1773," *Caribbean Quarterly* 38 (1973): 419–41.

46. BMM Minutes, 1757–1770, 91, 97, 112, 115, Swarthmore.

47. Larsen, "Profile of a Colonial Merchant," 13, 53, 56. For the Quaker strictures against buying prize ships and arming merchant vessels see *Epistles from the Yearly Meeting of Friends,* 77, 132, 135.

48. "A Narrative of the sufferings of seven young men of the people called Quakers," PYM Meeting for Sufferings, Miscellaneous Papers, 1756, f. 10, Swarthmore.

49. Moulton, ed., *Journal,* 63–64.

50. VYM Minutes, 1702–1836, 91–93, 102, Haverford.

51. PYM Epistle to Friends in Virginia, PYM Miscellaneous Papers, 1748–1762, 1757, f. 16, Swarthmore. For Woolman's joint authorship of this epistle see PYM Minutes, 1749–1779, 101, Haverford.

52. See, for example, *Epistle from our General Spring Meeting*; Moulton, ed., Journal, 47–50, 85–86, 98–101.

53. See, for example, *Epistles from the Yearly Meeting of Friends,* 340, 352–53.

54. Anthony Benezet, "An Account of the Behaviour and Sentiments of a Number of Well-disposed Indians Mostly of the Minusing Tribe," Brookes, ed., *Friend Anthony Benezet,* 479–85, 484; *An Account of a Visit Lately Made to the People Called Quakers in*

Philadelphia, by Papoonahoal, An Indian Chief (London, 1761), 19–20; Gregory Evans Dowd, *War Under Heaven: Pontiac, The Indian Nations and the British Empire* (Baltimore: Johns Hopkins University Press, 2002), 194; Jane T. Merritt, *At the Crossroads: Indians and Empires on a Mid-Atlantic Frontier* (Chapel Hill: University of North Carolina Press, 2003), 317–20; Ralph H. Pickens, "A Religious Encounter: John Woolman and David Zeisberger," *Quaker History* 79 (1990) 77–92, 79–80; "Relation by Frederick Post of Conversation with Indians, 1760," *Pennsylvania Archives* 1st ser. (1852–1856), 3:742–43; Minutes of Meetings with a Delegation of Minisink, July 11–16, 1760, HM 8249, 12, Huntington.

55. Letter from Nathaniel Holland, May 21, 1761, "Report of the trustees of the Friendly Association who attended the Indian treaty at Easton in the 8th month 1761," Friendly Association Minutes, 4:115, 140, Haverford; "John Hays' Diary and Journal of 1760," *Pennsylvania Archeologist* 24 (1954): 63–84, 67.

56. "Relation by Frederick Post," 3; Minutes of Meetings with a Delegation of Minisink, July 11–16, 1760, HM 8249, 5–6, Huntington; *Minutes of the Provincial Council of Pennsylvania*, 10 vols. (Harrisburg, Pa.., 1852), 8:488. See Benezet, "Account," Brookes, ed., *Friend Anthony Benezet*, 479; *Account of a Visit*, 3–4.

57. Minutes of Meetings with a Delegation of Minisink, July 11–16, 1760, HM 8249, 2, Huntington.

58. Minutes of Meetings with a Delegation of Minisink, July 11–16, 1760, HM 8249, Huntington; *Minutes of the Provincial Council of Pennsylvania*, 8:484–91; "Relation by Frederick Post"; "John Hays' Diary and Journal of 1760," 67, 73–74. See Robert S. Cox, "Supper and Celibacy: Quaker-Seneca Reflexive Missions," in David Curtis Skaggs and Larry L. Nelson, eds., *The Sixty Years' War for the Great Lakes, 1754–1814* (East Lansing: Michigan State University Press, 2001), 243–75, 246–48; James, *People Among Peoples*, 96–100.

59. *Minutes of the Provincial Council of Pennsylvania*, 8:490; Benezet, "Account," Brookes, ed., *Friend Anthony Benezet*, 482; *Account of a Visit*, 13

60. Benezet, "Account," Brookes, ed., *Friend Anthony Benezet*, 479–84; *Account of a Visit*; Christian Schultze to Israel Pemberton, December 1, 1760, Report of the trustees, Friendly Association Minutes, 4:59, 143, Haverford; Minutes of Meetings with a Delegation of Minisink, July 11–16, 1760, HM 8249, 12–18, Huntington; "Some Account of a Visit of Divers Friends Made to the Indians," *Indiana Magazine of History* 32 (1936): 267–68; Anthony Benezet, "An Account of Papunhank's Second Visit to Friends the 4th of 8th month, 1761," Brookes, ed., *Friend Anthony Benezet*, 485–92, 488; John Woolman, "The substance of some conversation with Paponahoal the Indian Chief at AB in presence of Jo. W-n AB Etc.," Pemberton Papers, 13:23, HSP.

61. Woolman, "The substance of some conversation," Pemberton Papers, 13:23, HSP.

62. Woolman, "The substance of some conversation," Pemberton Papers, 13:23, HSP; Benezet, "Account of Second Visit," Brookes, ed., *Friend Anthony Benezet*, 488–89; Moulton, ed., *Journal*, 122–23.

63. Minutes of Meetings with a Delegation of Minisink, July 11–16, 1760, HM 8249, 6, Huntington; *Minutes of the Provincial Council of Pennsylvania*, 8:488. See Minutes of the Provincial Council of Pennsylvania, June 14, 1715, July 12, 1720, *Pennsylvania Archives* 1st ser. 2:599–600, 3:93; Henry J. Cadbury, ed., "Caleb Pusey's Account of Pennsylvania,"

Quaker History 64 (1975): 37–57, 49; James H. Merrell, *Into the American Woods: Negotiators on the Pennsylvania Frontier* (New York: Norton, 1999), 163–64; J. William Frost, "'Wear the Sword as Long as Thou Canst': William Penn in Myth and History," *Explorations in Early American Culture* 4 (2000): 13–45, 23–24; James O'Neil Spady, "Colonialism and the Discursive Antecedents of Penn's Treaty with the Indians," in William A. Pencak and Daniel K. Richter, eds., *Friends and Enemies in Penn's Woods: Indians, Colonists, and the Racial Construction of Pennsylvania* (University Park: Pennsylvania State University Press, 2004), 18–40, 26.

64. Gregory Evans Dowd, *A Spirited Resistance: The North American Indian Struggle for Unity, 1745–1815* (Baltimore: Johns Hopkins University Press, 1992), 31–32; Pickens, "Religious Encounter," 79–80; Report of the trustees, Friendly Association Minutes, 4:140, William Edmonds to Israel Pemberton, July 19, 1760, Pemberton Family Papers, box 1036, file 2, Haverford; Earl P. Olmstead, *David Zeisberger: A Life Among the Indians* (Kent, Ohio: Kent State University Press, 1997), 384–85 n5; Craig D. Atwood, *Community of the Cross: Moravian Piety in Colonial Bethlehem* (University Park: Pennsylvania State University Press, 2004), 70–73.

65. Woolman, "The substance of some conversation," Pemberton Papers, 13:23, HSP. In the summer of 1760, the Friendly Association gave Papunhank coats, blue cloth, ruffled shirts, silk handkerchiefs, calico gowns, and a variety of other apparel. See Papers Relating to the Friendly Association, 4:83, Haverford.

66. Benezet, "Account," Brookes, ed., *Friend Anthony Benezet*, 483; *Account of a Visit*, 15–17; Woolman, "The substance of some conversation," Pemberton Papers, 13:23, HSP. Minutes of Meetings with a Delegation of Minisink, July 11–16, 1760, HM 8249, 13, Huntington.

67. PYM Minutes, 1749–1779, 162, Draft of Israel Pemberton to Benjamin Hersey, and others, January 14, 1762, Friendly Association Minutes, 4:263, Haverford; Miscellaneous Papers of Philadelphia Yearly Meeting, 1748–1762, 1762, 8a, Swarthmore.

68. Articles of the New Jersey Association, 975B, 1–2, Haverford.

69. Moulton, ed., *Journal*, 122.

70. Journal manuscript, Woolman Collection, Box 2, 280, HSP. See I Timothy 5:22.

71. Moulton, ed., *Journal*, 122–23.

72. PYM Miscellaneous Papers, 1748–1762, 1759, f. 21, Swarthmore. For Woolman's and Stanton's joint authorship of this epistle see PYM Minutes, 1747–1779, 129, Haverford.

73. PYM Minutes, 1747–1779, 178, 183, Haverford.

74. PYM Minutes, 1747–1779, 226, 231, Haverford.

75. PYM Miscellaneous Papers, 1748–1762, 1763, f. 14, Swarthmore. For Woolman's and Pemberton's joint authorship of this epistle see PYM Minutes, 1747–1779, 180, Haverford.

CHAPTER 7. NOT IN WORDS ONLY: CONSPICUOUS INSTRUCTIVE BEHAVIOR

1. Moulton, ed., *Journal*, 87.

2. PYM Minutes, 1747–1779, 119–20, 172, 177, 182–84, 207, Haverford.

3. Moulton, ed., *Journal*, 154,

4. Moulton, ed., *Journal*, 55.

5. Marietta, "Conscience, the Quaker Community, and the French and Indian War," 18; Ketchan, "Conscience, War and Politics."

6. Woolman, "Plea for the Poor," 253; Journal manuscript, Woolman Collection, Box 2, back page 4, HSP. See also Woolman, "Conversations," Comly and Comly, eds., *Friends' Miscellany*, 354.

7. Woolman, "Plea for the Poor," 252, 255.

8. 1753 Ledger, 216–17; On Gaskill's Quakerism see BMM Minutes, 1757–1770, 14, Swarthmore.

9. Evans, Journal, Comly and Comly, eds., *Friends' Miscellany*, 10: 27–30; "Memoirs of Joshua Evans," Comly and Comly, eds., *Friends' Miscellany*, 1:302–3.

10. Moulton, ed., *Journal*, 161–62, 162 n8.

11. Grundy, ed., *Resistance and Obedience*, 44.

12. 1753 Ledger, 211, 216.

13. Moulton, ed., *Journal*, 156.

14. Abner Woolman, Journal, Chapter XXXVIII, Haverford.

15. Evans, Journal, Comly and Comly, eds., *Friends' Miscellany*, 10:18.

16. "Germantown Friends' Protest Against Slavery, 1688," Frost, ed., *Quaker Origins*, Document 3; Philadelphia Monthly Meeting, *An Exhortation and Caution to Friends Concerning the Buying or Keeping of Negroes* (Philadelphia, 1693), 2; Hepburn, *American Defense*, 23–24, 31–32; Elihu Coleman, *A Testimony against the Antichristian Practice of Making Slaves of Men* (Boston, 1733), 12–17; Ralph Sandiford, *A Brief Examination of the Practice of the Times* (Philadelphia, 1729), 62.

17. Benjamin Lay, *All Slave-keepers That Keep the Innocent in Bondage Apostates* (Philadelphia, 1737), 19, 34–35; *Memoirs of the Lives of Benjamin Lay and Ralph Sandiford*, 40–41.

18. See Ruth Ketring Nuermberger, *The Free Produce Movement* (Durham, N.C.: Duke University Press, 1942), 5.

19. Grundy, ed., *Resistance and Obedience*, 44–45.

20. Moulton, ed., *Journal*, 53–55, 156..

21. Woolman, *Some Considerations Part Second*, 27.

22. 1753 Ledger, 236, 238, 238 contra.

23. Evans, Journal, Comly and Comly, eds., *Friends' Miscellany*, 10:18, 33–36.

24. William Hunt, Journal, 81, Haverford; *Memoirs of William and Nathan Hunt*, 47–48.

25. PYM Minutes, 1747–1779, 121, Haverford.

26. Moulton, ed., *Journal*, 117–18; *Pennsylvania Gazette*, April 1, 1762.

27. WMM Miscellaneous Papers, Proposals for Printing Books, Swarthmore.

28. Moulton, ed., *Journal*, 119.

29. Amelia Mott Gummere, *The Quaker: A Study in Costume* (New York: Benjamin Blom, 1968); Frost, "From Plainness to Simplicity," 19–21; Leanna Lee-Whitman, "Silks and Simplicity: A Study of Quaker Dress as Depicted in Portraits, 1718–1855" (Ph.D. dissertation, University of Pennsylvania, 1987), 35–56.

30. George Churchman, Journal, 1:32, Haverford.

31. Moulton, ed., *Journal*, 119–21.

32. Moulton, ed., *Journal*, 119–20, 190; Woolman, "Plea for the Poor," 255, 266.

33. Cadbury, *John Woolman in England*, 95, 97, 102.

34. Fox, *Journal*, 1:107–8.

35. Kenneth Carroll, "Sackcloth and Ashes and Other Signs and Wonders," *Journal of the Friends Historical Society* 53 (1975): 314–25; Carroll, "Quaker Attitudes Towards Signs and Wonders," *Journal of the Friends Historical Society* 54 (1977): 70–84; Carroll, "Early Quakers and 'Going Naked as a Sign'," *Quaker History* 67 (1978): 69–87; Carla Gardina Pestana, "The City upon a Hill Under Siege: The Puritan Perception of the Quaker Threat to Massachusetts Bay, 1656–1661," *New England Quarterly* 56 (1983): 323–53, 331. See also Leo Damrosch, *The Sorrows of the Quaker Jesus: James Naylor and the Puritan Crackdown on the Free Spirit* (Cambridge, Mass.: Harvard University Press, 1996), 115–76.

36. A copy of verses in praise of an eminent old speaker . . . Joseph Rule," Catchpool manuscripts, 1:313, Friends House; see also "A poem composed by Joseph Rule on his sweet experience of a retired life in a hermit like manner, among the mountains, woods, and bushes in Wales," Catchpool manuscripts, 1:73; R. Hingston Fox, "Joseph Rule, The Quaker in White," *Journal of the Friends Historical Society* 11 (1914): 36–38; Joseph J. Green, "Joseph Rule, The Quaker in White," *Journal of the Friends Historical Society* 2 (1905): 64–68; "Joseph Rule, the White Quaker," *Proceedings of the Wesley Historical Society* 4 (1904): 165–67; *Dr. Free's Remarks Upon Mr. Jones's Letter* (London, 1759), 63–64; Francis De Valangin, *A Treatise on Diet, or the Management of Human Life* (London, 1768), 340–41.

37. Moulton, ed., *Journal*, 120.

38. See Sobel, *Teach Me Dreams*, 64.

39. For indications of Woolman's preoccupation with cleanliness see Moulton, ed., *Journal*, 168, 190.

40. Moulton, ed., *Journal*, 190.

41. Philotheos Physiologus, *The Country-Man's Companion, or, A New Method of Ordering Horses and Sheep* (London, n.d.), 123–24.

42. *Memoirs of the Lives of Benjamin Lay and Ralph Sandiford*, 67; John Hunt, "Notices of Benjamin Lay," Comly and Comly, eds., *Friends' Miscellany*, 4:275. Lay's estate inventory reveals, however, that at the time of his death in 1759 he owned finer clothes than this. See Gummere, *The Quaker*, 44–45.

43. Woolman, "Plea for the Poor," 250, 259, 266; Philip Boroughs, "John Woolman's Spirituality," in Heller, ed., *Tendering Presence*, 1–16, 7.

44. Cadbury, *John Woolman in England*, 96.

45. Abner Woolman, Journal, Chapter XXIII, Haverford.

46. "Memoirs of Joshua Evans," Comly and Comly, eds., *Friends' Miscellany*, 1:303.

47. Evans, Journal, 21–24, 32.

48. Fox, *Journal*, 1:363.

49. George Churchman, Journal, 2:7, 8, Haverford.

50. Report of the trustees, Israel Pemberton to Mary Pemberton, August 5, 1761, Friendly Association Minutes, 4:139, 153, Haverford; *An Account of the Behavior and Sentiments of Some Well Disposed Indians Mostly of the Minising Tribe* (Stanford, N.Y., 1803), 16–17.

51. Report of the trustees, Friendly Association Minutes, 4:143, 151, Haverford.

52. Account dated April 7, 1761, Friendly Association Minutes, 4:83, Haverford.

53. Minutes of Meetings with a Delegation of Minisink, July 11–16, 1760, HM 8249, 14–15, 17, Huntington; Report of the trustees, Accounts signed by Israel Pemberton, December 3, 1761, Friendly Association Minutes, 4:143, 151, 251, Haverford.

54. Letter from Nathaniel Holland, May 21, 1761, Friendly Association Minutes, 4:115, Haverford.

55. See, for example, Benezet, "Account," Brookes, ed., *Friend Anthony Benezet*, 483. See also *Account of a Visit*, 16–17. Partly under the influence of the Quakers' published writings, this view of Papunhank survives in the scholarly literature. See Dowd, *Spirited Resistance*, 31; Alfred A. Cave, *Prophets of the Great Spirit: Native American Revitalization Movements in Eastern North America* (Lincoln: University of Nebraska Press, 2006), 15; Lee Irwin, *Coming Down from Above: Prophecy, Resistance, and Renewal in Native American Religions* (Norman: University of Oklahoma Press, 2008), 127.

56. Letter from Nathaniel Holland, May 21, 1761, Friendly Association Minutes, 4:115, Haverford.

57. See, for example, Christian Schultze to Israel Pemberton, December 1, 1760, Friendly Association Minutes, 4:59, Haverford.

58. Israel Pemberton to Mary Pemberton, August 5, 1761, Friendly Association Minutes, 4:153, Haverford.

59. Report of the trustees, Friendly Association Minutes, 4:151, Haverford; Minutes of Meetings with a Delegation of Minisink, July 11–16, 1760, HM 8249, 15, Huntington.

60. Letter from Papunhank, Job Chillaway and David Owens, September 15, 1761, Israel Pemberton to Tonquakena, October 31, 1761, Letter from Nathaniel Holland, November 12, 1761, Israel Pemberton to Papunhank, March 20, 1762, Friendly Association Minutes, 4:191, 195, 199, 223, 235–36, 236, 239, 243, 271, Haverford; Minutes of Meetings with a Delegation of Minisink, July 11–16, 1760, HM 8249, 18, Huntington; Merritt, *At the Crossroads*, 305.

61. PYM Ministers and Elders Minutes, 1735–1774, 441, Haverford.

62. Moulton, ed., *Journal*, 122–23, 127.

63. Moulton, ed., *Journal*, 123–24. See Pslam 34:7.

64. Moulton, ed., *Journal*, 123–24, 131–32; JW to Sarah Woolman, June 8, 1763, William Lightfoot to Sarah Woolman, June 13, 1763, Woolman Collection, Box 1, 7, 8, John Pemberton to Israel Pemberton, July 2, 1763, Pemberton Papers, 16:109, HSP; Gummere, ed., *Journal*, 88–89, 92–93; Whitney, *John Woolman*, 291–93, 314–15. For Lightfoot's position in the Friendly Association see Extract from the minutes of the Friendly Association, April 19, 1762, Pemberton Papers, 15:134, HSP.

65. Moulton, ed., *Journal*, 126, 127, 129, 137.

66. Moulton, ed., *Journal*, 123, 128, 129–30, 132, 134.

67. Moulton, ed., *Journal*, 126.

68. Moulton, ed., Journal, 128.

69. Moulton, ed., *Journal*, 125, 128.

70. Pickens, "Religious Encounter," 85, 89; Olmstead, *David Zeisberger*, 385 n5;

Merritt, *At the Crossroads*, 304; *John Papunhank: A Christian Indian of North America: A Narrative of Facts* (Dublin, 1820), 11–13.

71. Moulton, ed., *Journal*, 128, 134.

72. Moulton, ed., *Journal*, 135.

73. Moulton, ed., *Journal*, 132.

74. Moulton, ed., *Journal*, 134. For an indication of Quaker-Moravian relations as it affected outreach toward Indians, see William Edmonds to Israel Pemberton, July 19, 1760, Pemberton Family Papers, Box 1036, file 2, Israel Pemberton and others to "Netawallwaleman, and the rest of the head men of the Delaware Indians of Kekailammapaikung, and to John Papunehung, and the rest of the Indian Brethren at Welhick Thuppeck and all other Indians living beyond the Ohio, to whom this may come," July 8, 1773, Pemberton Family Papers, Box 1036, file 1, Haverford.

75. Moulton, ed., *Journal*, 132–4.

76. Benezet, "Account," Brookes, ed., *Friend Anthony Benezet*, 479–85, 483; see also *Account of a Visit*, 17.

77. Pickens, "Religious Encounter," 84–86; *John Papunhank*, 13.

78. Pickens, "Religious Encounter," 85–86, 89; Olmstead, *David Zeisberger*, 385 n5; Merritt, *At the Crossroads*, 304.

79. PYM Minutes, 1749–1779, 189, Haverford; John Pemberton to Israel Pemberton, July 2, 1763, Pemberton Papers, 16:109, HSP, Gummere, ed., *Journal*, 91–3; Whitney, *John Woolman*, 311–15.

80. JW to Uriah Woolman, June 4, 1763, Gratz Mss., Case 8, box 25, JW to Israel Pemberton, June 16, 1763, Pemberton Papers 16:98, JW to Sarah Woolman, June 8, 1763, Woolman Collection, Box 1, 7, HSP; PYM Ministers and Elders Minutes, 1735–1774, 444, Haverford; Gummere, ed., *Journal*, 88; Whitney, *John Woolman*, 291–92; Moulton, ed., *Journal*, 124.

81. Silver, *Our Savage Neighbors*, 191–226; Ketchum, "Conscience, War, and Politics; Marietta, "Conscience, the Quaker Community, and the French and Indian War;" Sloan, "'Time of Sifting and Winnowing;" William Smith, *A Brief View of the Conduct of Pennsylvania, for the Year 1755* (London, 1756), 23.

82. Moulton, ed., *Journal*, 135. See also John Pemberton to Israel Pemberton, July 2, 1763, Pemberton Papers, 16:109, HSP, Gummere, ed., *Journal*, 92–93 and Whitney, *John Woolman*, 314–15; Kenny, *Peaceable Kingdom Lost*, 116; Anderson, *Crucible of War*, 533–34.

83. Dowd, *War Under Heaven*, 194–96; Kenny, *Peaceable Kingdom Lost*, 128–29, 133–34, 167; Merritt, *At the Crossroads*, 305–6.

84. Israel Pemberton to John Allen, April 8, 1768, Message from the Friendly Association to Netalwalem and the rest of the Delaware Indians at Kaikailammapakung, May 18, 1771, Friendly Association Minutes, 4:403, 4:423, Haverford; Journal manuscript, Woolman Collection, Box 2, 142, HSP; Moulton, ed., *Journal*, 134 n26.

85. Merritt, *At the Crossroads*, 317–20; Olmstead, *David Zeisberger*, 385 n5; William Edmonds to Israel Pemberton, July 19, 1760, Pemberton Family Papers, box 1036, file 2; Israel Pemberton and others to "Netawallwaleman, and the rest of the head men." For events in Wyalusing in the 1760s and early 1770s, see Amy C. Schutt, "Forging Identities: Native

Americans and Moravian Missionaries in Pennsylvania and Ohio, 1765–1782" (Ph.D. dissertation, Indiana University, 1995), 90–121.

86. Silver, *Our Savage Neighbors*, 191–226; Kenny, *Peaceable Kingdom Lost*, 147–45; Eustace, "Sentimental Paradox"; Sloan, "Time of Sifting and Winnowing."

87. Moulton, ed., *Journal*, 142–43.

88. Moulton, ed., *Journal*, 138–39; *The Life and Travels of John Pemberton, A Minister of the Gospel of Christ* (London, 1844), 49–52; PQM Minutes, 1723–1772, 319, 321; PYM Ministers and Elders Minutes, 1735–1774, 453, Haverford; BQM Minutes, 1686–1767, 319, Swarthmore.

89. See generally Marietta, *Reformation*.

90. BMM Minutes, 253, 255, 263–64.

91. Moulton, ed., *Journal*, 145.

92. Moulton, ed., *Journal*, 145–46.

93. Kenneth Lane Carroll, *Joseph Nichols and the Nicholites: A Look at the "New Quakers" of Maryland, Delaware, North and South Carolina* (Easton, Md.: Easton Publishing, 1962), 26.

94. Moulton, ed., *Journal*, 145; Carroll, *Joseph Nichols*, 42.

95. Carroll, *Joseph Nichols*, 43.

96. Moulton, ed., *Journal* 150–52.

97. Woolman, "Plea for the Poor," 271.

98. "A Testimony from Friends of Mount Holly, New Jersey, concerning William Boen Comly and Comly, eds., *Friends' Miscellany* 1:183–84; William Boen's marriage certificate, May 3, 1763, Gummere, ed., *Journal*, 608–9.

99. "A Testimony from Friends of Mount Holly, New Jersey, 1:184.

100. Henry J. Cadbury, "Negro Membership in the Society of Friends," *Journal of Negro History* 21 (1936): 151–213, 153; PQM Minutes, 1723–1772, 373, back p. 6, Haverford.

101. Cadbury, "Negro Membership," 168.

102. 1769 Ledger, index page; Woolman, *Some Considerations*, 11; see also Woolman, "Plea for the Poor," 268–72.

103. Moulton, ed., *Journal*, 152–53.

104. Moulton, ed., *Journal*, 152–53.

105. Woolman, "Plea for the Poor," 270, 271–72.

106. Letter from Abner Woolman, 1770, in Abner Woolman, Journal, 7–8, Haverford; see also ibid, Chapter XXXIII.

107. Moulton, ed., *Journal*, 156.

108. Woolman, "Plea for the Poor," 271.

CHAPTER 8. THE DEEP: CROSSING THE SEA

1. Moulton, ed., *Journal*, 40–42.

2. Moulton, ed., Journal, 107.

3. See, for example, Fox, *Journal*, 1:273, 561, 2:151, 214, 317–18, 460; Sandiford, *Brief Examination*, 2; Hume, *Remarks on Small Pox*, 16.

4. Larson, *Daughters of Light*, 105; Henry J. Cadbury, "Sailing to England with John Woolman," *Quaker History* 55 (1966): 88–103, 94; Samuel Emlen to Sarah Emlen, June 6, 1772, Letters of Samuel Emlen, 1772–1797, 23, HSP; Moulton, ed., *Journal*, 169.

5. JW to Sarah Woolman, June 23, 1760, Woolman Collection, Box 1, 6, HSP.

6. Moulton, ed., *Journal*, 113.

7. Moulton, ed., Journal, 113, 114.

8. JW to Jane Crosfield, December 12, 1760, Woolman Manuscripts, Swarthmore. See Acts 27:9–28:31. For more on Crosfield and her travels see PYM Ministers and Elders Minutes, 1734–1774, 415, Haverford; George Crosfield, ed., *Memoirs of the Life and Gospel Labours of Samuel Fothergill* (Liverpool, 1843), 397–99.

9. Moulon, ed. *Journal*, 108, 112.

10. JW to Israel Pemberton, November 17 and n.d., 1761, Pemberton Papers 15:74, 111, HSP.

11. Woolman, *Some Considerations Part Second*, 7.

12. Ibid., 38, 39–40, 43.

13. Benezet, *Observations on Inslaving*, 3–5.

14. Anthony Benezet, *A Short Account of that Part of Africa Inhabited by the Negroes* (Philadelphia, 1762).

15. PYM Ministers and Elders Minutes, 1734–1774, 422, 425–26, Haverford.

16. Churchman, *Account*, 205.

17. George Churchman, Journal, 1: 26, 28–29, Haverford.

18. Churchman, *Account*, 204–6.

19. PYM Ministers and Elders Minutes, 1734–1774, 430, Haverford.

20. Slaughter misdates some of Woolman's most important writings from this period, particularly *Considerations on Pure Wisdom* and the draft passages from that essay rejected by the Overseers of the Press. See Slaughter, *Beautiful Soul*, 209–14. *Considerations on Pure Wisdom* was composed and printed in 1768.

21. Journal manuscript, Woolman Collection, Box 2, back page 1, HSP.

22. Woolman, "Plea for the Poor," 246–47, 258.

23. Woolman, "Conversations," Comly and Comly, eds., *Friends' Miscellany*, 1:341. For the manuscript of this piece see Journal manuscript, Woolman Collection, Box 2, back pages 15–27.

24. Woolman, *Considerations on True Harmony*, 31.

25. Journal manuscript, Woolman Collection, Box 2, back page 3, HSP. See also Woolman, *Considerations on Pure Wisdom*, 22–23.

26. Woolman, "Plea for the Poor," 258.

27. Woolman, *Considerations on True Harmony*, 2.

28. PYM Meeting for Sufferings to LYM Meeting for Sufferings, 1766, Invoice from Mary Hinde, 1768, PYM Sufferings Miscellaneous Papers, 1766, 6, and 1768, 7; Anthony Benezet to Sophia Hume, July 25, 1767, Ms. 163, f. 25; LYM Sufferings Minutes, 32:68–69, Friends House.

29. BMM Minutes, 1757–1770, 275, Swarthmore.

30. Anthony Benezet, *A Caution and Warning to Great Britain and her Colonies* (Philadelphia, 1766), 3, 4.

31. Journal manuscript, Woolman Collection, Box 2, back pages. 5–14, HSP.

32. Woolman adopted a similar rhetorical strategy in a brief discussion of the slave's experience in *Considerations on Pure Wisdom*, 15–17.

33. Moulton, ed., *Journal*, 297–98. See also Robert E. Spiller, "John Woolman on War," *Journal of the Rutgers University Library* 5 (1941): 60–61.

34. BMM Women's Minutes, 1747–1799, 107, PYM Ministers and Elders Minutes, 1734–1774, 468, Haverford.

35. PYM Ministers and Elders Minutes, 1734–1774, 489–90, 500, Haverford.

36. JW to Israel Pemberton, April 4, 1769, Pemberton Papers, 21:1, HSP.

37. Moulton, ed., *Journal*, 153 n58.

38. JW to ?, October 16, 1769, Woolman Collection, Box 1, 3, HSP; see also JW to ?, October 22, 1769, file 851, Haverford.

39. See Thomas Maxwell to James Pemberton, January 1, 1767, October 2, 1769, January 17, 1770, Pemberton Papers, 19:29, 21:75, 106, HSP.

40. JW to Israel Pemberton, November 11, 1769, Pemberton Papers, 21:85, HSP.

41. Gummere, ed., *Journal*, 109–11, 284n; Henry J. Cadbury, *John Woolman in England*, 35.

42. It has sometimes been suggested that Woolman and Smith had been childhood friends, though there is no contemporary evidence to support that assertion and Smith's diary suggests that they barely noticed each other until the 1750s. See Slaughter, *Beautiful Soul*, 409 n21; Livesay, "John Woolman: Persona and Person," 173–75.

43. Moulton, ed., *Journal*, 156–58.

44. See Cadbury, *John Woolman in England*, 30.

45. PYM Minutes, 1747–1779, 77, BMM Minutes, 1737–1756, 308, BMM Minutes, 1757–1770, 47, 70, 181, 194, 286, Swarthmore; BMM Women's Minutes, 1747–1799, 56, Haverford.

46. JW to John Smith, April 16, 1760, in Gummere, ed., *Journal*, 59.

47. George Churchman, Journal, 1:29, Haverford.

48. Moulton, ed., *Journal*, 159.

49. Gummere, ed., *Journal* 112; Slaughter, *Beautiful Soul*, 289–90; on Asher's marriage see BMM Women's Minutes, 1747–1799, 125, Haverford; Gummere, ed., *Journal*, 523.

50. Gummere, ed., *Journal*, 113.

51. 1769 Ledger, 183 contra. See also Moulton, ed., *Journal*, 160.

52. Moulton, ed., *Journal*, 185–86.

53. Woolman, *Epistle*, 2. See Galatians 2:20.

54. Moulton, ed., *Journal*, 186.

55. See Benezet, *Short Account*, 45. The mines of Potosi were a familiar part of the critique of Spanish imperialism in the English-speaking world. In an essay addressed to the colonists of New Jersey and Pennsylvania, Thomas Tryon referred to them as a model that the English should avoid. See Phusiologus, *Country-man's Companion*, 103.

56. Journal manuscript, Woolman Collection, Box 2, 280, HSP.

57. John Woolman, Essay on Silver Vessels, January 20, 1770, Woolman Manuscripts, Swarthmore. A page number—181—appears on the manuscript identifying it as the missing page 181 from Woolman's 1769 Ledger. See Matthew 19:12, Genesis 35:1–4.

58. Moulton, ed., *Journal*, 186–87.

59. *New Jersey Archives* ser, 1, vols. 32, 33, 35 (Somerville and Trenton, N.J., 1924–31).

60. *New Jersey Archives* ser, 1, 33:169, 33:269, 25:599.

61. Journal manuscript, Woolman Collection, Box 2, back page 14, HSP.

62. Journal manuscript, Woolman Collection, Box 2, 282, HSP. In the early 1770s Woolman repeatedly used the phrase "the spirit of this world" to designate corrupting influences. See Woolman, *Considerations on True Harmony*, 4, 6; Woolman, *Epistle*, 6. This was a common usage. See, for example, Churchman, *Account*, 196.

63. Journal manuscript, Woolman Collection, Box 2, 282, HSP.

64. Samuel Neale, Journal, quoted in Gummere, ed., *Journal*, 118.

65. BMM Minutes, 1757–1770, 336, 340–41, Swarthmore.

66. Moulton, ed., *Journal*, 161–62, 162 n8.

67. PYM Minutes, 1747–1779, 263, 279, Haverford; *Epistles from the Yearly Meeting*, 381–82.

68. These numbers have been assembled from BQM Minutes and PYM Ministers and Elders Minutes, Haverford.

69. Account of Woolman's illness and death, in Moulton, ed., *Journal*, 304.

70. BMM Minutes, 1770–1781, 24, Swarthmore.

71. PYM Ministers and Elders Minutes, 1735–1774, 515, 518, Haverford; LYM Ministers and Elders Minutes, 1767–1773, 247, Friends House.

72. 1753 Ledger, 203, 206; 1769 Ledger, 6 contra.

73. Abner Woolman's will, 9309–9315C, NJSA; *New Jersey Archives* ser, 1, vol. 35 (Trenton, N.J., 1931), 599.

74. Abner Woolman, Journal, appendix, 57–60, Haverford.

75. JW to John Woolman Jr., June 14, 1772, Port D/67, Friends House.

76. John Comfort's and Mary Woolman's marriage certificate, Woolman Collection, Box 1, f 9, HSP; BMM Women's Minutes, 1747–1799, 131, Haverford.

77. 1769 Ledger, 42–43. The house in Figure 11 is identified as the Comfort home in John Warner Barber and Henry Howe, *Historical Collections of New Jersey* (New York, 1845), 114. The structure depicted matches the plans Woolman developed for the Comfort house. The house now used as the John Woolman memorial is sometimes identified as the Comforts' home, but it was constructed in 1783. See Perinchief, ed., *The Woolman Family*, introduction. Slaughter identifies the house in this picture as John and Sarah's home. Slaughter, *Beautiful Soul*, 192.

78. Gummere, ed., *Journal*, 536.

79. JW to John Comfort, Woolman Collection, Box 1, 12, HSP.

80. Deed of trust to Stephen Comfort, April 27, 1772, Woolman Collection, Box 1, 11, HSP.

81. JW to Caleb Carr, April 28, 1772, quoted in Cadbury, *John Woolman in England*, 30.

82. Moulton, ed., *Journal*, 183–84, 188 n15; JW to John Townsend, June 19, 1772, Spriggs Manusctips 1:66, Friends House; JW to Reuben and Margaret Haines, July 31, 1772, Comly and Comly, eds., *Friends' Miscellany*, 1:10–11.

83. Elizabeth Smith's traveling certificate, Woolman Collection, Box 2, 3, HSP. See also BMM Women's Minutes, 1747–1799, 131, Haverford.

84. JW to Elizabeth Smith, April 28, 1772, Woolman Collection, Box 2, 3, HSP.

85. Note from Francis B. Gummere, February 1930, Woolman Collection, Box 2, 3, HSP.

86. PYM Women's Minutes, 1681–1814, 164, Swarthmore.

87. Gummere, ed., *Journal*, 538.

88. Allison, ed., *Memorials of Rebecca Jones*, 29.

89. *Pennsylvania Gazette*, October 14, 1772. See also PYM Women's Minutes, 1681–1814, 157, Swarthmore.

90. John Hunt, Journal, Swarthmore.

91. Moulton, ed., *Journal*, 122, 144.

92. BQM Women's Minutes, 1686–1845, 115, Swarthmore; BMM Women's Minutes, 1747–1799, 139, Haverford.

93. Allison, ed., *Memorials of Rebecca Jones*, 29.

94. Woolman, "Plea for the Poor," 266.

95. The table shown in Figure 12 belonged to Asher Woolman, and may well be the walnut table Asher inherited from John's father Samuel in 1750. See Samuel Woolman's estate inventory 4761–4766C, NJSA; Jonathan L. Fairbanks, *American Furniture, 1620 to the Present* (New York: Richard Marek, 1981), 313; Charles L. Venable, *American Furniture in the Bybee Collection* (Dallas: Dallas Museum of Art, 1989), 4–5.

96. Moulton, ed., *Journal*, 165.

97. John Cox, "Sketches and Recollections," 24, Dillwyn Parrish Recollections and Sketches, HSP.

98. See JW to Israel Pemberton, April 15, 1772, Pemberton Papers, 23:114b, HSP.

99. Cadbury, *John Woolman in England*, 8, 120–24; *Memoirs of William and Nathan Hunt*, 74–75; William Bispham, *Memoranda concerning the Family of Bispham in Great Britain and the United States of America* (New York: Privately printed, 1890), 235; Samuel Emlen to Sarah Emlen, May 2, 1772, Letters of Samuel Emlen, 1772–1797, 19, HSP; 1769 Ledger, 3. Henry J. Cadbury expresses some uncertainty as to whether the John Bispham who boarded the ship was thirty-eight-year-old John Bispham Sr., his twelve-year-old son John, Jr., or one of a few other possible John Bisphams. This question is largely settled by Emlen's description of the boy as a "lad."

100. *Pennsylvania Gazette*, June 13, 1765, February 20, August 28, 1766, October 15, 1767, May 5, 1768, May 18, November 2, 1769, May 24. November 1, 1770, April 18, July 11, September 19, September 26, 1771, April 16, 1772; see also Cadbury, "Sailing to England," 89–90.

101. Moulton, ed., *Journal*, 164.

102. See Sarah Logan to Sarah Emlen, September 9, 1772, quoted in Cadbury, "Sailing to England," 98.

103. Moulton, ed., *Journal*, 167–68.

104. See Marcus Rediker, *Between the Devil and the Deep Blue Sea: Merchant Seamen, Pirates, and the Anglo-American Maritime World, 1700–1750* (Cambridge: Cambridge University Press, 1987), 192.

105. Samuel Emlen to Sarah Emlen, November 4, 1772, Letters of Samuel Emlen, 55, HSP.

106. Cadbury, "Sailing to England," 94. See also Samuel Emlen to Sarah Emlen, June 6, 1772, Letters of Samuel Emlen, 23, HSP.

107. Moulton, ed., *Journal*, 178–79.

108. Journal manuscript, Luke Howard Manuscripts, Friends House, 22.

109. Moulton, ed., *Journal*, 179.

110. Samuel Emlen to Sarah Emlen, May 2, 1772, Letters of Samuel Emlen, 1772–1797, 19, HSP.

111. Moulton, ed., *Journal*, 166, 168–69, 170; see also 179–80.

112. Moulton ed., *Journal*, 167, 169, 170, 172, 178, 179–80.

113. Moulton, ed., *Journal*, 172.

114. Rediker, *Slave Ship*, 251–53; Walter E. Minchinton, "Characteristics of British Slaving Vessels, 1698–1775," *Journal of Interdisciplinary History* 20 (1989): 53–81, 70–71.

115. Moulton, ed., Journal, 171.

116. Compare John Woolman, *The Works of John Woolman, in Two Parts* (Philadelphia, 1774), 215, with John Woolman, *The Works of John Woolman, in Two Parts* (London, 1775), 184.

117. Compare Woolman, *Works* (Philadelphia, 1774), 226–27, with Woolman, *Works* (London, 1775), 193.

118. Moulton, ed., Journal, 179–80.

119. See Gummere, ed., *Journal*, 488–510.

120. Gummere, ed., *Journal*, 495, 497, 503, 504.

121. Gummere, ed., *Journal*, 505–6.

122. Journal manuscript, Woolman Collection, Box 2, back page 2, HSP. See also Woolman, *Considerations on True Harmony*, 31.

123. Moulton, ed., *Journal*, 184.

CHAPTER 9. A MESSENGER SENT FROM THE ALMIGHTY:
ENGLAND AND DEATH

1. Moulton, ed., *Journal*, 155.

2. Mary Andrews, Book of Extracts, MS Box 28 (1), 14, Friends House.

3. Samuel Emlen to Sarah Emlen, June 6, 1772, Letters of Samuel Emlen, 1772–1797, 23, HSP.

4. Moulton, ed., *Journal*, 166, 173.

5. Samuel Emlen to Sarah Emlen, June 6, 1772, Letters of Samuel Emlen, 1772–1797, 23, HSP; Moulton, ed., *Journal*, 179 n71.

6. William Hunt to Uriah Woolman, June 25, 1772, in *Memoirs of William and Nathan Hunt*, 88–90, 88.

7. JW to Sarah Woolman, June 13, 1772, Journal manuscript, Woolman Collection, Box 2, 283, HSP.

8. Moulton, ed., *Journal*, 181.

9. Cadbury, *John Woolman in England*, 20, 42.

10. See Cadbury, *John Woolman in England*, 51–52.

11. John Pemberton to Joseph Row, April 28, 1772, MS Vol. 163, 3, Friends House.

12. John Townsend to Sarah Woolman, November 9, 1772, Woolman Manuscripts, Swarthmore.

13. Cadbury, *John Woolman in England*, 51.

14. John Townsend to Sarah Woolman, November 9, 1772, Woolman Manuscripts, Swarthmore.

15. Moulton, ed., *Journal*, 102–5.

16. Moulton, ed., *Journal*, 155.

17. Gummere, ed., *Journal*, 530; 1769 Ledger, 29; JW to "J.C.", May 10, 1769, Woolman Manuscripts, Swarthmore.

18. Woolman, "Plea for the Poor," in Moulton, ed., *Journal*, 246–47.

19. John Townsend to Sarah Woolman, November 9, 1772, Woolman Manuscripts, Swarthmore.

20. JW to Israel Pemberton, Jr., November 17, 1761, Pemberton Papers, 15:74, HSP.

21. JW to Sarah Woolman, June 23, 1760, Woolman Collection, Box 1, 6, HSP.

22. Moulton, ed., *Journal*, 102–5.

23. Sophia Hume, *Remarks on the Practice of Inoculation*, 7 n.

24. See William Forster to Rebecca Haycock, August 16, 1772, Mss. vol. 77, f. 2, Friends House.

25. Hume's published works include *An Exhortation to the Inhabitants of the Province of South Carolina* (Philadelphia, 1748), *An Epistle to the Inhabitants of South Carolina* (London, 1754), *Extracts from Divers Ancient Testimonies of Friends and Others* (London, 1760), *Caution to Such as Observe Days and Times, A Short Appeal to Men and Women of Reason* (Bristol, 1765), *Remarks on the Practice of Inoculation,* and *The Justly Celebrated Sophia Hume's Advice and Warning to Laborers* (Newport, R.I., 1769). Several of her works appeared in multiple editions. I am unaware of any evidence to support Amelia Mott Gummere's assertion that Woolman helped revise Hume's work in 1748. See Gummere, ed., *Journal*, xii. Some of her correspondence with Benezet is in MS Vol. 163, Friends House. For more on Hume see Thomas Wagstaffe, *Piety promoted, in brief memorials, and dying expressions, of some of the people called Quakers. The ninth part* (London, 1796), 12–15; Cadbury, *John Woolman in England*, 57–58.

26. JW to Sophia Hume, June 13, 1772, in Gummere, ed., *Journal*, xii.

27. JW to Israel Pemberton, April 15, 1772, Pemberton Papers, 23;114b, HSP.

28. Samuel to Sarah Emlen, June 30 and July 5, 1772, Letters of Samuel Emlen, 1772–1797, 27, 31, HSP.

29. JW to John Townsend, July 31, 1772, quoted in Cadbury, *John Woolman in England*, 53.

30. Journal of Deborah Morris, quoted in Cadbury, *John Woolman in England*, 91, 93.

31. Letter from Samuel Emlen, September 15, 1772, quoted in Cadbury, *John Woolman in England*, 18.

32. Journal of Deborah Morris, quoted in Cadbury, *John Woolman in England*, 93.

33. Moulton, ed., *Journal*, 182, 184, 185.

34. Moulton, ed., *Journal*, 182–83.

35. For a sense of the treatment of such horses in England, see J. Crofts, *Packhorse, Waggon and Post: Land Carriage and Communications Under the Tudors and Stuarts* (Toronto: University of Toronto Press, 1967), 127; Howard Robinson, *The British Post Office: A History* (Princeton, N.J.: Princeton University Press, 1948), 126–29; W. T. Jackman, *The Development of Transportation in Modern England* (London: Frank Cass, 1962), 317–20.

36. Moulton, ed., *Journal*, 183.

37. Moulton, ed., *Journal* 190.

38. JW to John Wilson, September 22, 1772, Port. 6/34, Friends House.

39. Moulton, ed., *Journal*, 190.

40. Woolman, *Considerations on True Harmony*, 4–5.

41. Letter from Samuel Emlen, August 14, 1772, quoted in Cadbury, *John Woolman in England*, 18.

42. JW to the children of Stephen Comfort, September 16, 1772, in Gummere, ed., *Journal*, 137.

43. Cadbury, *John Woolman in England*, 44, 71.

44. JW to John Townsend, June 19, 1772, quoted in Cadbury, *John Woolman in England*, 53.

45. Cadbury, *John Woolman in England*, 81.

46. JW to John Townsend, July 31, 1772, quoted in Cadbury, *John Woolman in England*, 53–54.

47. Moulton, ed., *Journal*, 184–85.

48. Moulton, ed., *Journal*, 188; Cadbury, *John Woolman in England*, 82–3, 89–90. 99–100, 109.

49. Cadbury, *John Woolman in England*, 77, 81.

50. BMM Women's Minutes, 1747–1799, 131, Haverford; *Collection of Memorials*, 340–41.

51. See William Forster to John Birkbeck, September 1, 1772, Mss. vol. 77, f. 2; William Forster to Morris Birkbeck, September 24, 1772, Ms. Vol. 77, f. 13, Friends House.

52. William Forster to Rebecca Haycock, August 16, 1772, Mss. vol. 77, f. 2, Friends House.

53. Elizabeth Wilkinson, Journal, 1761–1763, 69, Haverford.

54. The quotation is from "Memoirs of Joshua Evans," Comly and Comly, eds., *Friends' Miscellany*, 1:300.

55. See Marietta, "Conscience, the Quaker Community, and the French and Indian War."

56. See Elihu Robinson's Diary, MS R3/2, Friends House. For background on the political debates surrounding tithe collection see Stephen Taylor, "Sir Robert Walpole, the Church of England, and the Quakers Tithe Bill of 1736," *Historical Journal* 28 (1968): 51–77.

57. Account of Woolman's illness and death, in Moulton, ed., *Journal*, 301. See also Testimony of the York Quarterly Meeting, March 25, 1773, in Gummere, ed., *Journal*, 328.

58. PYM Meeting for Sufferings to LYM Meeting for Sufferings, 1766, Invoice from Mary Hinde, 1768, PYM Sufferings Miscellaneous Papers, 1766, f. 6, and 1768, f. 7; Anthony Benezet to Sophia Hume, July 25, 1767, Ms. 163, f. 25; LYM Sufferings Minutes, 32:68–69, Friends House.

59. Brookes, ed., *Friend Anthony Benezet*, 272–73, 290–93, 417–18.

60. On the Somerset case, see William R. Cotter, "The Somerset Case and the Abolition of Slavery in England," *History* 79 (1994): 31–56; James Oldham, "New Light on Mansfield and Slavery," *Journal of British Studies* 27 (1988): 45–68. On the reaction to the Somerset case, see Carretta, *Equiano the African*, 206–9.

61. Cadbury, *John Woolman in England*, 67.

62. Anthony Benezet, *Observations on the Inslaving, Importing and Purchasing of Negroes* (Germantown, 1760), 2.; Anthony Benezet, *Some Historical Account of Guinea* (Philadelphia, 1771; reprinted London, 1772), 74–75 n. Phillips P. Moulton incorrectly indicates that Benezet included this passage in the first edition of this piece in 1759. See Moulton, ed., *Journal*, 13.

63. Cadbury, *John Woolman in England*, 67.

64. See Breen, *Marketplace of Revolution*, 195–234.

65. Michael Zakim, "Sartorial Ideologies: From Homespun to Ready-Made," *American Historical Review* 106 (2001): 1553–86, 1554–59.

66. John Cox, "Sketches and Recollections," 25, Dillwyn Parrish Recollections and Sketches, HSP.

67. Elihu Robinson's Diary, MS R3/2, Friends House; Tabitha Hoyland to Sarah Tuke, August 9, 1772, quoted in Cadbury, *John Woolman in England*, 94.

68. William Hunt to Uriah Woolman, June 25, 1772, in *Memoirs of William and Nathan Hunt*, 88–89; John Fothergill to Samuel Fothergill, June 9, 1772, Port. 22, f. 126, Friends House.

69. Letters from Samuel Emlen, July 2, September 5 and 15, 1772, quoted in Cadbury, *John Woolman in England*, 17–18.

70. Cadbury, *John Woolman in England*, 58.

71. Mary Andrews book of extracts, MS Box 28 (1), 13–14, Friends House.

72. Tabitha Hoyland to Sarah Tuke, August 9, 1772, quoted in Cadbury, *John Woolman in England*, 94.

73. Cadbury, *John Woolman in England*, 58.

74. Morris Birkbeck to Richard Shackleton, October 28, 1772, Port. 5/33, Friends House.

75. Elihu Robinson's Diary, MS R3/2, Friends House.

76. William Forster to Rebecca Haycock, August 16, 1772, Mss. vol. 77, f. 2; see also William Forster to William Birkbeck, Jr., July 1772, Mss. vol. 77, f.1, Friends House.

77. John Fothergill to Samuel Fothergill, June 9, 1772, Port. 22, f. 26, Friends House.

78. William Hunt to Uriah Woolman, June 25, 1772, in *Memoirs of William and Nathan Hunt*, 88–89.

79. Letter from Samuel Emlen, July 2, 1772, quoted in Cadbury, *John Woolman in England*, 17–18.

80. John Styles, "Clothing the North: The Supply of Non-Elite Clothing in the Eighteenth-Century North of England," *Textile History* 25 (1994): 139–66; Beverly Lemire, *Dress, Culture, and Commerce: The English Clothing Trade Before the Factory, 1660–1800* (New York: St. Martin's, 1997).

81. Moulton, ed., *Journal*, 190.

82. Silvester Thompson to his father, February 25, 1842, MS 335, f. 171; Samuel Tuke to Henry Tuke Mennell, 1851, Mss.Box 13/14. Friends House.

83. Moulton, ed., *Journal*, 185. See Isaiah 11:6–7.

84. Testimony of the York Quarterly Meeting, March 25, 1773, in Gummere, ed., *Journal*, 327.

85. Account of Woolman's illness and death, , 301–2; Testimony of the York Quarterly Meeting, March 25, 1773, in Gummere, ed., *Journal*, 326; JW to Reuben and Margaret Haines, September 23, 1772, Woolman Collection, Box 2, 3, HSP; Thomas Thornburgh to John Eliot, September 28, 1772, Port. 15/4, Friends House.

86. Moulton, ed., *Journal*, 56.

87. Woolman, *First Book*.

88. Moulton, ed., Journal, 30.

89. Moulton, ed., *Journal*, 40, 45.

90. Abner Woolman, Journal, Appendix, Haverford. The full text of Abner's final words reads: "I have greatly desired a support that I may bear these heavy pains with patience, and said I have felt many pains in my life, but these pains are different from any that I ever felt before."

91. Abner Woolman, Journal, Chapters XIII, XVII, Haverford.

92. Churchman, *Account*, 208–12; *Collection of Memorials*, 326–31.

93. Crossfield, *Memoirs of Samuel Fothergill*, 521–52.

94. Moulton, ed., *Journal*, 189; James King to Thomas Smith, September 9, 1772, Port. 15/2,William Forster to John Birkbeck, September 15, 1772, MS Vol. 77, f. 9, Friends House; *Collection of Memorials Concerning Divers Deceased Ministers* (Philadelphia, 1787), 298–301; *Memoirs of William and Nathan Hunt*, 21–22; Journal of John Hunt, July 1, 1770–January 31, 1773, f. 19 contra, Swarthmore; JW to Reuben and Margaret Haines, September 23, 1772, Woolman Collection, Box 2, f. 3, HSP.

95. John Pemberton to Joseph Row, October 28, 1772, Mss. 163, f. 5, Friends House.

96. JW to Sophia Hume, June 13, 1772, in Gummere, ed., *Journal*, xii; Sea Journal manuscript, note on envelope, Luke Howard Collection, Friends House.

97. JW to John Eliot, September 27, 1772, LYM Sufferings Minutes, 34:138–39, Friends House; Samuel Emlen to Sarah Emlen, November 4, 1772, Letters of Samuel Emlen, 1772–1797, 55, HSP.

98. Moulton, ed., *Journal*, 191–92, 192 n21, 304; John Woolman, *Serious Considerations on Various Subjects of Importance* (London, 1773), 132–33; Thomas Wagstaffe, *Piety Promoted, in Brief Memorials* . . . (London, 1775), 215. Henry J. Cadbury speculates that the dreamer was Peter Harvey, but the details of the story—the request for a private interview on the

deathbed, the five hours spent with the dying man, the return of the man's family, and his peaceful death, correspond precisely with the account Woolman wrote of his brother's death. Furthermore, Abner's journal indicates that he was a visionary dreamer, and in 1770 and 1771 he was preoccupied with the Delaware Valley Quakers' indirect complicity with the slave trade—the subject of the dream recorded at the end of John Woolman's journal. See Cadbury, *John Woolman in England*, 112 n1.

99. Isaac Wilson to Mildred and Roberts, October 7, 1772, quoted in Cadbury, *John Woolman in England*, 131.

100. Gummere, ed., *Journal*, 111–114, 302; Moulton, ed., *Journal*, 159–62, 185–86; 1769 Ledger, 183 contra.

101. Account of Woolman's illness and death, 304; Woolman, *Serious Considerations*, 133; Wagstaffe, *Piety Promoted*, (London, 1775), 215–16.

102. Account of Woolman's illness and death, , 302–3.; Testimony of the York Quarterly Meeting, March 25, 1773, in Gummere, ed., *Journal*, 326–29, 327; Note taken by Thomas Priestman, September 29, 1772, transcribed by Samuel Comfort, March 1839, Journal manuscript, Woolman Collection Box 2, 262, HSP.

103. Account of Woolman's illness and death, 303.

104. Account of Woolman's illness and death, 305; Woolman, *Serious Considerations*, 135–36; Wagstaffe, *Piety Promoted* (London, 1775), 217–18.

105. Cadbury, *John Woolman in England*, 120–21.

106. Account of Woolman's illness and death, 303; Woolman, *Serious Considerations*, 131–32; Wagstaffe, *Piety Promoted* (London, 1775), 214.

107. Account of Woolman's illness and death, 304; Woolman, *Serious Considerations*, 134; Wagstaffe, *Piety Promoted* (London, 1775), 216.

108. Account of Woolman's illness and death, 303; Woolman, *Serious Considerations*, 131; Wagstaffe, *Piety Promoted* (London, 1775), 213–14.

109. Account of Woolman's illness and death, 303; Woolman, *Serious Considerations*, 131; Wagstaffe, *Piety Promoted*, (London, 1775), 214.

110. Account of Woolman's illness and death, 303; Woolman, *Serious Considerations*, 132; Wagstaffe, *Piety Promoted* (London, 1775), 214.

111. Woolman, *Serious Considerations*, 133; Wagstaffe, *Piety Promoted* (London, 1775), 215.

112. Account of Woolman's illness and death, 302.

113. Testimony of the York Quarterly Meeting, March 25, 1773, in Gummere, ed., *Journal*, 327.

114. Esther Tuke to "S.E.," October 14, 1772, Catchpool Manuscripts 2:215, Sylvester Thompson to his father, February 25, 1842, MS 335, f. 171, Friends House.

115. Account of Woolman's illness and death, 305; Woolman, *Serious Considerations*, 135; Wagstaffe, *Piety Promoted* (London, 1775), 217.

116. Account of Woolman's illness and death, 305; Woolman, *Serious Considerations*, 135; Wagstaffe, *Piety Promoted* (London, 1775), 217; William Tuke to Reuben Haines, October 26, 1772, postscript, with note from John Woolman, September 29, 1772, in Gummere, ed., *Journal*, 324–25.

117. Account of Woolman's illness and death, 303–4; *Some Account of the Life and*

278 Notes to Pages 220–224

Religious Labours of Sarah Grubb (Trenton, N.J., 1795), 3; Woolman, *Serious Considerations*, 132; Wagstaffe, *Piety Promoted* (London, 1775), 214; Samuel Tuke to Henry Tuke Mennell, 1851, Mss.Box 13/14. Friends House.

118. Account of Woolman's illness and death, 304; Woolman, *Serious Considerations*, 132; Wagstaffe, *Piety Promoted* (London, 1775), 214–15; Samuel Tuke to Henry Tuke Mennell, 1851, Mss.Box 13/14. Friends House.

119. *Some Account of Sarah Grubb*, 3.

120. Account of Woolman's illness and death, 304; Woolman, *Serious Considerations*, 134; Wagstaffe, *Piety Promoted* (London, 1775), 216.

121. Account of Woolman's illness and death, 302, 303, 305; Woolman, *Serious Considerations*, 136; Wagstaffe, *Piety Promoted* (London, 1775), 218; Esther Tuke to "S.E.", October 14, 1772, Catchpool Manuscripts 2:215–17, Friends House.

122. Account of Woolman's illness and death, 305; Sarah Hall to Deborah Shakleton, October 22, 1772, quoted in Cadbury, *John Woolman in England*, 101–2.; Woolman, *Serious Considerations*, 136–37; Wagstaffe, *Piety Promoted* (London, 1775), 218–19.

123. Account of Woolman's illness and death, 305–6; Woolman, *Serious Considerations*, 137; Wagstaffe, *Piety Promoted* (London, 1775), 219; William Tuke to John Eliot, October 7, 1772, Port. 15/4, Thomas Priestman to John Priestman, October 8, 1772, Port. 42/38, Friends House.

124. Morris Birkbeck to Richard Shackleton, October 28, 1772, Port. 5/33, Friends House.

125. Testimony of the York Quarterly Meeting, March 25, 1773, in Gummere, ed., *Journal*, 326.

126. Abner Woolman, Journal, Chapter XXIX.

127. Account of Woolman's illness and death, 304; Woolman, *Serious Considerations*, 132–33; Wagstaffe, *Piety Promoted* (London, 1775), 215.

EPILOGUE

1. William Tuke to Reuben Haines, October 26, 1772, postscript, in Gummere, ed., *Journal*, 325.

2. Thomas Priestman to John Priestman, October 8, 1772, Port. 42/38, Esther Tuke to "S.E.," October 14, 1772, Catchpool mss. 2:215, Friends House.

3. "On the death of John Woolman," Catchpool mss. 2:218, Friends House.

4. William Tuke to John Eliot, October 7, 1772, Port 15/4, "Some Expressions of Jno Woolman during his illness," Port 15/5–8, Elizabeth Tuke to "S.E.," October 14, 1772, Catchpool mss. 2:215, William Forster to Mary Fairbank, November 3, 1772, Mss. vol. 77, f. 16, William Forster to Elizabeth Forster, November 3, 1772, Mss. vol. 77, f. 17, "Reflections arising from well-known events," October 25, 1772, Port. 15/26–28, LYM Morning Meeting Minutes, 6:178, Friends House; *Memoirs of William and Nathan Hunt*, 156–59.

5. John Pemberton to Joseph Row, Philadelphia October 16, 1772, Mss vol. 163, f. 4, LYM Morning Meeting Minutes, 6:172–74, 178, LYM Sufferings Minutes, 33:172, 240,

Friends House; Samuel Emlen to Sarah Emlen, November 4, 1772, Emlen Correspondence, 55, HSP; Gummere, ed., *Journal*, 488–510; Woolman, *Serious Considerations*.

6. LYM Ministers and Elders Minutes, 2:295, LYM Sufferings Minutes, 33:279, LYM Morning Meeting Minutes, 2:191–93, Friends House. Although the piece was published as *An Extract from John Woolman's Journal in Manuscript, Concerning the Ministry* (London, 1773), scholars now question whether Woolman intended the piece to be included in his journal.

7. YQM Minutes, 5:127, Leeds; Testimony of York Quarterly Meeting, March 25, 1773, in Gummere, ed., *Journal*, 328.

8. John Pemberton to Joseph Row, October 28, 1772, Mss. vol. 163, f. 5, Friends House; PYM Sufferings Minutes, 1756–1775, 379, 384, 386, 392–94, 396, 399–401, 406, 413, PYM Sufferings Miscellaneous Papers, 1774, 3, Swarthmore; Gummere, ed., *Journal*, xiii–xiv; in his footnotes, Phillips P. Moulton comprehensively surveys the revisions made by the editorial committee. See Moulton, ed., *Journal*.

9. Slaughter is incorrect in stating that *Considerations on Pure Wisdom* was not reprinted in America until the nineteenth century. See Slaughter, *Beautiful Soul*, 214.

10. PYM Sufferings Miscellaneous Papers, 1774, 3, Swarthmore; John Woolman, *Works* (Philadelphia, 1774).

11. *Leeds Mercury*, October 13, 1772, quoted in Cadbury, *John Woolman in England*, 132.

12. Wagstaffe, *Piety Promoted* (London, 1775), 209–19.

13. LYM Morning Meeting Minutes, 6:224, Friends House; William Matthews, *The Life and Character of Thomas Letchworth* (Bath, 1786), 24–25; Thomas Letchworth, *A Morning and Evening's Meditation* (Philadelphia, 1766).

14. LYM Morning Meeting Minutes, 6:224–25, Friends House.

15. LYM Morning Meeting Minutes, 6:224–5, FHL; YQM Minutes, 5:193, Leeds.

16. Matthews, *Life of Thomas Letchworth*, 25.

17. See Moulton, ed., *Journal*, 187, n.14.

18. YQM Minutes, 5:193, Leeds.

19. Compare Woolman, *Works*, 1st ed. (London, 1775), 54, 197, with Woolman, *Works* (Philadelphia, 1774), 52–53, 233–36, and Moulton, ed., *Journal*, 58, 185–86.

20. Compare Woolman, *Works*, 1st ed. (London, 1775), 74, 78, with Woolman, *Works* (Philadelphia, 1774), 75, 80–86, and Moulton, ed., *Journal*, 71, 75–87.

21. Compare Woolman, *Works*, 1st ed. (London, 1775), 102–3, with Woolman, *Works*, (Philadelphia, 1774), 111–16, and Moulton, ed., *Journal*, 102–5.

22. Compare Woolman, *Works*, 1st ed. (London, 1775), 196–97, with Woolman, *Works* (Philadelphia, 1774), 235–38, and Moulton, ed., *Journal*, 186–88.

23. Compare Woolman, *Works*, 1st ed. (London, 1775), 184, 193 with Woolman, *Works* (Philadelphia, 1774), 215, 226–27, and Moulton, ed., *Journal*, 171, 180.

24. Compare Woolman, *Works*, 1st ed. (London, 1775), 126–27, with Woolman, *Works* (Philadelphia, 1774), 140–43, and Moulton, ed., *Journal*, 120–22.

25. Compare Woolman, *Works*, 1st ed. (London, 1775), 196–98, with Woolman, *Works* (Philadelphia, 1774), 229–33, 239, and Moulton, ed., *Journal*, 182–88, 190.

26. LYM Morning Meeting Minutes, 6:225, 230 , Friends House; Woolman, *Works*, 1st ed. (London, 1775), iii–iv.

27. YQM Minutes, 5:202, Leeds.

28. LYM Sufferings Minutes, 34:114, LYM Morning Meeting Minutes, 6:234–35, Friends House.

29. LYM Morning Meeting Minutes, 6:236, Friends House.

30. LYM Sufferings Minutes, 34:136–39, Friends House.

31. YQM Minutes, 5:211, Leeds.

32. See John Woolman, *A Journal of the Life, Gospel Labours, and Christian Experiences of that Faithful Minister of Jesus Christ*, John Woolman (Dublin, 1776).

33. Compare Gummere, ed. *Journal*, 488–510 with Woolman, *Serious Considerations*, 88–128.

34. Compare Moulton, ed., *Journal*, 303, with Woolman, *Serious Considerations*, 132.

35. See Moulton, ed., *Journal*, 14–15. The Fabians drew particularly on a shortened version of Woolman's essay "A Plea for the Poor," which was published in 1793 as John Woolman, *A Word of Remembrance and Caution to the Rich* (Dublin, 1793).

36. See Arthur Brayshaw, "The Kindlier Way," *Friends Quarterly Examiner*, July 1935, 210–19, 215; Gilbert, "John Woolman (1720–1772): Abolitionist and Animal Defender."

37. Woolman, *Works*, 1st ed. (London, 1775), iv.

38. See Rosenberg, "Thomas Tryon."

39. See Carretta, *Equiano the African*, 270–367.

40. John Newton's *An Authentic Narrative of Some Remarkable and Interesting Particulars in the Life of **** (London, 1764), had appeared eleven years earlier, but as Brycchan Carey notes, Newton's early work did not "amount to a full-scale attack on the [slave] trade." Brycchan Carey, *British Abolitionism and the Rhetoric of Sensibility* (London: Palgrave, 2005), 108.

41. See, for example, "Biographical Sketch of the Life of John Woolman," published in the Quaker *Juvenile Magazine* 4 (1813): 1–8; *The Negro's Friend: A Christian Testimony Against Slavery, Selected from the Works of John Woolman, and An Affecting Case related by Dr. Philip* (London, 1830?).

42. Gertrude [pseud.], "From the Genius of Universal Emancipation, John Woolman," *The Friend: A Religious and Literary Journal* 5 (June 23, 1832): 32.

43. See John Greenleaf Whittier to Charles Calistus Burleigh, September 24, 1840, in Pickard, ed., *Letters*, 1:446; Whittier, "To the Pennsylvania Freeman," February 26, 1839, in ibid., 1:336.

44. Anonymous poem quoted in Brookes, ed., *Friend Anthony Benezet*, 77.

45. Peter Williams, Jr., *An Oration on the Abolition of the Slave Trade* (New York, 1808), 22; Rosalie Murphy Baum, "Early American Literature: The Black Contribution," *Eighteenth-Century Studies* 27 (1994): 533–49, 539; William B. Gravely, "The Dialectic of Double-Consciousness in Black-American Freedom Celebrations, 1808–1863," *Journal of Negro History* 67 (1982): 302–17, 303.

46. See *Memoirs of John Woolman* (Philadelphia, 1810?), which was reprinted several times in Britain and America; "Saint John Woolman," *Eclectic Review* 5 (June 1861): 559–78; Dora Greenwell, *John Woolman* (London: Kitto, 1871); Thomas Green, *John Woolman: A Study for Young Men*, 2nd ed. (London: Headley, 1897). Most of these works discuss

Woolman's opposition to slavery briefly, but place greater emphasis on his humility and piety. Whether they emphasize Woolman's politics or his spirituality, many Quakers today continue to exalt him as the "Quaker Saint" or the "Quintessential Quaker." See Cady, *John Woolman*; Sox, *John Woolman*; Michael L. Birkel, *A Near Sympathy: The Timeless Quaker Wisdom of John Woolman* (Richmond, Ind.: Friends United Press, 2003).

47. B. Barton, "A Memorial of John Woolman," *The Friend: A Religious and Literary Journal* 3 (October 2, 1830): 51. See also *A Journal of the Life, Gospel Labours, and Christian Experiences of that Faithful Minister of Christ, John Woolman* (Warrington: Hurst, 1840), 337–39.

48. "A Testimony from Friends of Mount Holly, New Jersey, Concerning William Boen," Comly and Comly, eds., *Friends' Miscellany*, 1:183–86.

49. "Memoirs and Anecdotes of William Boen," Comly and Comly, eds., *Friends' Miscellany* 5:269–80, 280.

50. In 1922 Amelia Mott Gummere provided important information on Boen in her edition of the journal, and in 1941 Janet Whitney incorporated that material in her biography. See Gummere, ed., *Journal*, 608–9; Janet Whitney, *John Woolman, American Quaker* (Boston: Little, Brown, 1942). Nonetheless, recent works on Woolman have reverted to the old pattern of ignoring the Boen episode. See Sox, *John Woolman*; Slaughter, *Beautiful Soul*.

51. *Account of a Visit*; [Anthony Benezet], *Some Observations on the Situation, Disposition, and Character of the Indian Natives of this Continent* (Philadelphia, 1784), 23–35; *An Account of the Behavior and Sentiments of Some Well Disposed Indians*; "A Remarkable Indian Minister," *The Christian Disciple* (Boston) 6, 6 (1818): 178–81; *The Friend, or Advocate of Truth* 4 (1831): 25–27; *John Papunhank*.

52. See especially "Saint John Woolman," 570–74. For earlier, briefer references to Woolman's visit to Wyalusing see *Memoirs of John Woolman* (London, 1816), 27; *Memoirs of John Woolman* (Philadelphia, n.d.), 14–15. See also Greenwell, *John Woolman*, 39–40; W. Tegnmouth Shore, *John Woolman: His Life and Our Times* (London: Macmillan, 1913), 199. More general works that recount Woolman's trip to Wyalusing include *Some Account of the Conduct of the Religious Society of Friends towards the Indian Tribes in the Colonies of East and West Jersey and Pennsylvania* (London, 1844), 92–93; Rufus Jones, *The Quakers in the American Colonies* (London: Macmillan, 1911), 405; Rayner Wickersham Kelsey, *Friends and the Indians, 1655–1917* (Philadelphia: Associated Executive Committee of Friends on Indian Affairs, 1917), 29–32. In 1922 Amelia Mott Gummere published Woolman's account of his 1761 meeting with Papunhank in Philadelphia, but that information has had little influence on subsequent accounts of Woolman's 1763 trip. See, for example, Llewelyn Powys, *Thirteen Worthies* (London: Grant Richards, 1924), 148; Whitney, *John Woolman*, 309; Reginald Reynolds, *The Wisdom of John Woolman* (London: Allen & Unwin, 1948), 28; Cady, *John Woolman*, 13; Sox, *John Woolman*, 75; Slaughter, *Beautiful Soul*, 256–57, 261. One notable exception to the general pattern is Samuel M. Janney, *History of the Religious Society of Friends, from Its Rise to the Year 1828*, 4 vols. (Philadelphia: Ellwood Zell, 1867), 3:363.

53. The Woolman canon gained one important addition in 1793, when Woolman's essay "A Plea for the Poor" was published in a heavily edited version as *A Word of Remembrance and Caution to the Rich*. In the 1830s Isaac and John Comly printed other

supplementary Woolman material in their *Friends Miscellany*, but those pieces appear to have had very little impact.

54. Moulton, ed., *Journal*, 23.

55. Moulton, ed., *Journal*, 3; Cady, *John Woolman*, 171–72.

56. Henry Crabb Robinson, diary entry for January 22, 1824, quoted in Green, *John Woolman*, iii.

57. Vida Dutton Scudder, ed., *The Journal of John Woolman* (London: J.M. Dent, 1952, first published 1910), vii.

58. Moulton, ed., *Journal*, 3, citing E. L. Griggs, ed., *Collected Letters of Samuel Taylor Coleridge* (Oxford: Clarendon, 1956), 1:302.

59. The classic analysis of the role of biography in the formation of American culture is Sacvan Bercovitch, *The Puritan Origins of the American Self* (New Haven, Conn.: Yale University Press, 1977). For a discussion of the place of Quakers in the American biographical tradition, see James Emmett Ryan, *Imaginary Friends: Representing Quakers in American Culture, 1650–1950* (Madison: University of Wisconsin Press, 2009), 120–58. For comparisons between Woolman's journal and Franklin's autobiography see Slaughter, *Beautiful Soul*, 16–17; Cady, *John Woolman*, 131; Janet Whitney, ed., *The Journal of John Woolman* (Chicago: Regnery, 1950), vii.

Index

Acknowledgments

THE LAST WORDS my father spoke at a Quaker meeting for business related, at least indirectly, to John Woolman. David Morse, a member of Storrs Friends Meeting, wanted to travel to the Sudanese province of Darfur to protest the killings there. As he explained later, Morse hoped to model himself in part on Woolman, whose "challenge" had been "to make vivid the kidnapping of Africans 'some thousand miles off' to his mostly comfortable middle class audience." He wanted to follow Woolman's example not only in seeking to take dramatic action to confront distant suffering, but also in asking for guidance from his meeting first. Morse discovered that he could not get a visa to Sudan, and so he proposed instead to fly to Chad and enter Darfur from the west. When he asked the meeting whether this would be a wise decision, my father was skeptical. This is how Morse describes his response: " 'Chad? David, do you have any idea of the logistics involved in getting across the desert? How would you carry food?' He grilled me unmercifully." After a moment Morse "felt the meeting's rejection bear down on me with the weight of lead." (For the full story see David Morse, "Facing Evil: Genocide in Darfur," *Friends Journal* (September 2005): 6–15, quotes 10, 12).

Woolman's name comes up frequently in American Quaker meetings. I was raised in a Quaker family, and I heard him mentioned fairly often as I was growing up. Therefore as I acknowledge those who helped me write this book I should start with the people who introduced me to Quakerism: my father John Plank, my mother Eleanor Plank, my sister Margaret Plank, my brother David Plank, and Friends Meetings in Cambridge, Massachusetts; Bethesda, Maryland; Storrs, Connecticut; Cincinnati Ohio; Aberystwyth, Wales; and Evanston, Illinois. I am especially indebted to Oak Park Friends Meeting in Illinois, where I served as clerk for part of the time I was working on this book.

My Quaker background introduced me to Woolman, but it was not the immediate inspiration for this work. On the contrary, my research into Woolman's career grew out of my longstanding academic interest in the controversies surrounding the expansion of the British Empire in the eighteenth century. From the outset I wanted to avoid relying on anachronistic intuition or Quaker lore. Instead I hoped to find eighteenth-century documentation on every question that arose. That goal, of course, was impossible to achieve, but in my pursuit of it I was extraordinarily well served by the librarians and archivists I met during my research. I would particularly like to express my gratitude to Christopher Densmore of the Friends Historical Library at Swarthmore College, John Anderies and Ann Upton of the Quaker and Special Collections at Haverford College, and the staffs at the Historical Society of Pennsylvania, Library Company of Philadelphia, New Jersey State Archives, Huntington Library, British Library, Woodbrooke Quaker Study Centre, Leeds University Library, and Friends House Library.

My research was generously funded by the Charles Phelps Taft Memorial Fund and the McNeil Center for Early American Studies. I would like to thank the 2007–8 fellows at the McNeil Center, my former colleagues in the Department of History at the University of Cincinnati, and my new colleagues in the School of American Studies at the University of East Anglia, not only for affording me the time and space to work on this book, but also for hearing me ruminate on it and giving me their comments. I have presented papers on Woolman at several venues over the years, and I have received helpful feedback from more people than I can mention here, but the following individuals were among those who gave me useful leads and sharp advice: Brycchan Carey, Robert Duplessis, Jerry Frost, Dallett Hemphill, Jon Kershner, Mark Kharas, Marcelle Martin, Daniel Richter, Ellen Ross, Jonathan Sassi, and Michael Zuckerman.

At the University of Pennsylvania Press, Robert Lockhart has been involved in this work almost since its inception. He has been businesslike, direct, and attentive to the project at a fine level of detail. This is the third book I have written with Bob's expert assistance, and I am profoundly indebted to him. The anonymous readers of my manuscript also gave me strong advice, and I would like to thank the staff at the press generally, and particularly Alison Anderson.

Finally I profess my thanks to my wife Ina Zweiniger-Bargielowska, for filling my life with surprising joy. More prosaically I need to thank her for aiding me on this book project from the start, encouraging me, helping me refine my ideas, chasing down some sources, reviewing each book chapter during the process of writing, and critiquing successive manuscripts of the entire work. I am certain that without Ina, I would never have even started this book.